Climate Change and Threatened Communities

Praise for this book

Praise for the second edition

'The 15 case studies in the 2012 edition of this influential book forefronted the stewardship of indigenous peoples in the governance of 80% of the Earth's remaining biodiversity. The new edition brings these vital stories up to date, as indigenous stakeholders become recognized partners in governance.'

Steve Lansing, Santa Fe Institute and Complexity Science Hub Vienna

'In contrast to other natural disasters, it can be hard to envisage climate change: the case studies in this volume make it real, they give its phenomenological dimension. It can also be hard to envisage climate change as anything other than globally homogenous: the case studies in this volume show the diversity in the human experience of climate change, as it interacts with a host of local environmental, cultural, economic, and political variables. Finally, it is hard for policy makers to not see climate change as the singular priority of communities around the world: but the case studies in this volume show otherwise, as communities find that their even more pressing problems are those of resource scarcity, state oppression, ethnic conflict, and so on. Thus, the case studies in this volume demonstrate that climate change both is and is not a global problem, or the same global problem, of the premiere global problem for the world's societies. This volume thus shows that climate change is more complex, more 'messy', than most policy makers like to think; but however institutionally inconvenient, that is the problem that they need to recognize and tackle if they are to succeed.'

Michael R. Dove, Yale School of the Environment

Praise for the first edition

'*Climate Change and Threatened Communities* is a timely wake-up call and reminder of the local-level practical, theoretical and ethical issues raised by climate change. Scholarly and accessible, it illuminates the rights, interests, needs, and capacities of the many vulnerable and marginalized communities threatened by climate change. For all concerned with how communities can adapt to the mounting stresses, shocks, and uncertainties of climate change, *Climate Change and Threatened Communities* will be a rich source of insight.'

Professor Robert Chambers, Institute of Development Studies, University of Sussex

'This unique and significant book has global importance for three reasons. First, the chapters from the Americas, Africa, and Asia convincingly show that climate change is adversely affecting local communities around the world. Nine of the case studies, for example, show that communities are suffering from increasing climatic variation as is also the case with my own community studies in two other countries: Zambia and Laos. Second, the case studies demonstrate the impressive resiliency of the communities involved in trying to cope with climate change. Such adaptive resiliency in turn emphasizes the third reason which is the need for policy makers not just to realize that impacts of climate change vary from place to place but that such variance demands that they work closely with local people in assessing impacts and in formulating coping policies which in turn require further local participation in monitoring and adaptive management.

Thayer Scudder, Professor Emeritus of Anthropology, California Institute of Technology

'This book is extremely important for reminding us that poor rural people in Africa have a great deal of experience in adapting to long and short cycles of climate change and that this experience is not yet being sufficiently harnessed under the climate change adaptation programmes being initiated by donors and African governments. Such adaptation challenges many long-standing 'African' problems such as unsatisfactory tenure regimes, especially for pastoralists and transhumants and for those managing farm fallow systems, but will decision-makers take a sufficiently long view to see this and act appropriately? This book provides plenty of evidence as to why they should.'

Gill Shepherd, Visiting Senior Fellow, LSE, London, and Special Adviser Ecosystems, Commission for Ecosystem Management, IUCN

'This outstanding volume embodies the most complete synthesis to date of major views and well-documented case studies on climate change and its threat to humanity. As leading scholars in their field, the authors encapsulate the engaging theoretical orientations in this newly developing discipline of the effect of climate change on the great diversity of indigenous peoples and cultures around the globe. It is not only an up-to-date contribution to the current debate on global climate change, but also a fantastic handbook for students.'

L. Jan Slikkerveer, Professor and Director of the Leiden Ethnosystems and Development Programme (LEAD), Faculty of Science, Leiden University, The Netherlands

Climate Change and Threatened Communities

Vulnerability, Capacity, and Action

Second Edition

Edited by
Yancey Orr

Practical
ACTION
PUBLISHING

Practical Action Publishing Ltd
25 Albert Street, Rugby,
Warwickshire, CV21 2SD, UK
www.practicalactionpublishing.com

A catalogue record for this book is available from the British Library.

A catalogue record for this book has been requested from the Library of Congress.

ISBN 978-1-78853-421-5 Paperback
ISBN 978-1-78853-423-9 Electronic book

Citation: Orr, Y., (2025) *Climate Change and Threatened Communities: Vulnerability, Capacity & Action*, Rugby, UK: Practical Action Publishing http://doi.org/10.3362/9781788534239

Since 1974, Practical Action Publishing has published and disseminated books and information in support of international development work throughout the world.

Practical Action Publishing is a trading name of Practical Action Publishing Ltd (Company Reg. No. 1159018), the wholly owned publishing company of Practical Action. Practical Action Publishing trades only in support of its parent charity objectives and any profits are covenanted back to Practical Action (Charity Reg. No. 247257, Group VAT Registration No. 880 9924 76).

Cover design and Typesetting by: Katarzyna Markowska, Practical Action Publishing

The manufacturer's authorised representative in the EU for product safety is Lightning Source France, 1 Av. Johannes Gutenberg, 78310 Maurepas, France. compliance@lightningsource.fr

In memory of David W. Brokensha (1923-2017) whose pioneering work showed how society and the environment are intrinsically linked and whose life embodied many of the 20th century's achievements.

Contents

List of tables and figures   xi
About the editor   xii

1 Introduction   1
   A. Peter Castro, Dan Taylor and David W. Brokensha

2 Climate change and forest conservation:A REDD flag for
   Central African forest people?   17
   Philip Burnham and Simon Hoyte

3 Social vulnerability, climatic variability, and uncertainty in rural
   Ethiopia: A study of South Wollo and Oromiya Zones of eastern
   Amhara Region   37
   A. Peter Castro

4 Farmers on the frontline: Adaptationand change in Malawi   53
   Kate Wellard, Daimon Kambewaand Sieglinde Snapp

5 Risk and abandonment, and themeta-narrative of climate change   71
   Dan Taylor

6 Mobilizing knowledge to build adaptive capacity: Lessons from
   southern Mozambique   85
   L. Jen Shaffer

7 Climate change and the future of onion and potato production
   in Central Darfur, Sudan: A case study of Zalingei locality   99
   Yassir Hassan Satti and A. Peter Castro

8 Comparing knowledge of and experience with climate change
   across threeglaciated mountain regions   115
   K.W. Dunbar, Julie Brugger, Christine Jurtand Ben Orlove
   with updates by Karina Yager

9 Aapuupayuu (the weather warms up): Climate change and
   the Eeyouch (Cree) of northern Quebec   131
   Kreg Ettenger

10 'The one who has changed is the person': Observations and
   explanations of climate change in the Ecuadorian Andes   149
   Kristine Skarbø, Kristin Vander Molen, Rosa Ramos and
   Robert E. Rhoades

11 Good intentions, bad memories, and troubled capital: American
    Indian knowledge and action in renewableenergy projects   163
    Raymond I. Orr and David B. Anderson

12 Reclaiming the past to respond toclimate change: Mayan farmers
    and ancient agricultural techniques in the Yucatan Peninsula
    of Mexico   175
    Betty Bernice Faust, Armando Anaya-Hernández, and
    Helga Geovannini-Acuña

13 Can we learn from the past?Policy history and climate change
    in Bangladesh   195
    David Lewis

14 Local perceptions and adaptation to climate change: A perspective
    from Western India   207
    Dineshkumar Moghariya

15 Ethno-ecology in the shadow of rainand the light of experience:
    Local perceptions of drought and climatechange in east Sumba,
    Indonesia   221
    Yancey Orr, Russell Schimmer and Roland Geerken

16 Local knowledge and technology innovation in a changing world:
    Traditional fishing communities in Tam Giang Cau Hai lagoon,
    Vietnam   233
    Thanh Vo and Jack Manno

17 Conclusion: Some reflections on indigenous knowledge and
    climate change   245
    Dan Taylor, A. Peter Castro, and David W. Brokensha

    Resources for Communities on the Frontlines of Climate Change   251
    Compiled by Wendy B. Miles

    Index   262

List of tables and figures

Tables

4.1   Extreme weather events in Malawi and people affected: 1987–2009   56
4.2   Farmer perceptions of weather events and climate variability   58
4.3   Farmer strategies for combating climate variability and soil
      infertility in Simlemba, Kasungu   62

Figures

12.1 PALSAR image showing the areas subject to inundation   183
12.2 Geoeye IR high resolution image, showing more canals   184
12.3 GPR images showing the structure of the canal at Cauich   185
12.4 Location of Aguada 4 of Calakmul and archaeological explorations   186
12.5 a) Diagram of water management feature; b) Aguada 3, limestone
      paved floor   187

About the editor

Yancey Orr is Associate Professor of Environmental Science and Policy at Smith College in Northampton, Massachusetts and Fellow at the United States Studies Centre at the University of Sydney. An environmental anthropologist specializing in Indigenous knowledge and social science methods, his research takes place in North America, Southeast Asia and Australia.

Chapter 1

Introduction

A. Peter Castro, Dan Taylor
and David W. Brokensha

> Those things that have long gone together are as it were confederate
> within themselves: whereas new things piece not so well ... they
> trouble by their inconfirmity.
>
> Sir Francis Bacon

*Global climate change is one of the greatest challenges confronting humanity in the
21st century, raising not only urgent scientific and policy issues but also profoundly
ethical ones. The people least responsible for the world's present environmental
predicament are often the ones most at risk from it. This book presents 15 case
studies from across the globe examining how communities and their members
are responding to challenges and opportunities presented by climate change. The
29 authors come from many countries, varying educational backgrounds, and
different careers. The writers are united by their concern with portraying the
motivations, perceptions, and predicaments of people at the local level, generally
from poor or marginalized communities, confronting situations arising from
global warming. They seek to inform both specialist and wider audiences about
the importance of recognizing and respecting local knowledge, capacities, interests,
and, crucially, rights. The authors aim to promote both scholarship and action by
providing detailed insights about the capacities and constraints of communities,
while addressing significant practical, theoretical, and ethical issues. The case
studies are distinguished by the diversity of environmental settings (spanning
subarctic to equatorial regions), topics (ranging from customary farming practices
and industrial wind farms to indigenous cosmologies and the United Nations
Collaborative Initative on Reducing Emissions from Deforestation and Forest
Degradation (UN-REDD)), and approaches (ranging from phenomenology to
archaeology). We do not claim that these cases are a representative sample of
situations faced by all rural communities and indigenous groups worldwide;
however, we feel that the cases portray situations and predicaments faced by many
rural people in all continents, especially those relying on agrarian, fishing, and
foraging activities for their livelihoods.*

Introduction

In the drought-prone mountains near Bati in north-eastern Ethiopia, people recall several distinct times of severe hunger during the 20th century. The famine of 1984, for example, is called '77', in reference to its year (1977) in the Ethiopian national calendar. Some villagers still have a phobia about saying that number, so painful are their memories of death, deprivation, and dislocation. In the distant past a time of famine occurred that became locally known *Durbailli*, which can be translated as, 'The one that impoverished those who were not aware'. An elder explained its meaning. Some people saw hard times coming, and they took measures to get ready, such as selling cattle before prices collapsed due to distress sales and declining livestock condition. Others responded slowly to signs of impending trouble, and they suffered harshly for their lack of preparedness. People remembered the event not only as a time of local historical significance, but also as a valuable lesson about the importance of awareness, timely action, and survival. For the inhabitants of these highland communities, being prepared is an ongoing creative response to both immediate and long-term vulnerabilities and opportunities. These, for example, range from altering the planting dates for their drought-resistant sorghum according to the area's increasingly variable rainfall, to making use of remittances from family members engaged in labour migration as a diversified income strategy. A central message of our book is that such knowledge, wisdom, and action from communities and indigenous peoples need to be recognized and heeded, especially given the urgent and complex challenge of global climate change.

A warming Earth and hot controversies

Increased concentrations of carbon dioxide, methane, and other heat-trapping gases are warming the planet as measured worldwide by average air and ocean temperatures, large-scale snow and ice melting, and global average sea levels. The Intergovernmental Panel on Climate Change, the premier scientific body for research on the topic, has concluded that evidence for global warming is 'unequivocal' (Parry et al., 2007: 30). For the earth's climates to be changing is not unusual: they are always dynamic, fluctuating since time immemorial between overall wetter and drier, cooler and warmer periods. Past drivers of climate change consisted of natural phenomena such as variation in the earth's orbit or the position and size of land masses, which were beyond human influence. In contrast, the current pattern of greenhouse gas accumulation largely originates from anthropogenic sources, particularly industrialization (Parry et al., 2007). For more than 250 years attaining 'economic development' has involved massive consumption of fossil fuels, deforestation, and other greenhouse gas-emitting processes. While industrial lifestyles have spread, to varying extents, worldwide, a relatively small number of people are responsible for the bulk of such emissions. The United Nations Development Programme estimated in 2007 that the world's richest countries, which constitute 15 per cent of its population, were responsible for nearly half of all carbon dioxide emitted. As E.F. Schumacher (1973) observed long ago in *Small Is Beautiful: Economics as if People Mattered*, the 'achievement' of a highly unequal industrialized economy based on supposedly endless consumption and production is a dangerous illusion, ignoring inherent environmental limits and endemic social violence. Unfortunately, maintaining this illusion is in itself a major industry, with powerful interests and sincere sceptics rancorously contesting the existence or importance of global warming. Disbelief and apathy are also fostered by the fact that many uncertainties exist about the current and future manifestations and implications of global warming. Why incur costs and inconvenience for something that might not occur? Yet, as Andrew Revkin (1992) noted three decades ago, the crystal ball may be cloudy, but the message is clear: climate change is happening. Present-day political and social inertia only reduce our ability to respond in a timely and effective manner to these new and threatening circumstances.

Global climate change raises not only significant scientific and policy issues, but also profoundly ethical ones. The people least responsible for the world's present environmental predicament are often the ones most at risk from it (Singer, 2002; UNDP, 2007; Galloway McLean et al., 2009; World Bank, 2010). More than a billion people in developing countries live on less than US$1.25 per day, and their carbon footprints are very, very light. Although deforestation and agriculture account for approximately 30 per cent of global carbon emissions, a large number of rural households contribute only minimally to this process. Furthermore, as has been documented time and time again (to the extent that one truly appreciates 'research' to mean 're-search'), these same rural households often serve as effective natural resource managers, actively working to maintain the ecological integrity and biodiversity of forests, pastures, farmland, wetlands, marine areas, and other environments (for example, see Posey, 1999; Dove, 2006). Ironically, due to their agrarian, herding, fishing, or foraging livelihoods, which are closely connected to the Earth's hydrological cycle, and to their lack of buffers for hard times, they are highly vulnerable to extreme or erratic weather events generated by global warming. In Africa, for example, more than 70 per cent of the population depends on natural resources and agriculture for their livelihoods (Toulmin and Huq, 2006). It is estimated that over 40 per cent of rural Africans reside in arid and semi-arid environments, and yet only 4 per cent of Africa's cropland is irrigated (Juma, 2011: 8). Even those areas that rely heavily on irrigation, such as parts of South Asia, find their water sources threatened, whether by large-scale glacial retreat, shifts in rainfall that produce increased drought or floods, competing users, or environmental mismanagement (Leslie, 2005; Bates et al., 2008).

Care is needed, however, in depicting the nature and extent of climatic vulnerability among rural communities. Crisis narratives in the professional and popular media on rural livelihoods, poverty, and global warming often end up portraying communities and their members as hapless victims, incapable of exercising initiative without outside guidance. In contrast, our case studies document the diverse, dynamic, sophisticated, and effective strategies for survival devised by communities residing in areas characterized by high climatic risk. Without such practices, these communities would have disappeared long ago. These strategies and adaptations rely on detailed and long-term observations of local environments. Yet it is important to bear in mind that rural people do not reside in a timeless arena of simplicity and contentment. As revealed by our case study authors, local responses to shifting weather patterns are taking place in settings experiencing broader, sometimes dramatic, processes of change emanating from the local to the global levels. From the Canadian arctic to South Africa, communities are dealing with a multitude of political, economic, demographic, social, and cultural processes, including market liberalization, decentralization (at least nominally), introduction of new technologies, population growth, urbanization, labour migration, the spread of mass media, the rise of religious fundamentalism, and so on. Depending on circumstances, these changes may strengthen or weaken the capacity of communities and their members to respond to climate change. The emergence of famine in the war-torn and drought-ravaged southern Somalia in June 2011 sadly illustrates the complex linkage between social vulnerability and rainfall variability. Famine, death, and dislocation are not inevitable results of drought, but the outcome of long-standing insecurity, inadequate public service infrastructure, and other human institutional and behavioural processes.

We contend that the efforts of climate researchers, planners, and policy makers could benefit substantially by taking local knowledge and capacity for innovation into account. Indeed, recognition of this knowledge and capacity, as well as its foundational system of resource rights and use institutions, must serve as a starting point for action, building up climate change-oriented mitigation and adaptation activities around it, rather than doing 'top-down' planning. Environmental sustainability, poverty alleviation, and social justice are intimately linked, and local populations need to be engaged as active participants in the design and governance of interventions, not as a matter of courtesy or as a technical strategy, but because it is their right (Leach et al., 2010). At the same time, enabling or enhancing opportunities for local action also allows people to draw on their own capacities and creativity to adapt to, or mitigate, climate change within the complex social and physical environments in which they live (Toulmin and Huq, 2006; Desmarais, 2007; Juma, 2011). Overall, people are more likely to be open to recommendations when they have had a say in their formulation and adoption. Thus, both 'equity' and 'efficiency' reasons exist for participatory approaches to climate change adaptation and mitigation:

such strategies are responsive to social justice concerns and also more likely to succeed due to their reliance on local capacity.

In fact, many analysts contend climate change adaptations provide an opportunity for promoting reforms and technological innovations that can bring about a more just and sustainable global society (Adger et al., 2009; Ensor and Berger, 2009; Terry, 2009; Pelling, 2011). To do so, climate change adaptations need to go beyond reducing specific climatic risks; instead seeking to transform people's relationship to (and understanding of) nature, as well as their relationships across and within human societies. As Donald Nelson (2009) observes, such an approach requires new awareness, new thinking, new knowledge, and new analytical tools – all major challenges for an entrenched global consumer society informed by Western-dominated views of economy, technology, and science. In this regard the case studies presented here take on an importance by presenting perspectives and experiences that largely emanate from the 'periphery' rather than the 'core' of our global society.

Climate change adaptation presents the prospect for implementing global social reforms, but it also offers the opportunity for installing policies and technical approaches that work against the interests of communities. Concern about global warming, for example, is justifying a new wave of interventions aimed at so-called LULUCF activities – land use, land use change, and forestry. The United Nations Reducing Emissions from Deforestation and Forest Degradation Programme (UN-REDD) was established in 2008 and now supports conservation projects that are linked to carbon trading arrangements. Other climate change-inspired projects seek increased energy production, including promoting new 'greener' approaches such as wind farms, biofuel production, and various forms of hydropower as a counter to long-standing petroleum and coal extractive industries. As described in several chapters, REDD and these other approaches may offer important economic opportunities for communities and their members, but they also pose significant risks, especially the loss of local control of, or access to, local resources (also see Angelsen, 2009). Attempts to use conservation or development as reasons for interfering with, or taking control over, community resource use are not unprecedented, but connected to long-standing processes of state and market expansion that have resulted in community disruption, dislocation, and marginalization (Castro and Nielsen, 2001). Once again, climate change interventions need to take seriously issues of social justice, including issues such as the recognition of community and aboriginal tenure rights (Lynch, 2011). The notions of 'climate justice' and 'climate equity' – promoting principles of mitigation and adaptation that are just and equitable – are increasingly recognized as vital ingredients in climate change negotiations, planning, and interventions, even if their attainment still falls short (Adger et al., 2009; Terry, 2009; Pelling, 2011).

The case studies

We present 15 case studies from across the globe detailing how communities and their members are responding to challenges and opportunities presented by climate change. The 29 authors come from many countries, varying educational backgrounds, and different careers. The writers are united by their concern with portraying the motivations, perceptions, and predicaments of people at the local level, generally from poor or marginalized communities, confronting situations arising from global warming. They seek to inform both specialist and wider audiences about the importance of recognizing and respecting the knowledge, capacities, interests, and rights of local communities. The authors aim to promote both scholarship and action by providing detailed insights about the capacities and constraints of communities, while addressing significant practical, theoretical, and ethical issues. At the same time the case studies are distinguished by their diversity of environmental settings (spanning subarctic to equatorial regions), topics (ranging from customary farming practices and industrial wind farms to indigenous cosmologies and the UN-REDD), and approaches (from phenomenology to archaeology). We do not claim that these cases are a representative sample of situations faced by all rural communities and indigenous groups worldwide; but we feel that the cases portray situations and predicaments faced by many rural people in all continents, especially those relying on agrarian, fishing, and foraging activities for their livelihoods.

The case studies are grouped regionally, as will be described in the next section. The political and cultural units covered in the case studies vary with the different settings presented by the authors. The Cree communities in Quebec, Canada, studied by Kreg Ettenger, for example, have gained some powers of regional self-determination through treaties. In contrast, the villages described in A. Peter Castro's chapter on Ethiopia constitute the lowest rung in the country's administrative hierarchy. Many of the communities included in this book have experienced social exclusion due to their ethnicity, social class, or other cultural attributes. It should be noted that the authors sometimes differ in their conception of, and priorities about, local or indigenous knowledge. A major industry has grown in academia during the past four decades about the nature of indigenous knowledge, and it is beyond the scope and purpose of this chapter or book to review the nuances of these arguments (see Dove, 2006, for a useful account). The concluding chapter of the book, however, presents some reflections by the editors on the nature and continued relevance of indigenous knowledge in the context of climate change adaptation.

Africa

REDD is viewed by its proponents as offering a win–win solution to the problems of carbon emission, sustainable forestry management, and poverty alleviation. Philip Burnham questions whether the UN-REDD Programme offers effective and equitable tools for combating climate change in Central Africa's forest areas. He uses Cameroon's disappointing experience with donor-driven community forestry since 1994 as a lens for viewing probable limitations in the conception and implementation of REDD. Officials designed and implemented the policy with minimal public involvement, seeking instead to emphasize Forest Department priorities of commercial logging and centralized management. Despite provisions for timber revenue sharing with local communities, the latter have yet to see returns, raising doubts about future financial disbursements from REDD. Burnham is not completely dismissive of REDD, however, noting that the work of Jerome Lewis and others demonstrates the capacity of rural communities to engage in REDD-oriented forest monitoring and management. Thus, the issue may be identifying the appropriate social scale at which REDD can operate to provide economic benefits to forest dwellers.

Planning for climate change adaptations in food-insecure communities requires analysis of 'the complex structures and causes of present vulnerability, and how it may evolve over the coming decades' (Bohle et al., 1994: 37). A. Peter Castro explores the complex relationship between social vulnerability and climatic variability in the north-eastern highlands of Ethiopia. Plough-based agriculture, with its cropping system attuned to local agro-ecological conditions, has long sustained rural communities in South Wollo and Oromiya Zones of Amhara Regional State. As a result of socio-economic forces and national policies in the 20th century, however, these areas became highly vulnerable to chronic food insecurity and famine. Climate change in the region now appears to be increasing the unpredictability of rainfall. Despite their widespread poverty, villagers pursue a number of strategies to deal with the uncertainties of climate change and livelihood challenges. They are trying to adjust local farming practices to meet changing needs and new conditions, while also pursuing non-farm and off-farm opportunities. Many recent government policies, including land titling, relief safety nets, and infrastructure development appear to be increasing economic opportunities and strengthening livelihood pursuits, though their long-term outlook is uncertain.

Climate change is only one of many challenges facing rural communities. Kate Wellard, Daimon Kambewa, and Sieglinde Snapp examine the responses of smallholders in central and northern Malawi to long- and short-term changes to their physical and institutional environments. In portraying community, household, and individual strategies regarding resource use and economic activities, they highlight the importance of gender and other socio-economic attributes. It bears emphasis that the gender dimensions of climate change are overlooked, yet awareness and understanding of them are crucial for addressing gender justice (Terry, 2009). The authors demonstrate that people engage in a range of actions, including crop and livelihood diversification, and soil, water, and land management. They also document that communities and households attempt to build their knowledge and skills on risk assessment and management principles from a variety of sources. Their chapter urges development agencies to engage in genuine partnership with rural communities, strengthening local capacity to address complex local and wider risks.

Dan Taylor's chapter also addresses the issues of risk and vulnerability, focusing on the causes and implications of southern Africa's increased maize dependency in the face of growing environmental uncertainty. Drawing on research in Malawi, South Africa, and Zimbabwe, the author describes the rise of maize – including new hybrid varieties – which is supplanting long-standing grains such as sorghum and millet which were well suited to the region's drought-prone conditions. This substitution of staples signals not only an economic and dietary change, but a significant institutional and symbolic shift. Communities are experiencing 'de-agrarianization' and commoditization, creating a new 'calculus of risk' affecting social and physical reproduction. As a result, the rural poor face increasing uncertainty. Within this context global warming, as portrayed by official sources, donor agencies, and the mass media, is becoming a meta-narrative on development that largely expresses the positions of powerful interests, making it appear that the rural African poor are responsible for their own increased climatic vulnerability. Taylor calls for giving renewed attention to long-standing, resilient local resource management and agrarian practices.

L. Jen Shaffer examines attempts by poor communities in southern Mozambique's Matutúine District to increase their local capacity for dealing with global warming, shifting national policies, international conservation efforts, and other forces increasingly influencing their lives. The author argues that rural people are not simply waiting for development assistance to be delivered, but eagerly seek out available sources of information, including immigrants, mass media, local people with travel experience, outside researchers, and members of non-governmental organizations. The purpose of this learning process is not to supplant local knowledge, but to enlarge and supplement it, enhancing or strengthening people's ability to pursue livelihoods and engage in public decision-making. Outsiders who seek to contribute to this process need to recognize that this process involves two-way communication; those engaged in assistance activities need to learn about the communities, their capacities and needs, to be effective. Shaffer's point is one often repeated in development discourse; it bears reflecting not only on why it is often repeated, but also why such repetition is necessary. Planners and policy makers often assume that they know what the public wants and needs but such assumptions are frequently inaccurate or incomplete. There is no substitute for public participation.

Climate change poses a significant challenge for sustaining livelihoods and fostering peace in the violence-torn Darfur region of western Sudan. Yassir Hassan Satti and A. Peter Castro's paper examines the situation of onion and potato growers in Zalingei, West Darfur State. Fur communities in Zalingei have displayed considerable initiative and ingenuity in adopting these two horticultural crops on a small scale since at least the 1940s. Households developed irrigated farming practices based on traditional technology, while developing local varieties. During the 1980s the Jebel Marra Rural Development Project fostered the expansion of these crops through infrastructural development and extension services. The ability of households to act in recent years has been constrained by an overall lack of resources, as well as by broader socio-economic and political concerns, especially the region's large-scale violence. Droughts and desertification intensified competition for resources in Darfur's increasingly volatile political setting, setting off clashes among farming and herding groups. Many farming households fled their homes, residing in camps for internally displaced populations. The remaining farming communities must not only deal with security concerns but also changing climatic conditions. Future expansion of onion and potato production by smallholders will require investment in research, extension, and training regarding the new agro-ecological conditions arising from climate change. The authors emphasize that the participation of local people is crucial in devising climate change adaptations. Attempts to improve local livelihoods will also ultimately depend on the effectiveness of efforts to resolve conflicts and to promote reconciliation among Darfur's diverse populations.

The Americas and Europe

Glacial retreat in many parts of the world offers some of the most compelling evidence for global warming (World Glacier Monitoring Service, 2008). Declining glaciers and ice caps are having negative impacts on water supplies and sea levels. K.W. Dunbar, Julie Brugger, Christine Jurt, and Ben Orlove compare local perceptions of environmental change in three areas experiencing shrinking and thinning glaciers: the Peruvian Andes, the Italian Alps, and the North Cascades in the United States. Thus, their study differs from others in this collection in that two of their research sites involve populations from industrialized countries. As might be expected, their perceptions differed, reflecting their varying uses, reliance on, and interactions with the glaciers. Yet, people in all three sites felt that they were losing, in various ways, valuable local knowledge for adapting to environmental change. The authors suggest that engagement of the communities in climate change mitigation and adaptation efforts must take into account their existing relationships and concerns with the local environment. Overall, the case study serves as a reminder that global warming is not only being experienced in developing countries, but has significant economic and cultural implications for communities in industrialized nations as well.

For many societies, what constitutes local environmental knowledge is being generated within a context of rapid ecological, technological, and cultural change. Kreg Ettenger reports on dramatic adaptations occurring among the Cree in the subarctic region of northern Quebec. Until 40 years ago, the Cree were isolated, impoverished, and culturally marginalized foragers. Large-scale industrial development, especially hydropower dams, and a land claims settlement have transformed Cree lifestyles and institutions. Many Cree households, however, continue to engage in hunting, fishing, and gathering, albeit with the latest technology, in a landscape transformed by dammed rivers, deforestation, and other industrial development. Climate change, especially increasingly unpredictable ice conditions and more frequent occurrence of severe storms, is creating new risks for foragers. Along with shifts in wildlife populations, it is also causing people to alter long-standing strategies and techniques. Cree environmental knowledge and practices are undergoing rapid modification as they strive to keep up with the sweeping and complex transformations occurring in their homeland.

People worldwide have often associated climate change and intemperate weather with moral or religious connotations (Strauss and Orlove, 2003). Kristine Skarbø, Kristin Vander Molen, Rosa Ramos and Robert E. Rhoades show how some Kichwa villagers in Cotacachi, Ecuador, explain the area's increasingly warm temperatures and erratic rainfall in terms of people's disrespect for their customary spiritual beliefs and practices. The long-standing local agricultural calendar is intimately connected to their indigenous 'cosmovision' based upon respect for the natural world and its constituent supernatural elements. The authors hope that an awareness of the Kichwa's holistic and spiritual ideas may cause readers to reconsider their relationship with, and dependency on, nature; providing an important step in furthering environmental change. While their argument may appear utopian in the context of a globalized society supposedly driven by self-interest, it is important to bear in mind that social and moral motives also influence human behaviour (Wilk and Cliggett, 2007).

Raymond Orr and David Anderson also consider the importance of cultural values in examining the possible involvement of American Indian communities in climate change-related renewable energy projects. Once marginalized by dispossession, official paternalism, and discrimination, some indigenous groups now consider using their reservations for wind power, biofuels, and other green-oriented investments, seeing it as compatible with their self-identities as ecological stewards. Federal subsidies provide significant incentives. In addition, evidence of climate change is apparent in the American Southwest. Nevertheless, numerous factors have held back implementation of such endeavours, including bureaucratic and legal constraints, as well as mistrust of outsiders based on past history. Still, the authors are optimistic about the possibility of these enterprises getting under way; as such projects could generate renewable energy and wealth for communities. Recent pronouncements by several companies about corporate social responsibility and environmentally-friendly investment suggest that a space may be opening for greater collaboration between the private sector and local communities. However, it is important to bear in mind the considerable conflicts and tensions that often prevail in corporate–community relations. This was manifested, for example, in the infamous and long-lasting 'Amazon Chernobyl' lawsuit between Ecuadorian Indians and the Chevron Corporation (Donziger, 2004).

Betty Bernice Faust, Armando Anaya-Hernández, and Helga Geovannini-Acuña promote another kind of collaboration with local communities involving researchers who seek to discover possibly useful past indigenous land use practices. Based on archaeological excavations and ethnographic studies in Campeche, Mexico, the authors are seeking to reclaim a pre-Hispanic Mayan canal system involving raised fields. They believe that this technology may help increase food security among local families who are already hard-hit by global warming, neo-liberal policies, and other predicaments. The authors' work is still incomplete, as they have yet to fulfil their goal of working with farm households to re-establish the irrigation works. Their initiative underscores the potential value of collaboration between communities and action-oriented researchers.

Asia and Oceania

The last group of papers deals with Asia and Oceania. David Lewis notes that climate change is emerging as a priority in Bangladesh's national planning – including among foreign aid agencies – as rising sea levels and floods, due to the melting of glaciers and ice caps, pose grave threats. He warns about the importance of learning from past environmental interventions, using the example of Bangladesh's Flood Action Plan (FAP), a major donor-led initiative. Although largely forgotten today, the FAP received the support of the country's government, as well as millions of dollars in donor support, between 1989 and 1993. These parties eventually abandoned this unpopular 'top-down' initiative. Communities resisted it and new technical experts provided different advice about dealing with Bangladesh's complex environment. Lewis argues that the country's needs regarding climate change will be better served by participatory approaches that pay close attention to past policy experience.

People worldwide not only perceive environmental processes, including climate change, through their own observations, but through the lenses of the mass media and other sources. As Akhil Gupta (1998: 264) observed regarding 'indigenous' agriculture practices in northern India, farmers' knowledge consisted of 'a mix of hybridity, mistranslations, and incommensurability'. This complex 'mix' is evident in Dineshkumar

Moghariya's study of risk perceptions regarding climate change in rural Saurastra and Kutch regions of Western India. He points out that people's responses differed on the basis of location. Interviewees in the drought-prone areas perceive less risk than those living in the cyclone-prone areas. Moghariya reports that many villagers did not believe that their livelihoods, including farm productivity, would suffer due to climate change, despite future increase in temperature and uncertain or heavy rainfall, or the possible spread of new plant diseases. Several of them assert that innovations in agricultural science will address any unwarranted situations. Others claim that growth in off-farm sources of income would sustain them. Moghariya's respondents blame climate change on deforestation, burning fossil fuels, and overpopulation, though their explanations sometimes consist of reinterpretations of external sources illustrating the concepts of 'hybridity, mistranslations, and incommensurability'.

Yancey Orr, Russell Schimmer, and Roland Geerken also explore the nature of local understanding of climate change in east Sumba, Indonesia. They also observed that the national media influence east Sumbanese understanding of environmental relationships, but they generally do not dictate how individuals understand their local ecology. The authors contend that phenomenological experiences such as shade, moisture, dew, heat, and sunlight serve as the basis for local explanations of drought. These experiences also provide the means to reorganize outside information about global climate change. This use of individual experience largely explains why the Sumbanese ecological model focuses solely on the role of vegetation in altering climate patterns, while ignoring widely reported factors in the media such as industrial pollution and carbon emissions.

Rural communities are not experiencing global warming in isolation, but finding that it often 'magnifies already existing problems of poverty, deterritoriality, marginalization, and non-inclusion in national and international policy-making processes and discourses' (Crate and Nuttall, 2009: 12). Thanh Vo and Jack Manno's study of Tam Giang Cau Hai lagoon in Vietnam describes how local communities are attempting to adjust to climate change within a context of sweeping political, economic, and social change. Their country's embrace of neo-liberal policy, including heavy promotion of commercial aquaculture and fishing, has had enormous implications for resource use. The authors observe that adaptation occurs through innovations drawing upon local knowledge of weather patterns, currents, fish behaviour and other environmental features. It also depends on local social norms. They document how community members devised innovative structures known as net enclosed ponds that combine prawn aquaculture with their traditional-style fish corrals. However, the success, popularity and density of these ponds have brought additional problems to the lagoon users, further challenging local social and ecosystem resilience.

Conclusion

Climate change is one of the greatest challenges confronting humanity in the 21st century. Major negotiations, planning efforts, and investments are under way. There is the danger that these efforts will over-emphasize technical and financial approaches that will serve to further exacerbate the problems faced by vulnerable communities. The contributors to this book call for climate change efforts that address the rights, interests, needs, and capacities of rural people, including indigenous groups. These communities and groups must engage as active participants in the design and governance of climate change interventions. The justification for their inclusion in climate negotiations and subsequent action is more than a matter of common courtesy, technical strategy, or positive instrumental outcome: it is their right. Without climate justice, there will not be timely mitigation and adaptation to climate change; neither will there be development, or the social justice that will underpin a better world.

Author updates to the 2025 edition

For the rerelease of this volume approximately 12 years after its original publication, we have included updates for each chapter. The original authors updated their work for most chapters and when not possible, the editor or an expert in the field has provided analysis of developments in the academic fields relevant to the original studies. When updating their chapters, authors focused on how their field-sites have changed, developments in the academic literature regarding climate change or how their research has built on this original work.

References

Adger, W., Lorenzoni, I., and O'Brien, K. (eds) (2009) *Adapting to Climate Change: Thresholds, Values, Governance*, Cambridge University Press, Cambridge.

Angelsen, A. (ed.) (2009) *Realising REDD+: National Strategy and Policy Options*, Center for International Forestry Research, Bogor Barat, Indonesia.

Bates, B., Kundzewicz, Z., Wu, S., and Palutikof, J. (eds) (2008) *Climate Change and Water*, Intergovernmental Panel on Climate Change Secretariat, Geneva.

Bohle, H., Downing, T., and Watts, M. (1994) 'Climate change and social vulnerability: Toward a sociology and geography of food insecurity', *Global Environmental Change* 4: 37–48.

Castro, A. and Nielsen, E. (2001) 'Indigenous people and co-management: Implications for conflict management', *Environmental Science and Policy* 4: 229–39.

Crate, S. and Nuttall, M. (2009) 'Introduction: Anthropology and climate change', in S. Crate and M. Nuttall (eds), *Anthropology and Climate Change: From Encounters to Actions*, pp. 9–36, Left Coast Press, Walnut Creek.

Desmarais, A. (2007) *La Vía Campesina: Globalization and the Power of Peasants*, Fernwood, Halifax.

Donziger, S. (2004) 'Rainforest Chernobyl: Litigating indigenous rights and the environment in Latin America', *Human Rights Briefs* 11: 1–4.

Dove, M. (2006) 'Indigenous people and environmental politics', *Annual Review of Anthropology* 35: 191–208.

Ensor, J. and Berger, R. (eds) (2009) *Understanding Climate Change Adaptation: Lessons from Community-Based Approaches*, Practical Action Publishing, Rugby.

Galloway McLean, K., Ramos-Castillo, A., Gross, T., Johnston, S., Vierros, M., and Noa, R. (2009) *Report of the Indigenous Peoples' Global Summit on Climate Change: 20–4 April 2009, Anchorage, Alaska*, United Nations University, Darwin, Australia.

Gupta, A. (1998) *Postcolonial Developments: Agriculture in the Making of Modern India*, Duke University Press, Durham.

Juma, C. (2011) *The New Harvest: Agricultural Innovation in Africa*, Oxford University Press, Oxford.

Leach, M., Scoones, I. and Stirling, A. (2010) *Dynamic Sustainabilities: Technology, Environment, Social Justice*, Earthscan, London.

Leslie, J. (2005) *Deep Water: The Epic Struggle over Dams, Displaced People, and the Environment*, Farrar, Straus and Giroux, New York.

Lynch, O. (2011) *Mandating Recognition: International Law and Native/Aboriginal Title*, Rights and Resources Initiative, Washington, DC.

Nelson, D. (2009) 'Conclusion: Transforming the world', in W. Adger, I. Lorenzoni, and K. O'Brien (eds) (2009) *Adapting to Climate Change: Thresholds, Values, Governance*, pp. 491–500, Cambridge University Press, Cambridge.

Parry, M., Canziani, O., Palutikof, J., van der Linden, P., and Hanson, C. (eds), *Climate Change 2007: Impacts, Adaptation and Vulnerability*, Contribution of Working Group II to the Fourth Assessment Report of the Intergovernmental Panel on Climate Change, Cambridge University Press, Cambridge.

Pelling, M. (2011) *Adaptation to Climate Change: From Resilience to Transformation*, Routledge, New York.

Posey, D. (ed.) (1999) *Cultural and Spiritual Values of Biodiversity: A Complementary Contribution to the Global Biodiversity Assessment*, United Nations Environmental Programme and Intermediate Technology Publications, London.

Revkin, A. (1992) *Global Warming: Understanding the Forecast*, Abbeville Press, New York.

Schumacher, E.F. (1973) *Small Is Beautiful: Economics as if People Mattered*, Bond and Briggs, London.

Singer, P. (2002) *One World: The Ethics of Globalization*, Yale University Press, New Haven.

Strauss, S. and Orlove, B. (eds), (2003) *Weather, Climate, and Culture*, Berg, Oxford.

Terry, G. (ed.), (2009) *Climate Change and Gender Justice*, Practical Action Publishing and Oxfam, Rugby.

Toulmin, C. and Huq, S. (2006) 'Africa and climate change', *Sustainable Development Opinion*. International Institute for Environment and Development.

UNDP (2007) *Human Development Report 2007/2008: Fighting Climate Change: Human Solidarity in a Divided World*, United Nations Development Programme, New York.

Wilk, R. and Cliggett, L. (2007) *Economies and Cultures: Foundations of Economic Anthropology*, 2nd edn, Westview, Boulder.

World Bank (2010) *World Development Report 2010: Development and Climate Change*, World Bank, Washington, DC.

World Glacier Monitoring Service (2008) *Global Glacier Changes: Facts and Figures*, United Nations Environmental Programme, Nairobi.

About the authors

A. Peter Castro is Professor Emeritus of Anthropology in the Maxwell School of Citizenship and Public Affairs at Syracuse University in Syracuse, New York. He is an applied cultural anthropologist specializing in agrarian livelihoods, natural resource conflict management, and rural social change, especially in East Africa.

Dan Taylor is the Director of the British non-governmental organization Find Your Feet, and Tutor in International Development at the Open University. He has a PhD in Anthropology from University College London. He has agricultural and rural development experience in Latin America, Oceania, South Asia and southern Africa.

David W. Brokensha (1923-2017) is Professor Emeritus of Anthropology and Environmental Studies at the University of California, Santa Barbara. He was a Director of the Institute for Development Anthropology from 1976 to 2000.

Chapter 2

Climate change and forest conservation: A REDD flag for Central African forest people?

Philip Burnham and Simon Hoyte

Looking at the impacts of recent forest legislation in Cameroon, this paper as originally framed in 2011 highlighted potential implications of REDD+ initiatives (Reducing Emissions from Deforestation and Degradation) for inhabitants of Central African forests. Created without due attention to the systems of indigenous knowledge and resource tenure of forest peoples, community forests have not fulfilled their promise in bringing sustainable development and effective forest management and, in the context of weak governance, have raised questions whether national-level REDD programmes could offer effective and equitable tools for combating climate change. The closing section of the paper provides a review of some of the substantial work on these themes that has been produced since 2011. It also considers the ongoing efforts to involve local people in forest mapping and monitoring using locally adapted GIS methods.

Introduction

The general theme of our book poses several challenges for someone working in the forested regions of Central Africa. First there is the difficulty of predicting the likely effects of climate changes such as global warming on the forest environments of the Congo Basin. Will increasing temperatures be associated with decreasing rainfall and desiccation of forests, followed by progressive encroachment of savanna, or will increased temperatures lead to increased rainfall and forest expansion, as has sometimes happened in the past? Will increasing atmospheric carbon dioxide concentrations enhance or reduce carbon capture by tropical forests? We claim no expertise in climatology or forest ecology, and the sources that we have read do not give unambiguous answers to these questions. The answers are clearly dependent, at least in part, on the time scale one considers, since palaeoecological studies in Central Africa do show considerable fluctuation of forest cover when viewed over longer time periods (Brncic et al., 2007; Clark 2004; Lewis, S. et al., 2009; Maley, 1990, 2001; Stager, 2001). Over a shorter time period, such as the human lifespan, it may be that change in forest cover and species composition will be quite variable spatially and will not show a directionality that is clearly linkable with longer term trends in climate change. Moreover, as experienced by forest peoples, changes in climate may have effects that are unforeseen by outsiders. For example, our colleague Jerome Lewis reports (pers. com. 2010) that the Mbendjele Yaka hunters of the Congo forests with whom he has long worked complain to him about the recent "disappearance" of the dry season, a time when game is easier to hunt. Such possibly short-term changes, which forest peoples are used to dealing with, may of course not be reflective of longer term climate trends.

A second set of general issues that must be addressed when considering potential or actual adaptations of indigenous peoples to climate change relates to the fact that bodies of indigenous knowledge are necessarily deployed in particular political-economic contexts. In the case of the present-day peoples of the Central African forest zone, the relevant context is one that is dominated by large scale commercial logging, on the one hand, and by programmes of biodiversity conservation and forest management (many of which have been stimulated by concern about climate change) on the other. We will devote some attention to current relations between indigenous peoples, local communities and commercial loggers later in this paper, but we will begin by looking at the significance of indigenous knowledge for conserving forests in the context of international concerns about climate change. As we will see, discourses relating to climate change have had and will continue to have strong impacts on the lives of the inhabitants of the Central African forest zone. In many respects at the present time, these political-economic impacts are of much more immediate adaptational significance for Central African people than any discernible objective change in climate.

The emergence of REDD policies

Especially since the 1980s, anxieties about the impacts of climate change, along with closely linked worries concerning the loss of tropical forests and global biodiversity, have been manifested in the organisation of numerous international conferences and in the framing of several global agreements to respond to these perceived threats. While all of these initiatives have had demonstrable impacts on the inhabitants of the Central African forest zone, in the present paper we will be particularly focusing on the implications of the REDD concept. As explained in The Little REDD+ Book (Global Canopy Programme, 2009: 14): "The basic idea behind Reducing Emissions from Deforestation and Degradation is simple: Countries that are willing and able to reduce emissions from deforestation should be financially compensated for doing so." The '+' that is now often added to REDD is designed to draw attention to the possibility that "REDD could simultaneously address climate change and rural poverty, while conserving biodiversity and sustaining vital ecosystem services" (Global Canopy Programme, 2009: 14). In recent decades it has become standard for international REDD policy discussions to acknowledge the need to protect the interests of local, and particularly indigenous, people (e.g. UN-REDD Programme, 2009). However problems of scale combined with the common reliance on state-based solutions in the context of weak governance have tended to block the realisation of such good intentions. It is not within the scope of this short paper to consider all the complexities of REDD initiatives in Central African countries but by looking at some of the experiences over the past three decades of programmes of forest management in Cameroon, we hope to highlight some potential implications of REDD for the inhabitants of the Central African forests.

Cameroon's 1994 forestry law

A basic argument of the present paper is that international climate change and forest conservation agreements have local effects that are seldom adequately foreseen or dealt with by the signatories to such agreements. To illustrate this point, we will consider the case of Cameroon's 1994 forestry law – legislation that emerged as a result of the impacts of the international Tropical Forestry Action Plan (TFAP) agreement of 1985, the subsequent UNDP-FAO-inspired National Forestry Action Plan for Cameroon (UNDP-FAO, 1988), and the World Bank's (1992) World Development Report combined with its structural adjustment and decentralisation policies (see Ekoko, 1997).

As Winterbottom (1992: 223–4) noted in his review of the TFAP planning process in Cameroon, although the UN agencies had adopted guidelines stipulating the critical importance for the TFAP of the traditional knowledge and resource management practices of forest-dwelling people as well as broadly based and participative consultation on potential impacts, none of the recommended procedures were followed. The central concerns that dominated Cameroon's TFAP were sustainable forest management and biodiversity conservation in the context of increasing timber production to support the national economy. In his analysis of the political economy of the 1994 legislation, Ekoko (1997: 15; see also Nguiffo, 1994: 45) argues that "forest dwellers and NGOs were almost completely absent from the discussions" at the law's drafting stage. The one component of the legislation that did make a nod toward local community interests was the inclusion, at the insistence of the World Bank, of clauses on community forests under which a group of villagers could apply for 25-year exclusive use rights over a 5,000 hectare tract of forest to be exploited and managed by them according to a management plan agreed with the Forestry Department (Burnham and Graziani, 2004). That said, despite the fact that the World Bank's 1991 Operational Directive on Indigenous Peoples envisioned the informed participation of the people themselves through direct consultation in the planning of actions that affect them, no such consultation took place in preparing Cameroon's community forestry legislation (Burnham, 2000).

Despite this disappointing beginning, it remains the case that it is within community forests that, in legal terms at least, there is the greatest potential for local people to deploy their indigenous knowledge systems in forest management since the vast majority of Cameroon's humid forest zone has been gazetted for other purposes. Cameroon's 1994 forest law stipulated that a national forest management plan (commonly referred to as the "Plan de Zonage") be established that would divide the forested portion of the country into areas earmarked for various uses. While the "permanent forest estate" comprised extensive zones designated for sustainable logging by timber companies holding long-term licenses, other areas were allocated to biodiversity reserves, national parks, mining concessions, etc. The mapping for the national plan was carried out by a Canadian consultancy firm using remotely sensed data with no ground-truthing. In the major logging zones, the plan restricted farming activities, the major source of livelihood for the village populations of these districts, to narrow strips of land that typically extended only five kilometres on either side of the motorable roads (Joiris, 1997a: 43, 1997b: 101–2; Etoungou, 2003: 8). The methodological assumptions used by the consultants to establish the plan were designed to maximise the amount of forest earmarked for timber exploitation, and the consultants' report frankly admitted that the land allocated for agriculture would not be sufficient for the population's requirements over the long term (Côté, 1993: 33–34).

It is abundantly clear that this plan failed to take account of the actual modes of usage of Cameroon's forests by indigenous populations which display marked seasonal mobility and spatially extensive patterns of resource exploitation (Joiris, 1997b: 102) that are of key importance for these people in underpinning their capacities to adapt to environmental change. Although the farmers and hunter-gatherers that inhabit this zone do maintain their principal settlements today along the motorable roads, they also farm, hunt, fish and gather over very wide tracts of forest, establishing short- or longer-term encampments as required in favourable resource locations that, under the national forest management plan, are now reserved exclusively for logging, trophy hunting or biodiversity reserves. Detailed studies of Central African forest populations' systems of indigenous knowledge and patterns of usage of their forest environments have revealed complex mosaics of vegetation types that reflect the influences of not only relief, drainage, and other geomorphologic or climatological factors but also histories of human settlement. Depending on the time since their abandonment, the sites of former villages and fields each support distinctive vegetation types that are utilised in different ways by local people (Dounias, 1993, 1996; Hladik et al., 1990; de Wachter, 1997). This vegetational diversity is a key element in the adaptational potential of forest peoples in the face of climate change.

Moreover, as de Wachter's study (1997: 63, our translation) of the system of root crop agriculture and associated practices of hunting and gathering of the Badjwe people of south-eastern Cameroon shows, "... the impact of (Badjwe) root crop agriculture on the forest ... is not presently a menace to the primary forests of the Dja (river basin) and the landscape created by Badjwe root crop agriculture is a mosaic of primary and secondary forests capable of sustaining a level of hunting pressure greater than that of primary forest."

As we have argued in another context (Burnham, 1979), the high productivity of systems of root crop agriculture combined with the high levels of population mobility characteristic of many Central African peoples offer enhanced potential for adapting to changing social and environmental circumstances. Speaking of such Central African systems of root crop agriculture, Joiris (1997b: 101–102) argues (our translation): "Their economic system is complex. They require long agricultural fallow periods, and they manage vast forest tracts in ways that permit a long-term and sustainable exploitation of the fragile forest environment. Certainly, these societies have been subject to heavy prejudices in the colonial and post-colonial periods. However, one can reasonably argue that if their tropical forest ecosystems have maintained their astonishing diversity up to today, it is because, in spite of everything, these societies have well adapted economic systems." In other words, the systems of indigenous knowledge of Central African forest peoples are well adapted to sustainable forest management and offer considerable potential for playing an effective role within the emerging context of community forestry and REDD policies.

Cameroon's experience of community forestry

As already mentioned, the one element in Cameroon's 1994 forestry law that could be said to have taken some account of the interests and indigenous knowledge of the local inhabitants of the forest zone were the clauses establishing the possibility of creating community forests. However, the community forestry clauses were drafted in a form that was ill-adapted to the social realities of forest societies, which has ensured that they would be difficult to apply (Nguiffo, 1998; Burnham and Graziani, 2004). Moreover, this aspect of the law was distinctly unpopular with the Cameroon Forestry Department, which took the view that local communities were incapable of effectively managing forests and dragged its heels in implementing it. It was only as a result of pressure from the British government from 1995 that a Community Forestry Development Unit was eventually created within Cameroon's Ministry of Environment and Forests, with the brief to promote the application of the community forest legislation (MINEF, 1997).

Unfortunately, the subsequent history of the community forestry initiative in Cameroon has not been encouraging (Etoungou, 2003; Oyono, 2004a, 2004b; de Blas et al., 2011; Duguma et al., 2018). The politically uncentralised structures of the societies of Cameroon's forest zone along with the complex historical layering of local and state legal systems (Karsenty, 1999; Burnham, 2000; Burnham and Graziani, 2004: Oyono et al., 2007) combine to make collective decision-making and management of financially valuable resources extremely difficult – an outcome that would have been predictable had those who drafted the 1994 forestry legislation taken the trouble to inform themselves of the relevant ethnographic literature (e.g. Geschiere, 1982). The complex and expensive process of gaining the various governmental approvals to establish a community forest have typically proved to be beyond the capacities of local village community groups without the assistance either of external NGOs or of well-placed village elites (Etoungou, 2003; Oyono, 2004a). And many of the latter have shown themselves to be more interested in using the community forest legislation as a cover for illegal logging than for sustainable management of a village's forest resources for the collective good (Milol, 1998; Lewis, 2007: 6).

Despite the very evident problems affecting community forests in Cameroon, the concept remains popular among policy makers in Central Africa, with other modes of application being attempted in Gabon and Democratic Republic of the Congo. And given that Central African forests are such a valuable resource, whether one views them in terms of the value of their timber or in terms of their conservation values, it is largely in the context of community forests that local systems of indigenous knowledge are given any scope for ongoing application. Apart from their potential to deliver greater local participation in forest management and enhanced equity in revenue distribution (Karsenty et al., 2010: 8), community forests also have appeal for policy makers because they tend to be located in relatively populated areas that are under threat of deforestation from agricultural activities. Karsenty and colleagues (2010) advocate a 'payment for environmental services' (PES) approach to supporting community forests as part of a REDD scheme, a topic that we discuss further below.

Problems of equity in distribution of REDD benefits

While a fundamental principle underpinning current REDD proposals is that less developed countries that conserve their forests will be compensated by developed countries, there is considerable cause for concern that the local people inhabiting these forests may not receive an equitable share of these payments. Once again, the Cameroon case is very instructive in this regard. The 1994 law prescribed that a proportion of the taxes collected from loggers would be returned to the rural communes and villages to support local development projects. In this respect, the 1994 law did not represent an innovation since already for several decades legislation had been on the books to share such revenue. A Cameroon government body known as FEICOM was created in 1974 to redistribute tax revenues to communes and villages, but the performance of this body has been very unsatisfactory.

According to the 1994 law, the element of forestry taxes known as the 'annual forestry fee' was to be shared between the central government (50%), rural communes in the forest zones (40%) and village communities in the forest zones (10%). In 2006, Oyono, Cerutti and Morrison (2009; see also Cerutti et al., 2010) carried out a study of the actual distribution of forestry fees in a sample of communes and villages and found major irregularities in accounting and utilisation. At each stage of the disbursement process from central government, significant proportions of the funds went missing and, even for the proportion that did arrive at its proper destination, this was often not used for the intended purpose of promoting local development. As Oyono et al. (2009: 8) report, "numerous villages have yet to benefit from any projects while their forests are exploited (and) local communities believe the distribution and utilization of the annual forestry fee to be unfair and only contribute to increasing the wealth of the state, the mayors and the sous-préfets." In the circumstances, it is hardly surprising that, shortly after Oyono et al. completed their study, the Director of FEICOM Mr. Ondo Ndong was sentenced to 50 years in prison for embezzlement of 11 billion CFA (equivalent to £14,000,000) of the institution's funds (Dibussi, 2007).

The rural populations of Cameroon's forested zones are very used to such behaviour on the part of central government and, soon after the passage of the 1994 forestry law and in the absence of effective government implementation of its revenue-sharing provisions, an informal arrangement emerged. Village communities began to impose on logging companies their own tax of 1,000 CFA per cubic metre of timber extracted by threatening to block the passage of timber trucks. As a member of our research team observed in the area around Lomie in Cameroon's Eastern Province (Burnham, Graziani and Sharpe, 1998; Burnham and Graziani, 2004; see also Karsenty, 1999: 155 and Karsenty et al., 2010), this practice began to make available unprecedentedly large sums to local villages. However, it also increased tensions and promoted divisions within these communities, which lacked the collective structures to effectively manage this money for local development. In the main, the monies were shared out among individual villagers, who used them largely for personal consumption purposes.

As already discussed, under REDD+, developing countries would be paid by industrialised countries for preserving their forests to compensate for the latter's high levels of carbon emissions. However, one clear lesson to be drawn from the Cameroon case is that the inhabitants of the Central African forest region are not likely to benefit much from REDD payments unless some effective ways can be found to administer them. The World Bank's efforts to promote decentralisation and linked systems of taxation have not been generally successful in Central African countries (Bigombé-Logo, 2003; Etoungou, 2003; Olowu, 2003; Ribot, 2003) and, despite much talk of a commitment to continued 'capacity building', it would seem that we are still years away from effective realisation of these goals. And simply doling out sums of money to forest villages that lack structures to use them effectively for development isn't a satisfactory solution either, as we have seen.

REDD and the problem of scale – local, national, regional or global?

REDD programmes face a fundamental conundrum linked to questions of scale. On the one hand, deforestation needs to be prevented on a very large scale to make a significant impact on climate change. However, large scale programmes in Central Africa would be beset by serious difficulties. Firstly, the populations of the Central African forested zone are typically small and thinly dispersed, and the indigenous knowledge systems that they use to exploit their forest environments are intrinsically local in scale. Although Article 22 of the Rio Declaration states that: "Indigenous people and their communities and other local communities have a vital role in environmental management and development because of their knowledge and traditional practices", in practice, it is these very people who have husbanded the forest resources who risk being alienated from them by global REDD policies and legislation. Although on paper REDD policy statements usually acknowledge that it is essential to bring local people into the planning process, giving them an effective voice (much less fully free, prior and informed consent [FPIC]) has proved to be very difficult (see, e.g. Awana, 2010; Dkamela et al., 2009).

Then too, large scale monitoring of carbon stocks in tropical forests faces serious problems of measurement. From the outset of programmes such as CARPE in the 1990s (Biodiversity Support Program, 1993a, 1993b), considerable hopes have been expressed that the use of satellite imagery could serve as a means of assessing changes in forest cover over the great expanse of Central African forests. However, despite considerable efforts, large scale remotely sensed methods of assessing tropical forest carbon stocks are not yet sufficiently accurate to serve as a reliable basis for determining REDD payments. Bond et al. (2009: 29–30) explain in their report (see also Mayaux et al., 2005): "For the moment, current REDD measurements tend to combine high quality remotely sensed aerial estimates for deforestation and degradation with generalised carbon density numbers obtained from look-up tables and the literature. Such a combination of data with unequal certainties would jeopardise all the effort required to put in place accurate monitoring of gross deforestation, as the certainty of the final estimate will only be as good as the 'least best' uncertainty value" (but see Csillik et al., 2019).

Looking at the measurement issue from the ground up, Lewis's innovative work with several different Central African forest populations in conjunction with GIS software specialists Helveta has shown that local people can become effectively involved in forest management and monitoring through the use of adapted GPS technology (Lewis, J., 2008; Hopkin, 2007). By developing a visual icon-based system that can be run on a robust GPS handset, Lewis was able rapidly to train non-literate Mbendjele BaYaka in the Congo Republic to deploy their indigenous knowledge and create maps of their forest resources and ritual sites. On this basis, working with a local forestry company seeking Forest Stewardship Council certification for its timber, detailed maps of logging concessions could be drawn automatically by computer-aided design so that the company could avoid cutting trees or damaging sites of importance for local livelihoods and cultural sensitivities. In Cameroon, Lewis and Helveta have used a similar system to enable local people to monitor illegal logging (Lewis, J., 2007; Helveta, 2009), and this monitoring project is now being scaled up to national level. Based on this experience, the potential to develop a cost-effective system of sub-national or national scale carbon monitoring by local people as part of a REDD programme would seem apparent and would have the advantage of drawing on local people's intimate knowledge of their environment (see Skutsch, 2008).

Another unresolved issue is the question of at what geographical scale REDD+ activities should be pursued. Many commentators tend to favour using the national level, which has the advantage of being of broad enough scale to be significant for moderating climate change while also corresponding to the level of authority at which multilateral environmental agreements are ratified. However, as we have seen for Central African countries, national or regional scale REDD solutions face inherent problems of equity in distributing benefits. Other commentators favour sub-national REDD projects, which are typically referred to in the literature as 'payment for ecological services' (PES) projects (Karsenty, 2009; Karsenty et al., 2010), combined with a "gradual scaling up strategy" (Daviet, 2010). Not only do such more localised PES projects offer increased likelihood of equitable distribution of benefits to the local people involved but it is also at this scale that indigenous knowledge systems have the greatest potential to assist in well-adapted, sustainable forest management. As Bond et al. (2009: iv) explain in their recent review of REDD thinking: "The emergence of the concept of payments for ecosystem services has raised expectations among many stakeholders that ecosystems can be conserved through popular payments to ecosystem service providers rather than through unpopular measures of command and control ... The findings of this report are that payments for ecosystem services can create incentives for reducing emissions from deforestation and degradation. They are, however, not a universal panacea. A crucial issue is the overall national and forest governance framework. Under conditions of weak governance it is very difficult for payments for ecosystem services to be effective."

Author updates to the 2025 edition

Thirteen years have passed since this chapter was originally written, and much commentary has appeared over this period on the implications of REDD+ policies for forest peoples. Unfortunately, as we remarked in 2011 (and which is still true today), when we read many of the latest pronouncements on REDD+ in Central Africa, we are inclined to agree with Yogi Berra that "it's déjà vu all over again". As Bond et al. (2009: ix) aptly argued (see also Karsenty and Ongolo, 2012), "it is naïve to believe that it is easy to change and improve forest governance – there are many deep and vested interests in maintaining the status quo." Most of the warnings that we voiced in 2011 have proven true over the intervening period and, in this update we briefly review some of these ongoing problems, while pointing as well to some promising developments.

At a global level, the general verdict on the achievements of the REDD+ programme since its inception in 2005 is not encouraging. In 2018, the Center for International Forestry Research (CIFOR) published a collection of papers (Angelsen et al. (eds.), 2018) critically reviewing achievements of the previous ten years of the REDD+ initiative. Summarising some of their main findings, they noted (pp. xxii–xxiv), "Land tenure and the rights of indigenous peoples and local communities have been prominent on the REDD+ agenda since its early days. Implementation has resulted in some progress on tenure, but not enough to ensure a proper functioning of REDD+." As the CIFOR report also argued (p. xxii), "National forest monitoring systems will need to address participation, transparency, accountability and coordination to counteract the differences in the capacities, resources and powers of various stakeholders."

Regrettably, the Cameroon government has done little to formulate a coherent set of policies and structures to define and coordinate its REDD+ targets and activities. In particular, as was argued in the original version of this chapter and has been reiterated by several researchers subsequently (Dkamela et al., 2014), key lessons that could have been drawn from the experience of implementing Cameroon's 1994 Forestry Law regarding the necessity for an effective involvement of local communities and indigenous peoples in its REDD+ programme have not been taken on board by the Cameroon government (Freudenthal et al., 2011; Willis et al., 2016). Although the Cameroon government was happy to sign up for the REDD+ programme from the outset, evidently viewing it as a lucrative source of funding, it has dragged its feet in implementation (Republic of Cameroon, 2008; 2017). Despite the obvious necessity of revising Cameroon's 1974 national land tenure ordinance, which still retains the underlying French colonial principle that the bulk of the country's forest lands were "vacant and without master" and could therefore be considered to be state land (Egbe, 1996; Fisiy, 1996; Burnham, 2000; Awono et al., 2014b), no new land tenure legislation has been enacted.

With the Cameroon government demonstrably unwilling to address the major causes of deforestation in the form of industrial logging, mining and agribusiness, REDD+ activities have been restricted to a few, mostly small, "pilot" projects organised by local and international NGOs. While small projects are unlikely to reduce emissions at a scale that would significantly contribute to Cameroon's national REDD goals and do not form a part of an effectively coordinated national system (World Bank, 2021), they are nonetheless instructive in the context of this chapter with regard to the involvement of, and their impacts on, Cameroon's forest peoples.

Interestingly, given the perspective adopted in this paper, several of the local REDD+ projects so far undertaken in south-eastern Cameroon have been sited in community forests and have used the "payment for environmental services" (PES) approach to involve local inhabitants. Of course, this is not that surprising since, according to the Plan de Zonage of Cameroon's 1994 Forestry Law and in the absence of meaningful reform of Cameroon's 1974 land tenure law, there is little other space available for local communities to legally undertake forest-related activities. To take one example (Awono et al., 2014a; see also Awono et al., 2014b), community forests at the villages of Ngoyla and Mintom adjacent to the Dja Faunal Reserve have been used as the basis for a pilot project funded by the British government and managed by the Centre pour l'Environnement et le Développement (CED), a Cameroonian NGO working in conjunction with BioClimate, a UK-based environmental consultancy firm, and the Rainforest Foundation.

Although the community forestry management agreements in force in Ngoyla and Mintom permit timber and non-timber forest product extraction, the PES agreements between CED and the communities aimed to end logging, while also providing training in agroforestry methods so as to reduce emissions from traditional agricultural and gathering activities. It was hoped that carbon credits certified by the Plan Vivo Foundation (www.planvivo.org) could serve as a source of remuneration for community PES activities, although Awono et al. (2014a: 205) indicate that CED has expressed doubts about the viability of this plan given the risks and instability of the global carbon market. Potential problems also loom over the question of the equity of benefit sharing between Bantu farmers and indigenous Baka hunter-gatherers, although CED has attempted to develop management mechanisms to deal with this problem. On the other hand, the project is noteworthy for its demonstration of the usefulness of involvement of community members in mapping and monitoring forest resources.

Another REDD pilot project of a different design was established in the Ngoyla-Mintom area in 2010 by the World Wide Fund for Nature (WWF), using funding from the European Union (Freudenthal et al., 2011; Willis et al., 2016; see also Defo, 2020). This project adopted "a more ambitious 'landscape' approach extending across a vast area of forest in the Dja River basin with a view to creating a new IUCN Category I protected area" (Willis et al., 2016: 6). WWF's motivation for developing this project, which targeted extensive areas of forest in the zone officially reserved for large-scale commercial logging, was to protect these forests for biodiversity conservation while also contributing to achieving REDD targets. While the scale of the project has the potential to significantly reduce carbon emissions, it has been strongly criticised for failing to adhere to free, prior and informed consent guidelines, thereby riding roughshod over the rights and livelihoods of the indigenous Baka people and exacerbating the harmful impacts from extensive logging concessions across the Ngoyla-Mintom area (Willis et al., 2016; Nounah and Perram, 2019; Defo, 2020). Likewise, the WWF has been accused of supporting armed eco-guards in its protected areas who target the Baka with extreme abuse in the name of conservation (Hoyte and Clarke, 2020).

As we remarked in the original version of this chapter, there are serious risks that international agreements on climate change such as REDD will mandate forest management programmes which, in the context of the notably weak systems of governance in all the Central African states, will be both ineffectual and seriously prejudicial to the interests of the inhabitants of the forest zone. Unfortunately, as we have described in this 2024 update, some of these risks have become actualities in the forests of south-eastern Cameroon. On the other hand, and despite the fact that there are special challenges for REDD+ in working in commercial logging-dominated contexts, Jerome Lewis and Helveta have demonstrated that it is possible to devise locally adapted programmes of forest monitoring and management that meaningfully include local people. While it may seem counterintuitive to think that modern information technologies such as GPS and computer-aided mapping can assist indigenous peoples in deploying their knowledge systems in ways that contribute both to sustainable forest management and adaptive preservation of their livelihoods, one must not fall into the trap of thinking of systems of indigenous knowledge as existing in timeless isolation from global processes.

Over the past thirteen years, the original tools designed to facilitate participatory mapping and monitoring by the hunter-gatherers in this region have substantially evolved. Teaming up with Muki Haklay, an expert in Geographic Information Systems (GIS), the Extreme Citizen Science research group was born at University College London and the technology was refined resulting in a dedicated Android application named Sapelli Collector (after the sapelli African mahogany tree *Entandrophragma cylindricum*). This was initially tested alongside the Mbendjele BaYaka in Congo in 2012. The methodology was based on a socio-technical process whereby community members would instruct the researchers as to what they would like to map, and icons were formed and uploaded to create a Sapelli project for the relevant community; this was further refined and updated in an iterative manner based on community feedback (Stevens et al., 2014). The innovative features of the Sapelli tool were that for the users it was completely text-free, very adaptable, available to download on cheap Android smartphones, able to collect photo, audio and other media, and could send the data to a database automatically and in a periodic fashion, making use of pockets of mobile network across the landscape. The pioneering work by Gill Conquest, Michalis Vitos, and Julia Attenbuchner showed that non-literate hunter-gatherers could confidently understand and use introduced smartphones, the icon-based Sapelli Collector app, and satellite base-maps, while assessing the inherent power dynamics and ability of the community data to effect the change they envisaged (Conquest, 2013, 2014; Vitos, 2016; Altenbuchner, 2018).

With funding from the European Research Council, a new array of Sapelli Collector projects have recently been initiated. In Namibia, the technology was employed by the Ju|'hoansi to monitor intrusions onto their land by cattle ranchers and assist in game counts. In Kenya, Maasai community members created a Sapelli initiative with over 120 species of medicinal plants in order to facilitate intergenerational transfer of traditional knowledge. Fisher peoples in the Pantanal of Brazil adopted Sapelli to map their traditional fishing territory, leading to the creation of a large community reserve. And in Cameroon, initiatives alongside the Baka and Beti farmers empowered communities to report poaching, conduct biomonitoring of animals, report human-wildlife conflict, map important resource-use sites, collect evidence on eco-guard and other abuses, and even monitor the births and deaths in the village (see Chiaravalloti et al., 2022). The collaborations in Cameroon pushed the emphasis of co-design further by community members drawing their own icons – whether it be using sticks in the mud or charcoal on wood – which heightened the sense of ownership and bottom-up implementation (Hoyte, 2024). These diverse projects led to a formal outline of the methodology which centres heavily on an ethnographic foundation, FPIC (which is commonly abused – see Hoyte, 2022), community protocols, and data sovereignty, and additionally investigates ways in which communities can analyse and visualise their data independently (Moustard et al., 2021). When considering the context of REDD+ in Cameroon, the great advantage of Sapelli is that communities can collect data and evidence independently, whatever their level of literacy, and on their own terms. As our chapter has demonstrated, the hurdles of corruption and mismanagement have greatly compromised the potential for genuine community engagement with, and benefit from, REDD+ initiatives. However, with the availability of free but powerful tools such as Sapelli, those who possess the richest knowledge of the landscape but who remain the most marginalised and ignored can begin to collect data that are meaningful both to themselves and to decision-makers.

References

Altenbuchner, J. (2018) 'Towards inclusive GIS in the Congo Basin: an exploration of digital map creation and an evaluation of map understanding by non-literate hunter-gatherers', PhD dissertation, University College London.

Angelsen, A. et al. (eds.) (2018) *Transforming REDD+: lessons and new directions*, Center for International Forestry Research, Bogor, Indonesia.

Awana, A. (2010) 'Les autochtones de la forêt interpellent les gouvernants', *Le Messager*. March 31, 2010.

Awono, A., E. Barreau and H. Owona (2014a) 'Community Payments for Ecosystem Services in the south and east regions of Cameroon', in E. Sills et al. (eds.) *REDD+ on the ground: a case book of subnational initiatives across the globe*, pp. 203–221, Center for International Forestry Research, Bogor, Indonesia.

Awono, A., Somorin, O., Atyi, R. and Levang, P. (2014b) 'Tenure and Participation in Local REDD+ Projects: Insights from Southern Cameroon', *Environmental Science and Policy* 35: 76–86.

Bigombé-Logo, P. (2003) 'The decentralized forestry taxation system in Cameroon: local management and state logic'. World Resources Institute, Environmental Governance in Africa Series, Working Paper No. 10, Washington, D.C.

Biodiversity Support Program (1993a) *Central Africa: Global Climate Change and Development: Overview*, United States Agency for International Development, Washington, D.C.

Biodiversity Support Program (1993b) *Central Africa: Global Climate Change and Development: Technical Report*, United States Agency for International Development, Washington, D.C.

Bond, I., Grieg-Gran, M., Wertz-Kanounnikoff, S., Hazlewood, P., Wunder, S., and Angelsen, A. (2009) *Incentives to Sustain Forest Ecosystem Services: a Review and Lessons for REDD*, International Institute for Environment and Development, London.

Brncic, T., Willis, K., Harris, D. and Washington, R. (2007) 'Culture or climate? the relative influences of past processes on the composition of the lowland Congo rainforest', *Philosophical Transactions of the Royal Society: Biological Sciences* 362: 229–242.

Burnham, P. (2000) 'Whose forest? whose myth? conceptualisations of community forests in Cameroon', in A. Abramson and D. Theodossopoulos (eds.) *Land, Law and Environment: Mythical Land, Legal Boundaries*, pp. 31–58, Pluto Press, London.

Burnham, P. and Graziani, M. (2004) 'Legal pluralism in the rain forests of Southeastern Cameroon', in K. Homewood (ed.) *Rural Resources & Local Livelihoods in Africa*, pp. 177–196, James Currey, Oxford.

Burnham, P., Graziani, M. and Sharpe, B. (1998) 'The social and institutional context of forest resource utilisation and management in south-east Cameroon: the case of the Lomié Arrondissement', report to the Department for International Development, London.

Cerutti, P.O., Lescuyer, G. Assembe-Mvondo, S. Tacconi, L. (2010) The challenges of redistributing forest-related monetary benefits to local governments: a decade of logging area fees in Cameroon, *The International Forestry Review* 12 (2): 130–138.

Chiaravalloti, R., Skarlatidou, A., Hoyte, S., Badia, M., Haklay, M. and Lewis, J. (2022) 'Extreme citizen science: lessons learned from initiatives around the globe', *Conservation Science and Practice*, 4 (2).

Clark, D. (2004) 'Sources or sinks? The responses of tropical forests to current and future climate and atmospheric composition', *Philosophical Transactions of the Royal Society: Biological Sciences* 359: 477–491.

Conquest, G. (2013) 'Dodging Silver Bullets: Opportunities and challenges for an "Extreme Citizen Science" approach to forest management in the Republic of the Congo', MSc thesis: University College London.

Conquest, G. (2014) 'Designs for the Pluriverse? Assembling Power and Knowledge in Extreme Citizen Science', PhD upgrading proposal: University College London.

Csillik, O., Kumar, P., Mascaro, J., O'Shea, T. and Asner, G. (2019) 'Monitoring tropical forest carbon stocks and emissions using Planet satellite data', *Scientific Reports: NatureResearch*, [online] available from: https://www.nature.com/articles/s41598-019-54386-6.

Côté, S. (1993) *Plan de Zonage du Cameroun Forestier Méridional: Objectifs, Méthodologie, Plan de Zonage Préliminaire*, Canadian International Development Agency and Cameroonian Ministry of Environment and Forests, Yaounde.

Daviet, F. (2010) 'From Copenhagen to Cancun: forests and REDD', [online] available from http://www.wri.org/stories/2010/05/copenhagen-cancun-forests-and-redd.

de Blas, D., Ruiz-Pérez, M. and Vermeulen, C. (2011) 'Management conflicts in Cameroonian community forests', *Ecology and Society* 16 (1).

Defo, L. (2020) 'Six years of industrial logging in Ngoyla (East-Cameroon): what have been the outcomes for local populations?', *International Forestry Review*, 22.

de Wachter, P. (1997) 'Economie et impact de l'agriculture itinérante badjoue (Sud-Cameroun)', in D. Joiris and D. de Laveleye (eds.) *Les Peuples des Forêts Tropicales: Systèmes Traditionnels et Développement Rural en Afrique Équatoriale, Grande Amazonie et Asie du Sud-Est,* special issue of *Civilisations* 44: 62–93.

Dibussi, T. (2007) 'FEICOM corruption case: Ondo Ndong sentenced to 50 years in jail', [online] available from: http://www.dibussi.com/2007/06/feicom-corrupti.html.

Dkamela, G., Mbambu, F., Austin, K., Minnemeyer, S. and Stolle, F. (2009) 'Voices from the Congo Basin: incorporating the perspectives of local stakeholders for improved REDD design', World Resources Institute, Working Paper, Washington, D.C.

Dkamela, G.P., Brockhaus, M. Kengoum Djengni, F. , Schure, J., Assembe Mvondo, S. (2014) Lessons for REDD+ from Cameroon's past forestry law reform: a political economy analysis, *Ecology and Society* 19 (3).

Dounias, E. (1993) 'Dynamique et Gestion Différentielles du Système de Production à Dominante Agricole des Mvae du Sud-Cameroun Forestier', unpublished dissertation, University of Montpellier II.

Dounias, E. (1996) 'Recrûs forestiers post-agricoles: perceptions et usages chez les Mvae du Sud-Cameroun', *Journal d'Agriculture Traditionelle et de Botanique Appliquée* 38: 153–178.

Duguma, L., Minang, P., Foundjem-Tita, D., Makui, P. and Piabuo, S. (2018) 'Prioritizing enablers for effective community forestry in Cameroon', *Ecology and Society* 23 (3).

Egbe, S. (1996) 'Forest tenure and access to forestry resources in Cameroon: an overview', Paper prepared for Franco-British conference on land tenure and resource access in West Africa', International Institute for Environment and Development, London.

Ekoko, F. (1997) 'The political economy of the 1994 Cameroon forestry law', unpublished paper presented to the African Regional Hearing of the World Commission on Forests and Sustainable Development, Yaounde.

Etoungou, P. (2003) 'Decentralization viewed from inside: the implementation of community forests in East Cameroon', World Resources Institute, Working Paper No. 12, Washington, D.C.

Fisiy, C. (1996) 'Techniques of land acquisition: the concept of "crown land" in colonial and post-colonial Cameroon' in R. Debusmann and S. Arnold (eds.) *Land Law and Land Ownership in Africa*, Bayreuth African Studies No. 41, Eckhard Breitlinger, Bayreuth.

Freudenthal, E., Nnah, S. and Kenrick, J. (2011) 'REDD and rights in Cameroon: a review of the treatment of indigenous people and local communities in policies and projects', Forest Peoples Programme, Moreton-in-Marsh, U.K.

Geschiere, P. (1982) *Village Communities and the State*, Kegan Paul, London.

Global Canopy Programme (2009) *The Little REDD+ Book*, Global Canopy Programme, Oxford.

Helveta (2009) 'Forest community monitoring in Cameroon', [online] available from http://corporate.helveta.com/uploads/news/20100107015150-Helveta%20Cameroon %20CaseStudy_2009.pdf.

Hladik, C., Bahuchet, S. and de Garine, I. (eds.) (1990) *Food and Nutrition in the African Rain Forest*, UNESCO, Paris.

Hladik, C., Hladik, A., Linares, O., Pagezy, H., Semple, A. and Hadley, M. (eds.) (1993) *Tropical Forests, People and Food*, Parthenon Publishing Group, Paris.

Hopkin, M. (2007) 'Mark of respect', *Nature* 448: 402–3.

Hoyte, S. (2020) 'Cameroon: confronting environmental injustice and illegal logging in the rainforest through indigenous-led technology' in *Minority and Indigenous Trends 2020*, Minority Rights Group International, London.

Hoyte, S. (2021a) 'Co-designing extreme citizen science projects in Cameroon: biodiversity conservation led by local values and indigenous knowledge' in A. Skarlatidou and M. Haklay (eds.), *Geographic Citizen Science Design*, UCL Press, London.

Hoyte, S. (2021b) 'Decolonising protected areas: Sapelli in eastern Cameroon, [online] available ExCiteS Blog, https://uclexcites.blog/2021/01/17/decolonising-protected-areas-sapelli-in-eastern-cameroon/.

Hoyte, S. (2022) 'How not to consult indigenous people', [online] available Gorillas and Grandfathers Blog, https://simonhoyte.wordpress.com/2022/12/27/how-not-to-consult-indigenous-people/.

Hoyte, S. (2023) 'Gorillas and Grandfathers: Baka hunter-gatherer conceptions of the forest and its protection, and the implementation of biocultural conservation through Extreme Citizen Science in the rainforests of Cameroon', unpublished PhD dissertation, University College London.

Hoyte, S. (2024). Gorillas and Grandfathers: Baka hunter-gatherer conceptions of the forest and its protection, and the implementation of biocultural conservation through Extreme Citizen Science in the rainforests of Cameroon. Doctoral thesis (Ph.D), University College London

Hoyte, S., and Clarke, C. (2020) 'Violence, corruption, and false promises: conservation and the Baka in Cameroon', [online] available IWGIA https://www.iwgia.org/en/cameroon/3791-violence,-corruption,-and-falsepromises-conservation-and-the-baka-in-cameroon.html.

Joiris, D. (1997a) 'Introduction régionale: Afrique équatoriale', in D. Joiris, and D. de Laveleye (eds.) *Les Peuples des Forêts Tropicales: Systèmes Traditionnels et Développement Rural en Afrique Équatoriale, Grande Amazonie et Asie du Sud-Est,* special issue of *Civilisations* 44: 38–43.

Joiris, D. (1997b) 'La nature des uns et la nature des autres: Mythe et réalité du monde rural face aux aires protégées d'Afrique Centrale', in D. Joiris, and D. de Laveleye (eds.) *Les Peuples des Forêts Tropicales: Systèmes Traditionnels et Développement Rural en Afrique Équatoriale, Grande Amazonie et Asie du Sud-Est,* special issue of *Civilisations* 44: 94–103.

Karsenty, A. (1999) 'Vers la fin de l'état forestier?', *Politique Africaine* 75: 147–161.

Karsenty, A. (2009) 'REDD and PES perspectives in Central Africa', [online] available from: http://www.ecosystemmarketplace.com/documents/ acrobat/katoomba_xv/october_6_2009/Karsenty%20REDD%20and%20 PES%20in%20Central%20Africa.pdf.

Karsenty, A., Lescuyer, G., Ezzine de Blas, L., Sembres, T. and Vermeulen, C. (2010) 'Community forests in Central Africa: Present hurdles and prospective evolutions', *Proceedings of conference on Taking Stock of Smallholder and Community Forestry: Where do we go from here?* Montpellier, France, 24–26 March 2010.

Karsenty, A., and Ongolo, S. (2012) 'Can "fragile states" decide to reduce their deforestation? The inappropriate use of the theory of incentives with respect to the REDD mechanism', *Forest Policy and Economics* 18: 38–45, [online] available: http://dx.doi.org/10.1016/j.forpol.2011.05.006.

Karsenty, A., Vogel, A. and Castell, F. (2014) '"Carbon rights", REDD+ and payments for environmental services', *Environmental Science and Policy* 35: 20–29.

Lewis, J. (2007) 'Enabling forest people to map their resources & monitor illegal logging in Cameroon', *Before Farming* 2/3, [online] available from: http://www.waspress.co.uk/journals/beforefarming/journal_20072/ news/2007_2_03.pdf.

Lewis, J. (2008) 'Making the invisible visible: Designing technology for non-literate hunter-gatherers', paper presented at conference on *Subversion, Conversion, Development: Public Interests in Technologies,* Cambridge, 24 April 2008.

Lewis, S., et al. (2009) 'Increasing carbon storage in intact African tropical forests', *Nature* 457: 1003–1007.

Maley, J. (1990) 'L'histoire récente de la forêt dense humide africaine: essai sur le dynamisme de quelques formations forestières', in R. Lanfranchi and D.

Schwartz (eds.) *Paysages Quarternaires de l'Afrique Centrale Atlantique*, pp. 367–382, ORSTOM, Paris.

Maley, J. (2001) 'The impact of arid phases on the African rain forest through geological history', in W. Weber, L. White, A. Vedder, and L. Naughton-Treves (eds.) *African Rain Forest Ecology and Conservation: an Interdisciplinary Perspective*, pp. 68–87, Yale University Press, New Haven.

Mayaux, P., Holmgren, P., Achard, F., Eva, H., Stibig, H. and Branthomme, A. (2005) 'Tropical forest cover change in the 1990s and options for future monitoring', *Philosophical Transaction of the Royal Society: Biological Sciences* 360: 373–384.

Milol, A. (1998) 'Gestion des forêts communautaires au Cameroun: vers une nouvelle hierarchisation des chefferies traditionnelles?', in S. Bahuchet, D. Bley, B. Brun, N. Licht, and H. Pagezy (eds.), *L'Homme et la Forêt Tropicale*, pp. 487–499, Éditions de l'Université de Provence, Marseille.

MINEF (1997) *Attribution and Management of Community Forests: Manual of Procedures and Norms (Draft Version)*, Ministry of Environment and Forests, Yaounde.

Moustard, F., Haklay, M., Lewis, J., Albert, A., Moreu, M., Chiaravalloti, R., Hoyte, S., Skarlatidou, A., Vittoria, A., Comandulli, C., Nyadzi, E., Vitos, M., Altenbuchner, J., Laws, M., Fryer-Moreira, R., and Artus, D. (2021) 'Using Sapelli in the field: methods and data for an inclusive citizen science', *Frontiers in Ecology and Evolution* 9, [online] available from: https://doi.org/10.3389/fevo.2021.638870.

Nguiffo, S. (1994) *La Nouvelle Legislation Forestière au Cameroun*, Fondation Friedrich Ebert au Cameroun, Yaounde.

Nguiffo, S. (1998) 'In defence of the commons: forest battles in southern Cameroon', in M. Goldman (ed.) *Privatizing Nature: Political Struggles for the Global Commons*, pp. 102–119, Pluto Press, London.

Nounah, S. and Perram, A. (2019) 'De la coupe aux lèvres: le CLIP dans la réserve de faune de Ngoyla au Cameroun', Forest Peoples Programme, Moreton-in-Marsh.

Olowu, D. (2003) 'Local institutional and political structures and processes: recent experience in Africa', *Public Administration and Development* 23: 41–52.

Oyono, P. (2004a) 'Institutional deficit, representation and decentralized forest management in Cameroon: elements of natural resources sociology for social theory and public policy', World Resources Institute, Environmental Governance in Africa Series, Working Paper No. 15, Washington, D.C.

Oyono, P. (2004b) 'One step forward, two steps back? Paradoxes of natural resources management in Cameroon', *Journal of Modern African Studies* 42: 91–111.

Oyono, P., Cerutti P., and Morrison, K. (2009) 'Forest taxation in post-1994 Cameroon: distributional mechanisms and emerging links with poverty alleviation and equity', World Resources Institute, Environmental Governance in Africa Series, Working Paper, Washington, D.C.

Oyono, P., Ribot, J. and Larson, A. (2007) 'Or vert et or noir dans le Cameroun rural: ressources naturelles pour la gouvernance locale, la justice et la durabilité', World Resources Institute, Environmental Governance in Africa Series, Working Paper No. 22, Washington, D.C.

Republic of Cameroon, Ministry of Environment and Nature Protection (2008) 'The forest carbon partnership facility (FCPF) readiness plan idea note (R-PIN)'.

Republic of Cameroon, Ministry of Environment, Nature Protection and Sustainable Development (2017) 'REDD+ readiness in Cameroon: mid-term progress report'.

Ribot, J. (2003) 'Democratic decentralization of natural resources: institutional choice and discretionary power transfers in sub-Saharan Africa', *Public Administration and Development* 23: 53–65.

Skutsch, M. (2008) *Carbon Crediting for Forest Communities*, [online] available from: www.communitycarbonforestry.org.

Stager, J. (2001) 'Climatic change and African rain forests in the twenty-first century', in W. Weber, L. White, A. Vedder, and L. Naughton-Treves (eds.) *African Rain Forest Ecology and Conservation: an Interdisciplinary Perspective*, pp. 140–147, Yale University Press, New Haven.

Stevens, M., Vitos, M., Altenbuchner, J., Conquest, G., Lewis, J., and Haklay, M. (2014) 'Taking Participatory Citizen Science to Extremes', *IEEE Pervasive Computing* 13 (2): 20–29.

UNDP-FAO (1988) *Plan d'action forestier: Rapport pour la mission conjointe interagence de planification et de revue pour le système forestier du Cameroun*, United Nations Development Programme, Yaounde.

UN-REDD Programme (2009) *Engaging civil society in REDD - best practice in the Democratic Republic of Congo*, [online] available from: http://www.un-redd.org/UNREDDProgramme/CountryActions/DemocraticRepublicofCongo/tabid/1027/language/en-US/Default.aspx.

Vitos, M. (2016) 'Making local knowledge matter: design and evaluation of ICT tools for forest monitoring in the Congo-Basin' PhD dissertation: University College London.

Willis, J., Messe, V. and Olinga, N. (2016) The rights of Baka communities in the REDD+ Ngoyla-Mintom project in Cameroon, Forest Peoples Programme & Association Okani.

Winterbottom, R. (1992) 'Tropical Forestry Action Plans and indigenous peoples: the case of Cameroon', in K. Cleaver, M. Munasinghe, M. Dyson, N. Egli, A. Peuker and F. Wencélius (eds.) *Conservation of West and Central African Rainforests*, pp. 222–228, World Bank, Washington, D.C.

World Bank (1992) *World Development Report 1992: Development and the Environment*, World Bank, Washington, D.C.

World Bank (2021) *Nesting of REDD+ initiatives: a manual for policymakers*, The World Bank, Washington, D.C.

About the authors

Philip Burnham is Emeritus Professor of Social Anthropology at University College London and Honorary Director of the International African Institute. He has undertaken extensive field research in Cameroon since 1968.

Simon Hoyte is a post-doctoral researcher in environmental anthropology at University College London. His work is largely alongside the Baka hunter-gatherers in Cameroon, engaging with topics of community-led conservation, environmental justice, indigenous rights, and participatory mapping.

Chapter 3

Social vulnerability, climatic variability, and uncertainty in rural Ethiopia: A study of South Wollo and Oromiya Zones of eastern Amhara Region

A. Peter Castro

The smallholders of South Wollo and Oromiya live in an area of high climatic variability, including proneness to drought. Their plough-based system, with its cropping system attuned to local agro-ecological conditions, has long sustained intensive agriculture and substantial populations. However, a lack of access to productive assets, in combination with national policies and socio-economic forces, has rendered them vulnerable to famine and chronic food insecurity. Climate change in the region appears to be increasing the unpredictability of rainfall. Although there is no support for the claim of a widespread drying trend, the overall timing, distribution, and duration of rains within the wet seasons seem to be more erratic. Despite their widespread poverty, villagers pursue a number of strategies to deal with the uncertainties of climate change and livelihood challenges. They are trying to adjust local farming practices to meet changing needs and new conditions, while also pursuing non-farm and off-farm opportunities. Many recent government policies, including land titling, relief safety nets, infrastructure development, and extension of public services, appear to be increasing economic opportunities and strengthening livelihood pursuits, though their long-term outlook is not certain. In countries such as Ethiopia, addressing climate change is inseparable from issues of poverty alleviation and development.

Introduction[1]

In 1984, famine brought the rural communities of Wollo and northern Ethiopia to worldwide attention. Thousands of people died of starvation and hunger-related causes, and photographs of emaciated children and adults haunted the global media. This event severely discredited the Derg, the country's ruling junta, who had been celebrating their 10th year of Marxist revolution. Ironically, the Derg's rise to power had been propelled by another famine which had Wollo as its 'epicenter' (Mesfin, 1986). The imperial regime's slow and ineffective response to that humanitarian crisis provided the justification for deposing Haile Selassie after more than 40 years of governance. Severe droughts triggered both events, although, as will be discussed below, structural forces and other considerations set in motion the collapse of food provisioning. Climate change threatens to increase the vulnerability of Wollo's rural households, as their drought-prone environment becomes more unpredictable. This paper examines changes and continuities in the ways South Wollo communities and the national government have responded to climatic variability and uncertainty. Taking a long-term view, one sees both hopeful and troubling trends as households and officials try to deal with the challenges of livelihood and development in an increasingly uncertain context.

The setting

Ethiopia is a landlocked nation in the Horn of Africa. It has 85 million inhabitants, the second largest population on the continent (CSA, 2010). Most Ethiopians reside in the countryside and depend on agriculture for their livelihood. The country is among the poorest in the world, being ranked 157 of 169 according to the human development index; a composite of quality of life and economic output measures (UNDP, 2010). Although rapid economic expansion has taken place in recent years, fuelled in part by policies fostering greater market liberalization, most people are very poor by global measures. In 2005, more than three-quarters of its population lived on less than $2 per day (as calculated in purchasing power parity), and approximately two-fifths of them subsisted on less than $1.25; international measures of 'moderate' and 'extreme' poverty, respectively (World Bank, 2011).

Wollo is said to be 'the veritable heart of Ethiopia, physically, culturally and psychologically' (Mesfin, 1991: 18). The Amharic language supposedly originated in the area, yet the name Wollo is Oromiffa, reflecting its historical blending of Amhara and Oromo peoples and cultures. This study focuses on South Wollo and Oromiya Zones within eastern Amhara Regional State. South Wollo covers 17,067 km² and currently has 2.6 million inhabitants (CSA, 2010). Oromiya Zone (not to be confused with Oromiya Regional State) extends over 3,470 km² and has more than 485,000 residents. Each administrative zone is organized into smaller units called a *woreda*, which is subdivided into a number of *kebeles* (formerly peasant associations). More than 80 per cent of Ethiopia's population is rural, and South Wollo and Oromiya duplicate this pattern, with Dessie (160,000 population) and Kombolcha (90,000 residents) the only large urban centres. Most people are Muslims, though pockets of Orthodox Christians can be found. Wollo is renowned for the ability of its diverse cultural groups – Muslims and Orthodox Christians, Oromos and Amharas – to intermingle peacefully (Alemneh, 1990).

Agro-ecology, livelihoods and poverty

Local livelihoods and well-being in South Wollo and Oromiya are closely linked to land and weather. Rural households earn more than 90 per cent of their income from farming and livestock rearing (Little et al., 2006). A woman in South Wollo observed, 'It is with the support of nature that we survive.' The landscape consists of mountains, hills, and upland plateaux dissected by the Great Rift Valley. Sharp variations exist in elevation. South Wollo's highest peaks rise more than 3,500 metres above sea level, while Oromiya's eastern lowlands drop below 1,500 metres. Significant differences in rainfall and temperature patterns occur based on location and elevation. The lowest average annual rainfall (500 mm) and the hottest temperatures occur in the Oromiya lowlands, while westernmost South Wollo receives the most rain (upward of 2,000 mm) (Woldeamlak and Conway, 2007; Rosell and Holmer, 2007). There are two wet seasons: the *belg* rains from February to May, and the *meher* rains, from July to October, when the bulk of precipitation falls. The timing, amount, and reliability of the wet seasons also vary according to elevation, location and other factors. Droughts regularly occur in many areas, and farmers must often contend with poorly timed and distributed rains. Frost occurs in some highland areas, posing further risks to crops.

Customary farming practices are based on long-term experience with local environments and interpretations of current conditions. As in other parts of the northern highlands, people rely on a scratch plough drawn by a yoke of oxen or horses, effectively breaking the region's thick vertisol soils for cultivation. McCann (1995) points out that this 'simple but brilliantly adaptable tool' has supported intensive agriculture and substantial populations in the Ethiopian highlands for more than two millennia. Very little irrigation takes place, being limited to a few valleys with gravity-fed canals. In the late 1980s, only 1 per cent of Wollo's cultivated land was irrigated (Alemneh, 1990: 76). Thus, crops and agricultural calendars largely reflect elevation, rainfall regimes, temperature, and other local environmental conditions. People identify three main farming zones: *dega*, the cold uplands, where barley, wheat, peas, horse beans (fava beans) are the main cultigens; the *woina dega* or midlands, a temperate area favouring staples such as teff, wheat, maize, chickpeas, fenugreek, and vetch; and in the *kola* or lowlands, the hot, drier weather supports fields of sorghum, maize, chickpeas, millet and other crops. Households in *woina dega* and, wherever possible, in the *dega* and *kola*, sow their staple crops during both wet seasons. Many *dega* communities must confine their main planting to the *belg* rains, while *kola* farms often depend solely on the *meher* wet season. For areas prone to unpredictable rainfall, staples such as barley, teff (a highly nutritious indigenous grain used for *injera*, the national bread), sorghum and chickpeas provide reliable, drought-resistant crops (National Research Council, 1996). Yet, as will be discussed below, long-term practices are now challenged by apparent changes in rainfall patterns, declining soil fertility, and other concerns.

Livelihood pursuits are constrained by people's limited access to assets and income-earning opportunities. Land scarcity is a major problem throughout eastern Amhara region, where farms are about 20 per cent smaller than in the rest of the country (Little, 2008). Population pressures and redistribution of farmland by past and present governments have steadily reduced holdings. The BASIS survey of eight woredas in South Wollo and Oromiya recorded households as averaging only 0.8 hectares in 2001 (Little et al., 2006: 206). Communal lands for keeping livestock and other purposes are also under pressure due to increasing usage, conversion to government-run forest plantations, and formal or informal privatization, whether for farming or settlement (Pankhurst, 2003). While livestock serve as vital productive resources and as a buffer for dealing with contingencies, their accumulation is constrained by limited household capacity for upkeep, distress sales, and animal mortality. Most families lack sufficient draught animals and must engage in animal-sharing arrangements for ploughing. In 2003, almost two-fifths of South Wollo households surveyed by the BASIS project owned no oxen (Little, 2008). As in other parts of the Ethiopian highlands, households engaged in other forms of mutual cooperation that were generally 'informal, small-scale, and along gender demarcations' (Pankhurst, 1992: 79). For example, men might help in house construction, while women might share childcare or milling.

A limited number of non-farm and off-farm pursuits exist in the area, as officials only recently have encouraged such enterprises. Much of it consists of small-scale trading and shopkeeping, offering meagre returns (Devereux and Sharp, 2006). Few wage labour opportunities are available. The expansion of urban and peri-urban areas in South Wollo and Oromiya appears to be opening new business and employment opportunities, including for women (Pankhurst, 2003). Migration to Addis Ababa and other distant areas is increasing; for example, several households in Oromiya Zone reported that family members were in Djibouti and even Saudi Arabia. Nonetheless, labour migration and accompanying remittances are still a small-scale phenomenon. Low levels of educational achievement hinder the ability of many men and women to obtain higher-paying jobs. Overall income from all sources is very low in these communities; in 2001, more than 80 per cent of South Wollo and Oromiya households earned less than $50 per capita, far below the national average (Little et al., 2006). The area's widespread and chronic poverty is demonstrated by its reliance on safety-net and food-for-work schemes. Nearly 800,000 people in South Wollo alone received such help in 2009; about 30 per cent of its population (Gill, 2010: 118).

Two recent studies documented the precarious position of most households in South Wollo and Oromiya. The BASIS research project used ownership of productive assets (particularly livestock) and income to differentiate households according to economic status and viability, dividing them into four groups: 'very poor', 20 per cent; 'poor', 46 per cent; 'vulnerable', 13 per cent; and 'better off', 21 per cent (Little et al., 2006).

Devereux and Sharp's (2006) multifaceted study featured a self-assessment component of well-being and vulnerability, and community members placed their own households into the following grouping: 'destitute', 14.6 per cent; 'vulnerable', 54.9 per cent; 'viable', 27.5 per cent; and 'sustainable' 3.1 per cent. According to Devereux and Sharp, the self-reported data closely matched other data that had been collected. Both sets of authors observed that female-headed households were especially prone to poverty and destitution. For example, the BASIS study recorded that female-headed households on average had less than half the land and only 70 per cent of the total livestock of ones headed by men (Little et al., 2006).

In portraying the economic condition of South Wollo and Oromiya communities, one must be careful not to regard them as places of resigned passivity or lacking agency. People seek to respond to opportunities and hazards using the repertoire of ideas and actions open to them. This repertoire is socially distributed, reflecting differences in wealth, generation, gender, schooling, political connections, religion, and local agro-economic conditions. Furthermore, although community members often seek and welcome external assistance, accounts of relief or aid dependency syndromes are exaggerated (Little, 2008). On the contrary, many villagers recognize the necessity of obtaining assistance in times of need, yet they still feel uncomfortable doing so, as if they are 'begging'. A man in an Oromiya community, for example, after describing his worries regarding an ongoing drought, his poor harvest, a recent distress sale of oxen, and costly food purchases, stated, 'Things are getting worse, yet it is embarrassing to seek assistance.'

Vulnerability

At least six large-scale famines took place in Wollo during the 20th century (Dessalegn, 1991). Other severe localized food shortages occurred, many of them unrecorded by the wider society. A wide range of historical experience and cultural memory concerning famine and hunger exists across and even within South Wollo's and Oromiya's communities. Elders in the Oromiya lowlands recall several famines, extending back to the early days of Haile Selassie's imperial rule, if not earlier. These events often possess their own names, serving as both a memorial and as a warning for ongoing vigilance. In contrast, villagers in some of the grain-surplus areas of South Wollo claim that famine and severe food scarcity are largely unknown in their communities. For example, an elderly man in Jamma woreda claimed: 'We don't really know hunger.' People in some places, such as Legambo in South Wollo, contend that their homeland has become more prone to crop failure and food insecurity through time. The overall vulnerability of these communities, however, not only derives from their limited access to productive resources and climatic unpredictability, but also flows from their relationship to the national political economy.

Since imperial times Wollo has been one of Ethiopia's least developed provinces (Dessalegn, 1991). It produced no major cash crop and contained no mineral that might attract investment in infrastructure to overcome its rugged terrain. Exploitative tenancy, taxes, and other practices during the time of Haile Selassie deprived people of their entitlement to sufficient food (Sen, 1981). The Wollo famine of 1972–73 severely eroded the authority of the emperor, who was deposed by the Marxist-oriented Derg. They implemented several reforms aimed at raising living standards and decreasing rural vulnerability, including tenure reform (nationalization and redistribution of farmland), farm collectivization, conservation campaigns, a famine early warning system, literacy promotion, and business nationalization. Popular support for some policies eroded quickly as the interventions proved fruitless or even counter-productive. Peasants generally disliked land nationalization, collectives, conservation enclosures (with large tracts of pasture converted into tree plantations), trade restrictions, and increased taxes (Marcus, 2002; Pankhurst, 2003). Severe state repression intensified opposition throughout the country, with movements arising along ethnic, regional, and other social divisions (de Waal, 1991).

Famine in Wollo, Tigray, and elsewhere during 1984–85 seriously undermined the Derg's legitimacy. Officials ignored early warning reports of crop failures. Dessie and Kombolcha experienced exceptionally poor *meher* rains in 1984, causing it to be the driest year since records started in the 1950s (Woldeamlak and Conway, 2007). Drought and crop failures served as the trigger, but analysts emphasized that the famine revealed deeper problems: failed agrarian policies, inattentive or inept government, and peasant resource scarcity (Jansson et al., 1987; Mesfin, 1991; Dessalegn, 1991), as well as ongoing conflict and military activities (de Waal, 2001; Marcus, 2002). Others favoured overpopulation (Hardin, 1985) and even human-induced climate change (Brown and Wolf, 1985). The Derg's efforts to address the famine's structural causes through large-scale involuntary population movements were highly unpopular. Poor planning and inept management added to the unhappiness of resettlement, which shifted people to sparsely inhabited lowlands. Villagization, which placed people in concentrated settlements, was similarly mishandled.

By 1991, the Ethiopian People's Revolutionary Democratic Front (EPRDF), a coalition led by Meles Zenawi, defeated the Derg and took over the national government. Promising democracy and prosperity through a mixed economy, the EPRDF government initiated some market reforms while retaining certain aspects of past policies. Peasant agriculture fell into the latter category. Officials reaffirmed land nationalization, seeking to prevent land sales and the movement of rural people into the cities (Marcus, 2002: 236). The new government initially implemented more land redistributions to accommodate demobilized soldiers, resettlement scheme returnees, and other landless people. This action increased tenure insecurity. Interviews in 1999 and 2001 indicated that many people in South Wollo and Oromiya linked redistribution with increasing land scarcity and decreasing farm productivity. People also expressed reluctance regarding the government promotion of Green Revolution technology as input loans had to be repaid regardless of the harvest. Drought, erratic rain, and unfamiliarity with the new technology made these loans risky propositions.

A severe food crisis in eastern Amhara region and other areas tested the EPRDF's legitimacy in 1999. Despite enhanced crop/food monitoring capacity, both the national government and its international partner organizations were caught unawares by the scope and magnitude of the event, which became the worst food crisis since 1985. Officials announced in December 1998, that a near record harvest was expected, and that only 224,600 people in South Wollo and Oromiya would require emergency food aid. By May 1999, officials realized that they needed to triple that number (Castro, 1999). Emergency food needs increased elsewhere as well. With the country engaged in a bitter border war with Eritrea, international donors were sluggish to respond to this appeal. The event brought the nation 'to the edge of a major disaster', with nearly 10 million people ultimately receiving food aid (Hammond and Maxwell, 2002). Many households lost substantial livestock through distress sales and death; however, large-scale starvation and dislocation had been averted. Asset recovery often took upwards of three years in the BASIS study area, with people relying on assistance received from kin and others within their local social networks, food aid transfers, wage labour, trade and other strategies (Little et al., 2006). Returning to their pre-1999 drought conditions usually meant that households still had few productive assets and limited food stocks. Certain hard-hit areas were slow to regain their oxen for ploughing. As late as 2007, for example, some households in Legambo woreda of South Wollo still relied on horses for ploughing.

Shortly after the 1984 famine, Mesfin (1991) interviewed households in South Wollo and nearby Shewa about their perceptions of climate and drought. Despite the Derg's promotion of atheism, the vast majority of people attributed drought solely to God. A few respondents cited deforestation and soil erosion; Mesfin noted that people had been bombarded with deforestation and soil erosion as causes of drought to little effect. My interviews in South Wollo and Oromiya between 1999 and 2007 suggested that people still generally attributed climate patterns to God. For example, I asked a man in Bati woreda: 'Is there a way to predict the weather?' His response: 'We always trust God'. In the midst and immediate aftermath of the 1999–2000 food crisis, however, a few people shifted their perspective, linking drought and crop failure to unpopular policies. Land redistribution, started by the Derg and retained in its early years by the EPRDF, was especially singled out. Women in a Kutaber woreda focus group reported in 1999 that land redistribution 'brought drought'. Men in a Werebabo woreda focus group called it 'a bad and cursed activity', associating it with crop failure. An elderly man in Bati woreda insisted that redistributions were linked with 'rough rains', declining farm production, and 'hunger'. Two elderly men in Legambo woreda pointed out in 2001 that since the EPRDF had come to power their area experienced droughts, late rains, and similar problems causing 'deepening poverty'. These critical comments were not made lightly. People often feared reprimand for expressing such ideas.[2] It should be noted that I did not record such views after 2001, as impacts of the 1999 crisis receded, and as policies and times changed.

Recent Ethiopian history shows that both rural households and the national governments are highly vulnerable to the impacts of severe drought. In the wake of the 1999 crisis, officials implemented several steps to enhance national capacity for disaster preparedness (Hammond and Maxwell, 2002). Serious droughts and food shortages in 2003 and 2008 reinforced the need for action. Officials sought to improve famine early-warning monitoring and the targeting and delivery of relief assistance. A new safety net programme launched in 2005 sought to strengthen the long-term food security capacity of households and local communities (Sabates-Wheeler and Devereux, 2010). Road and other infrastructure projects, including along the main route connecting Dessie with Addis Ababa, promised greater connectivity to the nation and the wider world. The government initiated land titling to assuage tenure insecurity, and it promoted agricultural intensification through use of Green Revolution technology, small-scale irrigation, tree planting, and conservation projects. Other community development efforts include interventions aimed at increasing people's access to education, health care, and other public services. Some government initiatives have been controversial, particularly the leasing of large tracts of farmland to private investors and foreign firms for commercial purposes (Cotula et al., 2009). Resettlement has been revived as well. The long-term ability of these policies and interventions to deal with such challenges as population growth, rising demand for development, calls for more democratic governance, and the threat of inflation remains to be determined (Gill, 2010).

Similarly, households in South Wollo and Oromiya have pursued a range of actions aimed at enhancing their well-being, including intensifying farming, engaging in trade, seeking off-farm employment (including labour migration abroad), and taking advantage of public services to bolster their human capital. Particularly since the 1984 famine, people have experimented with different farming practices, including planting new crop varieties, trying chemical fertilizers, using irrigation, planting trees, and altering the timing of their planting (see Alemneh, 1990). In pursuing such agendas, they frequently faced numerous obstacles, such as a lack of access to capital or to technology appropriate to local conditions. Competition over the use and management of common property resources (water, pasture, forest) appeared to be increasing in some places, provoking tensions and conflicts (Pankhurst, 2003). For example, disputes arose in the Gimba area, where rapid peri-urban growth and the government's leasing of a tract of pasture to a private investor reduced the communal lands available to local households. Despite these challenges, when God favours the area with good weather, the efforts of farmers are rewarded, if modestly. But nowadays even nature seems as unpredictable as ever, if not more so.

Uncertainty

Global climate change poses one of the major human development challenges for the 21st century (UNDP, 2007). How it will affect the people of South Wollo and Oromiya is unclear, if not controversial. In the midst of the 1980s famine, Brown and Wolf (1985) suggested that in Africa land degradation caused by rapid population growth might be causing localized climate change, particularly increased drought. A recent report examining Ethiopian rainfall patterns from 1960 to 2004 found that it had decreased in the north-east, south-east, and south-west (FEWS, 2005). The authors identified a warming trend in the southern Indian Ocean as the main culprit for this shift, and they warned that food aid demand would spike as farm productivity declined. Other studies disagreed with the claim of widespread drying trends, including ones focusing on the nation (Cheung et al., 2008), Addis Ababa (Conway et al., 2004), where 100 years of rainfall records existed, the highlands (Nyssens et al., 2004, which examined evidence for the past 20,000 years), Amhara Regional State (Woldeamlak and Conway, 2007), and even South Wollo (Rosell and Holmer, 2007). Several studies found no significant changes or trends in overall annual rainfall totals. However, in many areas, including South Wollo (Rosell and Holmer, 2007), rainfall variability appeared to be increasing. The timing, distribution, and duration of rains within wet seasons seemed to be more unpredictable. Related aspects of weather such as amount of cloud cover and temperature may also be changing in some areas.

Household interviews supported the notion that rainfall variability seemed to be increasing. A man in Bati woreda in the Oromiya lowlands stated, 'What we call good times – if Allah is willing – is when we have good rains in April'. He quickly added, 'The problem is that now only in rare cases do we have good rains in April'. The late rains that year had substantially delayed his sorghum crop. When interviewed in August 2002, he pointed to the fields and said, 'By this time the children would have access to stalks that taste like sugar cane. But now look – nothing.' Visited a year later, he reported that the rains continued to be erratic. The man pointed out that people defined a wet season 'as a continuous time of rainfall. In the past, the rains would not stop. Now there seems to be a gap between rains'. In the high mountains of Dessie Zuria woreda of South Wollo, a man stated that 'the weather changed, becoming hotter than before'. People in his community planted their main crop during the *belg* rains that fall from February to May. Crops planted later may encounter frost, poorly timed rains, and other problems. In response to changing weather patterns, they planted during the *meher* rains from July to October. Some individuals devoted up to half their land to this experiment. He reported, 'The last time we had good fields but heavy rains and frost occurred at harvest. The *meher* experiment doesn't seem to work'. Nonetheless, some households in the *belg* agricultural areas still attempt to obtain a *meher* crop. Some people, particularly in the lowlands, reported that changes in weather appeared to affect the prevalence of insects and crop diseases that attacked the crops.

People try to deal with the challenges of nature in creative ways, whether through individual or collective efforts, including expanding irrigation, experimenting with crop varieties, altering planting practices, and using chemical fertilizers. In pursuing these strategies, they are encountering a range of obstacles. For example, at Maybar Lake in South Wollo, households competed to siphon water for irrigation, and these canals reduced the flow for downstream users, particularly for a stream that served a communal grazing ground. Such situations call for greater social coordination, including availability of conflict management institutions (Pankhurst, 2003). Others encountered constraints in obtaining greater technical advice regarding water harvesting, cultivation practices, or new planting stocks. This situation did not signal an exhaustion of possibilities in terms of agricultural production, but unfulfilled opportunities for innovation and investment, combining local and external knowledge and capacities.

Conclusion

The smallholders of South Wollo and Oromiya live in an area of high climatic variability, including proneness to drought. Their plough-based system, with its cropping system attuned to local agro-ecological conditions, has long sustained intensive agriculture and substantial populations. However, lack of access to productive assets, in combination with national policies and socio-economic forces, has rendered them vulnerable to famine and chronic food insecurity. Climate change in the region appears to be increasing the unpredictability of rainfall. Although there is no support for the claim of a widespread drying trend, the overall timing, distribution, and duration of the rains within the wet seasons seem to be more erratic. Despite their widespread poverty, people in South Wollo and Oromiya pursue a number of strategies to deal with the uncertainties of climate change and livelihood challenges facing them. They are adjusting local farming practices to meet changing conditions, while also increasingly pursuing non-farm and off-farm opportunities. Despite being both absolutely and relatively impoverished, the people of South Wollo and Oromiya are not without agency, capacities, creativity, and priorities. Their involvement in all facets of planning and implementing climate change adaptation and mitigation efforts is essential.

National policies have always cast a strong influence over the fate of South Wollo and Oromiya communities. In the past, many official actions (as well as inaction) increased rural vulnerability. The occurrence of famine is not an act of nature, but the outcome of social processes strongly reflecting peasant marginalization. Recent changes in government policies, particularly land titling, relief safety nets, infrastructure development, and public services, are widening the scope for local livelihood pursuits. The rise of labour migration is increasing the importance of remittances to the rural economy. Whether these interventions and changes will prove effective in fostering widespread economic growth and livelihood remains to be seen. Nonetheless, the Ethiopian government should continue to promote policies that widen people's chances for gaining access to productive resources, for enhancing their human capital, and for allowing them to develop their capacities. Addressing climate change in Ethiopia is inseparable from issues of poverty alleviation and development.

Author updates to the 2025 edition

In June 2018, I travelled to South Wollo for the first time in nearly a decade. It was a quick visit, featuring an invited talk at Wollo University in Dessie, the zonal capital, about my work with the BASIS project. Wollo University, founded in 2005, was one of several recently established universities and colleges in Ethiopia. Another, Mekdela Amba University, had been recently opened in South Wollo at Tulu Awliya, in what had been part of Gimba pasture until only a few years earlier (Mengistu, 2005). These institutions embodied a feeling of hope for the region and for the country as a whole, widening access to higher education while also strengthening national research capacity. I felt their presence was especially vital for addressing the challenge of climate change. Given the diverse and complex patterns of climate change in the country, including significant intra-regional variation within Wollo's farming zones (Rosell and Holmer, 2015; Yimer et al., 2018), the spread of such institutions was not only promising but necessary. As noted by Amogne Asfaw and Hassen Yimer (2024), two scholars from Wollo University, climate change interventions need to be based on local context-specific details. During this same period Teferi Abate Adem (2019: 19) carried out a brilliant ethnographic study elucidating how Amharic-speaking farmers in two South Wollo villages 'think and talk about variability in the timing, amount, duration, and spatial distribution of rainfall during, as well as across, their respective crop-growing wet seasons'. Teferi (2019: 33–34) highlighted their 'God/Allah-centered' cultural models of nature, including climate change, yet observed the, 'strong complementarity between farmers' pragmatic, household-level agronomic responses to erratic rains, and their village-wide rain-making prayers and seasonal agricultural rituals'. His study suggested several promising directions for future research.

Further reasons for hope emanated from the national level. Ethiopia's economy had been among the fastest growing in the world for several years. Its rapidly increasing urban and peri-urban centres especially reflected this expansion, for better or worse. In Dessie, for example, businesses, residences, and related infrastructure now engulfed the adjacent highly productive farmlands of Gerado. Hope in the country also rose as a new prime minister, Abiy Ahmed, had recently taken over, promising political and economic reforms, as well as an end to the war with Eritrea. Alas, things turned out differently. What unfolded in Amhara State, including Wollo, and some other parts of the country was death, destruction, disruption, and displacement, with the Tigrayan War, ethnic struggles, and now fighting between the national armed forces and Amhara militias that were once their allies. Exploring how and why this sad predicament occurred, as well as its heavy human toll, are beyond the scope of this chapter (for example, see Amnesty International, 2020; Alemayehu, 2022; Tamrat Anbesaw et al., 2022; Sisay Sahlu, 2024). Dessie and nearby rural areas which escaped violence in the war to oust the Derg during the 1980s were now very hard-hit by these conflicts. Violence, instability, and control measures such as curfews and travel restrictions add enormously to the challenges and burdens of seeking to address climate change. Climate justice requires not only social justice, but a firm commitment to peacemaking and reconciliation as a response to conflict and societal tensions. There can be no other way.

Notes

[1] This study draws on information collected from 1999 to 2007, while I was a member of the BASIS-Collaborative Research Support Program (funded by the United States Agency for International Development), which dealt with food security and asset recovery from drought and other shocks. While I gratefully acknowledge the contributions of participating institutions and project colleagues, I alone am responsible for the interpretations presented here, including any errors. The reissuing of this collection offers me the opportunity to acknowledge my gratitude to many individuals involved in the BASIS study: Peter D. Little, the late Workneh Negatu, the late Yigremew Adal, Mengistu Dessalegn Debela, Kassahun Kebede, Yared Amare, Degafa Tolossa, Alula Pankhurst, Priscilla Stone, Dilu Shakeke, and Tegegne Gebre-Egziabher. I also thank for their assistance and support during my 2018 visit to South Wollo: Teferi Abate Adem, Hassen Hussein, Goshu Wolde Tefera, Dawit Gebremariyam, and Jemu. The Maxwell School of Citizenship and Public Affairs at Syracuse University provided funding for the 2018 trip.

[2] In 2001, I mentioned some of these local views during an informal workshop in Addis Ababa. I recall that an audience member essentially accused me of being a stooge for anti-government propaganda.

References

Adem, T.A. (2019) 'Vernacular explanations of rainfall variability in highland Ethiopia'. In G. Bennardo (ed.) *Cultural Models of Nature: Primary Food Producers and Climate Change*, pp. 19–37, Routledge, London and New York.

Alemayehu, E. (2022) 'The Scene of Wollo University during the Invasion of TPLF Led Force', *Abyssinia Journal of Business and Social Sciences* 7: 1–18.

Alemneh, D. (1990) *Environment, Famine, and Politics in Ethiopia*, Rienner, Boulder.

Amnesty International (2020) *Beyond Law Enforcement: Human Rights Violations by Ethiopian Security Forces in Amhara and Oromia*, Amnesty International, London.

Anbesaw, T., Zenebe, Y., Asmamaw, A., Shegaw, M., and Birru, N. (2022) 'Post-traumatic stress disorder and associated factors among people who experienced traumatic events in Dessie town, Ethiopia, 2022: A community based study', Frontiers in Psychiatry, 25 Oct, 13: 1026878.

Asfaw, A. and Yimer, H. (2024) 'Trend analysis of climate change-induced extreme events in drought-prone areas: A case of Legambo district in South Wollo zone of Amhara National Regional State, North Central Ethiopia', *Abyssinia Journal of Business and Social Sciences* 9: 41–56.

Brown, L. and Wolf, E. (1985) 'Reversing Africa's decline', *Worldwatch Paper* 65.

Castro, A. (ed.) (1999) 'Kebele profiles', BASIS Horn of Africa Program, Addis Ababa.

Cheung, W., Senay, G., and Singh, A. (2008) 'Trends and spatial distribution of annual and seasonal rainfall in Ethiopia', *International Journal of Climatology* 28: 1723–34.

Conway, D., Mould, C. and Woldeamlak Bewket (2004) 'Over one century of rainfall and temperature observations in Addis Ababa, Ethiopia', *International Journal of Climatology* 24: 77–91.

Cotula, L., Vermeulen, S., Leonard, R. and Keeley, J. (2009) *Land Grab or Development Opportunity?* IIED/FAO/IFAD, London.

CSA (2010) 'Section B – Population' in Central Statistical Authority of Ethiopia, *Ethiopia Statistical Abstract 2009*, [Online] http://www.csa.gov.et/index.php?option=com_rubberdoc&view=category&id=71&Itemid=511 [accessed 7 July 2010].

de Waal, A. (1991) *Evil Days*, Human Rights Watch, New York.

Dessalegn, R. (1991) *Famine and Survival Strategies*, Scandinavian Institute of African Studies, Uppsala.

Devereux, S. and Sharp, K. (2006) 'Trends in poverty and destitution in Wollo, Ethiopia ', *Journal of Development Studies* 42: 592–610.

FEWS (2005) *Recent Drought Tendencies in Ethiopia and Equatorial-Subtropical Eastern Africa*, Famine Early Warning System Network, Washington, DC.

Gill, O. (2010) *Famine and Foreigners*, Oxford University Press, Oxford.

Hammond, L., and Maxwell, D. (2002) 'The Ethiopian crisis of 1999–2000: Lessons learned, questions unanswered', *Disasters* 26: 262–79.

Hardin, G. (1985) 'Overpopulation begets hunger: Food gifts don't help poor', *Hackensack Record*, 8 November, p. A–29.

Jansson, K., Harris, M., and Penrose, A. (1987) *The Ethiopia Famine*, Zed, London.

Little, P. (2008) 'Food aid dependency in northeastern Ethiopia: Myth or reality?', *World Development* 36: 860–74.

Little, P., Stone, M., Tewodaj Mogues, Castro, A. and Workneh Negatu (2006) 'Moving in place: Drought and poverty dynamics in South Wollo, Ethiopia', *Journal of Development Studies* 42: 200–25.

Marcus, H. (2002) *A History of Ethiopia*, 2nd edn, University of California Press, Berkeley.

McCann, J. (1995) *People of the Plow*, University of Wisconsin Press, Madison.

Mengistu, D. (2005) 'The commons: Changing resource uses and conflicts over a communal grazing area in Gimba', *Maxwell Review* 13: 4–9.

Mesfin Wolde Mariam (1986) *Rural Vulnerability to Famine in Ethiopia*, Intermediate Technology Publications, London.

Mesfin Wolde Mariam (1991) *Suffering Under God's Environment*, African Mountains Association and Geographica Bernensia, Berne.

National Research Council (1996) *Lost Crops of Africa*, Volume 1, National Academy Press, Washington DC.

Nyssens, J., Poesen, J., Moeyersons, J., Deckers, J., Mitiku Haile, and Lang, A. (2004) 'Human impact on the environment in the Ethiopian and Eritrean highlands – a state of the art', *Earth-Science Reviews* 64: 273–320.

Pankhurst, A. (2003) 'Conflict management over contested natural resources: A case study of pasture, forest and irrigation in South Wello, Ethiopia', in A. Castro and E. Nielsen (eds), *Natural Resource Conflict Management Case Studies*, pp. 59–80, Food and Agriculture Organization, Rome.

Pankhurst, H. (1992) *Gender, Development and Identity*, Zed, London.

Rosell, S. and Holmer, B. (2007) 'Rainfall change and its implications for belg harvest in South Wollo, Ethiopia', *Geografiska Annaler* 89: 287–99.

Rosell, S. and Holmer, B. (2015) 'Erratic rainfall and its consequences for the cultivation of teff in two adjacent areas in South Wollo, Ethiopia', *Norwegian Journal of Geography* 69: 38–46

Sabates-Wheeler, R., and Devereux, S. (2010) 'Cash transfers and high food prices: Explaining outcomes on Ethiopia's Productive Safety Net Programme', *Food Policy* 35: 274–85.

Sen, A. (1981) *Poverty and Famines*, Oxford University Press, Oxford.

Sisay Sahlu (2024) 'Kombolcha to Lalibela: a stifling voyage through conflict-torn Wollo', *The Reporter* March 30 [Online] https://www.thereporterethiopia.com/39422/ [accessed 9 September 2024].

UNDP (2007) Human Development Report 2007/2008: *Fighting Climate Change: Human Solidarity in a Divided World*, United Nations Development Programme, New York.

UNDP (2010) *Human Development Report 2010*, United Nations Development Programme, New York.

Woldeamlak Bewket and Conway, D. (2007) 'A note on the temporal and spatial variability of rainfall in the drought-prone Amhara region of Ethiopia', *International Journal of Climatology* 27: 1467–77.

World Bank (2011) *World Development Report 2011*, The International Bank for Reconstruction and Development, Washington, DC.

Yimer, M., Fantaw, Y., Menfese, T., and Kindie, T. (2018) 'Variability and trends of rainfall in north east highlands of Ethiopia', *International Journal of Hydrology* 2: 594–605.

About the author

A. Peter Castro is Professor Emeritus of Anthropology in the Maxwell School of Citizenship and Public Affairs at Syracuse University in Syracuse, New York. He is an applied cultural anthropologist specializing in agrarian livelihoods, natural resource conflict management, and rural social change, especially in East Africa.

Chapter 4

Farmers on the frontline: Adaptation and change in Malawi

Kate Wellard, Daimon Kambewa
and Sieglinde Snapp

This chapter examines how smallholders in central and northern Malawi are responding to climate change and other challenging aspects of their physical and institutional environments. It is concerned with human agency at the community, household, and individual levels, taking into account differences in gender and other social variables. The authors show how rural people attempt to build their knowledge and skills from a variety of sources. Their accumulated knowledge and farming practices – often embedded in locally distinct cultural traditions – have provided a basis for adaptation. A tremendous diversity of crop and livestock species, land use activities and craft production bear witness to the innovation and management skills of smallholders. The authors contend that development agencies must engage in a partnership with communities, helping rural people to strengthen local capacities for addressing climate change and other sources of vulnerability.

Introduction

Smallholder farmers in Malawi encounter complex changes in their social, institutional and biophysical environment on a daily basis. Increasing climatic variability – drought and floods – provides an additional challenge. Historically, farming systems and indigenous knowledge – often embedded in cultural traditions – have provided a basis for adaptation. A tremendous diversity of crop and livestock species, land use activities and craft production bear witness to the innovation and management skills of smallholders.

There is growing appreciation that human agency, agricultural practice and a biodiverse environment are essential to the resilience of poor communities. Yet policy makers often focus on technological fixes with a narrow understanding of how to support adaptation in the face of rapid change. This is illustrated by recent initiatives addressing food shortages in the face of the looming threat of climatic change in Africa. Intensified production has been promoted that privileges homogenized varieties, inputs and simplified planting arrangements. This includes fertilizer-dependent cereal cropping, and wetlands and seasonal gardens replaced with irrigation schemes. Such development frequently undervalues the role of local institutions, cultures and practices in managing and ensuring access to cultivated and semi-natural areas.

Climate variability has been a key feature of life in southern Africa. This is reflected in culture, including the importance of rain shrines among many Bantu-speaking people settled across much of Malawi. Traditional farming systems included complex intercrops of plants that matured at different times providing insurance in the face of erratic weather. Risk was also mitigated by reliance on indeterminate crops with the capacity to keep on flowering in the face of drought or pest attack.

This chapter documents the knowledge and processes of adaptation of smallholders to change over a generation in central and northern Malawi. It traces perceptions of changes in their physical and institutional environment and individual, household and community response strategies, including crop and livelihood diversification, and soil, water and land management. It shows how farmers from diverse groups attempt to build their knowledge and skills on risk assessment and management from a variety of sources. It also reveals the urgent need for development organizations to partner with smallholders and build on their knowledge and strategies to address complex local and wider risks.

Context

Malawi, a small landlocked country lying at the southern end of the East African Rift Valley, is one of the least developed countries in the world with an average gross domestic product (GDP) per capita of US$278 in 2008 (World Bank, 2009). Health and social indicators, though improving, are among the lowest in Africa, with infant mortality at 110 per 1,000 live births (ibid.), and average life expectancy at 54.6 years (UNDP, 2010) due to poor living conditions, food and water insecurity, poverty and diseases such as malaria and HIV/AIDS. The high and rapidly rising population (13.1 million, growing at 2.8 per cent per annum: Government of Malawi, 2009), limited cultivable area, and dual system of agriculture (smallholders and private estates), mean that 80 per cent of the population rely on very small landholdings (average farm size 0.28 hectares: IFAD, 2002). With only 2.3 per cent of cultivated land under irrigation (FAO, 2005), the vast majority of smallholder farmers are reliant on rain-fed agriculture under a unimodal rainfall system. Production levels vary from year to year, depending on prevailing weather and politico-economic factors. Fertilizer subsidies (targeted at up to 3 million resource-poor farmers) and the absence of major droughts have meant good harvests nationally for the five seasons to 2011. However, localized drought and flooding have affected production in different parts of the country, whilst an estimated 1 million vulnerable people are chronically food insecure (particularly in households headed by children, women, the elderly and disabled).

Perceptions of climate change – officials and farmers

Malawians are used to climate variability. Both meteorological data and farmer testimonies show a high degree of variability in rainfall totals, timing and distribution, over a fairly long time period (since the late 1970s). During the 2009/10 season, for example, parts of central and northern Malawi experienced late onset of the rains, high intensity rainfall causing localized flooding, a dry period of up to a month mid-season, and early cessation of rains.

Official reports on climate for Malawi are few. The National Adaptation Programmes of Action (NAPA, 2006: 25) includes only the following general narrative:

> Malawi receives an average of 850 mm of rainfall per year. This amount is adequate for rain-fed crop production and for recharging underground aquifers. However, the distribution and consistency of rainfall is very erratic and uneven, so that the whole of Malawi is prone to hydrological droughts. The worst affected areas are central-southern Karonga, the Bwanje Valley and the Shire Valley.

Data on rainfall, temperature and sunshine are recorded by the Meteorological Office. Time series records are held at district and station level, though obtaining them currently requires commissioning the Meteorological Office to visit the stations, transcribe historical data, check and compile it: not an option available to most farmers. The data are gradually being centralized and computerized and should soon be more accessible (R. Stern, pers. comm.). However, there are ongoing data limitations especially at local/ catchment level.

Generalizations about climate trends in Malawi are difficult, given variations in microclimates and terrain (Magrath and Sukali, 2009), as well as data limitations. Trends in daily temperature across southern Africa have been observed by New et al. (2006) based on evidence from meteorological services:

- Mean annual temperature has increased by 0.9°C between 1960 and 2006. This increase is most rapid in summer (December–February); slowest in September to November.
- The frequency of hot days and nights shows significantly increasing trends during all seasons.
- The frequency of cold days and nights shows significantly decreasing trends during all seasons except September to November.

Long-term rainfall trends are less clear and few trends at individual stations are statistically significant. However, looking at the region as a whole, New et al. (ibid.) find that the average regional dry spell length, average rainfall intensity and annual one-day maximum rainfall all show statistically significant increasing trends. They also found an indication of decreasing total precipitation, accompanied by increased average rainfall intensity concentrated on extreme precipitation days.

Interestingly, in southern Africa (and elsewhere) changing sea surface temperatures are believed by climatologists to be more important than changing land use patterns in controlling warm season rainfall availability and trends (Christensen et al., 2007). This is in contrast to received wisdom repeated by extension agencies and the media to farmers in Malawi: that deforestation is the main cause of climate change.

Headline figures on extreme weather events focus on the incidence of floods and droughts over the past two decades. Data compiled by the Centre for Research on the Epidemiology of Disasters (CRED) International Disaster Database record six years of drought affecting between 500,000 and 7 million people and floods affecting 200,000 to 500,000 (Table 4.1). However, localized events may not be included, for example the 1991 Phalombe flash floods that are reported to have killed more than 1,000 people and washed away villages and farms (NAPA, 2006).

Few detailed climate change scenarios have been constructed for Africa, given limited computational facilities, human resources and climate data. Projections of median air temperature increases for southern Africa by the end of the century lie between 3°C and 4°C, roughly 1.5 times the mean global response, for all seasons (Christensen et al., 2007). Precipitation projections are much more variable due to difficulties in modelling, data and deforestation projections. The overall picture is one of drying in much of the sub-tropics and an increase (or little change) in precipitation in the tropics (ibid.) (Malawi lies between latitudes 9° and 18°S.) Tadross et al. (2005, cited in Christensen et al., 2007), examining models for southern

Table 4.1 Extreme weather events in Malawi and people affected: 1987–2009

Disaster	Date	People affected
Drought	1987	1,429,000
Drought	Feb 1990	2,800,000
Drought	Apr 1992	7,000,000
Flood	Feb 1997	400,000
Flood	Jan 2001	500,000
Drought	Feb 2002	2,829,000
Flood	Dec 2002	246,000
Drought	Oct 2005	5,100,000
Drought	Oct 2007	520,000
Flood	Nov 2007	180,000

Source: EM-DAT CRED International Disaster Database

Africa, found projected decreases in early summer (October to December) rainfall and increases in late summer (January to March) rainfall over the eastern parts of southern Africa. Hewitson and Crane (2006, cited in Christensen et al., 2007) project increased winter precipitation in east and southern Africa. Rainfall intensity is also expected to increase (Tadross et al., 2005, cited in Christensen et al., 2007).

Projections of climate change impact by the World Bank (2009) show it affecting agriculture through higher temperatures, greater crop water demand, more variable rainfall, and extreme climate events such as floods and droughts. Projections for Malawi show average yields of main food crops (including maize, millet, sweet potato, rice, soybean, groundnut) decreasing by 5 to 10 per cent by 2050. They make a number of assumptions including no carbon dioxide fertilization and no or linear changes in land management practices.

Farmers are acute observers of weather patterns and events and have a number of ways of measuring and comparing these. Osbahr et al. (forthcoming) use as a benchmark for farmer perceptions a 'normal' climate year, which they find to be influenced by their perceptions of ideal rainfall necessary to service their (differing) needs. Other studies have sought to identify from farmer narratives periods when significant changes are perceived to have occurred. In Malawi, many farmers refer to the 1970s–80s as a watershed period, from when changes in timing, distribution (temporal and spatial) and intensity of rainfall, temperatures and wind direction could be observed (Table 4.2) (own survey). Perceptions of good and bad years vary from place to place but are generally consistent within a locality and between gender groups. The indicators used by farmers varied by gender and socio-economic status. Thus women were more likely to use availability of water and drying of wells and domestic water sources as reference points, whilst men growing cash crops referred to the availability of *dambo* (shallow wetland) water for tobacco seedlings during the dry season.

Local people also have indicators for when rainfall is imminent but there is general agreement that these are becoming less reliable. Other sources are the radio and extension agents, but these too have proven problematic. Malawi's history of autocratic rule (until 1994) and top-down extension services mean that farmers have tended to be predisposed to following the advice of extensionists, although they have maintained their local knowledge base to some extent. However, farmers are now questioning the adequacy of both knowledge systems:

We know when there will be rains or not. We know through *utatavu* (dancing waves). Secondly, there is a black bird called *kowera*. It chirps at dawn and at noon. When these two happen we know rains will be coming. We learnt these from our ancestors. It is knowledge handed down to us from our ancestors through generations. They used to be reliable in the past. Nowadays, they are not as reliable. (Kaunda villagers, Kasungu, 6 June 2010)

Table 4.2 Farmer perceptions of weather events and climate variability

Year	Location	Weather event	Source
pre 1970 1970s 2000s	Salima (Central Region)	First rains started October: ripened mangoes, prevented bush fires. Rains began starting in November Rains now starting December: shorter season	ActionAid (2006)
1970s–80s	Kasungu (Central Region): Chisazima	Rain started November, ended March/April. Sometimes fell for 2 weeks with intermittent breaks. Rain medium-heavy especially December–January. Planted beginning November. Hot season started August/September until December: it was very hot. Cold season started April if rains heavy until March: very cold due to moist soil. July: showers, sometimes heavy rains; sufficient water in *dimbas* (seasonal gardens).	Own survey
1984 1989 1997	Mdoka Ndaya	Last 'good' years: rain started November, ended February, good rainfall distribution, no floods. People planted early, finished weeding December, eating fresh maize February, harvested very well.	
2000	Chaguma	Rains good, no prolonged dry spells; good harvests. Very hot August–December, couldn't walk barefoot. Cold season began April, heavy showers July.	
2001/2 2004/5		Droughts. Rains started and dried up. People harvested nothing: cooked banana roots, maize husks. Reliant on piecework outside the area, food-for-work programmes	
2000s		Rains start late, intermittent with dry spells, finish early. Not all areas receive rain. Insufficient moisture for main season and cold season *dambo* cultivation, wells dry.	
1970s–80s	Mzimba (Northern Region): Ekwendeni	Rainfall started November/early December, heavy to April when beans planted. Rains heavy but no floods. Sometimes *chiperoni* (cold season showers) and *mzambwe* winds. Hot season started early September. October very hot could not sleep in iron-roofed houses. No winds except whirlwind; cold season windy.	Own survey
2000s		Rain coming late and finishing early. Can stop for several weeks. Very sunny, dries the crop. Windy, from different directions. Hot season started September: hot with 'dancing waves'. Could not walk barefoot especially at noon. Hot even during rains.	
2008/9		Last good year. Rain began beginning of December up to April, with dry spells of maximum 2 weeks. Good harvest and enough water in *dimbas*.	
1990s 2002	Nsanje (Southern Region)	Floods increasing in intensity and frequency Floods over knee height	ActionAid (2006)

There is no one who is good at predicting weather. This change of climate has made life difficult for everyone. Last year when rains started our Field Assistant told us 'this is not rain for planting so do not plant because you will regret it'. I tell you some took his advice but actually those who transplanted tobacco and planted their crops early are the only ones whose crops did well. I am grey-haired but I cannot predict rains. Not today. Only God can do that. The only thing we can do is to prepare our fields early and wait for the rains so that when it comes early we can plant early. (Chiota villagers, Mzimba, 1 July 2010)

Farmers directly relate perceptions of weather to their own livelihood and land management practices and other natural phenomena, with maize planting and harvesting dates as key markers. Whilst planting of the main crop used to be in October for the southern and central regions with weeding by Christmas and harvesting beginning in February/March, this has shifted back by between one and two months over the past 30 years, frequently with dry periods of two weeks or more, affecting crop development and management requirements (Table 4.2). Similarly, the availability of water has affected dry season *dambo* farming.

From the, albeit limited, available evidence there appears to be a convergence of perceptions (from both officials and farmers) that rainfall patterns across Malawi have changed over the last thirty years, increasing risk for cropping and livelihoods. At the same time climate narratives have been compounded by changes in population, the environment, and political, social and economic context.

Responses to climate change

Government institutions, non-government organizations and farmers have made varying responses to observed climate variations and constructed narratives. Actions are conventionally classified as either mitigation strategies (aimed at preventing or minimizing the process of climate change) or adaptation methods (to enable individuals or communities to cope with or adjust to the impacts of climate variation in their local areas) (Nyong et al., 2007). However, people combine elements of both in a complex set of livelihood strategies.

Government responses

Government responses to climate change appear to have been significantly influenced by external initiatives as part of the international climate change agenda. The National Environmental Action Plan (Department of Environmental Affairs, 1994), the first comprehensive attempt to identify and address environmental degradation issues including climate change, was developed to implement Agenda 21 following the 1992 Earth Summit (UN Conference on Environment and Development).

Since 2006, official response has centred on the National Adaptation Programmes of Action (NAPA) which Malawi, in common with other less developed countries, has developed under the United Nations Framework Convention on Climate Change (UNFCC) 'to enable Malawi to address her urgent and immediate adaptation needs caused by climate change and extreme weather events' (Environmental Affairs Department, 2006: 3). Developing the NAPA involved 'wide consultation with various stakeholders in public and private sector organizations, including local leaders, religious and faith groups, academicians, NGOs, civil society and highly vulnerable rural communities throughout the country' (ibid.: 3).[1] Whilst NAPA acknowledge farmers' ingenuity, operationalizing an approach which genuinely values local and traditional knowledge alongside formal science and technology into a workable climate change strategy is challenging:

> In most parts of Malawi, communities have tried to devise ingenious ways to cope with and adapt to the adverse impacts of extreme weather events, including shifting homes to higher ground, storing grain in local granaries, hunting small animals, gathering and eating wild fruits and vegetables, sinking boreholes and using traditional medicines to cure various ailments and diseases. However, some of these are not very effective. (ibid.: 6)

Linkages between documented community practices and the NAPA strategy are unclear. For example, activities under priority project (c) Improving agricultural production under erratic rains and changing climatic conditions so as to improve living standards and sustainable livelihoods of vulnerable communities, include:

- Mapping out vulnerable areas and identifying drought-tolerant crops such as cassava, millet, sweet potatoes;
- Multiplying and distributing appropriate crop and animal varieties;
- Training farmers and field extension staff on agricultural husbandry practices;
- Disseminating extension messages on the crops and animal varieties;
- Irrigation farming. (ibid.: 34)

Whilst activities certainly reflect some farmer groups' expressed needs (bearing in mind the complexities of farmer narratives), the approach is essentially a top-down transfer of technologies. Other programmes, such as the flagship Green Belt Initiative which aims to bring 1 million hectares under irrigation, have potential to reduce vulnerability to drought at national level. Issues of access to and management of the schemes, as well as choice of technologies, will be critical to reducing vulnerability for individual smallholders.

Non-governmental organizations

Non-governmental organizations (NGOs) have mushroomed in Malawi over the past two decades with the advent of multi-partyism. Many were set up as aid/development/relief organizations to combat poverty: some incorporate disaster risk reduction strategies into their programmes, and a number are now starting to include climate issues (Ziervogel et al., 2008). NGO adaptation activities to observed climate change include technological interventions and resource management strategies:

- Programmes to support agriculture-based livelihoods and food security (drought-resistant crops, fertilizer, winter cropping and irrigation technologies);
- Awareness raising, information sharing and training;
- Reforestation (wind protection, flood control, soil conservation);
- Catchment management (riverbank protection, river dredging);
- Social protection (pensions, child and disability grants). (ibid.)

National environmental NGOs, such as Coordinating Unit for Rehabilitation of the Environment (CURE) and Centre for Environment Policy and Advocacy (CEPA), together with international NGOs, including Oxfam (Magrath and Sukali, 2009) and ActionAid (ActionAid, 2006), actively monitor climate effects and put pressure on government to respond.

Communities and individuals

Resource-constrained smallholder farmers in Malawi face a complex set of risks and uncertainties. Ever-present and inter-related challenges include: rapidly changing government policies on inputs (fertilizer and seed) and crop pricing; health, water and food security issues related to poverty; and environmental change and disaster risk. Researchers from the Stockholm Environment Institute (Ziervogel et al., 2008: 32) have identified various strategies undertaken by individual farmers and communities in Malawi to cope with the realities of poverty, disaster risk and environmental change:

- Planting trees (to conserve watersheds and to protect houses from strong winds);
- Growing hybrid maize and cassava varieties that mature more quickly than local varieties (but only a few can afford these);
- Planting more drought-resistant crops such as cassava, sweet potatoes and soya;
- Planting crops earlier or later, depending on shifts in rainfall patterns in the local area;
- Not lighting bush fires;
- Constructing contour ridges to conserve soil and water;

- Boiling drinking water to avoid water-borne diseases in times of drought and floods;
- Adopting new planting technologies (e.g. single seeds only 25 cm apart);
- Engaging in small businesses (e.g. selling fritters, charcoal, fish, traditional beer);
- Doing casual work, or *ganyu* (e.g. within the village, making bricks or working on someone else's plot, or in town, working in construction);
- Some resort to crime and sex-for-food transactions.

However, as the Stockholm Environment Institute authors explain:

> It is difficult to determine to what extent these activities are needed due to anthropogenic climate change, over and above natural climate variability and other environmental and socio-economic stressors. Very few people refer to these activities as climate adaptation strategies although they articulate the connections between these activities and various forms of environmental change very clearly, which is equally important in supporting community-based adaptation. Other than in the very places where NGOs and/or government agencies are supporting and piloting specifically designed climate change projects, most of these adaptation activities are being undertaken in response to changes that have been experienced and not in response to warnings and guidance that have been issued. (Ziervogel et al., 2008: 32–3)

Evidence of 'multi-purpose' strategies by farmers to address multiple, interacting constraints – including, but not necessarily primarily, climate variability – is supported by our own research.[2] Farmers in Simlemba, a drought-prone area in northern Kasungu district, are using a variety of strategies to try to combat drought, flooding and low soil fertility (Table 4.3).

Table 4.3 Farmer strategies for combating climate variability and soil infertility in Simlemba, Kasungu (percentage of farmers interviewed[1])

Actions taken to combat	Drought	Flooding	Infertile soils
Plant drought-resistant crops	40.0	10.0	15.0
Apply compost/manure	7.5	12.5	25.0
Soil and water conservation	5.0	10.0	12.5
Plant early, use improved varieties	2.5	10.0	17.5
Plant trees	2.5	7.5	7.5
Irrigation farming	10.0	10.0	0
Business activities, livestock	10.0	5.0	2.5
Casual labouring	7.5	2.5	0

Note: [1] Number of farmers interviewed = 40

Source: Survey by the authors

Cropping

Women farmers explained how they were looking for crops which could help address both drought and soil fertility:

> In the past we used to grow local maize, groundnuts and local sweet potatoes, but now we are growing hybrid maize, groundnuts, soya beans, hybrid potatoes, tobacco and beans. Over the years our soil has lost its fertility so it is not fertile enough for local crops without applying fertilizer. We have been advised to start growing hybrid crops. We wanted crops which were early maturing – since rains often finish early – and high-yielding. (Women farmers in Mdoka village, Kasungu 1 June 2010)

Successive varieties of hybrid maize have been promoted in Malawi since the 1970s, initially to increase yields as part of a fertilizer package, but increasingly in response to the shorter growing season. Nationally there has been a decline in local maize, relative to hybrid varieties. Farmers in Mzimba report that they are now growing soya both as a cash crop and to improve soil fertility, and cassava as a drought-resistant crop. Farmers in Kasungu have also started growing cassava as it requires less rainfall and can tolerate dry spells. However, not all farmers are able to afford the cost of seed for high-yielding varieties of maize and other crops. The problem is exacerbated by the unpredictability of the 'planting' rains: farmers have to weigh up the risks of planting early and losing their seed or planting late and the crop not reaching maturity. Responses appear to vary from place to place as well as between farmers within one area:

> We dry plant as soon as possible after we finish making ridges. However, the problem with planting before the rains start is that if the rains become very heavy the seeds do not germinate well because the fields get waterlogged. It becomes *chimera* (chaff). So we are forced to replant, which is not easy or cheap. (Women farmers, Mdoka village, 1 June 2010)

> Sometimes crops dry up, so instead of doing other things, you are forced to patch in more seeds or completely replant. At times it can happen that you have no seeds yet your crops have dried up. You end up stranded. When that happens, and it has happened, we go to do *ganyu* (casual work) wherever it's available to buy seeds. (Men farmers, Mdoka village, 2 June 2010)

Asking for seeds from friends or relatives or doing casual work for seeds, cash or food are frequently reported strategies for coping with hunger and the effects of drought on cropping. The high variability of rainfall within a relatively small area (even from one valley to another) means that people may be able to go and weed on another farm whilst their own field has yet to be replanted. In other years (such as the 2001/2 drought in Kasungu) people who did not benefit from food-for-work interventions went to do *ganyu* for those who were beneficiaries and receiving 'more than enough'.

A number of other land management practices are described by farmers as attempts to conserve moisture in their fields, manage drought or mitigate it, as well as address other constraints. Most cannot be categorized simply as 'introduced' or 'indigenous' technologies, but show how farmers are attempting to address extremely difficult situations in different ways using their very limited resources:

- If there is a dry spell when we are weeding, we stop to keep moisture in the soil. We stop any activity in the field especially weeding or banking to avoid disturbing roots.
- Stopping weeding in the field only helps a very little. We just do it because we have run out of ideas.
- When rain comes late, it makes weeds grow in our fields before planting because the *zimalupsa* will make the soil wet. So this forces you to weed first before planting and weed again after planting crops. This is time consuming.
- We are making box ridges to hold water in our fields, planting napier and other grasses, making manure and planting legumes.
- We are also planting local trees like *msangu* (*F. albida*) to keep moisture in our fields and attract rainfall. (Farmers in Kasungu and Mzimba, 6 July 2010)

Farmers also talk of significant changes in dry season *dimba* (seasonally wet) garden cultivation. In the past (until the 1980s) *dimba* crops cultivated were mainly sugar cane and local vegetables, but a wide range of crops are now grown: tomatoes, rape, bananas, maize, rice, onions, potatoes, guavas. 'We are trying to grow *dimba* crops to supplement the harvests from the rainfed fields so that we do not end up selling or eating anything meant for seed' (farmers in Kasungu). However *dimbas* in many areas, particularly the drier northern part of Kasungu, are drying out so the number of farmers actually able to cultivate their *dimba* gardens is falling in all but the most favourable years. This has also impacted on cropping: 'We stopped growing sugar cane because there is not enough water in the *dimbas* due to poor rains so sugar cane dried up some years ago'. To access the water farmers have to dig shallow wells, a labour-intensive activity that is practised by tobacco farmers for their nurseries using hired labour. Women also undertake this task for household water supplies during the dry season. In a few areas local people are able to access water from one of the dams constructed under food-for-work programmes.

Tree planting and management

Trees – on both individual and community land – are seen as a key part of climate mitigation and adaptation. Given the strong extension and NGO messages on tree planting, it is not surprising that farmers repeat this mantra. However, observations of species and tree planting and management practices are more nuanced. People describe the multiple causes of local deforestation as well as efforts to overcome these and constraints they face in doing so:

> People planted blue gum trees to attract rain ... They gambled by planting blue gum trees. They should have planted trees like *mtondo* and *mkuyu*. Blue gum trees – and gmelina – do not do anything to attract rains. They just destroy the soil. This is why there is no change. We should plant local trees. These will block wind blowing and attract rains. (Chisazima villagers, Kasungu, 3 June 10)

> Trees attract rains but people felled them to sell at General Farming estate ... People are growing tobacco so they use trees to construct sheds and *mikangala*... Over-population has also led to destruction of trees as people want to construct houses. (Chaguma villagers, Kasungu, 4 June 2010)

> We should conserve the trees that we have and avoid bush fires... People set bush fires to hunt for mice. There should be a law to punish whoever lights bush fires... This depends on the cooperation of everyone here to successfully implement it. People sometimes do not obey chiefs these days, so to decide who should enforce the rules is a problem. (Chisazima villagers, Kasungu, 3 June 2010)

> We don't allow bush fires in the hills and wherever there are trees. If someone is found setting bush fires the village heads fine him a chicken ... We don't allow people to cut down trees for charcoal. Charcoal-making is destructive to trees. We only allow firewood. We also do not allow cutting down trees along streams. Instead we are planting trees along streams. (Chiotha villagers, Mzimba, 1 July 10)

These testimonies reveal variation between the two areas in terms of community environmental management strategies and ability to enforce regulations: the more commercially farmed and populous Kasungu apparently facing more challenges. The different land-inheritance traditions may also be a factor (Kasungu is matrilineal; men tend to be more migratory and less inclined to invest in their land). Politics at local level is evident, with differing interpretations of the role of the state in selecting and enforcing appropriate measures for environmental protection.

Farmers have a range of suggestions for strategies to address climate and other challenges – particularly soil fertility – facing them: digging wells and drilling boreholes (women in northern Kasungu); constructing dams and providing small-scale irrigation equipment; raising seedlings and planting indigenous tree species; land and crop management strategies – planting drought-resistant crops and varieties, applying compost and using crop rotation; and off-farm activities, including buying and selling produce and juice processing. Others discussed the need for better weather forecasts: 'Maybe we should be consulting the *mlangezi* (extension worker), but he no longer stays here'. Only one farmer commented: 'It is a sign of the last days, maybe we should just be brave for it'.

Conclusions

Farmers in Malawi have been observing climate variability for a generation. They face multiple shocks and stresses from the environment and social change to politics and the market. Many are calling for 'multi-purpose' strategies to address compounding causes and effects and mitigate future disasters. This goes beyond existing responses which rely heavily on sectoral and technological solutions – although functioning boreholes are clearly needed to make a difference to millions of families, and earth dams and irrigation technology could improve food security and provide cash incomes. Some new interventions, however, are perceived as worsening drought conditions. Responses to deal with outcomes of climate change, such as crop insurance against drought and flooding, have been targeted at semi-commercial farmers but could be a key part of a package of responses for the poorest farmers.

Farmers formulate their own strategies to address risk, by adjusting crops and varieties grown, planting dates, weeding patterns, and intensifying dry season farming. However, there is a clear message that they need more information on improved technologies (varieties, rainwater harvesting) and improved access to know-how and inputs to incorporate them into their farming. As political and traditional structures have weakened, community solutions to deforestation and land management may need to be supported by effective government policies and facilitated by development organizations sensitive to diverse needs and resources.

Farmers' traditional methods of forecasting weather are no longer effective, while Met office forecasts are not reaching down to community level. A proposed programme[3] to partner with schools and communities in data collection and analysis of trends would help inform farmers on risks. This could be a first step in closing the gulf between outsider and farmer knowledge systems.

Updates to the 2025 edition

Yancey Orr

The original article promoted the importance of cultural knowledge in addition to technical knowledge for how communities adapted to climate change. By aggregating local studies, other researchers (Crona et al., 2013) have built global knowledge structures of climate change. More recent studies (Pyhälä et al., 2016) which surveyed local knowledge research articles found that few of such studies actually represent the views of local populations regarding climate change and that without standardized terms, such local communities could not be compared or used for generalization.

In the original chapter, the authors expressed concern that agricultural intensification may make responding to climate change more difficult. This intuition has been supported by recent studies of monoculture which have shown that vegetation homogenization decreases water retention within soils (Levia et al., 2020).

Notes

[1] A model with farmers as part of climate change solutions has been endorsed by the World Bank: 'Countries can build on the traditional knowledge of farmers. Such knowledge embodies a wealth of location-specific adaptation and risk management options that can be applied more widely' (World Bank, 2009: 154). The International Assessment of Agricultural Knowledge, Science, and Technology for Development (IAASTD), also calls for the recognition of 'farming communities, farm households and farmers as producers and managers of ecosystems' (IAASTD, 2009: 4).

[2] Study of farmer perceptions of and responses to climate variability and risk and uncertainty in Kasungu and Ekwendeni Districts, carried out by D. Kambewa and K. Wellard, Bunda College, July–November 2010 with funding from McKnight Foundation

[3] Planned by the Malawi Meteorological Office and University of Reading.

References

ActionAid (2006) *Climate Change and Smallholder Farmers in Malawi: Understanding Poor People's Experiences in Climate Change Adaptation*, ActionAid International, London and Johannesburg.

Centre for Research on the Epidemiology for Disasters – CRED, Malawi country profile – natural disasters, EM-DAT: The International Disaster Database. [Online] http://www.emdat.be/result-country-profile [accessed 1 December 2010].

Christensen, J., Hewitson, B., Busuioc, A., Chen, A., Gao, X., Held, I., Jones, R., Kolli, R., Kwon, W.-T., Laprise, R., Magaña Rueda, V., Mearns, L., Menéndez, C., Räisänen, J., Rinke, A., Sarr A., and Whetton, P. (2007) 'Regional climate projections', in S. Solomon, D. Qin, M. Manning, Z.

Chen, M. Marquis, K. Averyt, M. Tignor and H. Miller (eds), *Climate Change 2007: The Physical Science Basis. Contribution of Working Group I to the Fourth Assessment Report of the Intergovernmental Panel on Climate Change*, Cambridge University Press, Cambridge and New York.

Crona, B., Wutich, A., Brewis, A., and Gartin, M. (2013) Perceptions of climate change: Linking local and global perceptions through a cultural knowledge approach. *Climate Change* 119: 519–531.

Department of Environmental Affairs (1994) *National Environmental Action Plan*, Department of Environmental Affairs, Lilongwe.

Environmental Affairs Department (2006) *Malawi's National Adaptation Programmes of Action: Under the United Nations Framework Convention on Climate Change (UNFCCC)*, First Edition, Ministry of Mines, Natural Resources and Environment, Global Environmental Facility, UNFCCC, UNDP Malawi, Lilongwe.

FAO (2005) *Irrigation in Africa in Figures: AQUASTAT Survey 2005*, FAO Water Report 29, Food and Agriculture Organization, Land and Water Development Division, Rome.

Hewitson, B., and Crane, R. (2006) 'Consensus between GCM climate change projections with empirical downscaling: precipitation downscaling over South Africa', *International Journal of Climatology* 26, 1315–37.

IAASTD (2009) *International Assessment of Agricultural Knowledge, Science and Technology for Development Executive Summary of the Synthesis Report*, IAASTD, Washington DC.

IFAD (2002) *Assessment of Rural Poverty: Eastern and Southern Africa*, International Fund for Agricultural Development Eastern and Southern Africa Division – Project Management Division, Rome.

Levia, D., Creed, I., Hannah, D., Nanko, K., Boyer, E., Carlyle-Moses, D., van de Giesen, N., Grass, D., Guswa, A., Hudson, J., Hudson, S., Iida, S., Jackson, R., Katul, G., Kamagai, T., Llorens, P., Ribeiro, F., Pataki, D., Peters, C., Sanchez Carretero, D., Selker, J., Tetzlaff, D., Zalewski, M., and Bruen, M. (2020) 'Homogenization of the terrestrial water cycle', *Nature Geoscience* 13: 656–660.

Magrath, J. and Sukali, E. (2009) *The Winds of Change: Climate Change, Poverty and the Environment in Malawi*, Oxfam International, Lilongwe.

National Statistical Office of Malawi (2009) *2008 Population and Housing Census*, National Statistical Office of Malawi, Lilongwe.

New, M., Hewitson, B., Stephenson, D., Tsiga, A., Kruger, A., Manhique, A., Gomez, B., Coelho, C., Masisi, D., Kululanga, E., Mbambalala, E., Adesina, F., Saleh, H., Kanyanga, J., Adosi, J., Bulane, L., Fortunata, L., Mdoka, M., and Lajoie, R. (2006) 'Evidence of trends in daily climate extremes over southern and west Africa', *Journal of Geophysical Research* 111: D14102, doi:10.1029/2005JD006289.

Nyong, A., Adisina, F. and Osman Elasha, B. (2007) 'The value of indigenous knowledge in climate change mitigation and adaptation strategies in the African Sahel', *Mitigation and Adaptation Strategies for Global Change* 12: 787–97.

Osbahr, H., Dorward, P., Stern, R., and Cooper, S. (2011) 'Supporting agricultural innovation in Uganda to climate risk: linking climate change and variability with farmer perceptions', *Experimental Agriculture*, Special issue 02, 47: 293–316.

Pyhälä, A., Fernández-Llamazares, Á., Lehvävirta, H., Anja, B., Ruiz-Mallén, I., Salpeteur, M., and Thornton, T. (2016) 'Global environmental change: local perceptions, understandings, and explanations', Special Feature: Small-Scale Societies and Environmental Transformations: Co-evolutionary Dynamics, Ecology and Society21(3): 25.

Tadross, M., Jack, C., and Hewitson, B. (2005) 'On RCM-based projections of change in southern African summer climate', *Geophysical Research Letters* 32: L23713, doi:10.1029/2005GL024460.

UNDP (2010) *Human Development Report 2010: The Real Wealth of Nations: Pathways to Human Development,* United Nations Development Programme, New York.

World Bank (2009) *World Development Report 2010: Development and Climate Change,* The World Bank, Washington, DC.

Ziervogel, G., Taylor, A., Hachigonta, S., and Hoffmaister, J. (2008) *Climate Adaptation in Southern Africa: Addressing the Needs of Vulnerable Communities,* Stockholm Environment Institute, Stockholm.

About the authors

Kate Wellard is a socio-economist researching, teaching and providing policy inputs on livelihoods and equitable, sustainable development. She has worked with government, NGOs and universities in southern, eastern and West Africa, including seven years at Bunda College, University of Malawi. She is currently Visiting Fellow at the Natural Resources Institute, UK.

Daimon Kambewa is a rural sociologist and senior lecturer working on institutions, policies and strategies for sustainable agriculture and rural development. He specializes in customary land tenure and wetlands management and local environmental knowledge and practices. He is Head of the Department of Agricultural Extension at Bunda College, University of Malawi.

Sieglinde Snapp is Soils and Cropping System Ecologist and Professor at the Kellogg Biological Station, Michigan State University, USA. Her research and teaching address sustainable principles of agro-ecology and biodiversity for integrated management. She is committed to trans-disciplinary, participatory approaches working in the US Great Lakes Region and Africa.

Chapter 5

Risk and abandonment, and the meta-narrative of climate change

Dan Taylor

The evidence for climate change is incontrovertible. However, the perspectives of the poor are neither considered nor requested in current narratives. Drawing on work in Malawi, Zimbabwe and South Africa this chapter will discuss the risk of maize dependency in the face of environmental uncertainty: this includes climate change but also other factors which lead to the abandonment of resilient systems of farming, and of farming as a livelihood. The abandonment of 'traditional' crops like sorghum and millet suggest a new 'calculus of risk' leading to a preference for maize, which has become the region's leading staple. The chapter also analyses the implications of making climate change a meta-narrative, with the tendency to subsume other obstacles to development within it.

Introduction

The evidence for climate change appears incontrovertible (Gleick et al., 2010). Less certainty exists regarding the implications of climate change for the lives and livelihoods of Africa's rural poor. Climate change mitigation and adaptation efforts can be pursued in ways that strengthen rural livelihoods, meet broad-based community development needs, and enhance poor people's overall capacities (UNDP, 2007; Adger et al., 2009). But a wide range of climate change policy, technical, and financial investment strategies are possible, and many of them may not address development needs. On the contrary, some climate change-related policies and actions may prove detrimental to the interests of Africa's rural poor. For example, public assistance flows may be diverted from poverty alleviation to climate change concerns (Michaelowa and Michaelowa, 2007). Furthermore, climate change-driven crisis narratives regarding food insecurity can be used to promote agrarian policies, favouring industrialized agriculture that marginalizes household producers and their long-term practices (Guttal and Monsalves, 2011).

The geographical area for my analysis will be southern Africa – Malawi, South Africa and Zimbabwe; three countries whose food security is under threat. In addressing this problem, I will illustrate how social change manifested in current agricultural practices has reinforced a particularly narrow approach to pursuing food security. This approach takes the form of dependence on a single crop – maize – with its attendant risks. People are abandoning indigenous crops better suited to the vagaries of African climates. For years this crop substitution has been heralded as a progressive change boosting regional food security (Byerlee and Eicher, 1997). Concerns about climate change are now being used to justify further intensification of African maize production, including introduction of genetically modified varieties (Vaidyanathan, 2010). Ironically, by increasingly focusing on maize production, rural households have been giving up a robust and resilient agro-ecosystem with a great capacity for mitigating and adapting to climate change.

I am concerned that climate change discourse is becoming an all-encompassing meta-narrative of change that often fails to distinguish local context from global problems; that fails to understand the difference between the particular determinants of poverty and its global discourse; and that fails to articulate the priorities of poor people rather than an undifferentiated notion of the common good. Calling for a return to indigenous grains and other crops may seem an unworkable, even naïve, argument. However, it is one that is gaining recognition. The National Research Council's (1996: xiii) three volume series on traditional African cereals, vegetables, and fruits highlights 'their potential for expanding and diversifying African and world food supplies'. Regarding pearl millet, for example, the National Research Council (1996: 79) states: 'a new era may be dawning. Pearl millet is supremely adapted to heat and aridity and, for all its current decline, seems likely to spring back as the world gets hotter and drier'. Yet, it must be acknowledged that promotion of these indigenous crops will be challenging. According to a report on Agriculture and Rural Development Day 2010, which took place in parallel with the United Nations Climate Change Conference in Cancún: 'An entrenched "culture of maize" is hampering efforts to help Africa cope with climate change, experts said at the sidelines of climate talks here' (Dube, 2010). With increased documentation of the detrimental impacts of global warming on maize yields (Lobell et al., 2011), the importance of indigenous grains is being reinforced.

What if 'maize is life'?

The crop preferences of farmers provide us with a perspective on the changing habits of farmers, their farming systems and the social organization that underpins agricultural practices. In this regard I look at maize and sorghum, both of which have been the major food security crops at different points in history.

Maize originated in Central America. Domesticated from the wild *teosinte*, maize *(Zea mays)* has been bred to become the high-yielding crop that we know today (Harlan, 1975). Introduced into the interior of southern Africa by the 17th century (Huffman, 2009), its spread over the past 100 years to become the dominant food crop of southern Africa has been nothing short of miraculous. Indeed maize's widespread adoption probably occurred no earlier than the first quarter of the 20th century (McCann, 2005), though any attempt to infer a date is speculative. Once a vegetable crop grown in the gardens of women for 'green' maize, it has spread into the fields of men as a subsistence and cash crop. Indeed a meal without maize in the form of *nsima* (Malawi), *sadza* (Zimbabwe) or *uphuthu* (Zulu, South Africa) is regarded as one unable to stave off hunger. Hence in Malawi it is said: *chimanga ndi moyo* (maize is life) (Smale, 1995).

This maize dependency is interesting because it raises the question why a once insignificant crop grown largely by women has become the dominant crop of the region. It is beyond the scope of my study to cover maize's long and complex history in southern Africa, though it bears noting that the crop's spread and dominance has been connected to broad processes of social change, including colonialism, commercialization and urbanization (see McCann, 2005; Huffman, 2009). Maize now has spread into areas considered marginal for its production due to low and highly unpredictable rainfall. This would suggest irrationality in farmers' choices; however, this is far from the truth.

The fact that maize is a cross-pollinator means that a yield decline can be mitigated through careful seed selection, which offers it resilience and the ability to adapt to changing environmental circumstances. Maize is not a drought-resistant crop, though farmers claim that some of the more 'traditional' varieties have drought-resistant characteristics; this explains why many farmers continue to select seed for their next planting from their own fields (Taylor, 1999). The standing crop is seldom seriously damaged by birds or diseases. Thus, maize is a versatile and adaptable crop which can be grown across a wide range of climatic conditions though its environmental limits are often exceeded by farmers in more marginal areas.

Yields per unit of land and labour from maize outstrip those of small grains – sorghums and millets – they have replaced. Maize also requires less labour for field management and food preparation. It does not require any threshing or winnowing. The advent of high-yielding varieties (HYVs) of maize, more often than not hybrids, can potentially outstrip the open pollinated varieties grown traditionally by farmers. Such high yield potential is only fully realized with the use of inorganic fertilizer, due to high plant nutrient requirements, and at least some supplementary irrigation. But there is a downside: seeds must be repurchased annually so as not to lose their hybrid vigour. However, farmers, either due to a lack of information or lack of access, often replant hybrids, with disappointing results. At the same time, the risk of investing in hybrid seeds in situations of recurrent drought is a deterrent to farmers who depend on their own crops for household food security. In addition, hybrid maize requires better post-harvest storage than most farmers are able to provide, leading to considerable post-harvest losses from pests or pre-planting germination. There has been some progress in addressing these limitations expressed in HYVs.

Maize is more often than not grown as a single crop in a field – monocropping – which is in direct contrast to the complex farming systems based on intercropping that characterized environmental utilization in the past. While the uniformity of the field makes it easier to manage, the risk of crop failure is higher.

Less than a century ago, sorghum and millet, indigenous to Africa, were the most important grain crops in southern Africa. In South Africa, for example, farmers use the generic term *amabele* for both, but the correct terms are: *amabele* for sorghum (*Sorghum bicolor*); *unyawothi* for pearl millet (*Pennisitum glaucum*); and *upoko* for finger millet (*Eleusine corocana*). At one time sorghum was the crop that underpinned food security, now it is forgotten by the many who would view maize-based systems as the current and historical norm. The declining importance of sorghum in socio-cultural terms is exemplified by sayings which allude to its past importance. The Zulu saying *usewadelile amabele* ('he who abandons sorghum, risks everything'; my translation) resonates with current patterns of change (Samuelson, 1923). Indeed, Samuelson translates the word *(ama)bele* as 'Kaffir-corn generally; means of living; life itself; existence', which contrasts with the newly found importance of maize in the region. As a signifier of 'life itself', it is hard to imagine the tremendous social change that has resulted in its relegation to a crop of minor importance.

Both sorghum and millet are drought-resistant crops. Indeed, the National Research Council (1996: 128) observes that sorghum can grow 'on sites so burning and arid that no other major grain – with the exception of pearl millet – can be consistently grown'. In addition, sorghum can withstand waterlogging and tolerate salinity, and it is one of the most photosynthetically efficient plants (National Research Council, 1996). Both crops continue to be grown for a variety of reasons. For example, in the lower rainfall areas of Zimbabwe, sorghum is the mainstay; pearl millet is grown for taste and finger millet for its storability (see van Oosterhout, 1993, on farmers' crop selection criteria). Such a system offers productivity and hence food security, satisfies gastronomic preferences, and reduces risk.

There is considerable justification for attributing sorghum's decline to public policy in which research on maize has received the preponderance of research funding. The National Research Council (1996: 127) claims that sorghum 'receives merely a fraction of the attention it warrants'. But neglect by scientists provides only a partial answer. The clue to sorghum's declining importance lies in its lower yield potential combined with its most limiting constraint – birds. Thus a local farmer in South Africa, Philemon Zwane (see Taylor, 1999), has distinguished between sorghum that is bird-proof, that is guarded, and that is protected by 'Zulu medicine'.

Farmers have three options open to them: to grow bird-proof varieties which are poor in taste, mainly for beer brewing; to guard against birds, with considerable demand on human resources; and to protect the crop with the use of 'traditional medicines'. The social organization required to watch against birds while the crop is 'ripening' requires people to plant at the same time – a task once co-ordinated by the chief and his council – and share the onerous burden of continuously guarding the crop at certain periods of its development. This time-consuming task can no longer be shared with children now at school and men who may be away, leaving the task to the women whose responsibilities are already onerous and for whom staying alone is arguably dangerous. Maize, which does not have to be guarded, provides a viable alternative, provided of course that rainfall is adequate.

This has obvious implications for climate change strategies because there is the need to match social as well as agricultural priorities with the changing nature of rural society.

The competing goals of climate change and development

The narrative of climate change cannot be divorced from risk and uncertainty in relation to farming systems in these environments. The abandonment of sorghum demonstrates a clear break with the past and in many senses constitutes a metonym for an entire agricultural and social system in which lives – at key times – needed to be organized around protecting crops from birds and other wild and domestic animals. The motivation to do so in the contemporary period does not appear to exist, given new preferences and priorities. Hence, once the crop of food security, sorghum is largely an abandoned crop in much of southern Africa, but it is also the most symbolic, given its designation as 'life itself'.

Farmers' uptake of certain crops and their abandonment of others is partly due to seed access, partly due to the efforts of extension services and, in the case of Malawi, government diktat, dating back to the Banda era. This is reflected in the promotion of hybrid maize by the extension services of all three countries, in the penetration of the private sector into remoter areas, and in current consumer preferences. This is particularly important in the Malawi case where seed is either given free or subsidized; likewise with fertilizer, where successive governments have established a patron–client relationship in supporting input subsidization. Furthermore, it should not be construed as cynicism to attribute voter behaviour to the timely availability of subsidized farm inputs which often precedes elections in Africa – fertilizers are votes! This form of patrimonialism has characterized Malawi but is equally applicable to Zimbabwe where, of late, land rather than fertilizer has been the medium.

Here is not the place to make the full argument for a more sustainable alternative. The case has been made by the International Assessment on Agricultural Knowledge, Science and Technology for Agricultural Development (2008), known as the IAASTD Report, which has convincingly expressed the view that a new vision for agriculture must be underpinned by an approach that is more environmentally benign (also see National Research Council, 1996).

Thus, the promotion of a high input strategy for the development of African agriculture can, on the basis of contemporary and past experience, proceed only with considerable risk. Climate change is the latest in this long list of risks posed to farmers on the continent, albeit with more serious consequences than others. The statement of the IAASTD panel of international experts that 'business as usual is not an option' calls for a radical rethink of what agriculture should look like in the future. The review, while not ruling out any options, came out in support of agro-ecology, a risk-reducing, resource-conserving, context-specific form of agriculture that attempts to mimic the natural ecosystem it has replaced. This includes the need for the conservation of agricultural and biological diversity on which wider ecosystems depend; a critical sustainability issue often overlooked. Indeed, the case for biodiversity has yet to receive the same attention as climate change but is critical in the lives of poor people alongside its importance in mitigation and adaptation strategies.

There is much to learn here from periods of African history when monoculture was not quite so prevalent and, indeed, polycultures which included a number of different crops occupying different agro-ecosystem niches were planted sequentially, and sometimes simultaneously, in the same field with overlapping periods of harvest. This extended the harvest period, and offered a higher likelihood of a successful agricultural outcome by ensuring that, at least, some food was always available for harvest. The probability of a successful harvest was ensured by combining crops with different growth habits, times to maturity, and drought and flooding resilience – hence reducing risk. While yields for individual crops might be lower, the yield for the entire field could be higher as grains, legumes, tubers and leaf crops would all be harvested, often at different times. However in contrast, much-publicized programmes such as the Alliance for a Green Revolution in Africa, the Millennium Development Project and the Malawi Input Subsidization Programme all fit within the same modernization conceptual framework: yield maximization, farming system simplification, and a heavy reliance on purchased inputs. But such an approach is the antithesis of the need by African farmers for strategies to mitigate risk through diversification – likewise for climate change.

But, if more agro-ecological approaches are to be introduced then there is the need to embed activities in the specific realities of farmers rather than assuming that climate change adaptation and mitigation and development are converging strategies. Michaelowa and Michaelowa (2007) in analysing the use of Overseas Development Aid (ODA) to fund climate change efforts have highlighted their conflicting priorities. Interpreting the Millennium

Development Goals (MDGs) as 'codified' efforts to eradicate poverty, they demonstrate the inherent contradiction of redirecting resources from poverty eradication to climate change when objectives are clearly divergent. The evidence for the presumption that climate change efforts can converge with economic growth, or development, is not borne out by either India or China, the two countries that have made most progress towards realizing the MDGs; in both cases considerable increases in greenhouse gas emissions have occurred. As they also show, 'mitigation strategies in developing countries provide politicians in industrialized countries with a welcome strategy to divert the attention of their constituencies from the lack of success in reducing greenhouse gas emissions domestically' (Michaelowa and Michaelowa, 2007: 6).

While there is the justifiable argument that the MDGs are not developmental (for example see Chang, 2010, for one perspective), it should be apparent that development takes precedence in the lives of the food insecure. From this perspective alone, it would be possible to argue that climate change strategies as currently conceptualized, do not take sufficient cognizance of the aspirations of Africa's poor.

Farmer perceptions of risk and climate change

Risk adversity, once exemplified by practices which promoted agricultural biodiversity, crop diversification and mixed farming, has been replaced in many cases by monocultural maize production combined with non- or off-farm activities such as out-migration where job seeking provides both an income and mechanism for investment in agriculture. Hence, it should be noted that farming for many may indeed constitute a part-time livelihood and only partially meet the needs of household food security. Migrants working in the mines of South Africa characterize the interplay of urban and rural opportunism in support of a livelihood; such activities complemented farming which is seldom sufficient in rural economies for which a cash income is increasingly essential. The penetration of the market into rural Africa negates the dichotomization of the rural and the urban which are essentially intertwined, and informs what course of economic action farmers may choose to follow.

There is a complex interplay of factors – from social to environmental through to economic – which underscores the decision-making that precedes whether to plant or to leave; abandoning farming for one or more seasons. A household as an entity, however, might well do both by delegating the more able to seek a temporary or permanent cash income elsewhere. The abandonment of crops like sorghum and millet, and their replacement by maize and paid work, suggests a new 'calculus of risk' in the face of existing and new threats to a successful agricultural outcome. When taken in combination with new needs and wants in an increasingly material-orientated world, abandonment could be of agriculture itself.

Often the need for cash in what constitutes a subsistence agrarian economy necessitates other income sources beyond that which farming can provide. In Malawi farmers may well sell maize in a time of scarcity in the assumption that donor aid will meet the shortfall in the 'hungry season' which, as an approximation, follows planting and ends with next harvest.

Risk adversity, abandonment and now climate change are interweaving narratives in the changing patterns of social and physical reproduction in which 'de-agrarianization' and commoditization lead to an uncertain future for the rural poor. This is exacerbated by smaller landholdings, divided as part of inter-generation transfers, leading to fewer crop rotations and fallows, lower soil fertility as nutrients are extracted by successive crops, and increased soil erosion as soil organic matter is depleted.

Farmers in sub-Saharan Africa are acutely aware of the risk of drought, arguing that rainfall is lower, less reliable and combined with higher temperatures. However, mitigation and adaptation strategies are neither articulated nor prioritized (Barbier et al., 2009; Mertz et al., 2009), which appears to be the norm unless questions related to changing weather patterns are interpreted as climate change (compare with Thomas et al., 2007). It is clear that farmers are acutely aware of changing environmental conditions, but the inference that this demonstrates an awareness of climate change is assumed.

Furthermore, the assumption that changes in weather patterns are synonymous with long-term climate change requires greater analysis. The unpredictability of the weather is particularly common in the discourse of communities, particularly the elderly, whose statements often refer to some 'golden age' in the not too distant past. However, the lack of verification is often a problem, with short-term weather perturbations given more importance than longer-term changes, because they are more clearly remembered.

In a South African study (Bryan et al., 2008), farmers were incorrect in their assumption that temperature increased and precipitation decreased. Whereas farmers' perceptions of long-term changes in climate appear correct for temperature, they were wrong for rainfall (where the attributed decline was not statistically significant). They make the important observation that farmers appear to focus more on 'short-term trends than long-term changes'. They also show that 62 per cent of farmers from their South African sample have taken no adaptation measures.

The efforts by non-governmental organizations to promote mitigation or adaptation to climate change are laudable, but normative statements of intended action, building on what is done anyway, do not substitute for real and lasting solutions (see for example Oxfam, 2009) – and often reflect a relabelling of existing sustainable agricultural programmes. This is confusing where contradictory policy messages are problematic; for example, in Malawi the competing messages, particularly by government and other agencies, of agricultural diversification combined with compost-making run parallel with maize intensification using HYVs and fertilizer.

Hence climate change as a phenomenon only becomes a part of popular discourse when awareness is raised, often by outside agencies. While consciousness of this threat to agriculture is important, it comes with the danger that it is interpreted by farmers that they are (solely) to blame for climate change through their practices, particularly as agents of deforestation, having cleared afforested areas for farming (B. Williams pers. comm., 2009). The view that Africa's poor with their insignificant carbon footprint are responsible for climate change is part of the same discourse in which victims of undesirable change become its perpetrators (Escobar, 1995).

Meta-narrative of climate change

This paper has highlighted the competing aims, discourses and actions that are part and parcel of the current discourse of climate change. The argument that human-made global warming is a challenge to be met by decisions and subsequent action taken at national and global levels should appear obvious. However it is equally apparent that the impact of individual resource-poor smallholders is inconsequential when measured in global terms, but their voices should nonetheless be heard in any such deliberations, lest the proposed solutions be detrimental to the interests of the poor (Msukwa and Taylor, 2011).

Climate change can be characterized as a meta-narrative which encompasses everything within it. On the positive side, a broad focus of climate change opens a space for the articulation of other, less popular, or more controversial, subjects. But in subsuming everything, climate change runs the danger of becoming an all-encompassing discourse of competing powerful interests; squeezing out the particular in favour of the more generic, popular and universal issues of our times. The more immediate and particular constraints faced by a given community may have little or no connection to climate change, but are part of a process of political marginalization and economic exclusion that is embedded in this global narrative. The need for agrarian reform, for property rights, for reliable livelihoods, for educational opportunities, for social justice in the face of inequity all have, at most, a tenuous connection to the issue of climate change. The discourse of development has become confused with a more recent and contemporary discourse of climate change. As Gregory et al. (2005: 2147) conclude: 'climate change is only one of several changes affecting food systems and that its relative importance varies both between regions and between different societal groups within a region'.

What then are the implications of this for the African poor whose view of agriculture is culturally specific and whose room for manoeuvre is increasingly constrained by the more macro issues of our time? Climate change is an important issue but less immediate than the struggle for everyday survival. If maize or sorghum have at different times constituted life and security, then the seamless connection between the environment – crop, soil and climate – and the farmer is essentially intertwined. Yet the discontinuity between maize and sorghum reflects the changing nature of African agrarian society in which risk and abandonment are ever present realities in the lives and livelihoods of Africa's poor.

Conclusion

This chapter has argued that the discourse of climate change and its ensuing policies should reflect the priorities of poor people and, in doing so, it calls for a greater focus on southern African smallholder production systems. In the past these were notable for their complexity embodied in a wide range of crops, which were eminently suitable for the region's highly variable rainfall regimes and drought-prone conditions. Times have changed and so has agriculture with maize, often grown in monocultures, becoming predominant. Yet the need for agricultural biodiversity as part of more diverse, robust and resilient farming systems is increasing in importance within the context of climate change.

Returning to agrarian systems characterized by a higher degree of biodiversity will be challenging. There is the continual threat that governments and powerful market stakeholders will seek to meet the challenges of rising populations and a growing global demand for food through more intensive use of industrial farming technology, including greater reliance on hybrid maize. However the actions of poor people cannot be ignored. Both their impact on, and their need for, biologically diverse environments must be considered. They are both utilizers of natural resources and custodians of agricultural and biological diversity. The challenge is to maintain as well as recreate agro-ecosystems that provide a diverse range of food in a context where more systemic, uniform agricultural systems are becoming the norm.

The need to recognize and appreciate the diverse and complex management systems that have characterized African agriculture is becoming increasingly important as social change is manifested in the abandonment of long-term farming practices suited to local environmental conditions. These practices may become extremely relevant to global food security given current uncertainties about if, how, where and when the process of global warming becomes irreversible. The more resilient crops that have typified African farming systems for centuries could well constitute the building blocks of agriculture for the future. Whether this will be enough is uncertain, but sorghum, not maize, may become synonymous with life once again.

Updates to the 2025 edition

Yancey Orr

Recent studies anticipate that the increased heat and longer summers will threaten maize production in southern Africa. Climate models predicting more common extreme temperatures (number of days above 35°C) suggest that maize farmers may respond by changing their planting dates (Mangani et al., 2023). These changes may reduce the time for maize plants to mature and reduce yields. Systematic literature reviews of maize and climate studies in Africa show that drought is the major concern for agricultural production (Du and Xiong, 2024). Drought and temperature extremes may reduce maize yields by as much as 33 per cent if temperatures rise by 4°C (Pörtner et al., 2022). Based on such climate and agricultural changes, Africa will likely need to import more grain in the decades to come (Zhai et al., 2020).

References

Adger, W., Lorenzoni, I. and O'Brien, K. (eds.) (2009) *Adapting to Climate Change*, Cambridge University Press, Cambridge.

Barbier, B., Yacouba, A., Karambiri, H., Zoromé, M. and Somé, B. (2009) 'Human vulnerability to climate variability in the Sahel: farmers' adaptation strategies in northern Burkino Faso', *Environment Management* 43: 790–803.

Bryan, E., Deressa, T., Gbetibouo, G. and Ringer Gbetibouo, C. (2008) 'Determinants of Adaptation to Climate Change in Ethiopia and South Africa', International Food Policy Research Institute and Centre for Environmental Economics, South Africa, [online] available from: http://gecafs.org/documents/PP05Bryan.pdf [accessed 10th May 2010].

Byerlee, D. and Eicher, C. (eds.) (1997) *Africa's Emerging Maize Revolution*, Rienner, Boulder.

Chang, H. (2010) 'Hamlet without the Prince of Denmark', in S. Khan and J. Christiansen (eds.) *Towards New Developmentalism: Market as Means rather than Master*, Routledge, Abingdon [online], available from: http://www.econ.cam.ac.uk/faculty/chang/pubs/HamletwithoutthePrinceofDenmark-revised.pdf [Accessed 25th May 2010].

Du, S. and Xiong, W. (2024) 'Weather Extremes Shock Maize Production: Current Approaches and Future Research Directions in Africa'. *Plants* 13(12): 1585.

Dube, J. (2010) 'Experts: African maize culture militates against climate adaptation', Climate Change Media Partnership, December 10, http://www.climatemediapartnership.org/reporting/stories/experts-african-maize-culture-militates-against-climate-adaptation/

Escobar, A. (1995) *Encountering Development: The Making and Unmaking of the Third World*. Princeton University Press, Princeton.

Gleick, P., Adams, R., Amasino, R., et al., (2010) 'Climate change and the integrity of science', *Science* 328: 689–690.

Gregory, P., Ingram, J., and Brklacich, M. (2005) 'Climate change and food security', *Philosophical Transactions: Biological Sciences* 360: 2139–2148.

Guttal, S. and Monsalve, S. (2011) 'Climate crises: defending the land', *Development* 54: 70–76.

Harlan, J. (1975) *Crops and Man,* American Society of Agronomy and Crop Science Society of America, Madison.

Huffman, T. (2009) 'A cultural proxy for drought: ritual burning in the Iron age of Southern Africa', *Journal of Archaeological Science* 36: 991–1005.

International Assessment of Agricultural Knowledge, Science and Technology for Development (2008) 'Agriculture at a Crossroads', Island Press, Washington D.C. [Online] Available from: http://www.agassessment.org/reports/IAASTD/EN/Agriculture%20at%20a%20Crossroads_Global%20Report%20%28English%29.pdf [accessed 9 June 2010].

Lobell, D., Bänziger, M., Magorokosho, C. and Vivek, B. (2011) 'Nonlinear heat effects on African maize as evidenced by historical yield trials', *Nature Climate Change* 1: 42–45.

Mangani, R., Bunn, K.M., and Creux, N.M. (2023) 'Projecting the effect of climate change on planting date and cultivar choice for South African dryland maize production'. *Agricultural and Forest Meteorology* 341 (15): 109695.

McCann, J. (2005) *Maize and Grace: Africa's Encounter with a New World Crop 1500–2000,* Harvard University Press, Cambridge.

Mertz, O., Mbow, C., Reenberg, A. and Diouf, A. (2009) 'Farmers' perceptions of climate change and agricultural strategies in rural Sahel', *Environmental Management* 43: 804–816.

Michaelowa, A. and Michaelowa, K. (2007) 'Climate or development: is ODA diverted from its real purpose?', *Climate Change* 84: 5–21.

Msukwa, C. and Taylor, D. (2011) 'Why can't development be managed more like a funeral? Challenging participatory practices'. *Development and Change Vol. 21, No. 1 (February 2011), pp. 59-72.*

National Research Council (1996) *Lost Crops of Africa,* Volume 1, National Academy Press, Washington, D.C.

Oxfam International (2009) *The winds of change: climate change, poverty and the environment in Malawi.* Oxfam, Oxford.

Pörtner, H.O., Roberts, D.C., Adams, H., Adler, C., Aldunce, P., Ali, E., Begum, R.A., Betts, R., Kerr, R.B., and Biesbroek, R. (2022) *Climate Change 2022: Impacts, Adaptation and Vulnerability.* IPCC: Geneva, Switzerland.

Samuelson, R. (1923) *King Cetywayo Zulu Dictionary.* Durban Commercial Publishing Company, Durban.

Smale, M. (1995) '"Maize is life": Malawi's delayed Green Revolution', *World Development* 23: 819–831.

Taylor, D. (1999) *Field of Futility or Hidden Hope? Agricultural Knowledge and Practice of Low Resource Farmers in the KwaZulu-Natal Province of South Africa,* unpublished Ph.D. thesis, University College London.

Thomas, D., Twyman, C., Osbahr, H. and Hewitson, B. (2007) 'Adaptation to climate change and variability: farmer responses to intra-seasonal precipitation trends in South Africa', *Climatic Change* 83: 301–322.

UNDP (2007) *Human Development Report 2007/08,* United Nations Development Programme, New York.

Vaidyanathan, G. (2010) 'A race to introduce GM corn before Africa's climate worsens', *New York Times* March 30, http://www.nytimes.com/cwire/2010/03/30/30climatewire-a-race-to-introduce-gm-corn-before-africas-c-40010.html

Van Oosterhout, S. (1993) 'Sorghum genetic resources of small-scale farmers in Zimbabwe', in W. de Boef, K. Amanor and K. Wellard with A. Bebbington (eds.), *Cultivating Knowledge: Genetic Diversity, Farmer Experimentation and Crop Research*, pp. 89–95, Intermediate Technology Publications, London.

Zhai, R., Tao, F., Lall, U., and Elliott, J. (2020) 'Africa Would Need to Import More Maize in the Future Even Under 1.5° C Warming Scenario', *Earth's Future* 9(1): e2020EF001574.

About the author

Dan Taylor is the Director of the British non-governmental organization Find Your Feet, and Tutor in International Development at the Open University. He has a PhD in Anthropology from University College London. He has agricultural and rural development experience in Latin America, Oceania, South Asia and southern Africa.

Chapter 6

Mobilizing knowledge to build adaptive capacity: Lessons from southern Mozambique

L. Jen Shaffer

This case study highlights the efforts of rural residents in southern Mozambique to build and strengthen their individual and community adaptive capacity for current and future climate, political, and economic uncertainties by mobilizing knowledge from many sources. Their attempts to integrate indigenous knowledge (IK) and information from outside sources demonstrate rural people's initiative, creativity, and adaptive potential, underscoring the opportunities for collaboration between local communities and outside policy and science experts. However, avenues for exchange between community members, officials, and scientists are sometimes limited by government distrust, paternalistic attitudes that dismiss 'bush' knowledge, differential distribution of IK by gender and other social variables, and a lack of understanding by all parties about how to effectively mobilize indigenous expertise for regional and national adaptive capacity building. External agents who seek to foster local adaptive capacity need to be willing to learn from rural communities, and to share, adapt, and integrate their own technical expertise with local IK.

Introduction

Communities in Matutúine District, southern Mozambique, like many others throughout Africa and the developing world, are currently experiencing unprecedented environmental, social, and economic challenges (Boko et al., 2007). Ronga residents of this district historically relied on the landscape, and their knowledge of such, to thrive during good years and survive environmentally unstable periods. However, ongoing climate change, new national and international conservation policies, and endemic poverty threaten local adaptive capacity for responding to current and future climate uncertainties. These changing conditions call for the development and adoption of new tools and strategies, as well as the reworking of old. In this chapter, I examine how rural residents of Matutúine District are mobilizing knowledge from many sources to build and strengthen their individual and community adaptive capacity. These local attempts to integrate indigenous knowledge (IK) and new knowledge from outside sources highlight the value of IK in building adaptive capacity, some of the challenges these efforts face, and potential opportunities for collaboration between local communities and outside policy and scientific experts.

Building appropriate adaptive capacity

Uncertainty about future environmental, social, and economic changes, and their potential effects, constrains adaptation to current and future climate change. Predicted climate changes will likely exceed the past experiences and current adaptive capacity of indigenous and other traditional populations (Boko et al., 2007; Salick and Byg, 2007). Variation in, and continuing changes to, site-specific socio-ecological conditions at the local level hinder development of successful climate change adaptation approaches at regional, national and international levels. Building appropriate adaptive capacity to meet the combined environmental, social, and economic uncertainties developing countries face will require mobilization and integration of IK with technical/technological knowledge from outside local communities.

Mobilizing knowledge builds adaptive capacity – the set of 'preconditions necessary to enable adaptation, including social and physical elements, and the ability to mobilize these elements' (Nelson et al., 2007: 397). Like other facets of culture, knowledge between and within groups varies due to factors including experience, gender, livelihood activity, socio-economic status and educational achievement. Sharing newly acquired and previously known information held individually or collectively contributes to increased adaptive capacity as it diversifies the number of resources that may be accessed and used (Sabates-Wheeler et al., 2008). Disagreements over knowledge ownership, veracity, and value can limit knowledge mobilization, sharing and integration if trust, open communication, and a willingness to assess and adopt new ideas are not shared by partners in this effort.

As 'a cumulative body of knowledge, practice, and belief, *evolving by adaptive processes and handed down through generations* by cultural transmission, about the relationship of living beings (including humans) with one another and with their environment' (Berkes, 1999: 8, my emphasis), IK incorporates ideas of flexibility and change, as well as permanence and tradition. This holistic knowledge system contains information relevant to appropriate adaptive capacity building such as site-specific socio-ecological conditions, adaptive resource management practices that have sustained communities through stable and uncertain periods, and memories of responses to past environmental changes and challenges (Nyong et al., 2007; Salick and Byg, 2007). Ongoing integration of new observations, experiences, and knowledge allows community and individual IK to grow and evolve.

However, synergies between climate and other socio-ecological changes, as well as the magnitude and frequency of possible climatic changes, will likely outpace IK growth and evolution. In this respect, contributions from outside sources can assist local communities in their adaptive capacity building and climate change adaptation efforts.

Technological and technical support from regional, national and international institutions offers basic information about climate change processes, rapid responses to problems, expertise, and access to financial and infrastructural resources that do not exist in the community. Early warning systems at the national and international level assist communities in emergency preparations for extreme climate events like cyclones, floods, and droughts (Coelho and Littlejohn, 2000). During and after these events, these support systems can aid and sustain populations over the short-term until households and communities get back on their feet. The extent of long-term climate changes, however, may overwhelm the ability of government institutions and non-governmental organizations (NGOs) to provide adequate and timely assistance to all communities. International adaptation fund discussions have produced general commitments for assistance, but arguments over responsibilities, vulnerability definitions and rankings, and implementation stall actual progress on deliverables (Paavola and Adger, 2006). Furthermore, some outside approaches exacerbate ongoing problems and increase vulnerability within communities because they fail to account for highly variable, socio-ecological conditions at the local level. Technologies supplied to communities by government agencies or NGOs may work in the general sense, but expensive maintenance or lack of suitability for local conditions reduces their utility over the long term. Inflexible national policies or international agreements can prohibit and restrict adaptive strategies like migration or natural resource use that individuals and households used historically to reduce vulnerability or mitigate the effects of climate or other environmental variability (Agrawal, 2009; Nyong et al., 2007).

Both IK and outside approaches have advantages and disadvantages. Knowledge of site-specific conditions places adaptive capacity end-users in a good position to understand whether the resources and strategies being offered for adaption will work in a particular context, given the projected climate conditions. Community mobilization of knowledge must be met by similar efforts at the regional, national and international levels. Integration of IK strategies and tools into the development and application of strategies and tools by government institutions and NGOs remains underutilized (Nyong et al., 2007; Salick and Byg, 2007). However, this integration is key to delivering timely, effective and appropriate assistance to local communities as they build adaptive capacity for climate change.

Challenges to adaptive capacity in Matutúine District

Matutúine District incorporates 5,403 km² of Maputo Province in southern Mozambique. Despite close proximity to the capital Maputo, most of the district's approximately 37,000 residents are spread across the landscape in small rural communities linked by shared historical, cultural, and familial ties. I conducted ethnographic research primarily in Madjadjane and Gala, having populations of 331 and 114 respectively, where 90 per cent of residents identify themselves as Mazingiri Ronga. These communities are located adjacent to Reserva Especial de Maputo (REM), which protects 700 km² of rich coastal savanna-forest biodiversity at the heart of the Maputaland Centre of Endemism (Soto, 2009; Smith et al., 2008).

Climate variability has shaped human–environment interactions between Ronga communities and the landscape of Matutúine District for at least 500 years. A dual economy of swidden agriculture and foraging recognizes the climatic hazards of a region governed by seasonal rainfall, an 18-year wet/dry oscillation, flooding, and drought (Tyson et al., 2002). Additional livelihood activities like fishing, goat and cattle herding, mat and charcoal production, beekeeping, reserve work, and tourism take advantage of the area's rich biodiversity to supplement household resources and generate income.

Daily subsistence use of various resources throughout the landscape support Ronga assertions that, 'Our land provides many things'. This statement minimizes the important sustaining role of local cultural institutions, social networks, and infrastructure in providing natural resource access. Personal experience, observations, and community memory passed along via inter- and intra-generational teaching affords the knowledge and skills equally necessary to local adaptive capacity. Matutúine's residents historically relied on the adaptive capacity found in their IK system to survive the ravages of Mozambique's Civil War, manage during drier periods, and cope with the effects of floods and droughts (Shaffer, 2009). Recent climate, socio-political and economic changes challenge key aspects of local adaptive capacity.

Regional climate projections for southern Mozambique suggest severely degrading living conditions as the climate evolves over the coming decades. A substantial rise in the numbers of hot days and nights, perhaps as much as 20–50 per cent by 2060, will offset increasingly rare cold days and nights (McSweeney et al., 2008). Various downscaled models predict an average temperature increase of 1–3°C by mid-century, with the greatest expected changes around the start of the agricultural growing season in October (Boko et al., 2007; Girvetz et al., 2009). Rainfall is expected to decrease during the dry season and early growing season, but increase towards the end of the growing season in February and March (Boko et al., 2007; Girvetz et al., 2009; McSweeney et al., 2008). These seasonal shifts will likely be accompanied by heavy rainfall events when precipitation does fall. Altered temperature and precipitation patterns jeopardize both the wild and agricultural vegetative production on which humans and other species depend. Expected overall declines in maize production of approximately 30 per cent by 2030, for example, threaten rural and urban food security as maize is the region's dietary staple (Lobell et al., 2008). Projections for bigger, more frequent droughts in southern Mozambique parallel increases of strength and frequency for the El Niño Southern Oscillation (ENSO) (Coelho and Littlejohn, 2000). Warming Indian Ocean waters will likely increase the intensity of cyclones and resulting floods; however, other aspects of climate variability like ENSO make predicting cyclone frequency and tracks uncertain (McSweeney et al., 2008). Both floods and droughts endanger human health, local livelihoods and wildlife communities via destruction of crops and wild vegetation. Flood and drought events can also create situations where water supplies become contaminated with faecal coliform bacteria and increase opportunities for transmitting water-borne illnesses like cholera. Lastly, stagnant water left over from receding floodwaters supports the growth of malaria-carrying mosquitoes – a potential issue in Matutúine District where malaria remains endemic.

Residents of Madjadjane and Gala already note rising temperatures, later starts for summer rainfall, increased variability in rainfall timing and amount, and greater unpredictability in extreme events. Analysis of temperature and precipitation data for the past 45 years, as well as investigations of regional ENSO teleconnections and other large-scale climate factors, supports local observations (Coelho and Littlejohn, 2000; Shaffer, 2009). Furthermore, local livelihood activities, which depend on vegetative production and water availability, have already been hindered by these recent climate changes. Residents connect their climate observations to: walking further for water as scratch wells, NGO-built cisterns and pumps, lakes, and rivers dry up; reduced crop yields and forage quality for livestock; fewer wild fruits and lower honey production; and increased wildlife conflict with elephants over crops. Fishers describe increased competition with crocodiles as fish concentrate in shrinking lakes and river pools (Shaffer, 2009).

In the socio-political realm, new conservation policies worry Matutúine's residents because past experience indicates that policy changes reduce access to resources utilized when drought or floods compromise agricultural production. Designation of the district's landscape as part of the Lebombo Transfrontier Conservation Area (TFCA) provides additional protective measures for wild plant resources. However, agreements between Lebombo TFCA partners, Mozambique, Swaziland, and South Africa, jeopardize local access by requiring policy alignment (Soto, 2009). Residents of Madjadjane and Gala retain rights to harvest wild plants for personal consumption within REM boundaries under Mozambican law. This unique arrangement could end because South African protected area policies forbid or severely restrict such harvests. Fencing of the TFCA Futí River Corridor for wildlife movement between REM and South African reserves is desired by communities to reduce wildlife conflict, but limits access to fertile soil and water. Further encouragement by REM staff to relocate outside REM boundaries for safety reasons also restricts resource access. When households relocate they lose resource access rights granted through ancestral ties to place and must ask for permission to use land and wild resources from the chief and council of their new community. Participation in NGO-sponsored ecotourism activities often requires residents to give up harvesting rights to communal areas, as seen in Madjadjane, and may not adequately compensate for lost resource access. Mozambique's conservation policies remain open to alternative strategies (Nhantumbo and Anstey, 2009; Smith et al., 2008; Soto, 2009), but the uncertainties of future climate changes could further limit access to livelihood resources via additional regulations to protect dwindling populations of native plants and animals.

Increasing participation in global markets has brought rapid economic change to Matutúine District. Historically, labour migration took young men to the capital and South Africa to earn money for remittances and starting their own household. Following the Civil War, many who fled Matutúine District to Maputo and South Africa because of fighting, chose to stay because of better employment and educational opportunities. These opportunities, and the chance to participate in what is seen as a more exciting urban culture, continue to draw men and women, ages 15 to 45, out of the district. While remittances provide limited relief to cash-poor households in a region of endemic poverty, migratory labour and education undermine local IK. Children begin learning necessary knowledge and skills as soon as they begin walking, and young people in the community solidify their IK between the ages of 15 and 35. During this period, youths acquire in-depth experiential IK of medicinal plants for treating humans and livestock, burning landscape for different livelihood activities, learning their community's and people's history, constructing homes, making household tools, and producing art from local materials, growing various crops well, and harvesting wild foods (Shaffer, 2009, 2010). When youths lose contact with knowledgeable elders during this formative period, they miss significant opportunities to practise the skills they learn under experienced guidance and to make the socio-ecological observations necessary to notice long-term changes when they occur.

Mobilizing knowledge to build community capacity

Residents of Madjadjane and Gala have little control over climatic changes, national conservation or economic policies, aid agency requirements, or the market forces that shape Mozambique's growing economy. In the face of current and future climate uncertainties, community members hold out hope for assistance from the government and NGOs but past experience suggests they will need to do much on their own. As a result, they are focusing efforts on maintaining current IK, and acquiring new knowledge and skills from sources outside the community.

Life stories, personal observations and community history are IK sources that speak to how people have responded to environmental changes and major events in the past. Application during daily activities actively maintains IK about wild food sources, medicines, construction materials, livelihood practices, local species, biophysical conditions including climate, and disturbance processes like fire. For example, households collect, dry, and store macuácuá (*Strychnos madagascariensis*), a wild fruit, each year to ensure food security during drought and flood events. Farmers draw on long-term climate observations and fire IK to clear and prepare small plots for cultivation (Shaffer, 2010). Family and friends share their observations, skills, and experiences informally at home, in the marketplace, or as they work together in the fields, workshops, or out in the bush. Sometimes IK is shared in more formal settings like religious gatherings, community council meetings, or REM and community meetings for planning purposes. In 2003, expectations for a drier period based on IK of long-term wet/dry cycles, led to discussion between Madjadjane's chief and local council members concerning strategies to deal with anticipated decreases in water availability. The discussion resulted in households moving closer to the Futí River and making accommodations to ensure that everyone in the community had access to arable land adjacent to the river or in places where groundwater was known to remain close to the surface. Primary school teachers in Madjadjane and Gala reinforce Ronga IK in their environmental science lessons, linking what students know about local plants, animals, weather, and the environment to new information about erosion, waste disposal, conservation, and climate change. Residents have also shared their IK with visiting researchers and the International Union for Conservation of Nature (IUCN) because they wish to document and preserve this knowledge for future generations.

New sources of information about climate and livelihood diversification come from radio broadcasts, visitors, government officials, NGOs, and family members who travel far from home. Rádio Moçambique broadcasts weather, climate and environmental information in both Portuguese and some local languages. Researchers, government officials and NGO workers share information about climate change, conservation, and the environment during community meetings and informal conversations. Two NGOs working in Matutúine District, HELVETAS and the IUCN, offered courses in ecotourism, English, and commercial beekeeping as part of training projects for alternative livelihoods that support biodiversity conservation and community-based natural resource management (CBNRM). An end to project funding and weak local financial management capacity jeopardize sustainability of local CBNRM (Nhantumbo and Anstey, 2009), but the skills and knowledge people have acquired open up new livelihood opportunities. Programme attendees have shared what they learned with family and friends. A honey cooperative in Madjadjane has successfully employed many traditional honey collectors in the manufacture of quality products for Maputo and South African markets, as well as improving local crop pollination. New community members who come to the area for employment at REM and marriage contribute new skills and knowledge. When the Civil War ended, a couple of men from Inhambane married women in Madjadjane and started a sleeping/floor mat industry which employs many local men and women. The success of this cottage industry depends on Madjadjane's location along a national highway and the sustainable harvest of mbungo (*Cyperus papyrus*) from the Futí River. Family members working in Maputo or South Africa as migratory labourers share new information over the phone or during holiday visits. Returning labourers bring new techniques and skills into the community, such as one commercial farmer in Gala who introduced citrus production and large-scale farming following his stay in South Africa.

What lessons can be learned?

People often cannot wait for outside assistance when confronted by the combination of climate and other socio-ecological changes, on top of the magnitude and rate at which they are occurring. As the case of Matutúine District shows, communities and individuals are already searching, reaching out, and using whatever means at their disposal to acquire the knowledge and skills they may need to adapt. These mobilization efforts have increased adaptive capacity and resilience, but uncertainties surrounding future changes make it difficult to say if these efforts will be enough.

Although this chapter emphasizes adaptive capacity building for future climatic uncertainty in local communities by community members, similar efforts within Mozambique's government and scientific institutions are under way (Ribeiro and Chaúque, 2010). Capacity building at the regional and national levels better prepares officials and scientists for dealing with the uncertainties of future climate change and its impacts at multiple scales. Local community involvement in this capacity building through information sharing, collaborative learning and joint decision-making can result in the development of socially and environmentally appropriate policies, tools, and management plans. Mozambique's ongoing decentralization, a commitment to community participation in governance, mainstreaming of climate change adaptation into all aspects of government, and inclusion of gender in the National Adaptation Program for Action indicate a desire to include IK and local perspectives in national and regional adaptive capacity building (Ribeiro and Chaúque, 2010). However, avenues for exchange between IK practitioners, government officials, and scientists are often limited by government distrust, attitudes that dismiss 'bush' knowledge, differential distribution of IK within communities by gender, social status and experience, and a lack of understanding by all about how to effectively mobilize IK for regional and national adaptive capacity building.

Based on the experiences of Madjadjane and Gala, several activities could support knowledge mobilization for adaptive capacity building at community, regional and national levels. These include:

Basic information sharing, even general regional model predictions, can assist communities with long-term planning and understanding the causes and consequences of climate changes. Opening dialogue with communities also helps climate scientists gain better information about the site-specific, socio-ecological effects of climate change (Shaffer, 2009).

Training expands the range of available livelihood options by providing people with the skills needed to successfully participate in expanding market and business opportunities above the entry level. Diversification may also allow residents to better respond to climate uncertainty as they have a wider range of options to tap into as conditions change.

Developing infrastructure, such as roads, dependable transportation, banks, clinics, and schools, expands opportunities to use mobilized knowledge by supporting a wider range of livelihood activities and allows people to improve the quality of life they enjoy in their chosen home. Application of climate change adaptation funding to improve clinics and access to health care would be just one potential way to assist district residents as they respond to ongoing climate changes. Local communities may require assistance with finding outside funding and tools to develop their own infrastructure where government involvement is constrained by limited financial resources and foreign debt.

Facilitating discussion and planning for the uncertainties of current and future changes contributes greatly towards building adaptive capacity. Work by Cuomo et al. (2008) found that contrary to popular belief, residents of traditional communities do not necessarily have many formal opportunities to discuss and share information about IK and environmental and climatic changes. In addition to discussion of IK during community council meetings, the ethnographic research supporting this chapter stimulated conversations amongst community members in Madjadjane and Gala about their IK, the value of local history, and what the future may hold for their children. Community presentations about ongoing and completed research projects or during development of regional and national management plans can facilitate collaborative learning and joint decision-making between IK practitioners, government officials, and scientists.

Adaptive policies increase the likelihood of achieving balance between sustainable development, environmental conservation and protection, and improved quality of life for all citizens. This ideal, enshrined in Mozambique's constitution, requires a commitment to open communication between government and local communities, as well as openness to alternatives, management flexibility, and ongoing reassessment to ensure a best fit for local socio-ecological conditions as they evolve (Ribeiro and Chaúque, 2010; Soto, 2009).

Conclusions

Past experience with climatic and other environmental variability has shown Matutúine District's residents that preparing for an uncertain future requires mobilizing all of the knowledge, skills, and tools available. Maintenance of IK keeps livelihood options open. Integration of new information from outside sources with Ronga IK allows local residents to use available natural, human, and social resources found in Matutúine District in new ways. With the exception of charcoal production, these new ventures, including ecotourism, a honey cooperative, and a sleeping/ floor mat cottage industry, are sustainable. Mobilizing available knowledge also provides access to new resources and known resources in new ways. These actions demonstrate the effectiveness of combining IK with outside information, through mobilization efforts at the local level, in building adaptive capacity and resilience for uncertain future climate change.

Knowledge integration for building climate change adaptive capacity from various sources requires drawing on the knowledge of different groups, and a deep understanding of local socio-ecological conditions to recognize what will work. Ideally, communities and individuals would have the ability to choose and/or the time to modify those technologies and technical solutions offered by government institutions and NGOs that best suit local socio-ecological conditions. This isn't always possible. Adaptive capacity needs to maintain flexibility through ongoing reassessment and acquisition of new knowledge, access, and resources so that individuals and communities may respond to future, unknown changes. Where regional, national and international organizations cannot provide assistance or respond too slowly or inadequately, individuals and communities may turn to their own experts and information networks for insight, and use their access to outsiders to acquire new knowledge and skills. This local process of adaptive capacity building can best be supported by researchers, government institutions, and NGOs willing to learn from indigenous and other traditional communities, and share, adapt and integrate their technological and technical knowledge with local IK.

Author updates to the 2025 edition

Twelve years on and counting, mobilizing knowledge at the community level remains crucial for building adaptive capacity in the face of ongoing climate change and future climate uncertainty. This chapter explored how community residents undertook various knowledge mobilization tasks to enhance and expand their adaptive capacity in an environmentally and culturally appropriate manner. These actions included preserving their IK, seeking out new information from diverse external sources, and integrating what they learned with their IK to update and expand their knowledge base. As demonstrated in this case study from southern Mozambique, community-initiated action is essential but constitutes only part of the collaborative effort necessary for developing sustainable and appropriate climate solutions to the challenges faced by communities globally.

Climate adaptation discussions increasingly identify knowledge co-production as a transformative approach to foster collaboration between scientists, policymakers, and local community members necessary to appropriately address context-specific issues (Harvey et al., 2019; Norström et al., 2020). Ideally, by harnessing the collective expertise of diverse stakeholders, applied co-production initiatives should facilitate the development of novel and context-specific solutions to the local challenges posed by a changing climate. The inclusivity of this approach is also expected to improve the efficacy of both short-term responses and long-term adaptive strategies through participation of local residents, thereby promoting equitable and just climate action. However, comparative analysis of diverse knowledge co-production projects highlight limitations that can undermine the positive outcomes promised by this cluster of collaborative methods. These include time constraints and project boundaries that may impede the development of long-term relationships, mutual respect, and recognition of local community agency, all of which are essential for successful outcomes (Harvey et al., 2019; Latulippe and Klenk, 2020).

Self-organization through knowledge mobilization activities by residents of Madjadjane and Gala, as well as other similarly situated indigenous and traditional communities globally, offers a unique opportunity. By seeking the information they need to address challenging contextual conditions, residents extend their networks, establish new relationships, and build trust, which lays the groundwork for potential collaboration. Frequent, supportive interactions with partnering scientists and policymakers, which respect community agency, knowledge sovereignty, and diverse ways of knowing and doing, enable groups to effectively work toward meaningful, shared goals (Latulippe and Klenk, 2020; Norström et al., 2018). Difficult, yet rewarding, this collaborative dynamic for knowledge co-production nurtures resilience and enhances the adaptive capacity of communities to ongoing and future climate challenges.

Acknowledgements

I wish to thank the residents of Madjadjane and Gala for their assistance in this research, as well as D. Nelson and P. Tschakert for extensive discussions on adaptive learning, adaptive capacity, resilience, and vulnerability. This research was supported by a US Student Fulbright scholarship and by DDIG #BCS-0720077 from the National Science Foundation.

References

Agrawal, A. (2009) 'Local institutions and adaptation to climate change', in R. Mearns and A. Norton (eds.) *Social Dimensions of Climate Change: Equity and Vulnerability in a Warming World*, pp. 173–197, World Bank, Washington, D.C.

Berkes, F. (1999) *Sacred Ecology: Traditional Ecological Knowledge and Resource Management*, Taylor & Francis, Philadelphia.

Boko, M., Niang, I., Nyong, A., Vogel, C., Githeko, A., Medany, M., Osman-Elasha, B., Tabo, R. and Yanda, P. (2007) in M. Parry, O. Canziani, J. Palutikof, P. van der Linden and C. Hanson (eds.) *Africa. Climate Change 2007: Impacts, Adaptation and Vulnerability. Contribution of Working Group II to the Fourth Assessment Report of the Intergovernmental Panel on Climate Change*, pp. 433–467, Cambridge University Press, Cambridge.

Coelho, J. and Littlejohn, G. (2000) 'El Niño 1997–1998: Mozambique case study', report for the United Nations Environmental Programme.

Cuomo, C., Eisner, W. and Hinkel, K. (2008) 'Environmental change, indigenous knowledge, and subsistence on Alaska's north slope', *The Scholar and Feminist Online 7.1*.

Harvey, B., Cochrane, L., and Van Epp, M. (2019) 'Charting knowledge co-production pathways in climate and development', *Environmental Policy and Governance* 29: 107–117.

Latulippe, N. and Klenk, N. (2020) 'Making room and moving over: knowledge co-production, Indigenous knowledge sovereignty and the politics of global environmental change decision-making', *Current Opinion in Environmental Sustainability* 42: 7–14.

Nelson, D., Adger, W. and Brown, K. (2007) 'Adaptation to environmental change: contributions of a resilience framework', *Annual Review of Environment and Resources* 32: 395–419.

Norström, A. V., Cvitanovic, C., Löf, M. F., West, S., Wyborn, C., Balvanera, P., ... & Österblom, H. (2020) 'Principles for knowledge co-production in sustainability research', *Nature Sustainability* 3(3): 182–190.

Ntantumbo, I. and Anstey, S. (2009) 'CBNRM in Mozambique: the challenges of sustainability', in H. Suich and B. Child (eds.) *Evolution & Innovation in Wildlife Conservation: Parks and Game Ranches to Transfrontier Conservation*, pp. 257–274, Earthscan, London.

Nyong, A., Adesina, F. and Elasha, B. (2007) 'The value of indigenous knowledge in climate change mitigation and adaptation strategies in the African Sahel', *Mitigation and Adaptation Strategies for Global Change* 12: 787–797.

Paavola, J. and Adger, N. (2006) 'Fair adaptation to climate change', *Ecological Economics* 56: 594–609.

Ribeiro, N. and Chaúque, A. (2010) *Gender and climate change: Mozambique case study*, report for Henrich Böll Foundation Southern Africa, Cape Town.

Sabates-Wheeler, R., Mitchell, T. and Ellis, F. (2008) 'Avoiding repetition: time for CBA to engage with the livelihoods literature?', *IDS Bulletin* 39: 53–59.

Salick, J. and Byg, A. (2007) *Indigenous peoples and climate change*, Report of Symposium, 12–13 April 2007, Environmental Change Institute, Oxford, UK.

Shaffer, L. (2010) 'Indigenous fire use to manage savanna landscapes in southern Mozambique', *Fire Ecology* 6: 43–59.

Shaffer, L. (2009) 'Human-Environment Interactions on a Coastal Forest-Savanna Mosaic in Southern Mozambique', Unpublished Ph.D. dissertation, Department of Anthropology, University of Georgia, Athens.

Smith, R., Easton, J., Nhancale, B., Armstrong, A. Culverwell, J., Dlamini, S., Goodman, P., Loffler, L., Matthews, W., Monadjem, A., Mulqueeny, C., Ngwenya, P., Ntumi, C., Soto, B., and Leader-Williams, N. (2008) 'Designing a transfrontier conservation landscape for the Maputaland centre of endemism using biodiversity, economic and threat data,' *Biological Conservation* 141: 2127–2138.

Soto, B. (2009) 'Protected areas in Mozambique', in H. Suich and B. Child (eds.) *Evolution & Innovation in Wildlife Conservation: Parks and Game Ranches to Transfrontier Conservation*, pp. 85–110, Earthscan, London.

Tyson, P., Cooper, G., and McCarthy, T. (2002) 'Millennial to multi-decadal variability in the climate of Southern Africa', *International Journal of Climatology* 22: 1105–1117.

About the author

L. Jen Shaffer, is Associate Professor of anthropology at the University of Maryland, College Park. Her research interests centre on human–environment interactions in African savannas.

Chapter 7

Climate change and the future of onion and potato production in Central Darfur, Sudan: A case study of Zalingei locality

Yassir Hassan Satti and A. Peter Castro

Climate change poses a significant challenge for sustaining livelihoods and fostering peace-building in the troubled Darfur region of western Sudan. This paper explores the situation of onion and potato growers in Zalingei, Central Darfur State.[1] Horticultural crops for local and export markets offer Sudan's farmers a potentially significant source of income. Fur communities in Zalingei started adopting onion and potato cultivation on a small-scale since at least the 1940s, developing irrigated farming techniques using traditional technology and adapting local crop varieties. During the 1980s the Jebel Marra Rural Development Project fostered the expansion of these crops through infrastructural development and extension services. Thus, local cultivators displayed considerable initiative and ingenuity in combining their long-term knowledge of local environmental conditions and farming practices with recently introduced technologies. Their ability to act in recent years, however, has been constrained by an overall lack of resources, as well as by broader socio-economic and political concerns, particularly the region's endemic violence. Droughts and desertification intensified competition for resources in Darfur's increasingly volatile political setting, setting off clashes among farming and herding groups. Many households have fled to camps for internally displaced populations. The remaining farming communities must not only deal with security concerns but also changing climatic conditions. Future expansion of onion and potato production by smallholders will require investment in research, extension, and training regarding the new agro-ecological conditions arising from climate change. The chapter especially emphasizes that the participation of local people is crucial in devising climate change adaptations. Attempts to improve local livelihoods, however, will also ultimately depend on the effectiveness of efforts to resolve conflicts and to promote reconciliation among Darfur's diverse population.

Introduction

Climate change poses a significant challenge for sustaining livelihoods and fostering peace-building in the Darfur region of western Sudan. Covering an area as large as Spain, Darfur is part of the Sahel, the belt of semi-arid to semi-humid grasslands and wooded savannas bordering the Saharan desert. Rainfall, which generally occurs in the region between May and September, is highly variable from year to year. The Global Humanitarian Forum (2009) suggests that the Sahel is among the most physically vulnerable areas to climate change due to its proneness to drought, as well as the strong reliance of its inhabitants on rain-fed farming and herding. The rapid increase in Darfur's population, from 1.3 million in 1973 to 8.2 million people today, has added to the stress on the physical environment to support people, crops, and livestock (Darfur International Conference on Water for Sustainable Peace, 2011). Periods of drought and decreased rainfall in recent years, with their negative impacts on water supplies and vegetation cover, contributed to the circumstances that have fuelled conflicts between agriculturalists and herders in Darfur. In the 1990s, for example, the lack of dry season forage led pastoralists in Central Darfur to allow their cattle to graze on onion and potato fields, causing considerable damage and losses for the growers (Satti, 1999). While the linkages between climate change and the emergence of large-scale conflict in the region are complex and contested (O'Fahey, 2006; Kevane and Gray, 2008; Leroy, 2009), it is clear that promotion of peace-building must take into account issues of sustainable resource management and livelihood restoration. This chapter presents a case study of the implications of climate change for onion and potato growers in the Zalingei locality of Central Darfur State. Horticultural crops for local and export markets offer Sudan's agriculturalists a potentially significant source of income. Onions are the nation's most important vegetable in terms of crop area and value of harvest (Elbashir and Imam, 2010). Central Darfur has been one of the main centres of onion production (HCENR, 2000). The crop was introduced long ago into Sudan, and farmers selected and adopted onion cultivars to fit with their circumstances and priorities regarding taste, appearance, and storability. These local types and landraces have been 'found to be superior to exotic material under experimental and farm conditions' (Mahmoud et al., 1996). Most of Sudan's onion harvest is consumed locally, though some exports occur to European and Gulf countries. Growing potatoes in Sudan may have begun as early as the 1920s (Baldo et al., 2010). In the 1940s the crop started to spread to various parts of the country where conditions were suitable for its production (Elrasheed and Awad, 2009). Potatoes have emerged as one of the leading vegetable crops in the country. However, a recent study of the impact of climate change on global potato production indicates that the Sahelian region of Sudan will likely be adversely affected by shifts in rainfall and temperature patterns, reducing both crop quality and overall harvests (Haverkort and

Verhagen, 2008). Irrigation may enhance production, but Darfur region currently faces a critical water situation related to dry conditions, conflict, and insecurity (Darfur International Conference on Water for Sustainable Peace, 2011). Drought, destruction of water management infrastructure, and dislocation of large populations have reduced people's access to water supplies. In addition, increased temperatures will adversely affect the storability of both harvested crops.

Our analysis seeks to shed light on the extent to which the adaptations of Central Darfur onion and potato growers are effective in reducing vulnerability to climate change. Overall, we argue that the knowledge and adaptations of farmers, such as those in Zalingei, need to be taken into account when considering responses to climate change. The case of the onion and potato farmers is particularly insightful because it illustrates how new technologies and practices – irrigated horticultural production – are integrated with, and draw upon, pre-existing knowledge and strategies. The practices of Zalingei households reflect adjustments to current conditions, as well as the inter-generational transfer of information acquired from their elders. Over centuries of pursuing livelihoods in the region, local people have experience of dealing with unpredictable and highly variable weather conditions. Their knowledge and adaptations may contribute to the formulation of appropriate strategies to mitigate and adapt to climate change. In addition, these locally based initiatives offer the possibility of cost-effectiveness, as they will not require the government to invest substantial sums in creating entirely new strategies.

Our study is divided into four sections. The first section briefly introduces the environment, society and rural economy of the Zalingei locality in Central Darfur State. The second section focuses on understanding climate change from the perspectives of the Zalingei's inhabitants, who, by global standards, constitute a largely impoverished community. The third section gives details of the adaptation by the farmers, and the final part of the paper explores the future of the onion and potato production in Zalingei under the circumstances of local climate change. The paper concludes with policy recommendations regarding Zalingei's situation. It should be noted that our paper is based on recent fieldwork in Central Darfur State by Satti and on historical research on social aspects of Sudanese horticultural production by Castro.

The setting

Darfur region extends over an area as large as Spain in western Sudan. In 2012, it was subdivided into five states: West, North, East, Central and South Darfur. Central Darfur State covers more than 33,000 square kilometres, sharing borders with North, South, and West Darfur, as well as with Chad and the Central African Republic (UNOCHA, 2022; UNICEF, 2022). It features a marked agro-climatic gradient, with the Jebel Marra mountain range and plateau, which includes fertile and forested land, in the north. Lowlands in the south generally receive the most rain, averaging 1,200 mm per year in some places, and this rich savanna reflects the wetter conditions (Mohammed, 2009). Central Darfur had 1.6 million inhabitants in 2021 who are distributed in nine administrative localities, with Zalingei serving as the capital. Large numbers of people have fled the ongoing armed conflict, and are residing in camps for internally displaced persons or otherwise being hosted by urban or rural communities. The service sector of the state is limited to only very basic administrative activities. The inadequacy of the transport sector and other physical infrastructure contributes significantly to the current economic fragility of Central Darfur (Darfur International Conference on Water for Sustainable Peace, 2011).

The state's population can be divided ethnically and economically between Arab tribes who are pastoralists and non-Arab tribes who are mainly sedentary farmers; especially the Fur, the largest group in the Zalingei area. It is important to bear in mind that intermarriage and other socio-economic relations occurred across these ethnic and economic boundaries promoting peaceful coexistence in the region. Communities had worked out means to share water and pastoral resources, including migratory herding corridors (Leroy, 2009). The region's inhabitants also shared common values, including ones based on their Islamic faith. The *hakura* land tenure system, dating back to the Fur Sultanate that once ruled the region, also fostered peaceful relations by managing access to, and use of, natural resources among various social groups in an inclusive manner. A confluence of political, socio-economic, and environmental factors, however, fuelled intense armed conflicts throughout Darfur region, including Central Darfur, since the late 1980s (O'Fahey, 2006; de Waal, 2007; Leroy, 2009; Satti, 2009). More than 2 million people, including from Fur communities near Zalingei (Young et al., 2009), left their homes to escape the armed violence and chronic insecurity. Internally displaced persons comprised about one-fifth of the population in Central Darfur (UNICEF, 2022)..

Zalingei locality is situated west of the Jebel Marra mountain range and plateau, a volcanic massif whose highest peaks rise 3,000 metres above sea level. The Jebel Marra serves as its chief supplier of water, including seasonal streams which flow through the area's valleys, farmland and pastures during the rainy season. Almost two-thirds of Zalingei's annual average total of approximately 570 mm falls during July and August (ClimateData.Eu), and the rest generally occurring between June and September. As noted earlier, however, considerable variation occurs from year to year, and the region has experienced repeated droughts in recent decades. The town of Zalingei, with an estimated population exceeding 330,000 in 2021, serves as a local administrative and trading centre (UNICEF, 2022). According to a 1988 survey by the Jebel Marra Rural Development Project, more than 90 per cent of the town's inhabitants engaged in agriculture (Morton, 1993: 34). Since the onset of armed violence in 2003, several large camps for internally displaced persons are situated near the town. Although largely from rural backgrounds, the inhabitants of these camps are compelled by ongoing insecurity circumstances to pursue 'semi-urbanized livelihood strategies' in trying to obtain income (Young et al., 2009). These activities include selling firewood and tea, making bricks, construction labour, working as house servants, and reliance on remittances.

The main economic activity of Zalingei locality traditionally revolves around farming and animal breeding. Barbour (1954: 178), who visited the Zalingei area in the late 1940s, described Fur communities 'strung out along the watercourses ... subsist[ing] on the cultivation of rain crops during the summer'. Farmers relied primarily on rain-fed sorghum and millet, drought-resistant grains, along with sesame, chillies, okra, groundnuts, and other crops, some of which were grown among *haraz* (*Faidherbia albida*) trees, valuable for their nitrogen-fixing property and for providing fodder and numerous other useful products. Barbour also observed that local farmers had small irrigated plots near the seasonal streams, relying on hand-drawn shallow wells for watering. They grew onions 'a favourite crop ... generally eaten small and green', and also 'irrigated potatoes in the winter [were] becoming a general practice' (Barbour, 1954: 178). He noted that the potatoes were grown for local consumption, to sell to resident officials posted from eastern Sudan, and for sale in El Fasher. Potatoes were also grown in the area in rain-fed plots. A widely grown variety shared the name of the locality, Zalingei, and was probably introduced from seed of Dutch origin during the 1940s (Baldo et al., 2010). Lebon and Robertson (1961: 38) also recorded irrigated onion production in the late 1950s, noting that farmers maintained 'carefully tended plots, each plot about three feet square', watered from a hand-drawn well. Near settlements, however, a small number of local farmers had adopted the *shadoof*, a weighted beam with an attached container to hold water, permitting water to be drawn more quickly. Radwanski and Wickens (1967) also recorded small-scale irrigated potato production at Zalingei in the 1960s. Use of the *shadoof* for irrigation spread among farmers during the 1970s, demonstrating their initiative and willingness to adopt new practices (Morton, 1993: 34–5).

Irrigated agriculture expanded in Zalingei during the Jebel Marra Rural Development Project, which operated in Central Darfur between 1981 and 1992. Supported by the European Union, this project sought to build up the area's development infrastructure, including smallholder irrigation, while increasing extension and other public services (Morton, 1993; El Nur, 2009). A large-scale survey prepared for the project by its Monitoring and Evaluation Department (2008) furnishes a snapshot of irrigation in Zalingei for the 1987/88 crop year. Of the 954 households interviewed from 60 villages, the survey included 160 households from 10 villages in Zalingei locality and another 27 households from two villages from within Zalingei town (Monitoring and Evaluation Department, 2008: 1). In Zalingei locality, 77 per cent of households reported using irrigation, watering an average area of 0.30 hectares. They stated that 60 per cent of their plots were devoted to onion, 14 per cent to watermelon, 10 per cent to sugar cane, 4 per cent to okra, and 13 per cent to 'other crops', which included chilli, potato, and tomato. In Zalingei town, 48 per cent used irrigation, covering an average area of 0.023 hectares. These farmers devoted 91 per cent of their irrigated land to onion, with the rest producing watermelons (Monitoring and Evaluation Department, 2008: 39). In both places the sale of onions was an important source of income to families, amounting to 33 per cent of the value of all sales for Zalingei locality and 60 per cent for Zalingei Township's (Monitoring and Evaluation Department, 2008: 43). The survey did not report locality-specific information about methods of irrigation, but it noted that 79 per cent of the plots in the entire project area were supplied by a *romboya*, a leather bucket or gourd that drew water from shallow, hand-dug wells. Another 9 per cent were stream-fed, 8 per cent used pumps, and 5 per cent involved the use of a *shadoof*. The report underscored the importance of irrigation especially for cash cropping of horticultural vegetables and fruits. These commodities have become an essential part of the food systems in local towns such as Zalingei, El Geneina, and Wadi Salih.

Water is also a vital resource for the pastoralists who regularly settle in Zalingei as part of their migratory movements (Satti, 2009). Local customs and rules specify that nomadic groups who arrive at the area regularly with their animals may benefit from crop residues after the harvest. The pastoralists have dry season grazing rights, with the resulting manure a boost to local farming. Herders also enjoy access to drinking water for themselves and livestock, as well as access to grazing along their migratory corridor. Decreased rainfall and declining rangeland vegetation have led migratory pastoralists to seek new sources of water and pasture, intensifying competition for such resources and contributing to tensions (Leroy, 2009). Violent conflicts in recent years have drawn attention to social and economic divisions between herding and sedentary communities. However, as noted earlier, the pastoral and farming sectors – though separate – have also been complementary and linked by social and economic exchanges in which each is influenced by the other (El Amin, 1999). Competition for water or other resources does not inevitably result in conflict or violence. However, where multiple and complex forces generate widespread societal hostility and tensions, such competition can help trigger disputes.

Climate change, farmer vulnerability and responses

Climate change, as commonly used today, refers to human-driven long-term changes in weather patterns worldwide. Emissions of greenhouse gases from fossil fuel combustion, deforestation, urbanization, and industrialization cause variations in solar energy, temperature, and precipitation. These changes in climate may influence agriculture in a positive or negative way, depending, for example, on increases or decreases in the reliability and amount of rainfall or shifts in the length of the growing season. While global in scope, the phenomenon of climate change is ultimately experienced at the local level. For small-scale farmers such as Zalingei's onion and potato producers, climate change poses a threat to their long-term livelihood, despite their use of irrigation. Their vulnerability occurs in part because climatic shifts may diminish the water resources that they depend on. As already mentioned, the Darfur region currently faces a critical water supply situation due to the cumulative effects of drought, conflict, and inadequate infrastructure (Darfur International Conference on Water for Sustainable Peace, 2011). Unpredictable and insufficient rainfall also obviously reduces harvests for rain-fed crops. Warmer temperatures associated with global warming threaten specific crops such as potato, whose quality suffers in terms of processing and storability (Haverkort and Verhagen, 2008). For onions, higher temperature and humidity increase the risk of post-harvest losses due to mould and other problems (El-Nagerabi and Ahmed, 2003). Furthermore, widespread desertification and related environmental changes in the region constitute potential long-term influences on food security and human health. Climate change may also contribute to greater competition over natural resources, adding to social tensions.

In a landscape as contested as Darfur's, it is perhaps not surprising that even the issue of how climate is changing is debated among experts and policy makers. A report by the United Nations Environmental Programme (2007: 60) stated that average annual rainfall at El Geneina in the neighbouring state of West Darfur had decreased by 24 per cent when compared over the periods 1946–1975 and 1976–2005: 564 mm to 428 mm, respectively. Several analysts claim that a marked decrease in rainfall and increase in temperature have occurred in Darfur since the 1970s or early 1980s (for example, see Ban, 2007). In contrast, Kevane and Gray (2008) state that while a 'structural break' toward less rainfall may have occurred around 1971, the period from 1972 to 2002 did not display a linear downward trend. In assessing these perspectives, it is wise to bear in mind Zakieldeen's (2009: 4) observation that, 'Sudan is one of the driest but also the most variable countries in Africa in terms of rainfall. Extreme years (either good or bad) are more common than average years'. Furthermore, rainfall not only has generally decreased between 1941 and 2001, it has become increasingly unpredictable in the country. Zakieldeen (2009: 4) points out: 'Declining and uncertain rainfall makes life very difficult for traditional farmers and herders and severely affects their livelihoods'.

Evaluating weather patterns is an integral part of an agriculturalist's life, as it greatly affects decision-making. Zalingei's onion and potato growers perceived climate change in the unfolding occurrence of clouds, winds, temperature, rain, and other features of the environment. These observations are vital to their agricultural livelihoods, which depend on the accurate interpretation of nature in order to carry out tasks in a timely and effective manner. For example, one to two months before the rainy season is set to start, if the rate of the temperature increases and if dense clouds appear high in the sky, then farmers predict that the coming wet season will have heavy rains. Conversely, low temperatures and fewer clouds are associated with less intense rainy seasons. Farmers use these observations to determine the best times for planting, or whether to prepare for an impending disaster. This experience is based on having lived in the area for generations, accumulating information about the climate, water flows, soils, plants, and so on; and it is knowledge that is passed on to their children. They have also inherited a stock of knowledge on how to respond to a range of environmental conditions. This stock of knowledge held by the farmers is not static, but added to, or modified, through ongoing interaction with their physical and social environments. The expansion of irrigated onion and potato production during the Jebel Rural Development Project from 1981 to 1992 offers an example of the dynamism. The project promoted farming practices such as irrigation that local farmers found appealing. Although some of them had engaged in it in the past, the project provided the infrastructure and extension advice to expand both the number of growers and the area under irrigation. Their adoption of these practices was filtered through their already existing knowledge of local soils, temperatures, rainfall, pests, and other relevant considerations, while they also learned-by-doing in terms of irrigating using pumps and other means. For example, potatoes have a relatively low tolerance for water stress so farmers needed to learn how to manage water to ensure a favourable harvest. Hence agricultural practices are dynamic, rather than being the static unfolding of traditional routines.

The ability of farmers to respond to changing climatic and other conditions does not depend solely on their individual or communal knowledge. It also requires attention to local institutions, including those that govern access to, and use of, natural resources. Land tenure arrangements in Darfur evolved over centuries offering community-based rights in the form of land titling, introduced during the Sultanate era (the *hakura* system), and subsequent changes introduced during British administration and Sudanese national governments. Conflicts which have arisen between farmers and pastoralists originate in disagreements relating to contested understandings of the long-standing *hakura* system. These disagreements and conflicts are also indicative of the breakdown of mutual respect between groups (Leroy, 2009).

Onion and potato production

Onions and potatoes, major horticultural cash crops in Zalingei locality, are produced in well-aerated, fertile sandy clay soils found near and along the valleys (wadis) where water for irrigation is plentiful. As described earlier, onion farmers had developed several local types and landraces of onion to meet their preferences and growing conditions. These local varieties have often served as the basis for 'new improved lines' which have been introduced to farmers (HCENR, 2000: 13). The Jebel Marra Rural Development Project and other extension services furnished some of these varieties. The major types of onions currently produced by the farmers in Zalingei locality are Kamlin, Saggai, and Furawya. The main varieties of potatoes used by local farmers are Holland alpha and Beladi. The amount of onions and potatoes harvested in Zalingei fluctuates from year to year. Variations in rainfall have been a major factor in influencing production despite the use of irrigation. The groundwater level decreases when there is less rain than usual. Thus, farmers must expend more money and effort to deepen boreholes or wells, and in lifting water to the surface. Warmer temperatures also reduce soil moisture, and declining soil fertility is a concern. Insects and other pests also attack crops, particularly when plants are in their early growth stages.

Violence and insecurity in the area have had a serious impact on farming, resulting in abandoned fields. While Fur farmers are regarded as the historical, well-established producers of onion and potatoes, they are increasingly displaced people. As mentioned earlier, episodes of armed violence have occurred in the region since the 1980s. Due to the brutal conflict between the Sudan government and rebel groups since 2003, however, large numbers of Fur households were forced to leave their villages. In doing so, the Fur have been compelled to abandon their onion and potato farms. They now live on the periphery of cities and towns as internal displaced persons. Others have fled to neighbouring countries as refugees. This disruption in livelihoods and productivity is indirectly connected to the impacts of climate change. The current war in Darfur between the government and the rebels originally started as a conflict between pastoralists and farmers, over access to land resources (Satti, 2004). As previously mentioned, the role of climate change in the Darfur conflict is debated by experts (Kevane and Gray, 2008; Leroy, 2009), though both drought and desertification have played roles in fuelling tensions.

Where local farming communities still operate, onion and potato growers adapt their own local methods to mitigate the effects of climate change, seeking to guarantee satisfactory yields and good quality harvests. Their adaptations reflect age-old knowledge, practical experience and newly introduced techniques and technologies. Some of these methods can be summarized as follows:

- Increasing the duration of irrigation to avoid the loss of soil due to wind erosion. In the past people irrigated from three to seven hours per week, now they often try to do so for ten to eleven hours to maintain soil moisture levels. However, using extra watering time increases the cost of irrigation, and runs into the potential problem of water availability.
- Planting earlier than usual to avoid insects and plant diseases. This task requires early preparation of seedlings, and offers the advantage of

a harvest arriving in the markets at a time of scarcity, bringing better profits to the producers.

- Using plastic pumps instead of a *romboya* or other customary means to avoid water loss during irrigation. Although this method is not traditional, it is an innovation widely used by local farmers as watering can take place in a faster manner.

These methods are useful and practical because they generally do not require a lot of money to construct or implement; rather, they largely depend on the experience and skills of the farmers. Although traditional knowledge is effective to some extent in mitigating the negative impacts of climate change, some difficulties call for action beyond the local level.

The future of onion and potato production in Zalingei locality

The future of Darfur depends on conflict resolution and peace-building efforts that allow farmers to sustain their agricultural livelihoods (Leroy, 2009). Onions and potatoes provide much-needed income to farmers in Zalingei locality, as well as an important source of food for urban dwellers. Parts of Western Darfur also appear to be environmentally suited to the production of high-quality seed potatoes (Baldo et al., 2010). Yet, the future of onion and potato production is threatened by climate change, as drought, heat, and related changes in agro-ecological conditions could undermine local capacity to sustain yields and to deal with post-harvest storability. Besides reduced water supplies, crop pests, crop diseases, and post-harvest losses due to mildew and other problems are direct threats to producers. Farm productivity is also at risk because of cultural changes and policy frameworks that weaken the ability of communities to manage their resources. Interventions are needed that address both the technical and social aspects of agriculture.

Other actions are important as well. There is the need to strengthen community institutions such as the farmers' union which provides improved seeds and services to households. The *hakura* land tenure should be reconstituted or enhanced so it can provide access to land to people desiring to engage in farming. These reinvigorated institutions can serve as local safety nets, while also furnishing a setting for establishing new community-level coping mechanisms. The relationship between agricultural research and extension should be strengthened in order to develop and create new plant varieties such as drought-resistant crops, cultivation practices, and post-harvest management strategies suitable for Central Darfur's agro-ecological conditions. Agricultural extension and meteorological services also need to work more closely together in order to provide better information to onion and potato farmers, as well as other local resource users. Furthermore, these services need to draw on the long-term, detailed agro-ecological knowledge and observations of community members.

Conclusion

Climate change adaptations must take into account indigenous knowledge, as well as local socio-economic conditions. Many decades ago farmers in Zalingei adopted onion and potato production to meet local needs and to pursue market opportunities. They adapted these crops to local technology and conditions. With the Jebel Marra Project in the 1980s and 1990s, they continued to adapt new technologies and practices into their existing repertoire of knowledge, expanding irrigated production of these crops. Today, the onion and potato farmers of Zalingei are willing and able to respond to the challenges posed by climate change in their area. Their ability to act, however, is limited by their overall lack of resources, as well as constraints arising from their wider social setting, especially the ongoing insecurity related to the recent history of violence in Darfur region. Farmers require support in terms of research, extension, and training regarding agriculture and their changing agro-ecological conditions. Just as crucial are the peace-building efforts that may enable internally displaced persons and refugees to be returned to their original villages. Restoration of the agricultural sector, including that of onion and potato production, depends on farmers' adaptation to climate change, but equally so on the success of the peace-building efforts that can resolve the conflicts of Western Darfur. The need to strengthen local capacity to manage natural resources is part of the solution, but conflict resolution must take place simultaneously.

Author updates to the 2025 edition

Large-scale violence and societal instability pose major challenges for efforts to deal with climate change, whether at the macro or micro levels. Sadly, Sudan, including Darfur region and Zalingei locality, offers a distressing case study. At present Sudan is engulfed in a humanitarian catastrophe of 'epic proportions' (Devi, 2023; Ali and Diamond, 2024). The eruption of warfare between the Sudanese Armed Forces and the Rapid Support Forces (established from Darfurian Arab militias formerly known as the Janjaweed and their allies) in April 2023 has shaken all aspects of life in the country, as civilians, public institutions, infrastructure, and food supplies have all been targeted or otherwise seriously impacted by violence and insecurity. After a year of fighting, 12 million Sudanese (of a total population of approximately 49 million) had fled their homes and 18 million people were acutely food insecure, including 5 million on the verge of famine (IOM, 2024; UNOCHA, 2024). Darfur has experienced some of the worst violence and levels of displacement. Meanwhile, international actions to deal with the humanitarian crisis and its underlying causes have been sluggish and inadequate.

The present dire predicament contrasts greatly with the situation in 2012, when *Climate Change and Threatened Communities* was initially published. The

Doha Peace Agreement of 2011 between the Sudan government and three major Darfurian rebel groups ushered in a time of cautious optimism. The Darfur People's Conference, held at Al Fasher in December 2011, resulted in the creation of Central Darfur State, including Zalingei locality, from West Darfur State. Projects and peace-building activities for 'early recovery' – a supposed transitional phase from humanitarian to development assistance – were launched by Sudanese and international non-governmental organizations, often with funding from the United Nations and other external sources. Although not aimed directly at addressing climate change, these projects sought to strengthen community economic and social resilience (Castro, 2018). Local achievements, however, could not tame the political and economic forces at the regional, national, and international levels driving instability and violence that have overwhelmed the country (de Waal, 2015).

Before the current war erupted, the International Potato Center issued a report highlighting the considerable potential for the crop in Sudan, highlighting Zalingei as a place with year-round production potential (Simpson et al., 2021). Local potato growers, along with onion farmers, have faced multiple challenges in the last decade. High rainfall variability and drought proved detrimental, as had crop pests, with low yields resulting in some farmers switching to red pepper and beans. Ongoing tensions and clashes between farmers and pastoralists over land and water undermined production as well. Some farmers abandoned their plots due to deliberate damage by pastoralists, with local reconciliation committees furnishing inadequate compensation. High fuel prices made it increasingly expensive to irrigate land. Brutal warfare and the collapse of governmental authority have caused many farmers and others, including most of the Ministry of Agriculture staff, to flee Zalingei for Chad and East Sudan. Official records and documents, including those vital for agricultural extension services, have been burned, destroying the local database that had been accumulated regarding onion and potatoes. So ends this very troubling update of Zalingei's, Darfur's, and Sudan's situation.

Notes

[1] Zalingei was located in West Darfur State when the first edition was published. It became part of the newly created Central Darfur State in 2012. For clarity's sake, we list its current designation.

References

Ali, Mutasim and Diamond, Y. (2024) *Breaches of the Genocide Convention in Darfur, Sudan (April 2023—April 2024): An Independent Inquiry,* Raoul Wallenberg Centre for Human Rights, Montreal.

Baldo, N., Elhassan, S. and Elballa, M. (2010) 'Occurrence of viruses affecting potato crops in Khartoum State-Sudan', *Potato Research* 53: 61–7.

Ban Ki Moon (2007) 'A climate culprit in Darfur', *Washington Post*, 16 June 2007.

Barbour, M. (1954) 'The Wadi Azum', The Geographical Journal 120:174–82. ClimateData. Eu, [Online] http://www.climatedata.eu/climate.php?loc=suzz0004&lang=en [accessed 27 July 2011]).

Castro, A. P. (2018) 'Promoting natural resource conflict management in an illiberal setting: Experiences from Central Darfur, Sudan,' *World Development* 109: 163–171.

Darfur International Conference on Water for Sustainable Peace (2011) *Donor Appeal Document*, UNICEF, UNEP, UNDP, UNAMID, FAO, Ministry of Irrigation and Water Resources of the Government of Sudan, Public Water Corporation, Ground Water Wadi Directorate, Khartoum.

Devi, S. (2023) 'Sudan facing humanitarian crisis of 'epic proportions,' *The Lancet* 402: 1737–1738.

de Waal, A. (ed.) (2007) *War in Darfur and the Search for Peace*, Justice Africa and the Global Equity Initiative, Harvard University, London.

de Waal, A. (2015) *The Real Politics of the Horn of Africa: Money, War and the Business of Power*, Polity, Cambridge.

El Amin, K. (1999) *Some Environmental Consequences of Human Response to Drought in Sudan Darfur Region*, University of Khartoum, DSRC Monograph Series No. 42, Khartoum.

Elbashir, H. and Imam, M. (2010) 'Status report on fruits and vegetables production and processing industry in Sudan', *2010 AARDO Workshop on Technology on Reducing Post-harvest Losses and Maintaining Quality of Fruits and Vegetables*, pp. 168–79, Taiwan Agricultural Research Institute, Taichung.

El-Nagerabi, S. and Ahmed, A. (2003) 'Storability of onion bulbs contaminated by Aspergius Niger mold', *Phytoparasitica* 31: 515–23.

El Nur, M. (2009) 'Land tenure and conflict in Zalingei area, Darfur', unpublished M.S. thesis, University of Khartoum, Development Institute and Research Center, Khartoum.

Elrasheed, M. and Awad, F. (2009) 'Economics of potato production and marketing in Khartoum State', *Journal of Science and Technology* 10: 80–91.

Global Humanitarian Forum (2009) *Climate Change – The Anatomy of a Silent Crisis*, Global Humanitarian Forum, Human Impact Report, Geneva.

Haverkort, A. and Verhagen, A. (2008) 'Climate change and its repercussions for the potato supply chain', *Potato Research* 51: 223–37.

HCENR (Higher Council for Environment and National Resources) (2000) *The Sudan's National Biodiversity Strategy and Action Plan*, Ministry of Environment and Tourism, Sudan Government, Khartoum.

International Organization for Migration (IOM), Displacement Tracking Matrix (2024), Sudan Mobility Update (01), May 29, 2024.

Kevane, M. and Gray, L. (2008) 'Darfur: Rainfall and conflict', *Environmental Research Letters* 3: 1–10.

Lebon, J. and Robertson, V. (1961) 'The Jebel Marra, Darfur, and its region', *The Geographical Journal* 127: 30–45.

Leroy, M. (ed.) (2009) *Environment and Conflict in Africa: Reflections on Darfur*, United Nations University for Peace, Africa Programme, Addis Ababa.

Mahmoud, M., Khidir, M., Khalifa, M., El Ahmadi, A., Musnad, H. and Mohamed, E. (1996) *Sudan: Country Report to the FAO International Technical Conference on Plant Genetic Resources*, Food and Agriculture Organization of the United Nations, Khartoum.

Mohamed, O. (2009) *The Role of Religion and Custom in Conflict and Peace in West Darfur*, Department of Sociology, University of Khartoum, Khartoum.

Monitoring and Evaluation Department, Jebel Marra Project (2008) Livelihoods in West Darfur: The Jebel Marra Project's 1988 Post Harvest Survey, Morton, J. and Company, London.

Morton, J. (1993) *Agricultural Development in Darfur Region*, Sudan, Unpublished PhD dissertation, London University.

O'Fahey, S. (ed.) (2006) *Environmental Degradation as a Cause of Conflict in Darfur: Conference Proceedings*, United Nations University for Peace, Addis Ababa.

Radwanski, S. and Wickens, G. (1967) 'The ecology of *Acacia albida* on mantle soils in Zalingei, Jebel Marra, Sudan', *Journal of Applied Ecology* 4: 569–79.

Satti, Y. (1999) *The Role of the Government in the Tribal Conflicts in Darfur*, unpublished Higher Diploma thesis, University of Khartoum, Development Studies and Research Institute, Khartoum.

Satti, Y. (2004) *The Role of Government Institutions and Civil Society Organizations in Peace Building in Darfur*, unpublished M.A. thesis, University of Khartoum, Development Studies and Research Institute, Khartoum.

Satti, Y. (2009) 'Pastoralism, land rights and migration routes in Darfur: the case of West Darfur State', in M. Leroy (ed.), *Environment and Conflict in Africa: Reflections on Darfur*, pp. 259–70, United Nations University for Peace, Africa Programme, Addis Ababa.

Simpson, H., Mikkola, J., and Parker, M. (2021) *Unleashing Potato's Potential in Sudan: A Scoping Mission Report*, International Potato Center, Lima.

UNICEF (2022) State Profile: Central Darfur.

United Nations Environmental Programme (UNEP) (2007) *Sudan: Post-Conflict Environmental Assessment*, UNEP, Nairobi.

United Nations, Office for the Coordination of Humanitarian Affairs (UNOCHA) (2022) Central Darfur State Profile, Updated March 2022.

United Nations Office for the Coordination of Humanitarian Affairs (UNOCHA) (2024) *Sudan Humanitarian Update*, 15 May 2024.

Young, H., Jacobsen, K. and Osman, A. (2009) *Livelihoods, Migration and Conflict: Discussion of Findings from Two Studies in West and North Darfur, 2006–2007*, Feinstein International Center, Tufts University, Medford.

Zakieldeen, S. (2009) *Adaptation to Climate Change: A Vulnerability Assessment for Sudan*, International Institute for Environment and Development, Gatekeeper Series, 142, London.

About the authors

Yassir Hassan Satti is Assistant Professor in the Peace Research and Development Centre at Eldaein University in East Darfur State. He has published several papers in the areas of conflict resolution, peace-building, livelihoods, gender, and development.

A. Peter Castro is Professor Emeritus of Anthropology in the Maxwell School of Citizenship and Public Affairs at Syracuse University in Syracuse, New York. He is an applied cultural anthropologist specializing in agrarian livelihoods, natural resource conflict management, and rural social change, especially in East Africa.

Chapter 8

Comparing knowledge of and experience with climate change across three glaciated mountain regions

K.W. Dunbar, Julie Brugger, Christine Jurt and Ben Orlove with updates by Karina Yager

Glacial retreat offers some of the most compelling evidence for global warming, while posing potential problems for water supplies and sea levels. The authors compare local perceptions of environmental change in three areas experiencing shrinking and thinning glaciers: the Peruvian Andes, the Italian Alps, and the North Cascades in the United States. Local perceptions differed, reflecting their varying uses, reliance on, and interactions with the glaciers. Yet, people at all three sites felt that they were losing, in various ways, valuable local knowledge for adapting to environmental change. The authors suggest that efforts to engage the communities in climate change mitigation and adaptation efforts take into account their existing relationships and concerns with the local environment. Overall, the case study serves as a reminder that global warming is not only being experienced in developing countries, but has significant economic and cultural implications for communities in industrialized nations as well.

Introduction

This chapter presents the results of multi-sited fieldwork across three glaciated regions: the Cordillera Blanca in the Peruvian Andes, South Tirol in the Italian Alps, and the North Cascades in the United States. Our goals in the study are to explore the ways in which communities living in these regions are experiencing change in their environments, and examine the concerns they may have about these changes. Indigenous knowledge increasingly plays a role alongside scientific work on climatic change (e.g. Cruikshank, 2005; Berkes, 2007; Orlove et al., 2008). It offers a means, very different from scientific terminology, for thinking and speaking about weather and climatic changes. Though overcoming epistemological and methodological differences is a challenge, indigenous knowledge can help to more specifically identify the ranges of variability and ways in which these changes are affecting ways of life for humans, animals and ecosystems. Further, perceptions of knowledge and past experiences with climatic changes are important indicators for how adaptation does or does not take place (e.g. Adger et al., 2009; Thomas et al., 2007; Vedwan, 2006).

Identifying as indigenous

Much work has been done on defining what it means to be indigenous, so we do not attempt to do so further here; however, the diversity of our study populations and the title of this volume compels us to briefly address the concept of indigeneity. In the Cordillera Blanca, the people who were interviewed for this research fit clearly into established categories of indigeneity since they have been settled in the area for millennia, trace strong cultural links with the pre-Columbian peoples, and speak a language of pre-Columbian origin. In South Tirol, the people have also been long settled in the area, and have a strong local identity, with many cultural and religious traditions and a deep attachment to South Tirol as their homeland. They use the word *einheimisch* to describe themselves; this word can be translated as indigenous, but also means native, local and home-grown. However, their linguistic and cultural affiliations mark them as German, and thus associate them with one of the major stocks of modern Europe.

In the US site, European-American settlers displaced the indigenous population in the late 19th century; the current residents are either descended from these settlers, or have moved into the area more recently. This population would seem to be entirely non-indigenous, especially because of the immediate contrast with Native American groups, who are stronger in western Washington than in many other parts of the contiguous United States. Nonetheless, many of the people interviewed in this site were descendants of the first settlers or long-term residents who make a living through the extraction or use of natural resources – mining, logging, farming, and hydropower – and augment it through hunting, fishing, and foraging, which require a specialized type of knowledge that is often part of indigenous identities in other settings. In the US case, we do not feel that their more recent migration into the area discounts them from providing compelling testimony to a changing climate, nor does it discount their concerns for the future of their environment.

Site descriptions

In each of the study regions, glacier retreat is well documented scientifically. From a 1970 baseline developed using aerial photographs, the national inventory of Peruvian glaciers shows that glaciers in the Cordillera Blanca have shrunk by 22 per cent in the last 25 years (INRENA, 2007). Throughout the Alps, there has been clearly recognizable glacial retreat since 1850 and very strong loss since 1985 (Paul et al., 2007). In the North Cascades, rising temperatures have contributed to a 40 to 60 per cent decrease in the volume of glaciers since 1984, higher snow levels and increased stream flow in the winter months, and a declining snowpack (Pelto, 2008). Another important aspect of climate in these regions is precipitation, which varies on very small spatial scales in each of these mountainous regions. The Cordillera Blanca has a marked seasonality, during the Southern Hemisphere winter the valley is arid with most of the yearly precipitation occurring between October and May. South Tirol experiences very dry climate conditions year-round. In contrast, the North Cascades is a temperate maritime climate with a significant annual precipitation, most of which falls during the winter and produces a heavy snowpack.

In the first two cases, the Cordillera Blanca and South Tirol, residents have experienced the impacts of climate change and observed, among other changes, dramatic glacier retreat. While glaciers have also retreated rapidly in the North Cascades, the awareness and concerns on the part of residents about glacier retreat are mixed. We feel this is in part due to the higher levels of precipitation in the North Cascades as compared to the Cordillera Blanca and South Tirol sites and also because of the differences in geomorphology between the North Cascades and the Alps or the Cordillera Blanca. The Cascades are a much younger mountain range, so stream valleys are still deeply incised and the terrain is too steep and rugged for settlements to be established close to glaciers. Settlements in the Andes and in the Alps are established near the tree-line, where glaciers are easily visible.

Cordillera Blanca

Our Peruvian study site is located in the Santa Valley at an elevation of 3,300 metres just under the Copa glacier (6,188 m). Here we focus on the *comunidad campesina* Siete Imperios, which has seven hamlets, consisting of approximately 500 people. While these seven hamlets have similar livelihood and governance structures, they differ markedly in their connections to irrigation ditches which channel glacial meltwater, newer potable water and electricity projects and also in terms of their line of sight with the Copa glacier and other glaciated peaks. Siete Imperios is bordered by two rivers that originate at the glacier and join together in the lower parts of the community, feeding into the Santa River, which flows into the Pacific Ocean.

Siete Imperios was established following the agricultural reform in the 1970s that dissolved large privately owned estates and deeded the land to newly established communities of indigenous families who continue to live and work there. Primarily subsistence agropastoralists since before the landed estates, the residents of the region grow crops nearly year round due to the combination of rainfall and the use of glacial meltwater. Families earn money through the occasional sale of livestock or surplus harvests, but also through short-term labour contracts with neighbours, municipal projects, or seasonal migration to work on large coastal plantations.

South Tirol

South Tirol lies in the north of Italy just at the border with Switzerland. The study area includes Sulden, Trafoi, and Stilfs, three villages in the municipality of Stilfs, which is located between 1,033 and 3,905 metres, and has approximately 1,000 residents. The municipality includes some of the highest mountains in the Eastern Alps including the Ortler (3,905 m) and Königsspitze (3,851 m).

Once based on animal husbandry and heavily irrigated agricultural activities, at the end of the 19th century, farming became increasingly difficult due to land tenure changes and inheritance systems. With the growing romanticism surrounding nature, villagers began to encourage visits to the mountains and the tourism industry was born. Many residents were fearful of the mountains, viewing them as a source of natural hazards like avalanches, rock falls, and other dangers. As scepticism towards the mountains diminished, tourism began to flourish and brought new economic opportunities. Through the various political shifts that occurred in the next decades, tourism became an income-generating activity, leading to a boom in the 1950s that survives as small-scale tourism across the municipality.

North Cascades

The North Cascades in Washington State are the most densely glaciated mountains in the contiguous US although few peaks are more than 3,000 m. Mountain streams run through the summer with the help of melting winter snow, feeding numerous large rivers and lakes. The glaciers, snowpack, rivers and lakes support a variety of salmon runs, which continue to be a main source of subsistence and cultural significance for indigenous people of the region. However, salmon and their recovery have become contentious subjects in the region. The glacial meltwater helps to keep the rivers cool in summer, providing more oxygen for fish and spawning salmon, and glacier retreat is likely to become an issue in the debate over salmon.

Our research focuses on two communities in parallel river valleys within the watersheds of Mt Baker, a 3,285 m active volcano. The town of Concrete in Skagit County is located at the confluence of the Baker and Skagit Rivers, at an elevation of 84 m with a population of about 500 within the town limits. The unincorporated community of Glacier in Whatcom County lies on the North Fork of the Nooksack River, at an elevation of 276 m with a population of about 100. Both sites lie adjacent to Mt Baker-Snoqualmie National Forest, much of which is being managed as wilderness and roadless areas, and near North Cascades National Park.

In the past most residents made their living through natural resource production on the surrounding public lands. Increasing federal regulation of these lands, coupled with the decline of natural resource production-based industries in the rural American West since the 1970s (Walker, 2003), has led to shrinking population and economic opportunity in Concrete and Glacier. Today residents look to recreation and tourism to boost local economies or commute to jobs in the cities to the west.

Experience with and knowledge of climate change

The knowledge addressed here resides in the minds of local people, in collective discussions and filtered through various organizations. In addition, the physical and built environments are sources of knowledge since the glaciers in these cases are not only visible, but also accessible. Across our sites, we examine knowledge from various sources: oral history, place names, visits to glacier fronts and surfaces, physical structures located on or near glaciers, paintings of mountains, photograph collections, written records of community meetings and local monographs. Such constructed knowledge plays a crucial role in responses to the effects of climate change. Recent work argues that expanding the range of knowledge is one of the critical domains that influence adaptation limits (see Adger et al., 2009; Berkes, 2007, among others).

Cordillera Blanca

In Siete Imperios, most of the knowledge about receding glaciers, shifting rainfall patterns and other climatic changes are a result of daily observation. In some cases the sources of knowledge originate from oral histories shared by parents or grandparents. For a handful of residents who had lived or worked outside of the community, their knowledge of climatic changes, and even the fact that there is a larger discourse on climate change, was influenced by a range of sources including government incentives, radio programmes, non-governmental organization (NGO) activities, and interaction with people experiencing environmental change on the desert coast or the rainforest. For a number of community members, climate change knowledge is also shared through the growing participation in the Seventh Day Adventist Church. Although the message from this church discourages actions to mitigate or respond to climatic changes, it does educate members on a larger discourse of global warming.

Throughout the valley, glacial loss and change is also captured in aerial photography by government and externally funded scientific research, but also in murals that urge people to protect the environment and save the glaciers. While the murals are publicly accessible, only those working for or with scientists have access to aerial photos.

Within Siete Imperios, almost every person interviewed for this research observed that the glacier has receded significantly in their lifetime. They quickly and easily point out places much lower on the mountain where they used to visit the glacier as they pastured animals, gathered special flowers and harvested ice to sell in the towns or use at home, usually for the creation of *raspadillas* (shaved glacial ice combined with flavouring and sugar). Most remember the glacier as a social place to gather as young adults or families, but reveal that hardly anyone visits now because it is much farther away and more dangerous due to the steep rock walls left by the most recent recession. They remark on its beauty, saying it is now 'only islands of ice which one cannot climb' and that it is 'deteriorating'. Older members of the community comment on the changing nature of the ice itself, claiming it is weaker, and does not last long enough to be worth gathering or bringing down to the village.

Farmers indicate that the seasonality which so marks the agricultural and cultural calendars is now much more chaotic. Rain, hail, wind or frosts that once occurred 'in their time' are now less predictable. Some residents claim that frosts and hails are more intense, much like rainfall which is also said to be harder and colder. These hard rains wash out seedlings, ruin entire harvests and leave standing water which encourages fungal growth on the hooves of their animals. They also exacerbate erosion and damage irrigation canals, paths, and roads. Temperature increases are also widely noted among residents. The diurnal extremes the Andes are known for are becoming more intense, with hotter days and much colder nights than those in the past. Irrigation periods that used to keep a field moist for a full week, only last a few days as the hotter, drier soil needs more water. Some families and the managers of communal woodlots have successfully experimented with planting trees at higher elevations, and local farmers are now able to cultivate some varieties of potatoes and corn on plots higher up the mountainside. As recently as a decade ago, it was not feasible to grow corn in Siete Imperios because of the cool climate at this altitude, but now nearly every family rotates it into their sequence of crops.

The people of Siete Imperios very clearly connect glacier recession with water availability. Although they have not yet seen devastating change in the hydrological regime of the area, many people fear for the viability of the near future. Most of those interviewed believe that the glacier will indeed disappear soon, and with it local water sources.

The concept of impending water scarcity has been a concern for many years in Siete Imperios, but the people have yet to see significant enough change to compel action. The hamlets that are the furthest away from the glacier already claim there is not enough water for irrigation during drier months. There have been several meetings over redistributing water between Siete Imperios and the communities which share the river border, and the growing urban centre of Marcara downstream. For now these redistributions are amicable discussions between community centres and no families report having less water due directly to these changes, but many are concerned about continued availability. Some are discussing allowing young adults to become full members of the community solely in order to increase the numbers they can report that need water, and thereby control more of the meltwater than nearby communities.

South Tirol

There are several glaciers that can be seen from the village of Sulden at the end of the valley, which is quite open and flat until it culminates at the Sulden glacier itself. The glaciers and surroundings have played an important role in the history of the village of Sulden: they have been feared, especially in times of growth (Christomannos, 1999 [1895]), but also admired for providing a good living for mountain guides. There are multiple sources of local knowledge in South Tirol: routine observation, oral histories, paintings and sculptures that depict the mountains, and also extreme events such as avalanches and landslides which serve as memory markers. Besides daily activities that provide views of the glacier, residents also hike near them, take tourists to visit them, and hear stories from their parents and grandparents.

There is also a tradition of documenting fluctuations of the glaciers in history books written by residents of the three communities (Hurton, 2004; Pinggera, 1997; Thöni, n.d.). Each village has its own special publications, which are a point of pride for the community, but are also used in larger discourses over resource management. Published histories are complemented by unpublished notes (Schöpf, 2008).

A further source of knowledge is the landscape itself and stories related to it. Different elements of the landscape – among them glaciers, roads, old paths, stones, constructions against natural hazards, sources of water, remains from World War II, or a tree with a carved sign – are part of the history. When villagers walk through the landscape, they tell stories about these features, incorporating them into an oral history.

Many scientific and expert studies are associated with local glacial changes and risk management. Typically, these studies and reports deal with different timelines or measurements than local knowledge. In addition to the larger studies, there are several organizations that work with a combination of both local knowledge and government experts, both of which are highly respected, to respond to environmental changes or disasters. While residents feel that neither local nor scientific knowledge can completely overcome the uncertainties involved in prediction or mitigation, local knowledge is based on both individual and collective experiences and therefore gains credibility.

The glaciers are considered to be important in many respects, and people have started to increasingly mention their worries about the retreat of the glaciers. Some residents were shocked about the rapid retreat of the glaciers. They pointed at the location where the ice of the *Trafoier Eiswand*, or the 'ice-wall of Trafoi', was melting. At that place, important fights took place during World War I, and it seems as if the memories are also in danger of melting away. This is a clear example of how place-names encode indigenous knowledge. Many of the villagers observe them and their movements carefully, and some called it sadly the 'beginning of the dying' of the glaciers and felt they ought 'to be left in peace'. One young woman interviewed had painted the glaciated peaks in order to have a memory of them before they became completely 'naked' and *schiech* (ugly and fearful) as the villagers express it. She was worried about the loss of their *Schönheit* (beauty), which has come up as an important aspect for the local people as well as for tourism. Other villagers were more concerned about future water availability, when the glaciers were gone. There is thought to be more uncertainty in terms of water availability than in earlier times. According to them, the weather is much more difficult to evaluate nowadays, and they talk about weather extremes, such as too much precipitation or drought.

Memories of natural hazards also have a significant impact on the perception of glaciers and glacial change. Interacting with natural hazards such as mudslides and flooding, as well as working towards protecting themselves from these events, has built knowledge about the changing environment. Many villagers claim that the knowledge once retained through this work, was lost when organizing was banned in the communities following World War I. The villagers tend to emphasize that in earlier days many people spent a great deal of their time working as mountain guides or farmers or at least tending a field for subsistence crops. They 'knew every stone and its name' in the surroundings. Even today, evaluation of the conditions takes place using all of the senses: especially listening and sometimes smelling.

North Cascades

As mentioned previously, residents of Concrete and Glacier do not live in the same proximity to, or with as accessible a view or reach of glaciers as do residents of the study sites in the Cordillera Blanca and South Tirol. How they are physically situated in relation to glaciers may have as much bearing on their awareness and concern about glacier retreat as the fact of their more recent migration into the area. In addition, as a result of copious average annual precipitation in the region, its inhabitants are less directly dependent on glacial meltwater for livelihoods than in the more arid climates of the Cordillera Blanca and South Tirol. In general, Concrete and Glacier residents' knowledge about changes in glaciers, climate, and other features of the landscape is influenced by the length of time they have lived in the area, the type of work they do, and their leisure activities.

As a result of their physical situation, and the fact that few residents' livelihoods still depend directly on the surrounding environment, residents of Concrete and Glacier are less likely to have direct experience of, or concerns about, glacier retreat. Those whose work or recreation provides views of the glaciers express 'shock' about how much change they can see.

Near Glacier there are several vantage points where there is a relatively close-up view of Mt Baker, so its residents are more likely to comment that Mt Baker looks 'more rocky' than in the past. In Concrete, residents remarked that the Sauk River turns brown in hot summers, and were aware that it was caused by the melting of a glacier that has come to be known as the Chocolate Glacier. Winter recreation in the North Cascades is more dependent on snowpack than glaciers, so winter recreationists are more aware of and concerned about the snow level, which is announced through mountain weather forecasts or discerned from the level above which the surrounding forested slopes are white.

Although they might not have experiential knowledge of glacier retreat, most study participants had heard about it: either on the news or the internet; from residents who work at North Cascades National Park which is conducting an ongoing study of glaciers within the park and disseminating findings at community outreach events; or from seeing comparative photographs that showed a particular glacier at some point in the past and more recently. Few are very concerned about it, however. Those who are express sadness over the loss of glaciers because of their beauty, or fear because they see glaciers connected cyclically to everything else in the ecosystem. They anticipate that the disappearance of glaciers will affect the forests growing on the mountains, the soil, the quality and quantity of the water in the rivers, the salmon, and the eagles that feed on the salmon. It will, in turn, affect their own lives, their communities, which depend economically on recreation and tourism, and 'the everyday operations and lives of everybody'. More often, residents did not see glaciers as important, in their lives or more generally. Many residents understand glacier retreat as part of a natural cycle that has been occurring for millions of years.

Changes in their environment that participants most frequently commented on were changes in their communities, changes in the forest since logging had declined, and changes in the weather. Many people agreed that winters were not as cold as they used to be generally, and summers were warmer and sunnier. A recurring remark from Concrete residents was that ancestors or 'old-timers' had told them that the Skagit River used to freeze in the winter. However, winter flows were lower before dams were built on the river. Believers in cycles of glacier advance and retreat were also likely to believe that weather changes were also cyclical.

The environmental hazards that participants mentioned most frequently were floods and the eruption of Mt Baker. In Concrete, some say that flooding on the Skagit is worse than it used to be. They do not attribute it to climate change, but to the cessation of dredging and channelling as a result of the various protective designations in the region. This observation illustrates a perception of the environment that many local residents who work or formerly worked in natural resource production share: it is being mismanaged due to too much government regulation. Their experience with the effects of new federal designations on the surrounding public lands and on their lives and communities is a kind of local knowledge that informs a sceptical view of climate change.

Differing experiences, knowledge and concerns

Comparison across the three sites indicates that the degree of knowledge and concern about glacier retreat in each depends heavily on the level and frequency with which residents interact with the glacier and how closely they tie their own livelihoods to the existence of glaciated peaks. Residents in the sites where livelihoods are dependent on natural resource production are more likely to perceive risk from glacial loss or change. In Siete Imperios, where livelihoods depend directly on the glacial meltwater for at least half of the year, and the residents see the glacier on a daily basis, the knowledge of glacial loss and the resulting concern is high and frequently discussed among residents. In South Tirol, where glaciers are also clearly visible and livelihoods depend largely on the beauty the glaciated peaks represent, knowledge of changes and concerns about glacial loss is also high. Where the landscape precludes residents from seeing glaciers on a daily basis in the North Cascades, and livelihoods are only tangentially dependent on mountain recreation, knowledge of glacial changes is less articulated and not as wide a concern throughout the local population.

For those in the North Cascades who were concerned about how glacier retreat would affect water availability, it was a much less immediate concern than to residents of Siete Imperios. Also, in the North Cascades the extensive investment in water infrastructure and the government support for water management creates a stronger sense of security about water supply than in Siete Imperios where recent water laws have changed access and control. Those in the North Cascades who were concerned about how glacier retreat would affect tourism were less clear about how this might happen than residents of the South Tirol who pointed out that ugliness of the mountains and the increased risk of mud and landslides threatens to reduce the number of tourists that visit the region.

Another element that seems to play a role in the level of concern over glacial changes is the relative degree of moisture or aridity in each site. In the more arid sites of the Cordillera Blanca and South Tirol, where meltwater is an important element of seasonal water availability and rainfall patterns are becoming less predictable, glaciers play a very important role in subsistence and livelihoods. Most study participants in the North Cascades did not see glacier retreat as affecting water availability, and were not experiencing other climatic or environmental shifts that gave them cause to worry about water levels. Residents here are more concerned about the effects that new federal regulations, state legislation, and salmon restoration plans would have on water availability and flood control. Similarly, knowledge and levels of concern also correspond to predictions of precipitation in each site. The Cordillera Blanca and South Tirol sites are expected to see more chaotic rainfall, which will disrupt glacial cycles and also force adjustments in water management. In the North Cascades, models predict rising snow levels and little change in precipitation patterns, so water availability is less of a concern.

Eroding local knowledge

The loss of physical places, such as glaciers and the surrounding environs, 'involve a loss of attendant cultural and social significance' that is sometimes less visible to economically oriented or large-scale calculations of climate change (Adger et al., 2009: 348; Turner et al., 2008). Standing out among the differences between the three sites is the consistency with which residents expressed concern that local knowledge thought crucial for adapting to changing environments is being lost. Though local residents in each site speak of loss when discussing the current depth of their communal knowledge on climatic and glacial changes, we refer to it as an erosion or weakening of knowledge, as it is a complex combination of generational change, market involvement, environmental change and a multitude of other factors that contribute to a feeling of loss. In addition, residents note changes in their surrounding environment that result in existing knowledge becoming less valid, and describe a sense that their world is becoming less knowable in the face of climate change. This feeling is also likely tied to a larger feeling of loss between older and younger generations, exemplified by things such as changing ties to the land, differences in farming techniques or shifting priorities. Descriptions and feelings of loss in these sites could also represent a generational critique of modern lifestyles that are less attuned and less responsive to changes in the environment.

In Siete Imperios, people worry that knowledge about farming, soil, manure, and ways of cooking and feeding families without purchased supplies is being lost. Knowledge about climatic changes and glaciers is changing as well. Residents used to sing at the entrance to the glacier before entering in order to encourage any impending small avalanches to fall before they enter the zone. This practice no longer occurs among younger generations, mostly because there is no longer a need for it as the glacier is much farther away and not as tall or expansive. Some say certain paths to the glacier are lost now from fewer people visiting the glacier.

Residents of South Tirol are convinced that the processes of becoming familiar with natural hazards, the structures built against them, and the natural environment in general are the basis of successful management of natural hazards. They believe that intuitive understandings are a key element for coping with uncertainty and the unknown. The point of view that considers factors like smell, silence, and intuitive understanding has not necessarily been shared by scientific experts, and residents fear that the process of becoming familiar with the landscape through a connection with it, as opposed to a study of it, is fading into the past.

Many of the long-time residents in the North Cascades are ageing and fear that the methods they used and the knowledge they gained working and foraging in the woods will die when they do. Although the technology and knowledge may be outmoded, they point to the importance of a kind of relationship between landscapes, livelihoods, and communities which they experienced, and which needs to be recognized, and perhaps recovered.

In each of the three sites residents are also at a loss when it comes to what can be done about melting glaciers. But their concern for a closer relationship between communities and their environment points to an understanding that the relationships that have helped them to survive thus far will serve them best in an uncertain future. Current climate change interventions in these sites vary; however, they are similar in that local knowledge is largely downplayed in favour of scientific or outside expert knowledge, which is not easily accessed. The valuation of scientific, expert knowledge leaves locals sceptical, but also in some cases powerless with regard to decision-making because they are no longer certain of their traditional environmental knowledge. In Siete Imperios, locals and outsiders share a concern about retreat, though language issues are a concern, as most adaptation interventions are communicated in Spanish, where many locals speak Quechua. Generally, locals in the North Cascades distrust scientists as either meddlers or environmentalists without concern for local livelihoods. The locals of South Tirol have a fine spatial resolution for hazards and feel that outsiders often misperceive risks, either exaggerating or minimizing them. Our research suggests that climate change adaptation initiatives for these communities should aim to take into account and enhance their existing relationships with their environments in order to encourage the accumulation of new knowledge and the development of new ways of living and coping in these changing environments.

Conclusion

This chapter discusses local knowledge of climate change in three sites (the Cordillera Blanca of the Peruvian Andes, South Tirol in the Italian Alps, and the North Cascades of Washington State, USA) where communities live near glaciers that have been retreating for decades. Though these communities are very different, they are each experiencing and observing glacial loss. In the Cordillera Blanca, residents are aware that glaciers are shrinking, and they are concerned that water availability will decrease in the future. Residents of South Tirol are also acutely aware of the changing glaciers. While they too are concerned for water resources, the glacier recession also evokes sadness over the loss of beauty and fear due to knowledge of glacial-related hazards. In contrast to these two sites, residents of the North Cascades were aware of changes in nearby glaciers, but did not consider the recession to have significant impact on their life. Commenting that glacial changes were 'a natural cycle', residents in the North Cascades were more concerned with changing social conditions in the communities than with environmental changes. Comparison across the three sites suggests that awareness and concern about glacier retreat on the part of nearby communities depends on interactions with glaciers and on the importance of glacier-related livelihoods in the local economy. Although the knowledge and concern about glacial loss differed between these sites, these communities shared a fear that local knowledge was being lost. Each community felt this knowledge was a vital element for their ability to operate effectively in their respective environments, especially as these environments continue to change.

Author updates to the 2025 edition

Karina Yager[1]

As originally put forth in this chapter, local and indigenous perceptions of glacier loss and their impacts on mountain livelihoods are multidimensional, closely tied to their daily life experiences. Documenting local knowledge regarding glacier loss continues to be an imperative task when identifying potential adaptive strategies to a rapidly changing alpine environment. Encouragingly, there is an increase in awareness and articulation of the understandings of glacier change, melt rate, surface area loss trends and its impacts on mountain socio-ecosystems. Unfortunately, rates of glacier loss are accelerating at the global scale (Rounce et al., 2023). The three main regions of study in this chapter are no exception and continue to be important mountain watersheds to monitor in terms of both scientific and local knowledge in assessing trends and societal impacts.

The glacierized peaks of the North Cascades of Washington are the largest concentration of glaciers in the continental US. Similar to the socio-ecosystem services provided by other mountain glaciers, the glacier meltwater from the North Cascades is important for downstream irrigation, fisheries, and power generation. In particular, glacier outflow is an important water resource during the dry summer months when precipitation levels fall. For example, the Skagit River watershed, which once contained 756 glaciers around 50 years ago, is the largest draining hydrological input into Puget Sound (Post et al., 1971). Summer glacier run-off is critically important to the Pacific Northwest's salmon populations, providing cool, nutrient rich waters ideal for migration and spawning for five native species of salmon (Wydoski and Whitney, 2003). The glaciers in this range have continued to rapidly diminish at a total cover loss of approximately 19 per cent from 1959 to 2009 (Riedel and Larrabee, 2016), a mean cumulative mass balance loss of 20–40 per cent from 1984 to 2006 across selected monitored glaciers (Pelto, 2008), and documented total loss of at least four glaciers in recent years.

Across the Alps, glacier loss is also prevalent and impacts tourism, water supplies, hydroelectric production, and poses potential hazards (Brunner et al., 2019). In the Tyrol region of Italy, glacier loss has even led to the redefining of national borders. Glacierized mountain peaks often constitute borders between countries, for example between India and Pakistan, and Chile and Argentina. In the Alps, glaciers define the borders between Italy and Switzerland, as well as Austria. Recognizing the accelerating loss of glaciers across the Alps, Italy and Austria signed agreements to facilitate the geopolitical implementation of 'moving borders' (Ferrari et al., 2018). Across the Alps, glacier loss in the coming decades is projected to result in total volume loss of around 50 by 2500, and their fate by 2100 dependent upon emission scenarios over the coming decades (Zekollari et al., 2019).

Since the 1930s, the glaciers of the Cordillera Blanca have decreased in their total area by 30 per cent, with warming temperatures threatening total loss of low-lying glaciers (Schauwecker et al., 2014). The glaciers of the Cordillera Blanca are important to downstream populations who depend on mountain water for mining, agriculture, hydropower and domestic use (Vuille et al., 2008), especially during the dry season when precipitation is low. Across the watersheds of the Cordillera Blanca, there is decreasing water availability, coupled with increasing water competition, which has direct implications for equity issues and increasing the vulnerabilities of rural and downstream communities (Lynch, 2012).

Given the accelerating trends of glacier loss across alpine regions, continued monitoring of the rapid response of glaciers to a warming climate and understanding the implications for downstream users is critical for identifying urgently needed adaptation measures.

Notes

[1]   Karina Yager is associate professor of Marine and Atmospheric Sciences at Stony Brook University.

References

Adger, W., Dessai, S., Goulden, M., Hulme, M., Lorenzoni, I., Nelson, D., Naess, L., Wolf, J., and Wreford, A. (2009) 'Are there limits to adaptation to climate change?' *Climatic Change* 93: 335–54.

Berkes, F. (2007) 'Understanding uncertainty and reducing vulnerability: lessons from resilience thinking', *Natural Hazards* 41: 283–95.

Brunner, M. I., Björnsen Gurung, A., Zappa, M., Zekollari, H., Farinotti, D., and Stähli, M. (2019) 'Present and future water scarcity in Switzerland: Potential for alleviation through reservoirs and lakes'. *Science of The Total Environment* 666: 1033–1047. https://doi.org/https://doi.org/10.1016/j.scitotenv.2019.02.169

Christomannos, T. (1999 [1895]) *Sulden–Trafoi, Tourismusverein im Ortlergebiete*, Bozen.

Cruikshank, J. (2005) *Do Glaciers Listen?* UBC Press, Vancouver.

Ferrari, M., Pasqual, E., and Bagnato, A. (2018) *A Moving Border: Alpine Cartographies of Climate Change*. Columbia University Press.

Hurton, J. (2004) *Sulden. Geschichte, Land, Leute und Berge*, Eigenverlag, Bozen.

INRENA (Instituto Nacional de Recursos Naturales) (2007) *Glaciares, Lagunas Altoandinas, Deglaciación y Cambio Climático*, [online] available from: http://inrena.gob.pe/irh/irh_proxy_glaciares.htm [accessed 12 October 2007].

Lynch, B. D. (2012) 'Vulnerabilities, competition and rights in a context of climate change toward equitable water governance in Peru's Rio Santa Valley'. *Global Environmental Change* 22(2): 364–373. https://doi.org/ https://doi.org/10.1016/j.gloenvcha.2012.02.002

Orlove, B., Wiegandt, E. and Luckman, B. (2008) *Darkening Peaks*, University of California Press, Berkeley.

Paul, F., Kaab, A. and Haeberli, W. (2007) 'Recent glacier changes in the Alps observed by satellite: consequences for future monitoring strategies', *Global and Planetary Change* 56: 111–22.

Pelto, M. (2008) 'Impact of climate change on North Cascade alpine glaciers, and alpine runoff', *Northwest Science* 82: 65–75.

Pinggera, G. (1997) *Stilfs, Geschichte eines Bergdorfes*, Gemeinde Stilfs, Stilfs.

Post, A., Richardson, D., Tangborn, W.V., and Rosselot, F.L. (1971) *Inventory of glaciers in the North Cascades*, Washington. US Geological Survey Professional Paper 705-A.

Riedel, J. L., and Larrabee, M. A. (2016) 'Impact of Recent Glacier Recession on Summer Streamflow in the Skagit River'. *Northwest Science* 90(1): 5–22.

Rounce, D. R., Hock, R., Maussion, F., Hugonnet, R., Kochtitzky, W., Huss, M., Berthier, E., Brinkerhoff, D., Compagno, L., Copland, L., Farinotti, D., Menounos, B., and McNabb, R. W. (2023) 'Global glacier change in the 21st century: Every increase in temperature matters'. *Science* 379(6627): 78–83. https://doi.org/10.1126/science.abo1324

Schauwecker, S., Rohrer, M., Acuña, D., Cochachin, A., Dávila, L., Frey, H., Giráldez, C., Gómez, J., Huggel, C., Jacques-Coper, M., Loarte, E., Salzmann, N., and Vuille, M. (2014) 'Climate trends and glacier retreat in the Cordillera Blanca, Peru, revisited'. *Global and Planetary Change* 119: 85–97. https://doi.org/https://doi.org/10.1016/j.gloplacha.2014.05.005

Schöpf, K. (2008) 'Die Geschichte von Sulden', Unpublished.

Thomas, D., Twyman, C., Osbahr, H., and Hewitson, B. (2007) 'Adapting to climate change and variability in southern Africa: farmer responses to intraseasonal precipitation trends in South Africa', *Climate Change* 83: 301–22.

Thöni, M. (n.d.) *Die Marienwallfahrt zu den hl. Drei Brunnen in Trafoi*, 8th edn, Eigenverlag, Trafoi.

Turner, N., Gregory, R., Brooks, C., Failing, L., and Satterfield, T. (2008) 'From invisibility to transparency: Identifying the implications', *Ecology and Society* 13: 7.

Vedwan, N. (2006) 'Culture, climate and the environment: Local knowledge and perception of climate change among apple growers in Northwest India', *Journal of Ecological Anthropology* 10: 4–18.

Vuille, M., Francou, B., Wagnon, P., Juen, I., Kaser, G., Mark, B. G., and Bradley, R. S. (2008) 'Climate change and tropical Andean glaciers: Past, present and future'. *Earth-Science Reviews* 89(3): 79–96. https://doi.org/https://doi. org/10.1016/j.earscirev.2008.04.002

Walker, P. (2003) 'Reconsidering "regional" political ecologies: toward a political ecology of the rural American West', *Progress in Human Geography* 27: 7–24.

Wydoski, R. S. , and Whitney, R.R. (2003) *Inland Fishes of Washington*, 2nd ed. University of Washington Press, Seattle.

Zekollari, H., Huss, M., and Farinotti, D. (2019) 'Modelling the future evolution of glaciers in the European Alps under the EURO-CORDEX RCM ensemble'. The Cryosphere 13(4): 1125–1146. https://doi.org/10.5194/tc-13-1125-2019

About the authors

K.W. Dunbar is currently writing her dissertation for the Anthropology Department at the University of Georgia after spending 18 months conducting research in the north-central Peruvian highlands.

Julie Brugger is a Postdoctoral Scholar in the Department of Environmental Science and Policy at the University of California, Davis. She received her PhD in Anthropology from the University of Washington.

Christine Jurt is a Research Associate in the Geography Department at the University of Zurich She received her PhD in Anthropology from the University of Bern.

Ben Orlove, an anthropologist at Columbia University, teaches in the School of International and Public Affairs, and is a research scientist at the International Research Institute for Climate and Society.

Update by:

Karina Yager is an associate professor in the School of Marine and Atmospheric Sciences at Stony Brook University in New York.

Chapter 9

Aapuupayuu (the weather warms up): Climate change and the Eeyouch (Cree) of northern Quebec

Kreg Ettenger

Climate change in the far north is impacting on many indigenous peoples, with subsistence activities especially threatened. Dangerous and unpredictable ice conditions, changing ecosystems, increased wildfires and other extreme events, and shifting wildlife patterns and populations are just a few of the threats to arctic and subarctic peoples. One indigenous group so affected is the Eeyouch (Cree) of northern Quebec. This chapter looks at some ways the Cree are being affected by, and are responding to, climate change in their homeland, called Eeyou Istchee.[1] Since the original version of this chapter was written, climate-related changes in this region have deeply intensified, with devastating and lasting consequences.

Introduction

The Cree of Quebec (also known as Eeyou or Eenou, plural Eeyouch/Eenouch, depending on the dialect)[2] live in mid-northern Quebec, a subarctic region east of James Bay and Hudson Bay. The total Quebec Cree population is around 21,000, most of whom live in 10 rural communities ranging in size from roughly 500 to nearly 5,000 residents. For much of their history the Cree lived a subsistence lifestyle based on hunting, fishing, and gathering. In the 17th century the European fur trade altered this existence, although the Cree were able to maintain many economic, social and cultural patterns well into the 20th century (Tanner, 1979; Francis and Morantz, 1987; Morantz, 2002).

In the last 50 years, mainly due to large-scale hydroelectric development and subsequent land claim agreements, rapid changes took place in Cree society. During this period, the Cree moved from a land-based economy to one based largely on community activities and income. Many families spend most of their time in communities to work and send children to school, while fewer than a quarter of all heads of household now work as fulltime hunters and trappers. Cree villages consist of contemporary houses with central heating, municipal water and sewage, and reliable electricity and communications (including internet). Modern offices, recreation complexes, and commercial centers are the norm. Air flights provide transportation of people and goods, and most communities are connected by road to the south. By all appearances, the Cree are set firmly in the 21st century.

At the same time, most Cree maintain strong connections with the land and their subsistence traditions. In addition to trappers who make a living off the land (supported in part by a government subsidy program), many families hunt, fish and gather at certain times of the year, focusing their efforts on key wildlife species and combining subsistence with social, cultural and recreational activities. Big game hunting takes place throughout the region, with moose, caribou and black bear being prime targets; small game such as ptarmigan, hare, and beaver are also harvested. Fish are caught using different techniques, including traditional gillnets and scoop nets as well as angling. Wild plant foods, especially berries, are gathered in large amounts. Other resources such as wood, bark and herbaceous plants are harvested for tools, crafts and medicines. In short, the Cree have retained many traditional skills and values and incorporated these into modern lifestyles. Climate change, however, now threatens the Cree's ability to continue key activities upon which both their economy and culture still depend.

Given that mean air temperatures in the Arctic are projected to rise by as much as 7°C (13°F) by the end of this century (ACIA, 2005), adaptation to climate change is necessary for northern communities (Peterson and Johnson, 1995; Ford et al., 2007). Many individuals and communities have already begun to develop adaptive strategies (Newton et al., 2005; Tremblay et al., 2008). The Eeyou of Quebec are being forced to quickly assess and adapt to climate-related changes in their homeland. These changes are affecting their ability to travel safely on ice and snow, to locate and harvest favoured wildlife species, and to engage in critical subsistence activities. In response they are taking steps to learn more about the nature of these changes and to adapt their harvesting strategies to compensate for the rapidly shifting environment.

Cree traditional knowledge, or *iyiyuu chischaaihtimuuin*, may be helpful in negotiating these changes, but is constrained by the nature and pace of rapid climate change. In other places in the Arctic, indigenous knowledge of residents has been combined with scientific data and models to form more complete understandings and predictions of climate change and its impacts (c.f, Barber et al., 2008; Krupnik and Jolly, 2002; Laidler, 2006; Riewe and Oakes, 2006). While scientific knowledge is useful for understanding large-scale processes, indigenous knowledge is vital in terms of understanding the impacts of change on local environments. It is also useful for generating and testing adaptations to the local impacts of climate change (Newton et al., 2005; Ford et al., 2007; Tremblay et al., 2008).

For the Cree, knowledge of environmental systems and processes, including the ability of different ecosystems and wildlife to adapt to fire and other natural forces, may be critical in helping them successfully adapt to the many changes associated with global climate change. Given the extent of change expected in arctic and subarctic regions in the coming decades, such adaptations will be crucial if the Cree hope to maintain their traditional subsistence activities into the future. Yet as I point out in this revised chapter, traditional knowledge may no longer be sufficient to respond to the kinds of changes that are now occurring in the region.

Environmental conditions and change in the James Bay region

The subarctic James Bay region of Quebec is characterized by boreal spruce forests punctuated by lakes, rivers, and extensive wetlands. The region's climate is extreme, with winter temperatures reaching -40°C (-40°F) and below, while summers can see temperatures above 32° C (90°F). Despite these extremes, many plant and animal species thrive. Black spruce is the major tree species; there is also balsam fir, tamarack, and jackpine, with white spruce along the seacoast. Poplar, birch, willows, and aspen line streams, rivers, and lakes. Blueberries, cranberries, and other woody plants provide food for wildlife and humans alike.

Farther north the taiga forest thins into forest-tundra at the edge of the Cree homeland. Mammals found in the region include moose, black bear, beaver, muskrat, otter, mink, porcupine, snowshoe hare, Arctic and red fox, wolf and caribou, among others. Marine mammals include ringed and bearded seals, polar bears, and beluga whales. Some 139 species of birds live or breed in the region, including more than 30 species of waterfowl. At least 16 fish species populate the lakes, rivers and streams, among them whitefish, brook trout, lake trout, suckers, sturgeon, and northern pike.

Climate change is just one of many environmental stresses affecting the region, which for several decades has undergone major transformations due to resource extraction (Hornig, 1999; Niezen, 2008). Logging has moved northward into the region since the 1950s, as has mining in more recent years. The greatest change, however, has come from hydroelectric development beginning in the 1970s (McCutcheon, 1996). The 'James Bay Project' dammed numerous rivers and created a massive infrastructure of roads, reservoirs, electricity generating stations and transmission corridors. These changes have brought outsiders ranging from casual tourists, to sport hunters and fishers, to temporary and permanent workers.

All of these factors have made an indelible imprint on the land and resulted in transformations to the region's ecology and wildlife. Climate change adds another layer of stress to which local systems, both ecological and human, must now adapt. Three particular types of impacts related to climate change are discussed here: effects on weather and seasons; on landscapes and ecosystems; and on wildlife. I conclude the chapter with a new description of the increased risk of wildfire due to hotter and drier conditions, leading to severe and prolonged fire seasons, with devastating consequences for landscapes, wildlife and people.

Weather and seasons

According to both scientific data and local observations, temperatures and weather patterns are changing in the region. Summer temperatures have increased and stretched into fall, while winters, which are generally shorter and warmer, see both more severe cold periods and periodic thaws. As one hunter put it during a series of consultations in the 1990s, 'The weather seems to have changed, and our rivers don't freeze anymore like they used to' (Scott and Ettenger, 1994: 147). Another stated, 'There's been a lot of changes in the seasons. Everything used to be really normal and you could predict how long the spring would be; now you can't predict anything' (Scott and Ettenger, 1994: 148). These observations are confirmed by regional weather stations. Late summer has seen significant warming from the 1950s through the 1990s, while midwinter periods are now generally colder; warmer fall and spring temperatures have shortened the overall length of winter (Beaulieau and Allard, 2003).

Weather and the length of seasons are critical factors for arctic and subarctic subsistence activities, as everything from travel to wildlife harvesting and storage depend upon them. A larger range of temperatures, more severe storms, greater frequency of winter thaws, and more ice storms and other high-impacts events can have devastating effects on wildlife and humans alike. The frequency of midwinter ice storms, as one example, is projected to more than double by 2080 in northern Ontario, roughly the same latitude as southern James Bay (Cheng et al., 2007). Changes observed so far with respect to weather and seasons in James Bay – hotter and drier summers, colder and snowier midwinters, warmer springs and falls, and more severe storms including icing events – all make the pursuit of subsistence activities more difficult, dangerous and uncertain for the Cree.

As an update, these regional trends have only accelerated as global temperatures continue to rise. The most recent year for which data are available, 2023, was 1.48° C warmer than pre-industrial averages globally, but Canadian temperatures saw nearly twice this level of warming, and the Canadian arctic warmed nearly three times as much (McBean, 2024). As described below, the Canadian wildfire season in 2023 was the worst in recorded history, a direct result of hot and dry conditions, a prolonged warm season, and a lack of both winter and summer precipitation in much of the subarctic.

Changing landscapes and ecosystems

According to both scientific studies and Cree observers, significant changes to local ecosystems are already occurring. To the north, on the coast of Hudson Bay near the community of Whapmagoostui, warming trends have led to melting permafrost and rapid erosion in the Manitounuk Sound area, altering the coastal landscape (Beaulieu and Allard, 2003). Warming waters in James and Hudson Bays are changing conditions for flora such as eelgrass (*Zostera marina*), with possible effects on associated fauna like geese and brants (Ward et al., 2005). Over the past decade, the decline of eelgrass beds has spread across much of the James Bay coastline, leading to declines in waterfowl populations and impacts on Cree hunting (Herodier, 2021).

As the tree line proceeds northward, taiga forest is encroaching upon the forest-tundra and tundra in the northernmost part of Eeyou Istchee (Lavoie and Payette, 1994; Gamache and Payette, 2005). In southern areas an increase in forest fires was predicted to result from hotter and drier summers. One study, using data from near the Cree community of Waswanipi, projected more than a doubling of risk of late-summer wildfires by the end of this century (Le Goff et al., 2009). These projections, as dire as they were, actually underestimated the problem, as described below. Land-based ecosystems are also changing as a result of less snow and ice cover, changes in precipitation, and other meteorological and hydrological changes.

These trends have only accelerated since the publication of the first edition of this book. Temperatures in the boreal region have continued to climb overall, seasonal patterns have continued to shift to hotter summers and warmer and shorter winters, and wildfires have increased in number and intensity, with 2023 representing by far the most severe and damaging wildfire season in Canadian history. In just one season, as much land burned due to wildfires in Canada (nearly 20 million hectares) as typically has burned for each of the last five decades (15–29 million hectares).

The effects of these changes on the boreal environment are still emerging, but it appears that there will be some transition from conifer to deciduous forests in response to repeated fires and other factors. Pioneer species such as birch and alder could replace spruce, tamarack and other climax tree species. Due in part to short-interval burning, where fires return within the period of normal wildfire recovery, climax forests may never return, and even smaller trees might not regrow (Shen, 2023). In some areas, especially where intense fires have killed off vegetation and consumed peat and humus, recovery might never fully occur.

Wildlife populations and migrations

Climate change is leading to shifts in wildlife populations and migration throughout the Arctic and subarctic (Gunn, 1995). Some large mammals, like moose, are following the shift of favoured habitats as they expand their range to the north. Other wildlife, including ice-dwelling marine mammals like seals and polar bears, are finding their habitat reduced to where their existence in the wild may be threatened (Derocher et al., 2004). Migratory birds have adjusted arrival dates in parts of northern Canada in response to warming trends, with some waterfowl arriving a month earlier than they did 70 years ago (Murphy-Klassen et al., 2005).

Canada geese (*Branta canadensis canadensis*), a critical species to the Cree, have changed migration patterns to the point where they are no longer a reliable source of food (see below). Another important species, the red-throated loon (*Gavia stellata*), is changing its flight pattern from near the coast to farther out to sea (Ettenger, 2002). Other species are finding either the weather or the habitat in the warming north more appealing. Giant Canada geese (*Branta canadensis maxima*), known locally as 'longnecks', have become a regular summer visitor to eastern James Bay in recent years. Meanwhile, lesser Canada geese (*Branta canadensis parvipes*) or 'shortnecks' are becoming less populous during their migrations (Giroux et al., 2024).

As a result of both climate change and possibly other factors, many mammals are in decline in the region. Perhaps the most drastic shift has occurred with caribou (*Rangifer tarandus*) populations, of which there are two subspecies (tundra and woodland) and two major herds (Leaf River and George River) in Quebec. The former has seen a decline of more than two-thirds since the early 2000s, while the latter has dropped by some 98 per cent in this time. This has led recently to an agreement between the Cree and neighboring Innu to limit hunting from this herd in response to the further pressure from 2023's wildfires on the herd's range (Bell, 2024). Other species have shown notable declines in the past two decades, including moose (Bell 2022) as well as a number of furbearing species such as lynx, marten, beaver, and foxes.

The 2023 wildfire season destroyed millions of hectares of forests and wetlands in Eeyou Istchee, with devastating losses of wildlife. Fires moved so rapidly, and left so few untouched areas, that many animals were no doubt killed directly; others would have died from injuries, lack of food and shelter, and exposure to predators within weeks or months of the fires. As the land recovers, some species will no doubt return more quickly while others, especially those adapted to the mature spruce forest ecosystem, might take years or decades to rebuild their numbers. Already threatened populations such as woodland caribou might be pushed past the tipping point.

Impacts on subsistence activities and the role of traditional knowledge

Climate change has impacted Cree subsistence activities ranging from transportation to the availability of key wildlife and plant species. These impacts are compounded by other changes such as dams, roads, logging and mining activities, and socioeconomic transitions. This makes it difficult to identify specific impacts of climate change; they are one of many forces affecting the ability of Cree families to engage in harvesting activities. It is possible, however, to highlight the ways in which climate change is interacting with other forces to affect Cree subsistence activities and traditional knowledge. I focus here on two types of impacts: those affecting travel and those affecting coastal hunting activities. In the former, climate change is leading to new risks and the need to develop new techniques and knowledge to adapt to these risks. In the latter, the changing climate is impacting local subsistence resources and the traditional knowledge base needed to acquire these resources. I conclude by looking at wildfires, a threat that could dwarf other impacts of climate change in the region.

Increased risk of travel on ice

The increased risk of sea ice travel associated with a warming environment has been well documented for Inuit and other Arctic peoples (Laidler, 2006; Barber et al., 2008; Ford et al., 2008; Tremblay et al., 2008). Less has been written about impacts of changing ice and snow conditions on subarctic groups like the Cree. The Cree use ice on rivers, lakes, and the ocean to travel more rapidly and easily throughout the winter. Travel on ice, however, is increasingly dangerous. In the spring of 2006 a well-known Cree hunter and community leader died when his snowmobile fell through ice, an accident attributed by some to 'unpredictable ice conditions and climate changes which have resulted in trappers being unable to predict weather patterns as they did before' (Iserhoff, 2006).

Predictive models of landfast (connected to shore) sea ice in the Canadian Arctic show thickness decreasing significantly, and dates of freeze-up and thaw changing by as much as two months by the latter part of this century (Dumas et al., 2006). Periods of freeze-up and thaw coincide with critical wildlife harvesting activities for the Cree and other subarctic groups, and many of their subsistence activities, such as waterfowl hunting, take place on or near coastal and inland waters. Even a slight change in the timing of ice formation or melting, or in the thickness and safety of the ice formed, can thus have major effects on travel, as this is when hunters and their families are moving to and from harvesting areas and hunting camps.

Travel dangers associated with climate change are amplified by other changes in Cree society. Since the early 1970s, for example, most Cree have switched from dog sleds to snowmobiles as the primary means of bush travel in the winter. Snowmobiles allow for faster travel, but give the traveler less time to respond to changing conditions, and also decrease sensitivity to one's surroundings due to engine noise and protective gear. In terms of knowledge, many young Cree do not possess the level of bush skills held by older residents, as less time today is spent in the bush than in generations past. Reading ice and other environmental conditions are skills that take years to master. One local tallyman (an experienced trapper who manages his family's hunting territory) refuses to allow winter visitors to his camp on an offshore island to cross sea ice unless he has personally checked conditions beforehand or travels with them as a guide (Ettenger, 2002b). In recent years sea ice conditions have become even less predictable and more dangerous due to a greater number and size of areas of open water (polynyas) as well as more frequent and larger storm events. In general, the combination of less predictable ice conditions, less knowledgeable hunters, and new technologies add up to a greater risk of loss of life or property than in the past, and the Cree communities are still figuring out just how to deal with this new level of risk.

At the community level, means of managing the risk of travel include alternative transportation and monitoring of ice conditions. One example comes from the coastal community of Eastmain, which has had to adapt to more dangerous ice conditions along the shores of James Bay and on nearby rivers. In a 1994 interview, one local official remarked on circumstances that led to changes in community practice with respect to spring travel:

> As a Public Safety Officer I have to monitor the ice [on the Eastmain River] every year in the spring. Because we had an accident one time in the spring; two people were driving across and one fell through the ice, and we lost that person.... So we have to drill holes around the beginning of April, start monitoring the ice, so that we can say what time we can close the river.... Because we don't want to lose people like that again, through the ice (Scott and Ettenger, 1994: 276–277).

Other local adaptations include a helicopter airlift program that transports people and goods to and from coastal waterfowl hunting camps once ice conditions are deemed unsafe. Helicopters have also been used in several instances when storms and wildfires, both of which have increased in number and intensity in recent years, have threatened families and workers in various parts of the territory. Nearly all Cree communities now have trained search and rescue teams, and some have specialized equipment such as Zodiak inflatable boats and scuba diving gear, to respond to the increased risk of travel in a changing environment. Educational programs are used to inform both local residents and visitors of the risks associated with travel in different locations and at different times of year. In some years, communities moved up dates of spring goose breaks to ensure that ice was still safe for travel (Diamond, 2010).

At the individual and family levels, Crees are also adapting their strategies and tactics to reduce risk. Some hunters are changing locations of harvesting activities to places where access is safer and more reliable, such as inland lakes and reservoirs instead of the coast of James Bay (Stephen Diamond, personal communication, July 2001). Others are using technologies such as GPS and satellite phones to communicate travel conditions to others, or to get up-to-date information themselves. Many Crees are switching from snowmobiles to more versatile ATVs; in communities such as Whapmagoostui these have become the primary form of local transportation in both summer and winter. This change corresponds with warmer winters and less snow in this region, as well as an expansion of local trail networks as communities choose safer land-based travel routes and decrease their use of sea and river ice for winter travel. And some hunters have simply reduced the amount of travel they do in the bush, choosing to locate their camps along major roads where they can be accessed by vehicle at all times of the year. While this may reduce the risk of travel, however, it also takes many families away from traditional harvesting areas, including the coastal waterfowl hunting camps that for generations have helped to define the coastal Cree (Scott, 1986).

Impacts on hunting: the case of coastal waterfowl

One critical harvesting activity for the Cree is waterfowl hunting, especially along the coasts of James and Hudson Bays, where five communities are located. As an indigenous people with subsistence harvesting rights, Cree are permitted to hunt waterfowl in the spring and summer as well as fall. Traditionally, birds like Canada geese, brants, loons, and ducks have been a major food source for the Cree. Spring and fall 'goose breaks' are also important times for family and community renewal, reinforcement of social ties, and passing on cultural traditions. Extended families typically spend time together in coastal goose camps; small children and elders participate in camp activities while youth are enculturated into hunting. In short, spring and fall waterfowl hunting have played a critical role in the maintenance of local subsistence economies and the social and cultural fabric of the Cree communities in recent decades (Scott, 1986). Climate change combined with other factors, however, is having a major impact on this activity.

Cree hunters have observed that the spring migration of waterfowl has changed in recent years, coming earlier and concluding more quickly than in the past (Scott and Ettenger, 1994). In former years, large flocks of geese would rest for days in coastal ponds and marshes, seeking open water for protection from predators and to feed on grasses and other foods. Cold weather and north winds would hold back the migration, keeping geese and ducks in areas where they could be hunted as they passed over ridges and settled in protected bays, channels and ponds (Scott, 1986). With warmer early springs, geese are less likely to remain in these areas, choosing to fly north to breeding grounds instead (Murphy-Klassen, et al., 2005; Diamond, 2010). Their flight paths tend to be high, making shooting difficult or impossible (Fred Tomatuk, personal communication, April 14, 1994).

Combined with more dangerous ice conditions, the spring goose hunt has become unreliable and in some years nearly absent. Given that outfitting a goose camp can cost each family thousands of dollars, the few geese harvested in recent years means a net economic loss for most families (Diamond, 2010). It also means the loss of an important food and the ability of hunters to pass along skills and knowledge to the next generation. Numerous older hunters have remarked about the decline in hunting knowledge among younger Crees, their lack of understanding of waterfowl biology and migration patterns, and the negative impacts their behaviors are having on other hunters (Scott and Ettenger, 1994; Ettenger, 2002a, 2002b). As a result of these changes, many Cree families have reduced their use of coastal hunting camps, and the number of waterfowl harvested each year has declined dramatically.

Cree hunters are responding to these changes in a number of ways, depending on the resources and knowledge available to them, the flexibility of their individual lifestyles, and other factors. One adaptation, previously noted, has been to change hunting locations to where wildlife is more easily accessed, such as along roads. Combined with modern communication methods, including cell and satellite phones, roads allow hunters to respond quickly to observed sightings of waterfowl, caribou and other wildlife. Cree hunters have also traveled as far south as the St. Lawrence and Ottawa Rivers to hunt geese on farmland (Fisher, 2009, 2010). Some hunters are using the internet to track migratory animals such as caribou, and to find new locations for hunting in response to changes in migratory patterns.

Hunters are also directing their efforts toward species or subspecies whose populations are increasing in the region. One example is the giant Canada goose, which many coastal hunters now take summer trips to target. On land, hunters harvest migrating caribou and other animals that may be in their areas for the first time in years. Their general response, as flexible and opportunistic foragers, is to hunt animals when and where available, using the road system and modern communications to locate and reach them. Subsistence harvesting rights that permit hunting throughout the year allow Cree hunters to be more flexible in their choice of prey and timing of activities. Still, these technologies and adjustments have not made up for the loss of critical resources and activities, including the spring coastal waterfowl hunt.

Author updates to the 2025 edition
Recent Eeyou responses to climate change

Since this chapter was first written, Eeyou communities and regional entities have made various attempts to assess, manage and ameliorate the impacts of climate change. For example, a joint 'Climate Change Project' was undertaken in 2009–11 to understand the impacts on hunting and other traditional activities (CTA et al., 2011). Major Cree entities including the Cree Trappers' Association (CTA), James Bay Advisory Committee on the Environment, Cree Regional Authority, and Cree Board of Health and Social Services of James Bay participated, with funding from Indian and Northern Affairs Canada.

Workshops and interviews were conducted in three communities (two coastal and one inland) to document local observations and to plan future actions. Major areas of concern were related to ecological impacts, wildlife losses, travel dangers, increased threats from wildfires, and hydrological changes. Proposed responses included the creation of local climate change committees, continued monitoring of climate change impacts, and the establishment of "security and awareness programs," mainly designed to make residents aware of the way that climate change is affecting travel safety and other hazards. The project also envisioned a GIS-based system for reporting observed impacts related to climate change in the region, which was subsequently funded and created. (The system used the "Cree Geoportal" website and is available at https://www.creegeoportal.ca/applications/climatechange/, although data collection for climate impacts ended in 2011 at the conclusion of the project.)

A regional conference in 2018 created a framework for understanding how climate change was affecting Eeyou Istchee and the Eeyou people, from health and diet to wildlife harvesting and other traditional activities. Three community reports (from Waskaganish, Whapmagoostui and Mistissini) were shared, all of which seemed to draw upon the results of the earlier project described above. The main outcome of this conference was a report (Bissonnette et al., 2019) that summarized major impacts experienced to date by the Eeyou communities and offered some general responses and strategies. Interestingly, while the report contains a short section on risks to hunting infrastructure such as cabins, the main threats seen were flooding and damage from black bears. Nothing was said about wildfire, which suggests that the events of 2023, discussed below, were beyond imagination at that time.

Eight priorities for the future were identified, including "protecting biodiversity and accessing wild food," "promoting Cree knowledge and land-based skills," "improving safety for travel and harvest," "intensifying Cree research and recording," "developing Cree educational programs," "ensuring water and food quality," "improving housing quality," and "implementing green technologies." By and large these replicate ideas generated in previous projects in response to economic development needs, impacts from regional development, and community perceptions regarding the loss of traditional knowledge and resource harvesting skills.

The work done over the past decade or so to address climate change in Eeyou Istchee, by and large, followed a standard template and assumed that climate change would be fairly gradual and incremental, not rapid and devastating. The strategies and methods discussed and proposed were based on the idea that having better knowledge and tools would allow the Cree to adapt in a sort of piecemeal fashion, based on local needs and threats as they emerged. Very little could have been done using these methods to prepare the Cree for the summer of 2023.

The devastating wildfires of 2023 and what the future holds

In 2023, the Cree experienced an apocalyptic season of wildfires that forever changed perceptions of how climate change would impact Eeyou Istchee, and what could be done in response. The 2023 wildfire season was the worst in Canadian recorded history, with some 20 million hectares (Mha) burned. Quebec received more than its fair share, with some 4.5 Mha of forests and muskeg (swampy woodlands and peat wetlands) consumed (Boulanger et al., 2024). While prior years had brought extensive fires in certain places, the summer of 2023 resulted in hundreds of fires, many of which raged for weeks and consumed thousands of square kilometers of boreal forests. Much of this destruction occurred in Eeyou Istchee, due to a combination of dry conditions, ample fuel, multiple fires occurring simultaneously, and the overwhelming size and intensity of many fires. In addition, with only a few Cree communities in a vast territory, firefighting efforts were spread thin, especially when compared to more populous areas farther south. Some fires raged unabated for weeks; others combined to form megafires, increasingly common in the warming north. Summer rains and normal cool spells were sparse, and many fires continued well into fall.

While fires can devastate northern forests, this was a new level of destruction for the Eeyouch and other northern residents. An estimated 12 per cent of the Cree homeland was burned by the fires (Blacksmith, 2024). And losses from wildfires are no longer confined to natural forests. Over the past few decades, an extensive network of permanent, well-constructed hunting camps has been established in the region, with structures ranging from modern cabins and traditional dwellings to outbuildings filled with equipment such as snowmobiles, outboard motors, generators, chainsaws, and the like. Cabins can cost upwards of Cdn $100,000 to build and equip, and an extended family encampment might contain several, or even dozens. An estimated 150 such camps burned in the 2023 fires, and many were not insured. Before this event, few cabins had been lost to fires, and fewer still to wildfires.

Affected families, whose traditional activities were centered on those camps, have not only lost significant economic resources. They have also lost vital links to their family "traplines" (managed land areas gained through inheritance), their vital bush foods (potentially worth tens of thousands of dollars per year), their focus for social gatherings such as goose camps and summer fishing camps, and, perhaps most importantly, their family memories and heritage. Family heirlooms like hunting rifles, photographs and goose down blankets were lost in the fires (Bell et al., 2023). It will take the forests decades to recover, and few families would have the resources, or the desire, to rebuild camps where there are no trees or clean water, no wildlife to harvest, and where all they see (and smell) is devastation. In the intervening years, the already tenuous connections that many Cree families have with their land and heritage could be permanently lost.

Conclusions

The steps being taken by the Eeyouch of Quebec – and by other northern Native communities in Canada and around the world – to adapt and respond to the effects of climate change are both admirable and necessary. But they might not be enough. The events of the past few years, from unprecedented heat waves to devastating wildfires that outstripped all capacity to manage them, show that climate change has radically and perhaps irreversibly changed life in northern environments. This is the reality that the Cree are now facing, as the devastation of the 2023 wildfire season made clear.

We are no longer living in a time when northern regions can adapt and recover in the face of occasional destructive events, such as large-scale wildfires, ice storms, or even hydroelectric reservoirs. The new adaptation is to "short-interval burns" that do not allow forests to recover before burning the same areas again (Whitman et al., 2019), so-called "zombie fires" that smolder through the winter before erupting again in the spring (Partlow, 2024), "extreme fire weather" (Jain et al., 2021) and extended wildfire seasons that stretch from spring to late fall, and "simultaneous megafires" (Bukovsky et al., 2022) that far exceed capacity to control or manage them. These fires threaten not only forests and wetlands, but cabins and other hunting property, northern communities (both indigenous and non-indigenous), and large-scale infrastructure such as power lines and hydroelectric installations.

When this chapter was first written in 2012, there was some hope that the worst impacts of climate change could be avoided through a combination of global actions and local efforts at adaptation and resilience-building. The Eeyouch were among those indigenous peoples worldwide who dedicated efforts to creating this resilience, at least on a modest scale. As recently as a few years ago, conferences and reports in Eeyou Istchee suggested that steps could be taken by the Eeyou communities to lessen the effects of climate change and strengthen wildlife harvesting and other community-based activities. An air of hopefulness ran throughout these efforts. The wildfires of 2023 were a devastating reality check to these hopes.

Notes

[1] Source for translation: http://www.eastcree.org/cree/en/dictionary/
[2] Cree spellings also include iyiyuu and iinuu, as well as syllabic (symbolic) versions.

References

ACIA (2005) *Arctic Climate Impact Assessment,* Cambridge University, New York. Available from: http://www.acia.uaf.edu/pages/scientific.html [accessed 20 June 2010].

Barber, D.G., Lukovich, J.K., Keogak, J., Baryluk, S., Fortier, L. and Henry, G.H.R. (2008) 'The changing climate of the Arctic', *Arctic* 61(Supp. 1): 7–26.

Beaulieu, N. and Allard, M. (2003) 'The impact of climate change on an emerging coastline affected by discontinuous permafrost: Manitounuk Strait, northern Quebec', *Canadian Journal of Earth Science* 40: 1393–404.

Bell, S. (2022) 'Declines in moose population a concern for Quebec Cree', *CBC News*, 10 February 2022. Available from: https://www.cbc.ca/news/canada/north/cree-moose-indigenous-bay-james-conservation-decline-population-1.6344246 [accessed 2 June 2024].

Bell, S. (2024) 'Quebec Cree and Innu leaders agree to reduce caribou harvest after summer wildfires', *CBC News*, 23 January 2024. Available from: https://www.cbc.ca/news/canada/north/cree-innu-caribou-northern-quebec-leaf-river-1.7092301 [accessed 2 June 2024].

Bell, S., Kitty, M., and Longchap, B. (2023) 'Lost in flames: As cabins burn with the forest in northern Quebec, Cree families are grappling with the resulting loss of culture, history, language and their ability to get out on the land', *CBC News*, 14 July 2023. Available from: https://www.cbc.ca/newsinteractives/features/lost-in-flames [accessed on 3 June 2024].

Bissonnette, J-F., Talec, P., Lloyd, K., and Del Vecchio, L. (2019) *Envisioning Responses to Climate Change in Eeyou Istchee: Report on the Regional Forum on Climate Change*, The Grand Council of the Crees (Eeyou Istchee)/ Cree Nation Government, Environment and Remedial Works, Montreal, Quebec, Canada.

Blacksmith, V. (2024) 'Wildfires and climate change are shifting the way some Quebec Cree hunt', *CBC News,* 5 May 2024. Available from: https://www.cbc.ca/news/canada/north/goose-break-forest-fores-quebec-cree-hunt-1.7191978 [accessed on 4 June 2024].

Boulanger, Y., Arseneault, D., Bélisle, A.C., Bergeron, Y., et al. (2024) 'The 2023 wildfire season in Québec: an overview of extreme conditions, impacts, lessons learned and considerations for the future', *bioRxiv* preprint version posted 22 February, 2024. Available at: https://doi.org/10.1101/2024.02.20.581257 [accessed 2 June 2024].

Cheng, C.S., Auld, H., Li, G., Klassen, J. and Li, Q. (2007) 'Possible impacts of climate change on freezing rain in south-central Canada using downscaled future climate scenarios', *Natural Hazards Earth Systems Science* 7: 71–87.

CTA, et al. (2011) *Climate Change in Eeyou Istchee: Identification of Impacts and Adaptation Measures for the Cree Hunters, Trappers and Communities*, Cree Trappers' Association, Eastmain, Quebec. Available from: https://www.creegeoportal.ca/wp-content/uploads/2022/06/FinalReportDMv5-coul.pdf [accessed 25 May 2024].

Derocher, A., Lunn, N.J. and Stirling, I. (2004) 'Polar bears in a warming climate', *Integrative Comparative Biology* 44: 163–76.

Diamond, J. (2010) 'Cree youth symposium postponed to June due to early goose break', News story posted 8 April 2010 on Grand Council of the Crees' website [online]. Available from: http://www.gcc.ca/newsarticle. php?id=204 [accessed 3 June 2010].

Dumas, J.A., Flato, G.M. and Brown, R.D. (2006) 'Future projections of landfast ice thickness and duration in the Canadian Arctic', *Journal of Climate* 19: 5175–89.

Ettenger, K. (2002a) *Cree Use, Management & Occupancy of the Offshore Region in Eastern James Bay & Southeastern Hudson Bay: Community Report for Eastmain*, Prepared for the Grand Council of the Crees (Eeyou Istchee)/ Cree Regional Authority, Montreal.

Ettenger, K. (2002b) *Cree Use, Management & Occupancy of the Offshore Region in Eastern James Bay & Southeastern Hudson Bay: Community Report for Waskaganish*, Prepared for the Grand Council of the Crees (Eeyou Istchee)/ Cree Regional Authority, Montreal.

Fisher, D. (2009) 'A cross-cultural hunting experience: The Fisher farm in Oxford Mills becomes a Cree hunt camp', Posted on Grand Council of the Crees' website 17 November 2009. Available from: http://www.gcc.ca/ newsarticle.php?id=192 [accessed 4 June 2010].

Fisher, D. (2010) 'Spring goose hunt in eastern Ontario', Posted on Grand Council of the Crees' website 17 May 2010. Available from: http://www. gcc.ca/newsarticle.php?id=206 [accessed 4 June 2010].

Ford, J., Pearce, T., Smit, B., Wandel, J., Allurat, M., Shappa, K., Ittusujurat, H. and Qrunnat, K. (2007) 'Reducing vulnerability to climate change in the Arctic: The case of Nunavut, Canada', *Arctic* 60(2): 150–66.

Ford, J., Pearce, T., Gilligan, J., Smit, B. and Oakes, J. (2008) 'Climate change and hazards associated with ice use in northern Canada', *Arctic, Antarctic, and Alpine Research* 40(4): 647–59.

Francis, D., and Morantz, T. (1983) *Partners in Furs: A History of the Fur Trade in Eastern James Bay, 1600–1870*. McGill-Queen's University Press, Kingston & Montreal.

Gamache, I. and Payette, S. (2005) 'Latitudinal response of subarctic tree lines to recent climate change in eastern Canada', *Journal of Biogeography* 32: 849–62.

Giroux, J-F., Idrobo, C.J., and Sorais, M. (2024) 'Bridging Cree knowledge and Western science to understand the decline in hunting success of migratory Canada geese', *Socio-Ecological Practice Research*, 03 May 2024. Available from: https://doi.org/10.1007/s42532-024-00182-0 [Accessed on 1 June 2024].

Gunn, A. (1995) 'Responses of arctic ungulates to climate change', in D.L. Peterson and D.R. Johnson (eds), *Human Ecology and Climate Change: People and Resources in the Far North*, pp. 89–104, Taylor & Francis, Washington, D.C.

Herodier, C. (2021) 'The decline of eelgrass on the coast means another Cree icon is disappearing as well', *The Nation*, 27 September 2021. Available from: http://nationnews.ca/community/the-decline-of-eelgrass-on-the-coast-means-another-cree-icon-is-disappearing-as-well/ [accessed 28 May 2024].

Hornig, J. (ed.) (1999) *Social and Environmental Impacts of the James Bay Hydroelectric Project,* McGill-Queen's University Press, Kingston & Montreal.

Iserhoff, A. (2006) *Presentation of the Grand Council of the Crees (Eeyou Istchee) and of The Cree Regional Authority on the Eastmain 1-A Rupert Project.* Available from: http://www.gcc.ca/archive/article.php?id=299 [accessed 3 June 2010].

Jain, P., Castellanos-Acuna, D., Coogan, S.C.P., Abatzoglou, J.T. and Flannigan, M.D. (2021) 'Observed increases in extreme fire weather driven by atmospheric humidity and temperature', *Nature Climate Change* 12: 63–70. Available from: https://www.nature.com/articles/s41558-021-01224-1 [accessed 25 May 2024].

Krupnik, I. and Jolly, D. (eds) (2002) *The Earth is Faster Now: Indigenous Observations of Arctic Environmental Change,* Arctic Research Consortium of the United States, Fairbanks, Alaska.

Laidler, G. (2006) 'Inuit and scientific perspectives on the relationship between sea ice and climatic change: The ideal complement?', *Climatic Change* 78(2–4): 407–44.

Lavoie, C. and Payette, S. (1994) 'Recent fluctuations of the lichen-spruce limit in subarctic Québec', *Journal of Ecology* 82: 725–34.

Le Goff, H., Flannigan, M. and Bergeron, Y. (2009) 'Potential changes in monthly fire risk in the eastern Canadian boreal forest under future climate change', *Canadian Journal of Forest Research* 39: 2369–80.

McBean, G. (2024) '2023 was the hottest year in history – and Canada is warming faster than anywhere else on earth,' *The Conversation*, January 11, 2024. Available from: https://theconversation.com/2023-was-the-hottest-year-in-history-and-canada-is-warming-faster-than-anywhere-else-on-earth-220997 [accessed 21 April 2024].

McCutcheon, S. (1996) *Electric Rivers: The Story of the James Bay Project*, Black Rose Books, Montreal.

Morantz, T. (2002) *The White Man's Gonna Getcha: The Colonial Challenge to the Crees in Quebec.* McGill-Queen's University Press, Montreal and Kingston.

Murphy-Klassen, H., Underwood, T., Shaly, S. and Czyrnyj, A. (2005) 'Long-term trends in spring arrival dates of migrant birds at Delta Marsh, Manitoba, in relation to climate change', *The Auk* 122(4): 1130–48.

Newton, J., Paci, C.D. and Ogden, A. (2005) 'Climate change and natural hazards in northern Canada: Integrating indigenous perspectives with government policy', *Mitigation and Adaptation Strategies for Global Change* 10: 541–71.

Niezen, R. (2008) *Defending the Land: Sovereignty and Forest Life in James Bay Cree Society,* 2nd edn, Prentice-Hall, New York.

Partlow, J. (2024) 'These wildfires never went out — they just moved underground', *The Washington Post*, 24 February, 2024. Available from: https://www.washingtonpost.com/climate-environment/2024/02/24/canada-wildfires-zombie-fires/ [accessed on 2 June 2024].

Peterson, D.L. and Johnson, D.R. (eds) (1995) *Human Ecology and Climate Change: People and Resources in the Far North,* Taylor & Francis, Washington, D.C.

Riewe, R. and Oakes, J. (2006) *Climate Change: Linking Traditional and Scientific Knowledge,* Aboriginal Issues Press, Winnipeg.

Scott, C. (1986) 'The socio-economic significance of waterfowl among Canada's aboriginal Cree: Native use and local management', in A.W. Diamond and F.L. Filion (eds), *The Value of Birds,* pp. 49–62, International Council for Bird Preservation, Cambridge, UK.

Scott, C. and Ettenger, K. (1994) *Great Whale Environmental Assessment Community Consultation: Final Report for Wemindji and Eastmain,* Vol 2., Part A, prepared for the Grand Council of the Crees (of Québec)/Cree Regional Authority, Montreal, August.

Shen, N. (2023) 'Ecologists say life will return to B.C. wildfire zone, but trees may never grow back', *CBC News,* 02 September 2023. Available from: https://www.cbc.ca/news/canada/british-columbia/wildfires-trees-wildlife-1.6955772 [accessed 20 May 2024].

Tanner, A. (1979) *Bringing Home Animals: Religious Ideology and Mode of Production of the Mistassini Cree Hunters,* Institute of Social and Economic Research, St. John's, Newfoundland.

Tremblay, M., et al. (2008) 'Climate change in northern Quebec: Adaptation strategies from community-based research', *Arctic* 61(Supp. 1): 27–34.

Ward, D., Reed, A., Sedinger, J., Black, J., Derksen, D. and Castelli, P. (2005) 'North American Brant: effects of changes in habitat and climate on population dynamics', *Global Change Biology* 11: 869–80.

Whitman, E., Parisien, M-A., Thompson, D.K., and Flannigan, M.D. (2019) 'Short-interval wildfire and drought overwhelm boreal forest resilience', *Scientific Reports* 9. Available from: https://www.nature.com/articles/s41598-019-55036-7 [accessed on 5 June 2024].

About the author

Kreg Ettenger is Associate Professor of Anthropology at the University of Southern Maine, where he teaches about indigenous peoples, the environment, tourism and other issues. He has worked in northern Quebec since 1994, conducting research on land use, forestry, heritage, tourism development and other topics in Cree communities.

Chapter 10

'The one who has changed is the person': Observations and explanations of climate change in the Ecuadorian Andes

Kristine Skarbø, Kristin Vander Molen, Rosa Ramos and Robert E. Rhoades[1]

This chapter reviews explanations of recent climatic change and its effects on agriculture from the perspective of the indigenous world view or 'cosmovision' of Kichwa farmers in Cotacachi, Ecuador. During recent years warmer temperatures and irregular rainfall have resulted in confusion regarding the agricultural calendar and higher instances of crop loss in this Andean community. Those villagers still rooted in the local 'cosmovision' link these changes to people's loss of respect for a living environment and weakened awareness of their intricate co-existence with the elements of nature. The chapter demonstrates that climate change not only involves technical and political economy discourses, but also for some people ideas and debates with moral and religious dimensions. The authors hope that the experiences and observations of these Kichwa farmers may serve as a reminder of our dependency on nature and that a reconsideration of our relationship to it will be necessary to abate current and future environmental change.

Introduction

Kichwa farmers in the highlands of Cotacachi, Ecuador explain that certain changes in the weather have disrupted the agricultural calendar in a way that is without referent in local memory. In this chapter we will review how the effects of climate change are perceived in the landscape and explained from the perspective of the local 'cosmovision', which exists today as a syncretism of Andean and Catholic beliefs (Sarmiento et al., 2008). This world view is reflective of that of the greater Andean tradition. It conceives of nature as alive and endowed with sentience and agency such that human–environment interactions are dialectical (Estermann, 1998; Apffel-Marglin and PRATEC, 1998). This is not the only lens through which climate change is perceived in the area. Government institutions, development organizations, telecommunication, and the formal education of youth also influence understandings of environment and climate. Here, however, we will focus on explanations from those who remain firmly rooted in the local cosmovision, primarily Cotacachi's elders. Like Turner and Clifton (2009), we believe that indigenous perspectives on human–environment relationships can offer insights for a world wanting to lessen its impact on the earth and construct a sustainable future. It is in this spirit that in the following pages we attempt to provide a channel for voices from Cotacachi on the issue of climate change.

Study area and methods

Cotacachi's 43 Andean communities cross the eastern slopes of the dormant Cotacachi volcano (4,939 m) located approximately 80 kilometres north of Ecuador's capital, Quito, in the province of Imbabura (PUCE, 2005). The communities' combined population is estimated to be 15,878 (UNORCAC, 2006). Although over 70 per cent of the working population is employed primarily in the neighbouring cities of Otavalo, Ibarra and Quito, agriculture continues to be important as slightly more than 84 per cent of the population owns and cultivates land, aiding livelihoods by supplementing inadequate income and seasonal unemployment (UNORCAC, 2006). While farmers with larger landholdings typically produce crops for sale in local and regional markets, the majority have only small plots (less than 1 hectare) where they grow food for household consumption. Fields span from 2,300 to 3,300 m in elevation and exhibit high agricultural biodiversity (Skarbø, 2006). Maize and beans are among the most commonly grown crops at lower altitudes, whereas higher up, tubers, grains and fava beans predominate. During the past decade maize has also been introduced into higher altitudes as warmer temperatures have allowed for its successful cultivation. Given that only 43 per cent of the population has access to irrigation water, most farmers depend on rainfall for the growth and maturation of their crops (UNORCAC, 2006).

Beyond and because of its millennia-old basis for subsistence in the area, agriculture also plays an important symbolic and material role in the constitution of culture and indigenous identity for the predominantly Kichwa population in Cotacachi (Rhoades, 2006). Although the locally grown diet is composed of a variety of foods, maize is the crop of primary cultural significance. It is considered the 'mother' of all crops and provides sustenance and social cohesion through a wealth of dishes consumed on everyday, festive and ritual occasions.

The information presented in this chapter was collected through participant observation, workshops and semi-structured interviews conducted by the authors in a 12-month period spanning 2009 and 2010. During this time, two of the authors lived with an indigenous family in the community of Turucu in Cotacachi's lowlands where they participated in agricultural and ritual activities throughout the year. Five workshops involving 200 participants were held, focusing on changes in weather and agriculture and explanations for their occurrence. Additionally, over 100 semi-structured interviews were conducted on a variety of climate- and agriculture-related topics with both men and women farmers between 20 and 90 years of age across 11 communities.

Climate and agriculture in Cotacachi: past and present

Farmers in Cotacachi explain that the year used to be divided into a rainy winter (September–April) and a sunny, windy summer (May–August), consistent with documentation of seasonality in neighbouring highland areas (Rovere and Knapp, 1988). Winter rains were punctuated by two *veranillos* (little summers): *el veranillo de las almas* (the little summer of Souls) in November, and *el veranillo del Niño* (the little summer of the Christ Child) in December. The agricultural calendar was fixed around this pattern. In lower altitudes, farmers typically intercropped maize with beans, fava beans, squashes, quinoa and lupines (*chochos*) in the early rains of September–December, and planted wheat and barley in the later rains of February and March. In March and April they would harvest some fresh maize but would leave most to dry on stalk for harvest in May and June. They would then plant fields with potatoes and peas, crops that thrive in the dry of summer, and harvest them in August along with the wheat and barley. Farmers then repeated the cycle when new rains began in September.

During the last years, however, Cotacacheños have noted increasingly irregular weather that deviates from the pattern described above. They report less rain overall and longer dry periods, lack of rain during what used to be wet winters and intense rain during what used to be dry summers. They further note decreasing levels in waterways and springs, as well as higher daytime temperatures. These changes pose challenges to local agriculture. The winter dry spells hinder the development of maize and beans. Rainy summers rot maize left to dry on stalk and leave potato and pea crops prey to blights. One farmer explains: 'My parents planted in accordance with the weather, winter or summer, as they knew in which season it would rain, they planted peacefully. Now they cannot do this anymore, because in the winter sometimes it rains and other times it is hot. One cannot plant anymore' (Workshop participant, 30 Nov 2009). Decreased water levels in local waterways further constrain agriculture by hindering irrigation and water use for livestock. Farmers also report greater loss of crops due to new pests and increased attacks of those already known, occurrences which may be associated with warmer temperatures and climatic change (Dangles et al., 2008).

When harvests are scarce, as they have been during the last decade, food security is threatened and the local diet changes as people tend to replace hearty local foods like soups and stews made from wholegrain quinoa, barley, wheat, cucurbits, maize and beans, with the purchase of less nutritious white rice and pasta. Lost harvests and more pests also inhibit the saving of seeds for the next year, threatening the maintenance of local biodiversity and the basis for future harvests. Summarized in the words of Cotacachi's mayor: 'There is a great climatic confusion [...]. There is disorganization, a confusion regarding the climate, regarding the time to sow, to harvest, and the effect is poverty, increased poverty. There is no production, there is no food, and because of this, there is malnutrition' (Alberto Anrango, 11 Nov 2009).

The lack of available local climate data makes it difficult to corroborate farmers' perceptions of change (Rhoades et al., 2006). However, farmers' observations are generally congruent with regional trends. Ontaneda (2007) reports high variability in rainfall in Ecuador's northern highlands during the past five decades, and decreased precipitation in more recent years (2000–2006). Throughout much of South America, including northern Ecuador, an increase in consecutive dry days as well as intense rainfall was registered during the last four decades of the 20th century (Haylock et al., 2006). In Latin America as a whole, the incidence and intensity of severe climate events such as El Niño/La Niña have also increased in recent decades (Magrin et al., 2007). These trends may partially explain farmers' observations of increased weather irregularity and reversed seasonality. The decreasing volume of the area's waterways is linked in part to the disappearance of Cotacachi's glacier during the last part of the 20th century (Rhoades et al., 2006). Andean tropical glaciers play an important role in regulating seasonal water availability and their retreat has been predicted to threaten water supplies (Bradley et al., 2006; Vuille et al., 2008). Farmers' observations of a warming environment are supported by climate data from the entire Andean region (Vuille et al., 2008; Vincent et al., 2005); in Ecuador's highlands mean temperatures on average increased by 0.9°C in the period 1960–2006 (Ontaneda, 2007).

Explanations of change

Many of Cotacachi's elders explain climate change and its effects as resulting from the loss of traditional beliefs and practices connected to the local cosmovision. This is an ongoing trend that they attribute to the formal education of youth and their lack of interest in agriculture, the 'modernization' and mechanization of agriculture, and sometimes to the increase of evangelicalism as well. As education exposes young people to alternative world views, activities and professional opportunities, they lose interest in agriculture and belief in the world view to which it has traditionally been tied. The contrast in perspectives within families is so generationally marked that when parents and elders share their beliefs, children often laugh and tell them that they 'are crazy to believe such lies'. The modernization and mechanization of agriculture, in turn, are said to distance people from direct interaction with the earth and negatively affect human and environmental health. Finally, evangelicalism is considered to challenge the local world view as its advocates reportedly discourage expressions of respect for the natural world which they misinterpret as adoration. As one woman explains: 'They [evangelists] come and say "you adore the earth and you are adoring the rocks, adoring the water, adoring the mountains", but we do not adore them, all that we do is respect them because we feel that they have life'. (40-year-old woman, Quitugo)

The local cosmovision

Traditional beliefs and practices in Cotacachi are founded upon respect for the natural world and its constituent elements. Mother Earth (*Pacha mama*), Mother Water (*Yaku mama*), Mother Rain (*Tamya mama*), Mother Cloud (*Fuyu mama*), Mother Wind (*Wayra mama*), Father Hurricane (*Akapana tayta*), Father Sun (*Inti tayta*), Mother Grain (*Grano mama*) and Mother Fruit (*Fruto mama*) are all alive. They are *personajes*: living elements that have personalities, roles and relationships to one another and to the local population as well. The two dormant volcanoes that dominate the area's natural landscape, *Mama Cotacachi* (Mother Cotacachi, also named *Urku rasu* (Snow-capped mountain) or *Urku mama* (Mother mountain)), and *Tayta Imbabura* (Father Imbabura), are also bestowed with life – they are God's (*Achi tayta*) stewards of the region, and bound by marital ties.

In order for there to be successful harvests and a secure food source, people throughout past generations have depended on the will and care of these *personajes*. Yet people are not passive subjects – their actions also affect the behaviour of the *personajes*; the communication is two-way. In awareness of their dependence on the natural world, people in Cotacachi have traditionally demonstrated respect for the elements of their landscape, through both daily activities and on ritual occasions. They have asked for permission before entering sacred springs and mountains, and they have carried out prayers, offerings (*ofrendas*) and masses (*misas*) for nature's elements – to keep them awake, to keep them happy, to remind them how important and revered they are among people, to call them to come or to ask them to withdraw. *Misas* and *ofrendas* were primarily carried out on sacred mounds (*tolas*). For example, people would throw grain and bean flours from atop *tolas* on days of fog in offering to Mother Cloud 'for her to be orderly, for what is happening now not to happen, for it to rain as it has to rain, and for the clouds to come down and sip from the springs, only to sip, and not to drink them dry' (Workshop participant, 20 Nov 2009). For Mother Earth, 12 counts of potatoes, maize, beans, fava beans and other foods would be blessed on a *tola* and buried in the centre of unproductive fields amidst prayer and throws of blessed water. For Mother Wind, 12 pieces of each crop would be blessed in the town of Ibarra, then buried in the Garden of *Mama Cotacachi*: a sacred place filled with wild flowers close to her summit.

Reverence was not only shown in rituals, it was also expressed through everyday life, asking Mother Earth's permission to enter fields and planting with what elders describe as 'faith and heart', in conversation with *Mama Cotacachi*: 'I am going to leave you in charge of these grains so that next year you return them to me multiplied'. An elderly man, frustrated by the carelessness of the young of today, explains:

> It is not only a question of working, weeding or watching the moon.[2] If a person weeds without having faith in God, he will not have a good harvest. [...] My mother always said that one has to believe in Mother Earth, one has to believe in God, in the Hurricane, in the breeze of the wind. 'One has to respect them so that they will also respect our crops', she said. When a crop was lost, she said, 'Who of you have faulted in your respect of Mother Earth? You have to regret and apologize'. (89-year-old man, Quitugo)

Effects of the loss of beliefs, respect and practices

When respect and communication are lost, it is thought that the natural world becomes upset and that agricultural production will invariably decline. Many elders and some young people explain the current climatic situation as punishment or a test of God, or Mother Earth. For example, some farmers describe the increase in pests and plant diseases as occurring because people have forgotten God; he drops handfuls of pests to the earth such that he might be newly remembered. Others explain that in the past they successfully eliminated the presence of pests by paying for mass, but, they say, having forgotten God and the life in nature, this no longer happens.

> Nature has life. Why do you think that when you bury a seed it grows? Because Mother Earth knows that she must make it grow. [...] I think that realizing this, we should start respecting our Mother Earth, our Lord. But since we do none of this, I think that it affects us, and because of this we also receive all these punishments. Well, they say that one should not say punishment, but they are making us remember that Mother Earth has life. (49-year-old man, San Pedro)

Elders note that during dry spells children are no longer gathered to call for Mother Rain, and so, they say, she remains absent. They also explain the lack of rain as caused by the removal of native vegetation which they believe 'call the rains' by drawing clouds to the area's waterways where they fill with water before releasing rain. During the last decades much native vegetation has been lost, ceding space to roads, construction and eucalyptus plantations. Without this vegetation it is thought that the clouds are unable to form and fill with water, and that instead winds blow them away.

In explanation of diminishing waterways some say that Mother Water sleeps when people do not make offerings to her, and that as she sleeps her volume diminishes. Since the implementation of water distribution systems during the last decades, community members no longer travel to the springs and waterways where they once made offerings to ensure the continued plenitude and availability of water. Tubing now delivers water to individual homes for which elders note that people have become physically and culturally removed from the resource. Some stress that this removal must be re-bridged as they note Cotacachi's youth as sharing a false sense of security about future water availability. They consider that ritual offerings to Mother Water should be restored among youth such that waterways remain plentiful. It is also believed that springs can dry from lack of demonstrated reverence by their users, flee in fright of loud noises and become covered by landslides only to re-emerge from the earth elsewhere – as far away as neighbouring mountains. In such cases the springs may return but only through ritual: ceremoniously calling the water and cleansing it with the help of a *yachak* (shaman) so as to cure it of its fright. Without this knowledge, belief in Mother Water as life bearing, and the awareness that water originates from the earth, elders express concern that the vulnerability of water as a resource will not be understood.

Elders also tell about dreams in which they have experienced revelations about the current climatic situation and about the importance of continuing the beliefs and practices that they know. In one workshop, an elder shared a dream of his, explaining the recent increased intensity of sunlight:

> I had a dream about Father Sun, where he said that he only opened his eye a little bit. This is why the sun is shining normally. But Father Sun said, 'When I get angry and open my eye wider, I will burn plants, houses, people, I will burn everything'. Father Sun says that in the coming years he will open his eye wide. Then, he will finish with all of us. Nobody will be saved. (80-year-old man, San Pedro)

Discussion and conclusion

Indigenous knowledge in Cotacachi – when considered as *a way of knowing the world* (Berkes, 2009) – exhibits resilience in the face of recent climatic change. The local knowledge system, grounded in the indigenous cosmovision, has been shaped by generations of local experience infused with new ideas through regional and global flows of people, information, goods, and non-native plants and animals throughout the past millennia. Even though some of its current content, like knowledge of weather prediction and the timing of agricultural tasks, seems to lose its utility in the face of climate change, on a more fundamental level, the cosmovision retains its explanatory power. The tales, teachings and cautionary dreams of elders offer precise frames of reference for the interpretation of climatic conditions for which local memory has no referent.

Yet, current cultural change is so strong that many young people reject the beliefs and practices rooted in the cosmovision, which according to elders provokes environmental change. Without the continued daily and ritual demonstration of reverence for Mother Earth, Mother Rain, Mother Wind, Mother Water, and Father Sun, they become disengaged and lose interest in performing the activities that sustain human life. Instead, they fall asleep, drift away, or become angry at both people and each other, the result of which is a less habitable environment. As one man states: 'It is not that the climate has changed. The one who has changed is the person, he has lost beliefs and all respect'. (89-year-old man, Quitugo)

Although understanding of climate change by Cotacachi's elders is culturally and locally contained, it might still offer reflection on some of the broader issues of climate change and human–environment interaction. From their perspective, the way people perceive the natural world, its workings and their relationship to it is of ultimate importance in shaping actions that in turn influence a shared environment. They point to our dependence on the natural world and the dialectic that characterizes our interactions with it, cautioning that to view nature as inherently static or as constant in regard to the provision of human needs is to underestimate the importance of our actions towards it.

Further, they caution against viewing the environment in purely mechanistic terms. One woman explains: 'the environmentalists say that one should not cut down trees because they filter the air, they give purity to the air, nothing more. But they only reach so far, they don´t arrive at the depth of it, that there must be contact and communication [with nature]' (40-year-old woman, Quitugo). According to this view, action based on physical understanding of the environment alone is insufficient and likely to be unsustainable. When we consider the impressive body of scientific information that exists on current climatic and environmental change against the lack of mitigating efforts around the globe, it becomes apparent that this knowledge alone seems to be an insufficient trigger of ameliorative action (Heyd and Brooks, 2009).

The roads toward more integrated and sustainable human–environment interactions may be many. The landscape perceptions and principles of interaction with the natural world contained in the knowledge system of Cotacachi's elders bear similarity to those of indigenous peoples in places such as the Pacific North West (Cruikshank, 2001), Tibet (Byg and Salick, 2009) and surely others as well. They are also related to views of nature and norms of behaviour formulated in more modern Western traditions, such as Deep Ecology (Naess, 1973, 1989). The case presented here offers an example of a holistic view of the world; a view that has old roots and still guides the lives of a few. It is our hope that the *Cotacacheños* cited above may remind us of our dependency on nature and that reconsideration of our relationship to it will be necessary to abate current and future environmental change.

Author updates to the 2025 edition

In the years following our study, anthropological research on climate change in the Andes has continued to provide ethnographic insights into the different knowledges and beliefs – Western scientific, religious, indigenous or cosmological, and other – that influence local explanations of environmental change and assignations of responsibility (Jurt et al., 2015; Paerregaard, 2020; Scoville-Simonds, 2018). As in the case of Cotacachi presented here, some of this work has focused primarily on describing those knowledges and beliefs (Paerregaard, 2013; Scoville-Simonds, 2018) while other studies have focused on how specifically they are enacted (Cometti, 2020; Stensrud, 2016). Much of the work in both areas shows how different knowledges and beliefs are not mutually exclusive, either through examples of syncretism in the case of the former (Schnegg et al., 2021) or through examples of complementary cultural (e.g. offerings to local waterways to increase abundance) and material practices (e.g. use of irrigation technologies to manage availability) in the case of the latter (Cometti, 2020; Stensrud, 2016). There has also been a call to advance this work beyond the mere documentation of such complementary practices in order to more fully understand the outcomes they produce (Stensrud, 2016).

Underlying this collective work is the acceleration of climate change and its impacts in the Andes (Dussaillant et al., 2019; Vuille et al., 2018). Those impacts influence not only the construction and enactment of different knowledges and beliefs but also the wellbeing of individuals, households, and communities, for example through increased threat and occurrence of glacial hazards, variation in water availability for agriculture, and relatedly, transitions from rural to urban livelihoods (Blackmore et al., 2021; Motschmann et al., 2020). Agreement around the need for urgent action to abate glacier retreat in the Andes has been growing among researchers, activists, and politicians, yet there is not necessarily consensus on what entities are most responsible for effecting action and what outcomes may be expected to result (Stensrud, 2016).

Amidst this lack of consensus, some researchers have begun to suggest that indigenous knowledges and beliefs should be given consideration beyond their documentation in such works as climate change ethnographies, to be included directly within climate science and adaptation policy (Harris, 2017). In particular, they ask what opportunities exist for the language of 'expertise' in science and policy to be broadened so that all stakeholders may be heard, different ways of knowing may inform one another, and new spaces of understanding may be created to inform climate action (Harris, 2017; Pajares et al., 2021). From this perspective, science and policy may be reconceptualized as processes in which to engage rather than as outcomes to be achieved, and it is noted that herein may be another role for anthropology (see also Crane et al., 2021). This role would be for anthropology to lend its capacity for reflexive analysis to considerations of procedural equity within, and distributional equity resulting from, those processes (Crane et al., 2021). As different countries in the Andes begin to develop and implement climate change adaptation policies (see for example Gobierno de Colombia, 2021; Gobierno del Ecuador, 2023; Gobierno del Perú, 2021), there may be increasing opportunities to do so. However, this will require policymakers to make space for ethnographers to engage in the collection and mediation of knowledges and actions informing and emanating from these potentially crucial plans.

In the end, as our then (in 2010) 89-year-old interviewee put it: 'the one who has changed is the person'. In order for these and other climate change adaptation and mitigation policies to be truly effective, they must thus account for the world views and human–environmental understandings underpinning people's actions.

Notes

[1] Robert E. Rhoades played a key role in inspiring and inciting the work behind this paper, but unfortunately left this world before its completion.

[2] During times past, farmers in Cotacachi used lunar phases as guides for the timing of agricultural activities. A smaller number of farmers continue this practice today.

References

Apffel-Marglin, F. and PRATEC (1998) *The Spirit of Regeneration: Andean Culture Confronting Western Notions of Development*, Zed Books Ltd, London – New York.
Berkes, F. (2009) 'Indigenous ways of knowing and the study of environmental change', *Journal of the Royal Society of New Zealand* 39: 151–56.
Blackmore, I., Rivera, C., Waters, W. F., Iannotti, L. and Lesorogol, C. (2021) 'The impact of seasonality and climate variability on livelihood security in the Ecuadorian Andes', *Climate Risk Management* 32: 100279.
Bradley, R.S., Vuille, M., Diaz, H.F., and Vergara, W. (2006) Threats to Water Supplies in the Tropical Andes, *Science* 312: 1755–1756.
Byg, A. and Salick, J. (2009) 'Local perspectives on a global phenomenon: Climate change in Eastern Tibetan villages', *Global Environmental Change* 19: 156–66.
Cometti, G. (2020) 'A Cosmopolitical Ethnography of a Changing Climate among the Q'ero of the Peruvian Andes', *Anthropos* 115: 37–52.
Crane, T. A., Roncoli, C., Meyers, J. and Hunt, S. E. (2021) 'On the Merits of Not Solving Climate Change', in L. Pedersen and L. Cliggett (eds.), *The SAGE Handbook in Cultural Anthropology*, pp. 480–501, Sage Press, Newbury Park, California.

Cruikshank, J. (2001) 'Glaciers and climate change: Perspectives from oral tradition', *Arctic*, 54: 377–93.

Dangles, O., Carpio, C., Barargan, A.R., Zeddam, J.-L., and Silvain, J.-F. (2008) 'Temperature as a key driver of ecological sorting among invasive pest species in the tropical Andes', *Ecological Applications* 18: 1795–1809.

Dussaillant, I., Berthier, E., Brun, F., Masiokas, M., Hugonnet, R., Favier, V., Rabatel, A., Pitte, P. and Ruiz, L. (2019) 'Two decades of glacier mass loss along the Andes', *Nature Geoscience* 12: 802–808.

Estermann, J. (1998) *Filosofía Andina*, Ediciones Abya-Yala, Quito, Ecuador.

Gobierno de Colombia (2021) *Plan nacional de Adaptación al Cambio Climático (PNACC), ABC: Adaptación Bases Conceptuales, Marco Conceptual y Lineamientos.* Available at: https://unfccc.int/documents/302817 [Accessed June 1 2024].

Gobierno del Ecuador (2023) *Plan Nacional de Adaptación al Cambio Climático del Ecuador (2023–2027).* Available at: https://unfccc.int/documents/627465 [Accessed June 1 2024].

Gobierno del Perú (2021) *Plan Nacional de Adaptación al Cambio Climático del Perú: un insumo para la actualización de la Estrategia Nacional ante el Cambio Climático.* Available at: https://unfccc.int/sites/default/files/resource/NAP-Peru-2021.pdf [Accessed April 11 2025].

Harris, D. M. (2017) 'Mountain-bodies, experiential wisdom: the Kallawaya cosmovisión and climate change adaptation', *Third World Thematics: A TWQ Journal* 2: 376–390.

Haylock, M.R., Peterson, T.C., Alves, L.M., Ambrizzi, T., Anunciação, Y.M.T., Baez, J., Barros, V.R., Berlato, M.A., Bidegain, M., Coronel, G., Corradi, V., Garcia, V.J., Grimm, A.M., Karoly, D., Marengo, J.A., Marino, M.B., Moncunill, D.F., Nechet, D., Quintana, J., and Rebello, E. (2006) Trends in Total and Extreme South American Rainfall in 1960–2000 and Links with Sea Surface Temperature, *Journal of Climate* 19: 1490–1512.

Heyd, T. and Brooks, N. (2009) 'Exploring cultural dimensions of adaptation to climate change', in W.N. Adger, I. Lorenzoni and K. O'Brien (eds.), *Adapting to Climate Change: Thresholds, Values, Governance*, pp. 269–282, Cambridge University Press, Cambridge.

Jurt, C., Burga, M. D., Vicuña, L., Huggel, C. and Orlove, B. (2015) 'Local perceptions in climate change debates: insights from case studies in the Alps and the Andes', *Climatic Change* 133: 511–523.

Magrin, G., Gay García, C., Cruz Choque, D., Giménéz, J.C., Moreno, A.R., Nagy, G.J., Nobre, C., and Villamizar, A., (2007) 'Latin America', in M. Parry, O. Canziani, J. Palutikof, P. van der Linden, and C. Hanson (eds.), *Climate Change 2007: Impacts, Adaptation and Vulnerability. Contribution of Working Group II to the Fourth Assessment Report of the Intergovernmental Panel on Climate Change*, pp. 581–615, Cambridge University Press, Cambridge, UK.

Motschmann, A., Huggel, C., Carey, M., Moulton, H., Walker-Crawford, N. and Muñoz, R. (2020) 'Losses and damages connected to glacier retreat in the Cordillera Blanca, Peru', *Climatic Change* 162: 837–858.

Naess, A. (1973) 'The Shallow and the Deep, Long-Range Ecology Movement. A Summary', Inquiry 16: 95–100.

Naess, A. (1989) *Ecology, Community and Lifestyle: Outline of an Ecosophy*, Cambridge University Press, Cambridge.

Ontaneda, G. (2007) *Evidencias del Cambio Climático en Ecuador. Actualización*, Instituto Nacional de Meteorología e Hidrología, Quito.

Paerregaard, K. (2013) 'Bare rocks and fallen angels: Environmental change, climate perceptions and ritual practice in the Peruvian Andes', *Religions* 4: 290–305.

Paerregaard, K. (2020) 'Communicating the inevitable: climate awareness, climate discord, and climate research in Peru's highland communities', *Environmental Communication* 14: 112–125.

Pajares, E., Calvo, E., Palacio, J.I., Munar, J.J., and Loret de Mola, C. (2020) 'Ancestral comprehensions for a policy for the future of the Earth: The narrative of the South American Andes in the face of the global climate crisis', *Pace Envtl. L. Rev.* 38: 383–422.

Pontificia Universidad Católica del Ecuador (2005) *El Cantón Cotacachi: Espacio y Sociedad*, Ediguias C. Ltda, Quito.

Rhoades, R.E., Zapata Ríos, X. and Aragundy, J. (2006) 'El cambio climático en Cotacachi', in R.E. Rhoades (ed.), *Desarrollo con Identidad. Comunidad, Cultura y Sustentabilidad en los Andes,* Abya Yala, Quito.

Rovere, O. and Knapp, G. (1988) 'Selection of climatic scenarios', in M. L. Parry, T. R. Carter and N. T. Konijn (eds.), *The Impact of Climatic Variations on Agriculture,* vol. 2: Assessments in Semi-Arid Regions, pp. 399–412, Kluwer Academic Publishers, Dordrecht.

Sarmiento, F.O., Cotacachi, C., and Carter, L.E. (2008) 'Sacred Imbakucha: Intangibles in the conservation of cultural landscapes in Ecuador', in J.M. Mallarach (ed.), *Protected Landscapes and Cultural and Spiritual Values,* vol. 2 in the series Values of Protected Landscapes and Seascapes, IUCN, GTZ and Obra Social de Caixa Catalunya, pp.114–31, Kasparek Verlag, Heidelberg.

Schnegg, M., O'Brian, C. I. and Sievert, I. J. (2021) 'It's our fault: A global comparison of different ways of explaining climate change', *Human Ecology* 49: 327–339.

Scoville-Simonds, M. (2018) 'Climate, the Earth, and God-entangled narratives of cultural and climatic change in the Peruvian Andes', *World Development* 110: 345–359.

Skarbø, K. (2006) 'Living, dwindling, losing, finding: Status and changes in agrobiodiversity of Cotacachi', in R.E. Rhoades (ed.), *Development with Identity: Community, Culture, and Sustainability in the Andes*, CAB International, Balfour, U.K.

Stensrud, A. B. (2016) 'Climate change, water practices and relational worlds in the Andes', *Ethnos* 81: 75–98

Turner, N. and Clifton, H. (2009) '"It's so different today": Climate change and indigenous lifeways in British Columbia, Canada', *Global Environmental Change* 19: 180–90.

Unión de Organizaciones de Campesinas e Indígenas de Cotacachi (UNORCAC) (2006) *UNORCAC en cifras*, unpublished manuscript, UNORCAC, Cotacachi, Ecuador.

Vincent, L.A., Peterson, T.C., Barros, V.R., Marino, M.B., Rusticucci, M., Carrasco, G., Ramirez, E., Alves, L.M., Ambrizzi, T., Berlato, M.A., Grimm,

A.M., Marengo, J.A., Molion, L., Moncunill, D.A., Rebello, E., Anunciação, Y.M.T., Quintana, J., Santos, J.L., Baez, J., Coronel, G., Garcia, J., Trebejo, I., Bidegain, M., Haylock, M.R., and Karoly, D. (2005) Observed trends in indices of daily temperature extrems in South America 1960–2000, *Journal of Climate* 18: 5011–5023.

Vuille, M., Carey, M., Huggel, C., Buytaert, W., Rabatel, A., Jacobsen, D., Soruco, A., Villacis, M., Yarleque, C. and Timm, O. E. (2018) 'Rapid decline of snow and ice in the tropical Andes: Impacts, uncertainties and challenges ahead', *Earth-science reviews* 176: 195–213.

Vuille, M., Francou, B., Wagnon, P., Juen, I., Kaser, G., Mark, B.G., and Bradley, R.S. (2008) 'Climate change and tropical Andean glaciers: Past, present and future', *Earth-Science Reviews* 89: 79–96.

About the authors

Kristine Skarbø is a PhD candidate of Anthropology at the University of Georgia. Her dissertation research explores dynamics in food and agriculture in the Ecuadorian Andes.

Kristin Vander Molen is a PhD student in Anthropology at the University of Georgia, and conducts research on agriculture in the Ecuadorian Andes.

Rosa Ramos is a farmer and community leader from the Kichwa community of Quitugo in Cotacachi, Ecuador.

The late **Robert E. Rhoades** was a Distinguished Research Professor in Anthropology at the University of Georgia. His extensive research spanned diverse themes and places, including agriculture and mountain communities in the Andes.

Chapter 11

Good intentions, bad memories, and troubled capital: American Indian knowledge and action in renewable energy projects

Raymond I. Orr and David B. Anderson

In response to the adverse effects of climate change on American Indian communities, tribal governments are focusing their resources toward environmentally sound social and economic activities. This response is based on a wide variety of cultural, economic, and legal factors: a contemporary identity that is linked to ecological stewardship; lifeways that are embedded in local environmental rhythms; and a desire to take advantage of federal subsidies that provide 'green jobs'. And, these factors in combination have led to a common desire throughout Indian Country to develop renewable energy production projects on reservation lands. Despite such interest, the development of these projects has been limited. This chapter explores legal and social obstacles faced by communities in planning and implementing such projects. Although numerous barriers exist, the authors are optimistic about the prospects of effective local participation in renewable energy production on American Indian reservations.

Introduction

Global warming poses in equal parts an ecological and ideological threat to indigenous North America. While American Indian communities' contributions to the causes of climate change have been relatively minimal, the consequences of climate change on these communities may prove substantial, with an acute impact on indigenous lifeways and knowledge systems through a change in customs and economies. As such, the effects of climate change represent a direct threat both to the sovereignty of the First Nations and Native communities, which seek to shape a progressive response to the challenges, and to the relationship that Native peoples have with the land. One response by American Indian tribes to address climate change has been to embrace development of renewable energy production on tribal lands. This response fits within their knowledge systems that understand humans as one of the land's most essential stewards.

We believe that two types of indigenous knowledge systems are present when American Indian tribes engage in renewable energy production projects. The first is the knowledge system that is typically cosmological and informs environmental stewardship. Second, less cosmological knowledge systems emerge, however, as tribes pursue renewable energy projects. These systems revolve around obstacles to the successful completion of such energy projects and satisfying ecologically responsible preferences. Following a broad definition outlined by Flavier et al. of *indigenous knowledge* as 'the information base for a society, which facilitates communication and decision-making' (1995: 479), we suggest that the inadequacies of Federal Indian law and policy, and the memories hewn from previous exploitative relationships form two other knowledge systems that erect barriers to the cosmological knowledge preference beholden to ecological responsibility. If 'Indigenous information systems are dynamic, and are continually influenced by internal creativity and experimentation as well as by contact with external systems' (Flavier et al., 1995: 479), then it stands to reason that community memory and policy context – both of which have substantial effect in Indian Country – must be included as a second type of indigenous knowledge system.

This chapter divides this second type of knowledge system into two categories of challenges: legal and sociological. The peculiar and often ambiguous legal standing of American Indian reservations in the United States, we argue, creates problems for securing both private and public funding of renewable energy projects. Though not typically associated with indigenous knowledge, the relationship between tribes and law, formed out of 'contact with external systems', certainly does create an 'information base for a society' (Flavier et al., 1995: 479) and one that is essential to decision-making. Possibly closer to the standard use of indigenous knowledge than federal legal relationships would be the conclusions that American Indians make about outsiders. This is both knowledge of, and a significant complication to renewable energy production which relies on non-indigenous technical expertise. A long history of exploitation of Native Americans by non-natives has endowed many in the indigenous community with a deep scepticism of outsiders which, in turn, forms a knowledge system that hampers partnerships needed to complete such technically advanced renewable energy projects.

Climate change and its impact on Native North America

Climate change disproportionally affects the poorest nations and communities. Despite often contributing less greenhouse gases per capita than their wealthier counterparts, developing nations are largely located in geographic zones that increase their vulnerability to weather-related catastrophes (Mendelsohn et al., 2006). And, this unequal aspect of climate change whereby those who were less responsible suffer more severely is a pattern replicated within marginal communities in many developed countries, including the United States.

It is predicted that climate change will impact American Indians earlier and with greater severity than other Americans. According to *Native Communities and Climate Change*, a study initiated by the Natural Resources Law Center at the University of Colorado, the effects of climate change will be widespread and adverse to North American indigenous communities due to their intimate relationships with the local environments (Hanna, 2007). In the Pacific Northwest, melting snow-caps and increased precipitation will continue to alter the hydraulic cycle. Such changes will disrupt salmon breeding and migrations patterns in the region that have been central to the ways of life for Pacific Northwestern indigenous communities. A warmer Alaska diminishes Arctic ice and modifies breeding and grazing of livestock and hunting grounds for seals, polar bears and caribou. Such change in game behaviour and availability would undermine the subsistence patterns of Arctic indigenous populations. In addition to reducing traditional game, thinner ice creates more difficult, dangerous and expensive travelling conditions for these groups as well as increasing the occurrence of erosion in their seaside villages.

American Indians in the South-western region of the United States are also susceptible to small variations in temperature and precipitation. An increase of 2°C in temperature may translate to a 20 per cent decline of water in the Colorado River Basin (Christensen et al., 2004; Udall, 2007). Such a decrease in water flow will affect tribes in this region that rely upon agriculture and livestock production for their economies. And, in addition to effects on the economic activities of tribes, these environmental changes will also put a strain on the harder-to-measure systems of tribal knowledge and culture (Cordalis and Suagee, 2008). For instance, water and river flow serve a significant role in political and religious life in the South-western region's Rio Grande Pueblos. Rainfall is limited in this region and these groups rely upon irrigation-based agriculture in which the flooding of fields requires a high degree of social coordination as in other communities throughout the world (Wittfogel, 1957; Lansing, 1991). Religious and political elites organize *corvée* labour and perform ceremonies that accompany seasonal changes. A prolonged change in the water level of the Rio Grande will disrupt these ceremonies and undermine both the harvest and the communal relationships that coordinate agricultural irrigation.

And, furthermore, it must be understood that this ecological disruption is an affront to the essence of the indigenous identity and knowledge. The claim that American Indians have a strong, if not intimate, connection with their ecological contexts is widely discussed in professional scholarship as well as popularized accounts of American Indians by Euro-Americans and Indians since the colonial era (Krech, 1999; Harkin and Lewis, 2007). The Native as environmentalist as a central component to American Indians' way of life goes as far back as representations of the *Noble Indian* or the

Noble Savage given by John Dryden in his *Conquest of Grenada 1670* (NB Jean-Jacques Rousseau is often, though erroneously, credited with coining the phrase 'Noble Savage'). Contemporary scholars typically refer to this as the 'Ecological Indian' (Krech, 1999).

A response by Native North America: renewable energy projects

We contend that indigenous knowledge contains both information and preferences. And concerned by these changes, and consistent with their tradition of environmental stewardship, many tribes are actively interested in acting to address climate change (Krakoff, 2008). Accordingly, many tribes are working to develop renewable energy production on tribal reservations (Cordalis and Suagee, 2008). Renewable energy generally is a segment of the contemporary economy that is rapidly growing in society at large and in American Indian communities (see, Reynolds, 2007; Nighthorse, 2002). In particular, the abundance of potential wind energy sites found throughout Native lands has led observers to declare that American Indian reservations could serve as the '[Saudi] Arabia of the Wind' (Melmer, 2002). According to a 2009 National Renewable Energy Laboratory report, there are at present 16 active commercial wind turbine sites operated on Native reservations, spread mainly across the Dakotas, the Great Plains and the Southwest (NREL Report, 2009).

Generally, these tribal renewable energy projects are particularly promising due to: tribes' legal status as semi-sovereign entities which allows for great flexibility and communal action; their cultural and religious beliefs that encourage stewardship of the land (Deloria, 1973); and their heightened vulnerability to climate change (Hanna, 2007). All of these qualities place American Indians in a uniquely advantageous position to develop and promote 'clean' energy. One of the more publicized projects is the Southern Ute Tribe's production of bio-fuels in South-western Colorado (Johnson, 2009). The Southern Utes have utilized substantial capital reserves from mining to generate the capacity to produce innovative types of bio-fuels. When asked about the implications of the project beyond monetary gain, the tribal chairman referenced the significance of the project in light of traditional tribal values of environmental consciousness: 'It's a marriage of an older way of thinking into a modern time' (Johnson, 2009).

However, 'success stories' regarding renewable energy projects, such as the Southern Ute, are surprisingly rare. Despite the Department of Energy appropriating funds for renewable energy feasibility studies on reservations as early as 1994 (conducting 17 feasibility studies in 1995 and 18 in 1996) (Sargent and Chabot, 1996), the first commercial wind turbine tribally owned and operated was not put into operation until 2003, nearly a decade later. Furthermore, only one of the 16 wind farms mentioned above had a production capacity greater than 1 megawatt (MW). American Indian groups have faced political, legal and social tensions that have clearly hampered such projects. Evidence of project stalling appears ethnographically even when it is generally avoided in media outlets and policy circles. When asked about how far his tribe is in developing renewable energy projects, a southwestern tribal council member replied, 'we talk about that all the time, it is something we are interested in, we have a consultant who is working on it for us but it hasn't gone far.' Similarly, as another tribal official said, 'there is a lot of talk but not much action' (Tribal leader interview, 2010). This chapter examines legal and social contexts that are not generally attributed as undermining renewable energy's potential on reservations.

Though enthusiasm has surrounded indigenous sustainable energy projects, the implementation of such projects has not been as widespread as desired and we propose that two types of impediments generally emerge: tribal and federal legal inadequacies that hamper tribal access to capital; and sociological scepticism from tribal leadership that jeopardizes partnerships.

The remainder of this chapter examines these two categories of impediments to American Indian renewable energy projects. Though not comprehensive in identifying all obstacles (technical problems are outside the scope of this project), each section highlights the sometimes hidden social, political and legal dynamics that account for the difficulty in getting renewable wind energy projects 'in the air'.

Tribal and federal legal inadequacies

Renewable energy production requires capital-intensive infrastructure. For example, industry-standard delivery cost for wind turbines is $1.37 million/MW of capacity (Morales, 2010). Thus, a wind farm with 10 MW or greater capacity has upfront costs into the tens of millions of dollars. Some tribes are able to draw upon large capital reserves from successful real estate, gaming, or other economic activity. However, most tribal ventures require outside capital funding. Potential capital sources include private investors and government grants and loans, though the current laws general are inadequate to support widespread access to such capital sourcing.

Public funding takes the form of government grants, subsidized loans or guarantees on tribal bond offerings, and tax incentives. Recently, federal funding has been more forthcoming. In early 2010 as part of the Stimulus Package, the Acoma Band of Pueblo was awarded $7 million in tribal economic development bonds issuance authority to be used toward construction of a 15 MW wind farm (Kamerick, 2010). This award matches the stated federal policy of supporting access to capital for tribes developing renewable energy production, as articulated by President Obama at the opening of the Tribal Nations Conference in November 2009: 'Up to 15 per cent of our potential wind energy resources are on Native American land, and the potential for solar energy is even higher [...] We are securing tribal access to financing and investments for new energy projects.' With similar grants to the Navajo Tribe and other native communities, there is promise that the federal government will uphold its commitment to provide increased access to capital to indigenous communities that are otherwise excluded from capital markets.

However, several changes to federal law and policy would increase the ability of indigenous communities to secure financing for, and facilitate the development of, renewable energy projects. Proposed Congressional legislation would take a significant step forward toward producing a much more conducive federal tax and regulatory environment. This legislation would amend the Tax Code to allow income tax-exempt tribal governments and tribal business entities to receive Production Tax Credits (PTCs) for their share of renewable energy produced, which they otherwise would not be entitled to receive given their tax status as governmental entities. Tribes can then either transfer these tax credits to private partners in the projects – which are of value to these non-tribal investors and therefore would decrease the cost of capital for indigenous communities – or the tribes can convert the credits into cash grants to meet their development costs in the projects. The proposed legislation would also simplify required leasing and right-of-way approval from the Department of Interior as well as delegate responsibility for conducting environmental impact studies on proposed projects to the tribal communities. Such legislation has been introduced repeatedly in Congress in some form over the past several years, most recently in 2010 as the Indian Promotion and Parity Act, but has stalled in committee each legislative session.

Although the public sector can play a significant role in supporting native renewable energy efforts, private funding from non-tribal investors will be the most significant capital source for widespread development of tribal renewable energy projects in the free-market economy. However, non-tribal investors are reluctant to invest with tribal partners because the legal systems that govern transactions on tribal lands are underdeveloped and unknown off the reservations. In particular, the majority of tribes lack a legal code for secured lending and other critical commercial transaction laws. Furthermore, the sovereignty of the tribal governments and attendant business associations leaves non-tribal partners uncertain of how and under what law contract disputes will be resolved. If a federal court determines that a tribal court has jurisdiction over a contract dispute, non-tribal partners find themselves at the mercy of unfamiliar tribal courts. Some non-tribal parties have responded to the uncertainty by demanding agreements that limit to as great an extent as possible the legal and other transactional uncertainty of these dealings – specifically by demanding waivers of sovereign immunity and forum selection clauses (McSloy, 2009). Regardless of the result, this legal uncertainty results in high transaction costs, which can effectively exclude many indigenous communities from capital markets (Miller, 2008). One non-tribal business partner remarked that 'doing business on a reservation is more difficult than doing business in China' (Barringer, 2008).

The tribes that have engaged in the most sophisticated financing transactions with non-tribal parties have adopted state statutory frameworks – and excluded unwritten traditional tribal practices from having legal effect – to provide a familiar legal framework for non-tribal counterparts (e.g. Mashantucket Pequot, which adopted into its tribal legal framework the secured transaction *UCC Article 9 code* from the State of Connecticut). Some tribes have taken a different approach to this dilemma and pushed through with reforms of tribal codes with input from state and federal government as well as non-tribal economic partners. The result in limited instances has been an updated and robust tribal code that strikes a balance between the legal needs of non-tribal counterparts as well as providing due respect to traditional and contemporary tribal practices and preferences. In general, such efforts to reform the tribal legal frameworks have been slow, though reform advocacy through promotion of model tribal codes (e.g. the Model Tribal Secured Transaction Act) created with indigenous input have been shown to have some success (Woessner, 2006). Nevertheless, these efforts remain critical to shaping a legal environment that makes non-tribal investors feel comfortable investing on tribal land while ensuring that the principle of sovereignty is not abandoned entirely.

Scepticism and partnerships

'Trust' is often viewed as critical to longer-term or large-scale business relations (Newell and Swan, 2000). In Francis Fukayama's controversial work, *Trust*, he argues that the degree of trust within a society is a powerful variable in explaining variation in global economic development (1995). Trust has historically been a rare commodity in Indian to non-Indian relations. In fact, the distrust could be the dominant feeling that emerged out of centuries of colonial engagement. American Indians in many instances interpret the colonial past as a warning for future engagements with outsiders and such sentiment is captured in the writing of Native author Elizabeth Cook-Lynn in *Anti-Indianism in Modern America*:

> [W]hite Americans, by and large, have no more respect for or understanding of native cultures and political status than they did during Jefferson's time, though they continue, as he did, to collect bones and Indian words and delay justice [...] Today, America's tongue is cloaked in ignorance and racism and imperialism as much as it was during the westward-movement era; and 'removal' is still the infuriating thrust of Indian/white relations. (2007: preface ix)

It would be a mistake to suggest that Cook-Lynn's interpretation captures all native feelings on the subject of white engagement and the degree to which the contemporary period of relations shows greater hospitality to Indians. American Indians are not unified in their interpretation of the results of engaging with outsiders, though ideologies similar to Cook-Lynn's are far more widespread than those who believe colonialism was a positive experience for Indians. Anger and distrust is not left in the past and can have deleterious effects on collaboration with federal agencies. In explaining the failure of a Sioux community to work with federal and state agencies toward needed flood preparedness before a village was destroyed by an overflowing river, a leader in the community believed that the history of abuse still sours contemporary relationships between Indians and outsiders, '[w]e have collective grief of many treaties broken and many sad memories. We lack trust in outsiders and even other Indians. We are a race that has been separated, and we feel disempowered. Then we further victimize ourselves' (Bender, 2003). Experiences with land takings, treaty breaking, and genocide have left American Indian communities sceptical of the benefits of interactions with outside groups (Pinel, 2007). This scepticism has significant ramifications for all economic development projects including even culturally appropriate renewable energy efforts. Renewable energy generally requires significant capital investment and expertise that most tribes do not possess in-house, therefore these projects require outside soliciting, a near continual presence of outsiders on reservations, and necessarily some trust between tribal and non-tribal partners. The role that outsiders can now have in tribal affairs is often limited by the quality of previous interactions. A tribal member who worked closely with his tribal government in the Southwest described business and tribal dynamics in the following way:

They've been 'burned' in the past. That is on their minds. It makes people here on the council edgy, always looking for someone to screw them. A lot of the time they [the tribal council or executive] want to be the first to call an outsider on something, try to make them look greedy or dishonest. This leads them to see things that aren't there a lot. (Tribal member interview, 2010)

Obviously, this severe scepticism sometimes leads to tensions between parties working on joint venture agreements. It is not uncommon that unexpected changes in projects make tribal leaders suspicious about trusting non-tribal partners. This mistrust can quickly jeopardize projects by placing current relationships into the sequence of deeply chequered relationships with business and government groups. Despite contemporary images that include vast casino wealth, most American Indians on reservations live in poverty and generally reservations have rarely felt the benefits of private industry. The absence of economic intervention (or the presence of extractive and exploitative economic projects) can be readily found on most reservations. These factors make American Indians still the poorest ethnic group in the United States. And, in this context, American Indians often find it difficult to believe the good intentions of outsiders even when the projects they seek to collaborate with them in are culturally appropriate and sustainable while also aimed at creating an outcome that tribal members want.

Conclusion

Climate change has an inherent pessimism in it. This feeling is compounded when those with the most to lose, in this case American Indians and indigenous peoples generally, have already lost so much in terms of their historical dispossession and social marginalization. In its focus on the current limitations of American Indian responses to climate change, this chapter's objective is not to deepen the despair. Describing what challenges exist inherently presumes a belief in the potential of overcoming these challenges. None of the aforementioned obstacles is so recalcitrant as to be completely unnavigable by clearer policy or greater awareness to a community's sensitivities. We remain optimistic about prospects of indigenous participation in renewable energy production in the American Indian reservation context because it is still occurring *in spite* of the challenges that it faces. However, tribal, federal, and state governments and other stakeholders must address the challenges identified above if the full potential of Native America's participation in renewable energy production is to be realized.

Updates to the 2025 edition

Yancey Orr

From 2010 to 2022, American Indian tribal governments have increased their engagement in renewable energy projects. During this period, the Federal Government spent over $120 million on 210 tribal-led energy projects (U.S. Department of Energy, 2024). This activity was partly spurred by incentives from the Federal Government to promote 'Green Energy' during this period. Further investment occurred from the Inflation Reduction Act's $720 million dedicated to Native peoples. Within this spending, $450 million was dedicated to Native renewable energy and efficiency programs (*Inflation Reduction Act Tribal Guidebook*, 2023). Tribal governments have also embraced self-reliance regarding meeting their needs, often called 'energy sovereignty' (Raimi and Davicino, 2023). Since the original publication of this work in 2011, sustainable and clean energy has increased the priority of American Indian tribes.

References

Barringer, F. (2008) 'Native Americans see profit in wind power', *New York Times*, [online] available from: http://www.nytimes.com/2008/10/10/world/americas/10iht-10wind.16835712.html

Bender, E. (2003) 'Disaster response for Native Americans complicated by history, money', *Psychiatric News* 38: 8.

Christensen, N., Wood, A., Voisin, N., Lettenmaier, D., and Palmer, R. (2004) 'Effects of climate change on the hydrology and water resources of the Colorado River Basin', *Climatic Change* 62: 337–63.

Cook-Lynn, E. (2007) *Anti-Indianism in Modern America: A Voice from Tatekeya's Earth*, University of Illinois Press, Champaign.

Cordalis, D., and Suagee, D. (2008) 'The effects of climate change on American Indian and Alaska Native tribes', *Natural Resources and Environment* 22: 45–9.

Deloria, V. (1973) *God is Red: A Native View of Religion*, Putnam, New York.

Flavier, J.M. et al. (1995) 'The regional program for the promotion of indigenous knowledge in Asia', in D.M. Warren, L.J. Slikkerveer and D. Brokensha (eds), *The Cultural Dimension of Development: Indigenous Knowledge Systems*, pp. 479–87, Intermediate Technology Publications, London.

Fukuyama, F. (1995) *Trust: The Social Virtues and the Creation of Prosperity*, The Free Press, New York.

Hanna, J. (2007) *Native Communities and Climate Change: Protecting Tribal Resources as Part of National Climate Policy*, University of Colorado Law School, Natural Resources Law Center Report, Boulder.

Harkin, M. and Lewis, D. (eds) (2007) *Perspectives on the Ecological Indian: Native Americans and the Environment*, University of Nebraska Press, Lincoln.

Inflation Reduction Act Tribal Guidebook (2023) The White House, https://www.whitehouse.gov/wp-content/uploads/2023/04/Inflation-Reduction-Act-Tribal-Guidebook.pdf

Johnson, K. (2009) 'A new test for business and biofuel', *New York Times*, 16 August.

Kamerick, M. (2010) 'Acoma, Ohkay Owingeh get $29M in new bonding authority', *New Mexico Business Weekly*, [online] available from: http://www.bizjournals.com/albuquerque/stories/2010/02/08/daily41.html

Krakoff, S. (2008) 'American Indians, climate change, and ethics for a warming world', *Denver University Law Review* 85, [online] available from: http://ssrn.com/abstract=1265804

Krech, S. (1999) *The Ecological Indian: Myth and History*, W. W. Norton and Company, New York.

Lansing, S. (1991) *Priests and Programmers: Technologies of Power in the Engineered Landscape of Bali*, Princeton University Press.

McSloy, S. (2009) 'Model Limited Sovereign Immunity Waiver (Short Form),' Appendix 4A, in *Matthew Bender's Asset Based Financing: A Transactional Guide*, Matthew Bender, Albany.

Melmer, D. (2002) 'Rosebud, Arabia of wind – its fable comes to life', *Indian Country Today*, 21 May.

Mendelsohn, R., Dinar, A. and Williams, L. (2006) 'The distributional impact of climate change on rich and poor countries', *Environment and Development Economics* 11: 159–78

Miller, R. (2008) 'American Indian entrepreneurs: Unique challenges, unlimited potential', *Arizona State Law Journal* 40: 1297–1341.

Morales, A. (2010) 'Wind turbine prices stagnant after slump in 2009', *Bloomberg.com*, [online] available from: www.bloomberg.com/news/2010-08-04/

wind-turbine-prices-stagnant-after-slump-in-2009-new-energy-finance-says.html

Newell, S. and Swan, J. (2000) 'Trust and inter-organizational networking', *Human Relations* 53: 1287–328.

Nighthorse C. (2002) 'Unlocking the potential of Indian tribal energy', *Indian Country Today*, 19 April.

Pinel, S. (2007) 'Culture and cash – how two New Mexico Indian Pueblos combined culture and development', *Alternatives: Local, Global, Political* 32(1): 9–39.

Raimi, D. and Davicino, A. (2024) 'Securing energy sovereignty: A review of key barriers and opportunities for energy-producing Native nations in the United States', *Energy Research & Social Science* 107,

Reynolds, J. (2007) 'Energy development: the potential of tribal power', *Indian Country Today*, 27 July.

Sargent, S. and Chabot, E. (1996) *American Indian reservations: a showplace for renewable energy,* paper presented at the Annual Conference of the American Solar Energy Society, Asheville, North Carolina, 13–18 April.

Udall B. (2007) 'Recent research on the effects of climate change on the Colorado River,' *Intermountain Climate Summary* 3: 2–6.

U.S. Department of Energy (2024) *Empowering Native Communities and Sustaining Future Generations*, Office of Indian Energy, January. https://www.energy.gov/indianenergy/articles/doe-office-indian-energy-overview-brochure

Wittfogel, K. (1957) *Oriental Despotism: a Comparative Study of Total Power*, Yale University Press, New Haven.

Woessner, P. (2006) 'A super model: new secured transaction code offers legal uniformity, economic promise for Indian country', *Community Dividend*, Federal Reserve Bank of Minnesota, [online] available from: http://www.minneapolisfed.org/publications_papers/pub_display.cfm?id=2277

About the Authors

Raymond I. Orr is a Lecturer in the School of Social and Political Sciences at the University of Melbourne. He received his PhD from UC Berkeley in Political Science. His research focuses on the intersection of intra-tribal indigenous politics and negotiations with the non-indigenous governments.

David B. Anderson is a civil litigator in Oakland, California. He received a J.D. from the University of California, Berkeley, School of Law. He has worked with numerous indigenous communities in the United States, Latin America, and Southeast Asia on economic and municipal development.

Chapter 12

Reclaiming the past to respond to climate change: Mayan farmers and ancient agricultural techniques in the Yucatan Peninsula of Mexico

Betty Bernice Faust, Armando Anaya-Hernández, and Helga Geovannini-Acuña

This chapter examines how archaeological research into past Mayan land use practices in Campeche, Mexico may contribute to increase farm productivity and food security for the region's smallholders. The area's rural communities are threatened by climate change, with the area's rainfall decreasing and less reliable in recent years. Harvests are diminished in both the traditional Maya practice of shifting cultivation (swidden) and the tractor cultivation introduced in the 1980s. Policies introduced as part of the North American Free Trade Agreement also place increasing economic pressures on local maize growers. Recent archaeological research in this area suggests that Pre-Hispanic, Maya canal systems with raised fields once drained floodwaters for later irrigation and household uses during dry periods. The authors call for collaborative efforts with local farmers to reconstruct this irrigation system on an experimental basis to determine if it can increase food production and complementary cash-cropping that forms part of family livelihoods today.

Introduction

In 2008, Mayan[1] farmers collaborated in a surface survey of the archaeological site of Cauich in Campeche, Mexico, where archaeologist Anaya identified the remains of a 500 m canal with indications of raised fields (Anaya and Faust, 2009). Hydraulic systems of this sort have been found in various sites across the Southern Maya Lowlands since Siemens and Puleston's first report of one in 1972. The farmers quickly grasped the explanation of how this system both conserved rainwater and drained fields flooded by storms. Now they want to rebuild it, a task which will require detailed information from archaeological excavation, soil analysis, and hydrological engineering. In this chapter we describe why both we and they think it may offer an appropriate response to local climate change that includes increases in both droughts and hurricanes.

Although government publications regarding rainfall in this region only begin with data from the 1980s, farmers report that changes began in the mid-1970s and include delay in onset as well as increases in both droughts and flooding. Their observations are similar to those made by other indigenous peoples, who are keenly observant of rainfall because they are closely dependent on local food production (IWGIA, 2008).

In the last decade, international news media have reported the more extreme climatic events that accompany global warming. Such news startles readers accustomed to the relatively stable climate of the 20th century, but Mayan Civilization also faced disruptive climate shifts with sea level variations of 3 m (Gunn et al., 1995), which led to the invention of this system in ~1500 BCE (Pohl and Bloom, 1996; Kunen, 2004). It was continually modified to accommodate shifts in climate as well as soil conditions in new locations. It successfully mitigated climate shifts for over a millennium, with the exception of two periods when prolonged droughts combined with political upheavals to result in the abandonment of major cities and a regional population decline (Gill, 2001; Gill et al., 2007). The last of these two catastrophes ended the Classic and inaugurated the Postclassic, a period when population densities were consistently lower. European contact brought epidemics of disease that repeatedly devastated Mayan populations until the late 20th century, when regional growth again reached levels that require agricultural intensification (Faust, 1998). Despite the use of tractors, fertilizers, and improved seeds, farmers now lose half or more of their crops to either drought or flooding during approximately two of every three years.

This chapter examines published research regarding the ancient Mayan canal system with reference to climate change, warfare, and variation in population densities as background to summaries of our own recent research on this system. We also compare this ancient system with current farming practices to evaluate its potential for mitigating the effects of contemporary climate change on food and water security in this Mayan region. We end with a description of the additional information needed before we can attempt reconstruction and experimental use of the ancient system. In short, this is a report of work in progress, evolving through partnership with local farmers in a long-term field site.

This work emerges from previous studies by the authors. Faust, an ethnographer, has done ethnographic research in Pich, Campeche since 1985, investigating indigenous agriculture, resource management, and processes of change. She and archaeologist Anaya co-directed the archaeological project in Cauich, a ranch whose owner resides in Pich. Archaeologist Geovannini reports her findings of a similar but even more complex system of canals and raised fields farther south, in the archaeological site of Calakmul. This information complements prior research on the extensive system of canals and reservoirs in nearby Edzná (Matheny et al., 1983).

The context

Indigenous knowledge is both creative and conservative of past successes in responding to climate shifts. Archaeology and history have interacted with ethnography to shift the popular mirage of 'timeless wisdom' to a working model of adaptation to environmental fluctuations that include anthropogenic ones through culturally constituted feedback loops. The resilience of such systems relies on cultural memory of past changes (political and environmental), as well as observation, experimentation, inventions, and adaptation of borrowed technologies to local conditions (e.g. Wilk, 1991; Crumley, 2000; Costanza, 2007). In the Mayan case, archaeology is particularly helpful in restoring cultural information lost during more than four centuries of colonial and national assimilation efforts.

Contrary to popular beliefs, the Maya have not disappeared; today they number over 2 million and live in the region occupied by their ancestors, now divided among the countries of Mexico, Guatemala, Belize, El Salvador, and Honduras. While their ancient civilization is best known for its stone architecture, beautiful artwork, logo-phonetic writing system, and astronomical knowledge (Sharer and Traxler, 2006), its agricultural achievements equally deserve respect. Many of these were developed in the Yucatan Peninsula, a challenging, tropical lowland environment that has no large rivers, few hills over 150 m, a six-month dry season, shallow soils on limestone rock, recurring droughts, and occasional hurricanes. The Maya conducted agricultural experiments in this area for three millennia when average global temperatures and local rainfall patterns varied significantly (Gill, 2001; Gunn et al., 2002). A severe 9th-century drought interacted with escalating warfare resulting in a system collapse across a region that included the greatest Maya cities of the Classic Period (e.g. Tikal, Calakmul, and Palenque), although some urban areas near plentiful sources of ground water continued until the 16th century when they were converted to Spanish colonial cities.

We propose to reconstruct an ancient Maya canal system that seems appropriate for present conditions of high population density and changing climate because it was developed and used for more than a millennium under similar conditions. In the 9th century, the Mayan population reached its peak; in some municipal areas the densities were similar to those of ancient states in Java and China (Rice and Culbert, 1990: 26). Then, an exceptionally dry period began, further aggravated by extreme droughts (Hodell et al., 1995; Gunn et al., 1995; Haug et al., 2003; Gill et al., 2007; McNeil et al., 2010). These no doubt exacerbated existing problems of political fragmentation and increased warfare documented in the hieroglyphs and iconography of this period (e.g. Webster, 2000).

The scarcity of domestic water supplies was probably even more immediately critical than food shortages and thus the likely trigger for political upheavals that escalated through positive feedback loops into a systemic collapse of the region's political-economic structure, accompanied by demographic collapse (Scarborough and Gallopin, 1995; Faust, 2001; Gill, 2001; Gunn et al., 2002; Gill et al., 2007). Lowered population densities[2] allowed the Maya to feed themselves using their earlier system of agriculture, a form of swidden that benefits from ecosystem services through a long fallow period, thus producing more food with less labour but using larger areas of land.[3]

Our interest in reconstructing the old canal system stems from our perception that the contemporary food security of Campeche State is at risk from climate change. The old system has multiple uses, including farm fishing, green manure production, and polycropping with basic grains, fruit trees and cotton. Archaeological research indicates that ancient Mayan communities adapted this technology to changing environments for centuries. We recently found the remains of two variants: one on the edge of the ancient Mayan city of Calakmul and the other in an upland valley in the sustaining area of Edzná. These differ in ways that indicate adaptation to local environments, both political and biophysical.

These ancient canal systems apparently supported a form of 'permaculture' that complemented long-cycle swidden[4] in the hills and intensive gardening in house yards and in-fields, close to permanent settlements. Various scholars have suggested that the narrow fields were 'irrigated' in some manner from rainwater stored in the canals (e.g. Matheny et al., 1983; Harrison, 1996; Whitman and Turner, 2001; Smardon, 2006). The use of stored rainwater for both irrigation and domestic use has the dual advantage of avoiding the energy cost of moving water up from deep wells and preventing chemical contamination from geological strata (primarily gypsum) which sometimes occurs in this region.

The subsurface irrigation mechanisms may be similar to those involved in the 'floating gardens' (*chinampas*) of Xochimilco near Mexico City. However, those are in reality earthen peninsulas constructed out from the shore of a natural lake, leaving areas of open water that resemble canals (Gómez-Pompa et al., 1982; Chapin, 1988). In contrast, the Mayans apparently "raised" their fields from a seasonal swamp by adding a layer of topsoil excavated from the canals, later supplemented by periodic additions of canal muck and a mulch of chopped water plants (Matheny *et al.*, 1983).

Thus, this work draws attention to the relevance of archaeological research for helping to strengthen community-based adaptations to climate change through the recovery of past indigenous knowledge and land-use practices relevant to current conditions. We present a description of the need for restoration of this system that includes analysis of the economic situation of the farmers in this area and a description of local climate change. This is followed by brief descriptions of the two canal systems we have found. Finally, we conclude with a short account of our collaboration with the farmers in preparations for the reconstruction of one of these systems and experimentation with its use. We seek to revive use of the canal system primarily for local food security including maize[5], vegetables, and fish (in the canals). Since cash income is also important for contemporary household economies (Wilk, 1991), the farmers will experiment with the production of Mayan cotton to meet international certification requirements as 'organic' and produced under 'fair trade' labour conditions.

Economic factors affecting maize farming in Campeche, Mexico

Maize has long been an important part of the Mayan diet and is still by far the largest crop grown in the state of Campeche, covering 1,500 km². Yet this is only a fraction of the state's territory of 57,924 km²; the remainder being occupied by cattle ranches, protected areas, community forest lands, commercial fruit orchards, and residential developments. Of the area cropped, only 0.6 per cent is irrigated (Gobierno del Estado de Campeche, 2004), leaving most lands vulnerable to droughts.

Contemporary population density is only 13 persons per km² (ibid.), contrasting with population estimates of over 20,000 inhabitants each for the three best known ancient Campeche cities (Edzná, Calakmul, and Champotón). Some scholars argue that these cities were maintained only by swidden agriculture and home gardens, but this seems dubious to us in the light of various ethnographic records of swidden production reviewed by Faust and Bilsborrow (2000: 84–89) that ranged from 1,480 to 289 kg/ha/ year where land was cropped for two years and re-grew to forest during the subsequent ten years. This system can provide sufficient maize to support a population density of between 20 and 30 persons/km², but only in areas with agricultural soils appropriate for this practice (for a description of ancient Mayan soil use see Fedick, 1996: 115–26). Thus, the population densities of ancient Mayan cities would have required more intensive agricultural systems in addition to long-cycle swidden.

The form of intensive agriculture currently in use is tractor cultivation of hybrid maize. Ranch owner Don Tránsito López provided a detailed account of the expenses that totalled $249/ha in 2008 (in US dollars), including fertilizer, herbicides, and tractor service to turn the soil.[6]

Regional statistics for tractor production during the same year (SAGARPA, 2008) include an average harvest of 2 tons/ha and an average price of $233/ ton paid to the producer. This produces a gross income of $466/ha, but after subtracting the costs of production, the net gain is only $217/ha without counting the cost of hand labour ($10/day) for planting, weeding, and harvesting or the cost of transportation.

Prices paid for maize at the farm in Mexico (when adjusted for inflation) have fallen disastrously since the 1994 commencement of the North American Free Trade Agreement and the associated increase in importation of maize from the USA (as predicted by the Zapatista leadership [e.g. Earle and Simonelli, 2005] and documented by Zahniser and Coyle, 2004). Young men have increasingly abandoned farming and migrate either to tourist zones (Re Cruz, 1996) or into the United States, seeking wages that will allow them to support families (Faust, 2004).

Even many of those who stay in the village abandon production for home use, preferring to dedicate their time to wage labour and use a fraction of their income to purchase tortillas or maize dough from *tortillerías*. These small, family-run factories purchase maize flour milled by Mexican agribusiness firms that increasingly use maize from US agribusiness. Thus household economies rely in part on inexpensive, mechanized maize production in the US combined with low transportation costs, both at risk from declining petroleum reserves and rising fuel prices.

An alternative to tractor production is the traditional, long-fallow swidden, which does not require purchased inputs; however, it costs more time in travel to dispersed fields and requires more land in fallow. Younger men who work full-time for wages have little time for this practice; thus, they often maintain only one small field near the village and pay for tractor services. Some help their fathers with the traditional *milpa* (maize plots) and share the harvest. Older men are frequently unable to find wage labour jobs and thus have the time to maintain the swidden tradition, but if their sons do not assist them they plant only a small area. By continuing the practice in miniature, they do maintain the knowledge necessary to recuperate it should conditions change; however, most are forced to depend at least in part on their adult sons.

Recent climate change affecting maize cultivation in Campeche, Mexico

In the region studied, global warming has created more frequent and intense storms than was the case at lower global temperatures (Gunn et al., 1995) and this trend is predicted to increase (Allen and Rincón, 2003: 27–8). In between the downpours, however, are weeks without rain. This may be in part a result of the regional deforestation for tractor cultivation of 700,000 ha in a massive rural development program of the Mexican federal government from 1972 to 1986 that was documented by J.M. Sandoval (1982) and M. Gates (1993). Research on the environmental effects of such large-scale deforestation in the tropics has been summarised by J. Shaw (2003: 6). In brief, the sun's rays are deflected from grasslands and crop lands far more so than from forest, which has greater leaf density and therefore more capacity to absorb these rays. The deflected rays from deforested areas heat the local atmosphere and disperse humidity that would otherwise form rain clouds, thereby decreasing local rainfall.

Local variation in rainfall is evident in data from 1982 through 1998 that was provided by CONAGUA (Comisión Nacional de Agua of the Mexican federal government) from their weather station at Nohyaxché, Campeche (CONAGUA, 1998). Over the 16-year period for which we obtained data, it varied from 26 to 63 mm during the two critical months when maize plants are growing (May and June) and between 8 and 26 mm during July, a month critical for the formation of the grain (ibid.). Vulnerability to climatic events does not end with crop maturity in August because both maize and beans are normally left on the plant to dry fully before harvesting for storage. During September and October, standing crops are often damaged by flooding from hurricanes. Thus, both the irrigation and drainage capabilities of the reconstructed canal system would be very helpful in present conditions. Analysis of daily data available from neighbouring weather stations (Maxcanú, Opichen, and Halachó), indicated gradual increases (from 1980) in the variation in rainfall by month and year. (Rodríquez, 2009). The onset of the yearly rainy season tended to begin later in the year and the number of days without rain increased during the agricultural season (ibid.). Comparative data from before 1972 might clarify the climate effects of the massive deforestation described above, but such information is not available.

The advantage of irrigation is clear to Mayan farmers, who have observed the modern systems installed for fruit production in the neighbouring Valley of Edzná, where the underground water table is less than 40 m below the surface; however, for Pich and other communities at relatively high elevations, the cost of pumping water from deep aquifers (>120 m) is enough to preclude such investments. Thus, the ancient system that saves rainwater for irrigation would be advantageous.

Research methods

We used interdisciplinary methods to construct our model of the ancient canal systems detected in Cauich and Calakmul. These include long-term ethnographic research with farmers in Cauich and neighbouring Pich; bibliographic research on climate change (present and past); interpretations of satellite images of the two systems; Ground Penetrating Radar (GPR), ground surveys by archaeologists; laboratory analysis of soil samples; and comparison with research reports of similar systems found in other lowland Mayan areas. At Calakmul, the former were complemented with analysis of LiDAR imagery and excavations on water reservoirs.

The methods we are using to plan reconstruction and experimental use of the raised field system include individual interviews with key informants, informal consulting on site, sharing of observations, and discussions with local farmers concerning epistemological and institutional constraints on funding (Ross et al., 2011).

Fieldwork results from two sites in Campeche, Mexico

Anaya and Faust (2009) found a relic canal system 23 km south of the ancient Mayan city of Edzná, on a private ranch in an elevated valley. Geovannini earlier reported (2008) another canal system farther south, on the border of the archaeological site of Calakmul, also in an elevated valley. Both these systems could have contributed basic grains, vegetables, fish, and cotton to dense urban populations during Pre-Columbian times and could potentially aid today's Mayan farmers in their struggles with climate change.

Cauich

Today Cauich is a ranch owned and worked by a resident of Pich. In Pre-Columbian times, it was likely an agricultural village within the sustaining periphery of the Mayan city of Edzná. In a survey of 225 ha of this site, Anaya identified 11 buildings that indicate continued occupancy from approximately 700 CE until the Mexican Revolution of 1910, subsequent to which the land was sold to the father of the present owner. Both father and son have used the land to raise cattle and grow maize, beans, squash and other produce, while residing in Pich. The son, don Tránsito López, continues these activities with his own sons. This continuity in agricultural use contrasts sharply with the 9th-century abandonment of the nearby Mayan cities of Edzná and Calakmul.

Associated with the oldest buildings in Cauich are the remains of a canal system that measures approximately 2 m wide by 500 m long (as yet the depth is unknown). It follows a natural gradient from west to east. Given the topography, storm waters would have drained from the valley into the canal, and eventually into an *aguada* with an underground drain (*such*). Don Tránsito reports it holds a pool of rainwater for only a few weeks, unlike most *aguadas* which conserve water for many months (interviews Nov. 8, 2010 and May 3, 2011). Aided by a cleaned and functioning canal system, this canal probably permitted cropping of an area that otherwise would have been a seasonal swamp.

Following Matheny et al. (1983) and Whitman and Turner (2001), we argue that canal systems such as that found in Cauich provided irrigation to raised fields. Anaya measured the raised fields by pacing and found them to be roughly rectangular and approximately 15 m long by 2.5 m wide. Rainwater could have been stored in the small canals between the fields at a depth sufficient to avoid rotting the roots of crops, but still provide subsurface irrigation through capillary action or possibly through the activity of micro-organisms in the soil. This would have made possible the cultivation of a second crop from September to December (dry season begins the first of November) and the protection of the main crop (May through to August) from periodic droughts. Other possible uses include vegetable cultivation by pot irrigation and fish farming, which has the additional advantage of minimizing mosquito larvae in the canals.

Author updates to the 2025 edition

Five years after the 2008 field season, in 2013 further geophysical prospection was carried out during the months of July and September. During this season, a radar ALOS PALSAR image was interpreted and verified in the field, (Akpinar Ferrand and Thomas III, 2013), identifying the areas subject to flooding as well as the extension of the canal system. Two images of different dates were used to highlight the differences between dry areas and wet areas. One image corresponded to the dry season in March 2010, the other corresponds to the rainy season in September of the same year. Both were combined into a single image and displayed in the red-green-blue (RGB) bands where the September image was assigned to the red and blue bands, while the March image was assigned to the green band. With this combination, the flooded areas under the vegetation cover appear in magenta, while the dry areas appear in green (Figure 12.1). Furthermore, during the field prospection, Akpinar Ferrand and Thomas III (2013) were able to detect among the crop fields, the silted vestiges of a system of minor canals. At the end of the prospection, another 2 km of the canal were identified, a series of smaller canals and two more *aguadas* measuring 18.29 m x 18.29 m with an approximate depth of 1.5 m and 21.3 m x 23.8 m with a depth of approximately 2 m, respectively. Likewise, it was observed that the canal system drained into an area of *suches*, or karst ponors. A ponor is a natural opening in the surface characteristic of karst landscapes where a surface current will flow into a groundwater system (Figure 12.1).

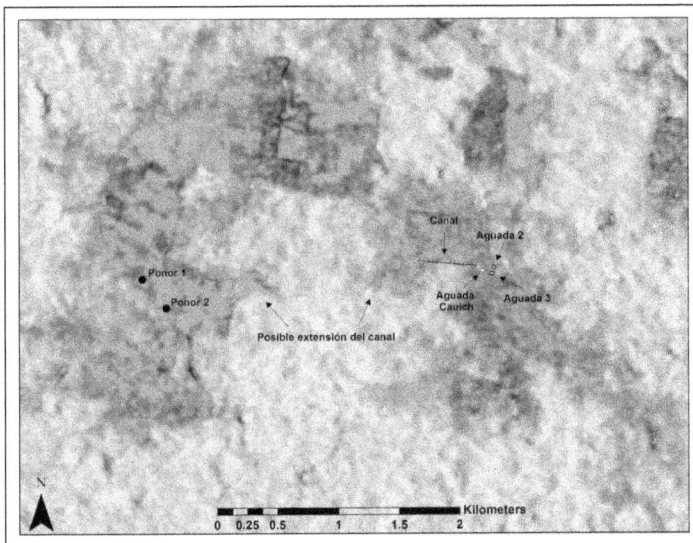

Figure 12.1 PALSAR image showing the areas subject to inundation (Processed by Benjamin Thomas III).

A high-resolution (2 m) Geoeye 1 satellite image corroborated not only the field observations, but also revealed that both the site and the canal system were much more complex than what could be observed in the field. In addition to the originally observed channel, at least three other large channels running from north to south were identified (Figure 12.2).

Figure 12.2 Geoeye IR high resolution image, showing more canals (Processed by Mandy Munro-Stasiuk).

Our research indicated that while the ancient inhabitants of Cauich invested in hydraulic works to harvest and store higher quality water for domestic use, they also had a particular interest in controlling seasonal flooding of low-lying farmlands, so they employed a considerable amount of work in a canal system built over a low hydraulic gradient environment. Ground Penetrating Radar (GPR) observations carried out by Dr. Munro-Stasiuk (2013) revealed that the extensive system of canals that drained excess water into the ponors area measured approximately 2 km long. Using PuleskoPro equipment and software with an interchangeable antenna that penetrates 4 m underground at 200 Mhz and up to 20 m deep at 50 Mhz, Munro-Stasiuk systematically conducted transects every 20 m, perpendicular to the channel, plus four more grids to obtain more detailed profiles.

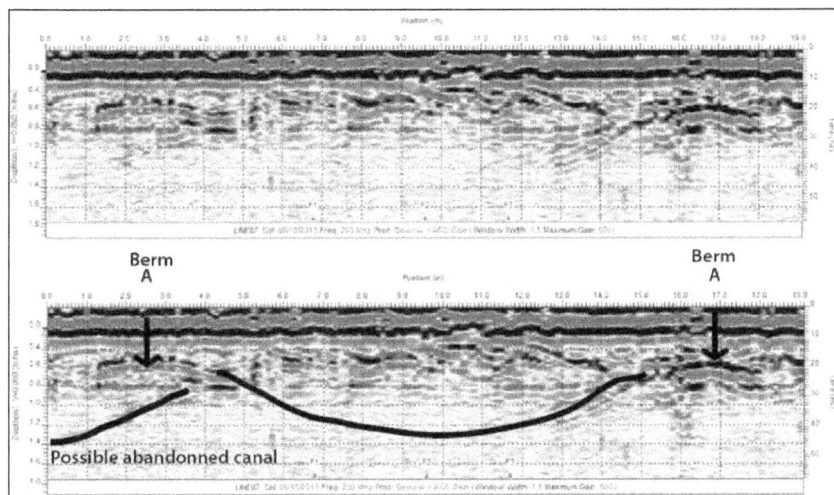

Figure 12.3 GPR images showing the structure of the canal at Cauich (Source: Munro-Stasiuk, 2013).

The canal was identified in practically half of the transects and in some sections, it appeared that it was used, abandoned and re-excavated. In other cases, you can clearly see its edges or walls (Figure 12.3). Likewise, long transects were detected that run parallel to the channel, showing minor channels perpendicular to them, approximately 10 m long and spaced about 90 m to 100 m apart. We think that they intersect the elevated fields where the main channel is at right angles. This pattern is consistent with the canal system reported for Edzná.

Calakmul

According to archaeologists, the city of Calakmul at its peak (600–900 CE) had an extension of ~30 km² with more than 6,000 buildings (Folan et al., 2001). It was built on a promontory, at the base of which Folan et al. (2001: 26) reported canals with possible agricultural use. Geovannini (2008) conducted a landscape evaluation to test this hypothesis.

Her analysis of remote images suggested canals of variable lengths, some in grids that include bounded fields and reservoirs. Geovannini (2008: 65–6) surveyed the fields on foot and found them to be flat with moderately deep soils. Using the FAO system (1976, Chapter 3.2.2.) for classification, she analyzed soil samples and identified the majority as Calcic Vertisols (*ya'ax hom* in Yucatec Mayan), used today for both swidden and tractor cultivation. She identified the other soils as Vertic Gleysols (*ak'alche'*); these are quite impermeable and thus suitable for use in lining canals and reservoirs.

Water collection methods developed by the ancient Maya in the Calakmul region offer valuable insights for sustainable water management in a tropical karst landscape. Recent research carried out in this region aided by LiDAR imagery (Brewer, 2016; Brewer et al., 2017; Dunning et al., 2016; Anaya Hernandez et al., 2017; Brewer and Carr, 2017; Brewer et al., 2017; Dunning et al., 2017; Dunning et al., 2018; Brewer, 2018; Dunning et al., 2022a; Dunning et al., 2023; Dunning et al., 2024) confirmed that due to the rarity of groundwater and perennial streams, the Maya built elaborate systems for water collection and storage, including reservoirs, smaller-scale tanks, chultuns (underground cisterns), and canals (Figure 12.4). Water was a fundamental component of Maya cosmology and agriculture was dependent on rain, which required water collection and storage in the rainy season for use in the dry season.

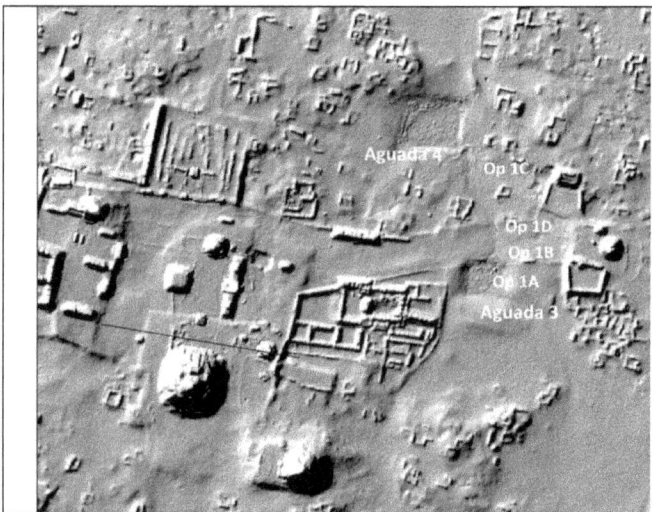

Figure 12.4 Location of Aguada 4 of Calakmul and archaeological explorations (Source: Kupprat et al. 2023).

The ancient Maya developed several specific technologies for water collection and storage such as sealing strategies with compacted clay, rammed earth, and limestone block and/or ceramic sherds paved floors for the reservoirs, deepening of reservoirs to increase storage capacity, control of water inflow and outflow and sand filters to maintain potability (Figure 12.5). The diversity and sophistication of these systems increased between the Middle Preclassic and Late Classic periods (ca. 800 BC – 900 AD).

In summary, the Maya's water collection and storage systems evolved from relatively simple adaptations of natural features in the Middle Preclassic to sophisticated, multi-scale systems that were integral to the urban fabric of Maya civilization by the Late Classic period. These systems were essential for the permanent settlement of the EIR and were a significant factor in the urbanization and development of the Maya lowlands.

(a)

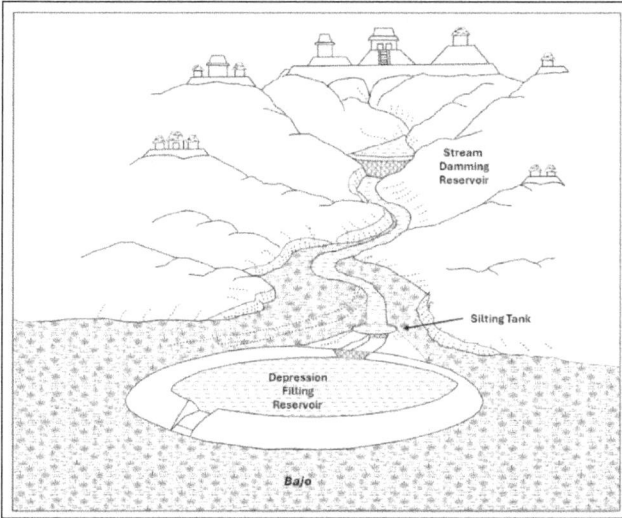

(b)

Figure 12.5 a) Diagram of water management feature (source: Dunning et al. 2022).
b) Aguada 3, limestone paved floor (source: Kupprat et al. 2023).

Indigenous–academic collaboration for rebuilding a canal system with raised fields

Both global average temperature and sea levels are already at the highest point faced during the past three millennia during which Mayans have farmed the Peninsula of Yucatan (Gunn et al., 1995, 2002). Both are predicted to continue rising, with associated increases in the frequency and intensity of local storms (Allen and Rincón, 2003: 27–8). Tractor cultivated crops are increasingly lost to flooding and drought, while the latter also devastates swidden fields on hillsides. Thus, we propose to 'reverse engineer' the water management system devised by the ancient Maya when responding to climate change. This proposed experiment contrasts with a previous one in Tabasco where the Chontal-Mayan farmers were not involved in planning, and the introduced system was modelled on one from a different climate zone (M. Chapin, 1988).

In our original work, we expressed our desire to reconstruct the water management systems in both Cauich and Calakmul. At that time, we considered this endeavour more feasible at Cauich than at Calakmul because the latter is located within a biosphere reserve. Paradoxically, this could be possible only at Calakmul. In 2014, a considerable section of the Prehispanic canal and the structures recorded during the 2008 field season were bulldozed by members of the Mennonite community in the region, who rented the land from the owner to cultivate their crops. On the other hand, the recent research carried out at Calakmul and hinterland, has shed bountiful information regarding technologies related to water management strategies. As before, the current research at Calakmul can potentially increase food security in a region where water is scarce.

In both the canal systems we have studied, the soils are predominantly Vertisols, which the International Union of Soil Scientists (IUSS, 2007: 95) recommends for use with the caveat that they require careful management of moisture, through both drainage and irrigation (a conclusion apparently reached by ancient Mayan farmers as well). The crop they recommend most highly is cotton (*Gossypium* sp.), pollen evidence for which has been found in several Mayan canal systems along with that for maize, beans, squash, and other cultigens (e.g. Matheny et al., 1983: 227; Pohl and Bloom, 1996).

Most of our farming colleagues are interested in growing staples for household use, but some wish to experiment with Maya cotton, fish farming, and vegetable production. We are engaged in participative planning with these farmers for future applied research, with frequent evaluations and modifications, as there are many unknowns. The first step will be to obtain detailed information concerning the original construction and use of this system. This will require excavation and consultation with hydraulic engineers, soil scientists, and those local farmers (Mayans and mestizos) who remember and use the knowledge of their ancestors.

These elders still recall how they managed the Pre-Columbian system that maintained village ponds for local use (Sandoval and Morales, 1982; Faust, 1998: 63–72,) until the government provided a modern water system. This information and local knowledge of soils, weather patterns, and techniques for cultivating the indigenous varieties of food crops are essential to the pilot project, in which we plan to test the system's capacity for mitigating the contemporary effects of climate change on water and food security in this region.

Acknowledgements

We thank La Trobe University in Melbourne, Australia, and Mexico's Instituto Nacional de Arqueología e Historia for their support of Geovannini's research in Calakmul, as well as the Consejo Nacional de Ciencia y Tecnología, the Centro de Investigación y de Estudios Avanzados del Instituto Politécnico Nacional, and the Universidad Autónoma de Campeche (all of Mexico) for their support of Faust and Anaya's project in Cauich. We are also indebted to Don Tránsito López, the owner of Rancho Cauich, and his family and workers, for their assistance and hospitality. We also want to express our gratitude to the University Press of Colorado for graciously allowing us to reproduce the diagram of Figure 12.2. The manuscript has been improved by suggestions from Jack Frazier, Anabel Ford, Joel Gunn, Ellen Kintz, Dan Leonard, various colleagues at professional meetings, and the editors of this volume.

Notes

[1] In this article we follow the practice of various ethnologists (i.e., M. Elmendorf and J. Nash) in using 'Mayan(s)' rather than 'Maya' for the people and the culture, as well as for the language. Archaeologists have traditionally used 'Mayan' only for the language and the term 'Maya' in reference to the culture and people. For interdisciplinary discourse, we prefer 'Mayan' as an adjective and 'Mayans' as a noun in order to minimize 'essentializing' interpretations by non-specialists.

[2] The mechanisms by which lower population densities were maintained from the 10th to the 16th centuries are unknown, but may well have included a variety known from ethnographic studies of other indigenous peoples (delayed marriage, abstinence during prolonged periods, breast feeding into the fourth year, use of plants known to be abortificants, and infanticide). Shortages of food and water also may have increased disease and lowered fertility rates. During the 16th century, Spanish chroniclers reported further Mayan population losses. Contemporary medical historians reviewing these documents, estimate the total loss at more than 75 per cent and the major factor as epidemics of Old World diseases. Epidemics continued to devastate Mayan populations until after the Mexican Revolution (1910–21) (Faust, 1998: 30–33).

[3] Various scholars have interpreted passages in early 16th-century Spanish documents as descriptions of raised fields and canals (see summaries by Faust, 1998; Whitmore and Turner, 2001); however, the areas mentioned were later abandoned and have not been authenticated by archaeological research. K. Mathewson (1984) documents river-fed irrigation systems in the Guatemalan Highlands, but those differ considerably from the lowland systems.

[4] This traditional system of agriculture is still common throughout the tropics. After two or three years of cropping, soil fertility is replenished by the re-growth of natural vegetation during a longer period, one whose length depends on climate, slope, soils, and subsoils. The term swidden is common in English, but in Mexico this system is usually referred to as *roza, tumba y quema* (slash-and-burn).

[5] Daltabuit et al. (1988: 50) report that in Cobá, Quintana Roo, Mexico, maize constitutes an average of 40 per cent of calories consumed, while Wilk (1991: 163) found that among the Kekchí of Belize the average daily consumption of maize by men provided 3,500 calories with 110 grams of protein while the consumption by women averaged 2,300 calories with 70 grams of protein. In both cases, during years with normal harvests, the consumption was adequate to meet the energy needs for the heavy physical labour involved in daily tasks.

[6] The 2007 exchange rate was $10.9 pesos to the US dollar, in 2008 it was 11.2, and in 2009 it was 13.5 (http://www.oanda.com/currency/historical rates [Accessed 14 November 2010]).

References

Akpinar Ferrand, E., and Thomas, B. III (2013) *Rancho Cauich Preliminary Field Report*. Informe de la temporada de campo 2013. Unpublished.

Allen, M. and Rincón, E. (2003) 'The changing global environment and the Lowland Maya: past patterns and current dynamics,' in A. Gomez-Pompa, M. Allen, S. Fedick, and J. Jiménez-Osornio (eds.), *The Lowland Maya Area: Three Millennia at the Human–Wildland Interface,* pp. 12–29. Food Products Press (Haworth), New York.

Anaya Hernández, A. andFaust, B. (2009) 'Una aproximación a la arqueohistoria ecológica de Cauich, Campeche', report for El Consejo de Arqueología del Instituto Nacional de Arqueología e Historia, México.

Anaya Hernández, A., Peuramaki-Brown, M., and Reese-Taylor, K. (2016) 'Introducción', in *Proyecto Arqueológico Yaxnohcah, Informe de las 2014 y 2015 Temporadas de Investigaciones,* edited by A. Anaya Hernández, M. Peuramaki-Brown, and K. Reese-Taylor, pp. 1–3. Report submitted to the Consejo de Arqueología del Instituto Nacional de Antropología e Historia, Mexico City.

Brewer, J. L. (2016) 'Investigaciones en aguadas de escala residenciales,' in *Proyecto Arqueológico Yaxnohcah, Informe de las 2014 y 2015 Temporadas de Investigaciones,* pp. 95–109. Edited by A. Anaya Hernández, M. Peuramaki-Brown, and K. Reese-Taylor, Report submitted to the Consejo de Arqueología del Instituto Nacional de Antropología e Historia, Mexico City.

Brewer, J. L., and Carr, C. (2017) 'Operation 22: Continuing Household Water Management Investigations at Yaxnohcah', in *Proyecto Arqueológico Yaxnohcah, Informe de la 2016 Temporada de Investigaciones,* pp. 125–148. Edited by K. Reese-Taylor and A. Anaya Hernández. Report submitted to the Consejo de Arqueología del Instituto Nacional de Antropología e Historia, Mexico City.

Brewer, J. L., Carr C., Dunning N. P., Walker D. S., Hernández A. Anaya, Peuramaki-Brown M., and Reese-Taylor K. (2017) 'Employing Airborne LiDAR and Archaeological Testing to Determine the Role of Small Depressions in Water Management at the Ancient Maya Site of Yaxnohcah, Campeche, Mexico'. *Journal of Archaeological Science: Reports* 13 (June): 291–302.

Brewer, J. L. (2018) 'Householders as Water Managers: A Comparison of Domestic-Scale Water Management Practices from Two Central Maya Lowland Sites'. *Ancient Mesoamérica* 29 (1): 197–217.

Chapin, M. (1988) 'The seduction of models, chinampa agriculture in Mexico', *Grassroots Development* 12: 8–17.

CONAGUA-Nohyaxché (Comisión Nacional de Agua, Estación Nohyaché) (1998) Resumen anual de datos climatológicos de la Estación Meteorological de Nohyaxché, Campeche, 1981–1998.

Costanza, R., Graumlich, L., Steffen, W., Crumley, C., Dearing, J., Hibbard, K., Leemans, R. Redman, C., and Schimel, D. (2007) 'Sustainability or collapse: what can we learn from integrating the history of humans and the rest of nature' *Ambio* 36: 522–527.

Crumley, C. (2000) 'From garden to globe: linking time and space with meaning and memory', in J. Tainter and S. McIntosh (eds.), *The Way the Wind Blows: Climate, History, and Human Action,* pp. 193–208, Columbia University Press, NY.

Daltabuit, M., Ríos, A. and Pérez, F. (1988) *Cobá: Estartegias Adapdativas de Tres Familias Mayas,* UNAM, Mexico City.

Dunning, N. P., Anaya Hernández, A. and Geovannini, H. (2016) 'Operaciones 13 y 19: Investigaciones en los reservorios', in *Proyecto Arqueológico Yaxnohcah, Informe de las 2014 y 2015 Temporadas de Investigaciones,* pp. 110–121. Edited by A. Anaya Hernández, M. Peuramaki-Brown, and K. Reese-Taylor. Report submitted to the Consejo de Arqueología del Instituto Nacional de Antropología e Historia, Mexico City.

Dunning, N. P., Hernández A. Anaya, Haggard A., and Carr C. (2017) 'Investigaciones en el Reservorio Brisa', in *Proyecto Arqueológico Yaxnohcah, Informe de 2016 Temporada de Investigaciones,* pp. 93–122. Edited by K. Reese-Taylor and A. Anaya Hernández. Report submitted to the Consejo de Arqueología del Instituto Nacional de Antropología e Historia, Mexico City.

Dunning, N. P., Brewer J., Carr C., Hernández A. Anaya, Beach T., Chmilar J., Grazioso Sierra L., Griffin R., Lentz D., Luzzadder-Beach S., Reese-Taylor K., Saturno W., Scarborough V., Smyth M., and Valdez F. (2022) 'Harvesting Ha: Ancient Water Collection and Storage in the Elevated Interior Region of the Maya Lowlands'. In J. Larmon, L. Lucero, and F. Valdez (Eds.), *Sustainability and Water Management in the Maya World and Beyond,* pp. 13–51. Boulder: University Press of Colorado.

Dunning, N. P., Brewer Jeffrey, Montgomery Shane, Cook Duncan, Carr Chris, and Kupprat Felix (2023) 'Investigaciones en el Reservorio Brisa', in *Proyecto Arqueológico Yaxnohcah, Informe de 2016 Temporada de Investigaciones,* pp. 233–270. Edited by F. Kupprat, A. Anaya Hernández, and K. Reese-Taylor. Report submitted to the Consejo de Arqueología del Instituto Nacional de Antropología e Historia, Mexico City.

Dunning, N. P., Montgomery, S., and Carr, C. (2024) 'Investigaciones en el Grupo Canche y la Aguada Changuis: Operación CLK18', in *Proyecto Arqueológico Bajo El Laberinto, Informe de la temporada 2023*, pp. 333–350. Edited by A. Anaya Hernández, K. Reese-Taylor, and F. Kupprat. Report submitted to the Consejo de Arqueología del Instituto Nacional de Antropología e Historia, Mexico City.

Earle, D. and Simonelli, J. (2005) *Uprising of Hope: Sharing the Zapatista Journey to Alternative Development*, Altamira, Walnut Creek.

FAO (Food and Agriculture Organization of the United Nations) (1976) *A Framework for Land Evaluation*. FAO Soils Bulletin 32, FAO, Rome.

Faust, B. (1998) *Mexican Rural Development and the Plumed Serpent,* Greenwood-Heinemann, Westport.

Faust, B. (2001) 'Maya environmental successes and failures in the Yucatan Peninsula', *Environmental Science and Policy* 4: 153–369.

Faust, B. (2004) 'The end of innocence: social consequences of the overuse of timber in a Maya community', in B. Faust, E. Anderson, and J. Frazier (eds.), *Rights, Resources, Culture and Conservation in the Yucatan Peninsula*, pp. 131–62, Greenwood, Westport.

Faust, B. and Bilsborrow, R. (2000) 'Maya culture, population, and the environment on the Yucatan Peninsula', in W. Lutz, L. Prieto, and W. Sanderson (eds.), *Population, Development, and Environment on the Yucatan Peninsula: from Ancient Maya to 2030*, pp. 73–106. International Institute for Applied Systems Analysis, Laxenburg, Austria.

Fedick, S. (1996) 'An interpretive kaleidoscope: alternative perspectives on ancient agricultural landscapes of the Maya Lowlands', in S. Fedick (ed.), *The Managed Mosaic*, pp. 107–31. University of Utah Press, Salt Lake City.

Folan, W., Fletcher, L., May, J. and Florey, L. (2001) *Las Ruinas de Calakmul, Campeche, México: Un Lugar Central y Su Paisaje Cultural*, Universidad Autónoma de Campeche, Mexico City.

Gates, M. (1993) *In Default: Peasants, the Debt Crisis, and the Agricultural Challenge in Mexico*, Westview.

Geovannini Acuña, H. (2008) *Rain Harvesting in the Rainforest: The Ancient Maya Agricultural Landscape of Calakmul, Campeche, Mexico*, Series: British Archaeological Reports S1879, Archaeopress, Oxford.

Gill, R. (2001) *The Great Maya Droughts: Water, Life and Death,* University of Texas Press, Austin.

Gill, R., Mayewski, P., Nyberg, J., Haug, G., and Peterson, L. (2007) 'Drought and the Maya Collapse', *Ancient Mesoamerica* 18: 283–302.

Gobierno del Estado de Campeche (2004) *Primer Informe Estadístico*, Campeche, México.

Gómez-Pompa, A., Morales, H., Ávila, E. and Jiménez, J. (1982) 'Experiences in traditional hydraulic agriculture', in K. Flannery (ed.) *Maya Subsistence. Studies in Memory of Dennis E. Puleston*, pp. 327–342, Academic Press, New York.

Gunn, J., Folan, W. and Robichaux, H. (1995) 'A landscape analysis of the Candelaria watershed in Mexico: insights into paleoclimates affecting upland horticulture in the Southern Yucatan Peninsula semi-karst', *Geoarchaeology* 10: 3–42.

Gunn, J., Foss, J., Folan, W., Domínguez-Carrasco, M. and Faust, B. (2002) 'Bajo sediments and the hydraulic system of Calakmul, Campeche, Mexico', *Ancient Mesoamerica* 13: 297–315.

Gurri, F. (2006) '25 años de colonización, sobreviviendo y garantizando el futuro en Calakmul', *Ecofronteras* 28: 2–6.

Harrison, P. (1996) 'Settlement and land use in the Pulltrowser Swamp archaeological zone, Northern Belize,' in S. Fedick (ed.) *The Managed Mosaic*, pp. 177–190, University of Utah Press, Salt Lake City.

Haug, G., Gunther, D., Peterson, L., Sigman, D., Hughen, K., and Aeschlimann, B. (2003) 'Climate and the collapse of the Maya civilization', *Science* 299: 1731–1735.

Hodell, D., Curtis, J. and Brenner, M. (1995) 'Possible role of climate in the collapse of the Classic Maya Civilization', *Nature* 375: 391–394.

IUSS (International Union of Soil Sciences, Working Group) (2007) *World Reference Base for Soil Resources 2006, first update 2007*. World Soil Resources Reports No. 103. FAO, Rome [Online] http://www.fao.org/ag/agl/agll/wrb/doc/wrb2007_corr.pdf [Accessed 30 June 2010].

IWGIA (International Work Group for Indigenous Affairs) (2008) Climate Change and Indigenous Peoples, special edition of *Indigenous Affairs* 1–2/08 [Online] http://www.iwgia.org [accessed 15 December 2010].

Kunen, J. (2004) *Ancient Maya Life in the Far West Bajo: Social and Environmental Change in the Wetlands of Belize*. Anthropological papers of the University of Arizona, No. 69, University of Arizona Press, Tucson.

Matheny, R., Gurr, D., Forsyth, W., and Hauck, F. (1983) *Investigations at Edzná Campeche, México. Vol. 1, Part 1: The Hydraulic System*, Brigham Young University, Papers of the New World Achaeological Foundation, No. 46, Provo.

Mathewson, K. (1984) *Irrigation Horticulture in Highland Guatemala*, Westview, Boulder.

McNeil, C., Burney, D., and Burney, L. (2010) 'Evidence disputing deforestation as the cause for the collapse of the ancient Maya polity of Copán, Honduras', *Proceedings of the National Academy of Sciences* 107: 1017–22.

Munro-Stasiuk M. (2013) GPR Prospection at Cauich, Campeche. *Rancho Cauich Preliminary Field Report*. Informe de la temporada de campo 2013. Unpublished.

Pohl, M. and Bloom, P. (1996) 'Prehistoric Maya farming in the wetlands of Northern Belize: more data from Albion Island and beyond,' in S. Fedick (ed.), *The Managed Mosaic: Ancient Maya Agriculture and Resource Use*, pp. 145–64. University of Utah Press, Salt Lake City.

Re Cruz, A. (1996) *The Two Milpas of Chan Kom: Scenarios of a Maya Village Life*. SUNY Press, Albany.

Rice, D.S. and Culbert, P. (1990) 'Historical contexts for population reconstruction', in T. Culbert and D. Rice (eds.), *Precolumbian Population History in the Maya Lowlands*, pp. 1–36. University of New Mexico Press, Albuquerque.

Rodríquez Castro, E. (2009) 'Las Plantas Medicinales Mayas: Un Estudio de los Factores de Riesgo Ambientales y Sociales en Maxcanú, Yucatán', Master's thesis, CINVESTAV del IPN [Online] http://www.cinvestav.mda.mx/ecología humana [January 16, 2009].

Ross, A., Sherman, K., Snodgrass, J., Delcore, H., and Sherman, R. (2011) *Indigenous Peoples and the Collaborative Stewardship of Nature: Knowledge Binds and Institutional Conflicts*, Left Coast Press, Walnut Creek.
SAGARPA (Secretaría de Agricultura, Ganadería, Desarrollo Rural, Pesca y Alimentación, Mexico) (2008) Maize Production in 2008 for Six Counties in Campeche State, Mexico. (Report provided by the Campeche office).
Sandoval Palacios, J. (1982) 'Development of Capitalism in Mexican Agriculture: Its Impact on the Humid Tropics: the Case of the Yohaltun Project in the Southeastern State of Campeche', unpublished Ph.D. dissertation, University of California at Los Angeles.
Sandoval Palacios, J. and Morales, A. (1982) 'Una aproximación metodológica para el estudio de un sistema hidráulico prehispánico en Yohaltún, Valle de Edzná, Campeche', *Boletín de la Escuela de Ciencias Antropológicas de la Universidad de Yucatán* 53: 13–27.
Scarborough, V. and Gallopin, G. (1994) 'A Water Storage Adaptation in the Maya Lowlands', *Science* 251: 658–62.
Sharer, R. and Traxler, L. (2006) *The Ancient Maya*, 6th edition. Stanford University Press, Palo Alto.
Shaw, J. (2003) 'Climate change and deforestation: implications for the Maya Collapse', *Ancient Mesoamerica* 14: 157–67.
Siemens, A. and Puleston, D. (1972) 'Ridged fields and associated features in Southern Campeche: new perspectives on the Lowland Maya', *American Antiquity* 37: 228–39.
Smardon, R. (2006) 'Heritage values and functions of wetlands in Southern Mexico', *Landscape and Urban Planning* 74: 296–312.
Webster, D. (2000) 'The not so peaceful civilization: a review of Maya war', *Journal of World Prehistory* 14: 65–119.
Whitmore, T. and Turner, B. (2001) *Cultivated Landscapes of Middle America on the Eve of the Conquest*, Oxford University Press, Oxford.
Wilk, R. (1991) *Household Ecology*, University of Arizona Press, Tucson.
Zahniser, S., and Coyle, W. (2004) 'US–Mexico corn trade during the NAFTA era: new twists to an old story', United States Department of Agriculture, Economic Research Service, Electronic Outlook Report, FDS-04D-01, www.ers.usda.gov [14 August 2010].

Chapter 13

Can we learn from the past?
Policy history and climate change
in Bangladesh

David Lewis

Using Bangladesh as its focus, this chapter asks whether we are doing enough to learn from past experiences to ensure that development actors can create coherent and effective responses to the new challenges of climate change. The author suggests that this learning requires less emphasis on new ideas and an unhelpful 'crisis narrative' of climate change, and closer attention to continuities in policy history and to ways of engaging more profoundly with local communities. At the heart of the argument is a short historical comparison between present day issues and the 1989–1993 Bangladesh Flood Action Plan (FAP), a major donor-led flood control initiative that now seems largely forgotten. The FAP was an essentially top-down initiative conceived by outside agencies and an unelected military government. After four years and millions of dollars spent, it was eventually abandoned in the face of a combination of resistance from local communities, recognition of the importance of local forms of indigenous knowledge, and new technical advice from experts who began to better recognise the limits of their understanding of Bangladesh's complex environment. Overall, the well-being of Bangladesh's people will be better served by participatory approaches that pay close attention to the complex yet crucial lessons of the country's recent development policy history.

Introduction

Climate change now looms very large over contemporary development efforts in Bangladesh, bringing together international donors and government, engineers, natural and social scientists, activists, NGOs and local communities. International development agencies have long exercised a high degree of power in Bangladesh, not just through the transfer of large-scale financial resources, but also in the ways they have shaped ideas, understandings and agendas for action (Wood, 1994). Yet development agencies like to focus on the here and now. It is striking how far earlier policy histories are only poorly remembered, or even sometimes entirely forgotten, within the 'perpetual present' of policy-making discourses (Lewis, 2009).

This chapter asks whether we are doing enough to learn from past experiences to ensure that contemporary development actors can create coherent and effective responses to the new challenges of climate change. It suggests that this learning will require less emphasis on new ideas and an unhelpful 'crisis narrative' of climate change and its impacts, and closer attention to continuities in and lessons from policy history to build ways of engaging more profoundly with local communities. At the heart of the argument is a short historical comparison between present day issues and the 1989–1993 Bangladesh Flood Action Plan (FAP), a major donor-led flood control initiative that now seems largely forgotten. The FAP was an essentially top-down initiative conceived by outside agencies and an unelected military government. After four years and millions of dollars spent, it was eventually abandoned in the face of a combination of resistance from local communities, recognition of the importance of local forms of indigenous knowledge, and new technical advice from experts who began to better recognise the limits of their understanding of Bangladesh's complex environment.

Bangladesh and climate change

There is a consensus that climate change is real, and is with us now. The Fourth Assessment Report of the Inter-Governmental Panel on Climate Change (IPCC) predicted that average global temperature may rise by around 3 degrees centigrade by the end of the current century and that sea levels could rise by 59 cm. More frequent periods of heat-wave and heavy rainfall are also predicted. The lack of international progress on negotiating reductions in greenhouse gas emissions has increased the need for urban and rural communities to take measures which will help them to adapt to the risks of increased storms, floods and landslides which are likely to impact negatively on their livelihoods and wellbeing. The United Nations Framework Convention on Climate Change (UNFCCC) specifies that developed countries are committed to helping 'particularly vulnerable' countries meet the costs of adaptation.

Within the donor community, the current trend is one of 'mainstreaming climate change into development and national planning' (Huq and Ayers, 2008). In the words of one UK Department for International Development (DFID) staff member, climate change has moved from the periphery 'to the centre' of all DFID's activities in Bangladesh. In 2007, the Government of Bangladesh (GoB) began incorporating the impacts of climate change into all its development activities and accordingly revised its interim Poverty Reduction Strategy Paper (PRSP). It adopted recommendations from the World Bank on climate change impacts into a new 25 year water sector plan, its coastal zone management programmes, and its disaster preparedness plans.

At a joint DFID and GoB meeting in London in 2008, the UK pledged £75 million additional funding over the coming five years, to help fight climate change through adaptation, technology transfer and mitigation, and through further international resource mobilisation to assist Bangladesh's efforts. The GoB also announced that it would add US$45 million of its own resources during 2009, and outlined its plans for a Multi-Donor Trust Fund (MDTF), a basket-funding mechanism for adaptation resources. In August 2009, the Ministry of Environment and Forests produced the *Bangladesh Climate Change Strategy and Action Plan 2009*, a detailed and comprehensive document that while perhaps short on implementation detail, appeared to signal that the GoB was itself taking the lead on the issue.

Media discourse on Bangladesh and climate change has become more intense, and increasingly draws on what some have termed a 'crisis narrative' (see Hartmann, 2010). In an article on the NGO Plan International's work in Bangladesh (*The Guardian*, 26 April 2008), Raekha Prasad wrote:

> One of Bangladesh's greatest potential problems is the creation of climate change refugees: people who can no longer farm on drowning coastal and river areas are forced inland to the country's already crammed cities.

Less cautiously, in a Reuters news agency article dated 14 April 2008, the headline screamed 'Bangladesh faces climate refugee nightmare'.[1] The term 'climate refugee' is particularly jarring for long-term observers of poverty and livelihoods issues in Bangladesh, because it implies a break with past behaviours as a result of recent climate trends, rather than a continuation and intensification of peoples' long-term livelihood strategies. It obscures the fact that for many people, moving around as a result of unstable riverine and coastal ecology is not a qualitatively new phenomenon, but has long been part of life and is an outcome of people's fragile livelihoods. Rivers regularly change course, and coastal areas are constantly eroded. A range of long term development initiatives – such as income generation, community organisation, land rights strengthening and infrastructure building – have long been engaging with such problems.

A report by Johann Hari in *The Independent* newspaper, under the heading 'Bangladesh is set to disappear under the waves by the end of the century' was particularly detailed. In Dhaka, he interviewed Bangladeshi climate scientist Dr Atiq Rahman, who provided basic facts which have informed the diagnoses of Bangladesh's situation: as sea levels rise, land is lost from the coastal areas, and as rivers flowing down into the delta from the melting Himalayan glaciers accelerates, more land is lost through more rapid soil erosion. The article pointed out that extreme weather events such as 2007's devastating Hurricane Sidr were increasing in frequency.[2] Hari reports stories told by coastal villagers about problems of salinity in drinking water, farmland which has become too damaged to grow crops, and coastal seas now too treacherous for fishing. On one island near Cox's Bazaar, he found two thirds of the land gone, and a population that had shrunk from 30,000 to 18,000 in 20 years. Hari also drew attention to fears that growing pressures on resources brought about by climate change could fuel disorder and religious intolerance. Linking Bangladesh's crisis with the need for the world's wealthy countries to take action on the causes of climate change, he concludes with the statement that 'if we carry on as we are, Bangladesh will enter its endgame'.

The Flood Action Plan (1989–93)

In Bangladesh's policy history, concerns about environment and human security in relation to flood control have from time to time attracted large-scale attention from the development community. The British colonial authorities, for example, commissioned a number of studies and public works during the early 20th century in the struggle to manage rivers and embankments (Iqbal, 2007). In the late 1980s, after many years of relative neglect,[3] international donors suddenly became interested in flood control once again after disastrous and well-publicised floods experienced in 1987 and 1988. Many environmentalists at that time had begun to link the recent floods to growing levels of soil erosion, which were believed to be the consequence of increasing Himalayan deforestation upstream in the mountains of Nepal.[4] The country's long-standing 'flood problem' suddenly became a donor priority and high profile international cause. In 1989, during what was to be the final year of the authoritarian government of General Ershad, a major multi-donor project known as the Flood Action Plan (FAP) began to take shape. The need for a comprehensive solution once and for all to Bangladesh's flood problem was given an extra fillip by reports that Madame Mitterrand, the wife of the French President who had been visiting Dhaka, had been alarmed to find water coming under her door (Boyce, 1990).

A communiqué from the G-7 summit held in July 1989 stated (World Bank, 1989: 23, quoted in Adnan, 1991: 8):

> Bangladesh ... is periodically devastated by catastrophic floods ... [There was] ... need for effective, coordinated action by the international community, in support of the Government of Bangladesh, in order to find solutions to this major problem which are technically, financially, economically, and technically sound.

Approved formally in May 1990, the proposed FAP included a total of 26 studies and pilot schemes, 11 'main' components and 15 'supportive' components. The aim was to construct tall embankments along both sides of Bangladesh's three main rivers, at an estimated cost of US$5–10 billion. This mega-project was to be one of the largest development projects ever undertaken. The French government joined with Japan, UNDP and USAID to engage a wide range of foreign experts, including engineers and later social scientists, to devise flood prevention and control schemes.

However, FAP became controversial for four main sets of reasons. First, the top-down manner in which the plan took shape in London under World Bank leadership raised important questions about accountability, consultation and participation. The donors had not considered lessons from earlier flood control measures before the plan was finalized, and nor was there any public consultation (Adnan, 1991). When the government of General H.M. Ershad fell in late 1990, a new interim government led by Justice Shahabuddin took power with a 'caretaker' role. A government task force on the FAP in February 1991 reported a range of concerns, particularly about the fact that the plan had not been opened to public debate (Custers, 1993).

Second, FAP's primarily technical emphasis on engineering solutions to problems of floods, based mainly on the construction of embankments and sluice gates, paid little attention to the potential of 'softer' people-centred solutions, drawing on past traditions of community management of floods, to build upon the generations of local experience of dealing with the problem.[5] FAP seemed blind to the political and administrative complexity of how such infrastructure could be effectively operated and equitably managed. Conflicts of interest quickly appeared within government and donor bureaucracies, and foreign consultancy teams. International opposition began to mobilise: for example, the US International Rivers Network argued that intervening in a powerful regional river system would actually worsen flooding (Custers, 1993). This view echoed far older – and largely forgotten – experiences from the British colonial period, when it was found that building river embankments seriously threatened local agricultural productivity, and contributed to the deterioration of rivers (Iqbal, 2007). As early as 1927, Calcutta Professor Prasanta C. Mahalanobis had produced a study of the North Bengal floods of 1922, which had argued that constructing embankments simply worsened floods in the long term, because they had the effect of raising river beds (Adnan, 2000).

Third, the project relied predominantly on donor country expertise gained from exotic contexts such as lowland water management in the Netherlands and flood control in the US Mississippi, both of which were potentially out of step with Bangladesh's own distinctive ecology and society. Even at a technical level (leaving aside history, politics and society), problems quickly became apparent. Experts have consistently failed to understand the complexity of Bangladesh's environment and natural resource systems. For example, the view of Bangladesh in the 1970s as a 'basket case' unable to feed its people was challenged in the 1990s when the intensification of agriculture brought the country close to food self-sufficiency (Bradnock and Saunders, 2002). Fourth, the establishment of the FAP quickly began to dominate development activities in Bangladesh. Hundreds of preliminary studies were commissioned to consider a wide range of water-related issues around the country, engaging large numbers of local and expatriate researchers, consultants and administrators, and drawing them away from work on other equally important issues. Development in Bangladesh, it seemed, had now become subordinated to the central problem of flood control.

By 1993, many of these limitations had become apparent, and FAP faded from view. The Dhaka embankment and another one built in Tangail were the only tangible results of what was to have been a show case mega-project, along with hundreds of word-processed studies which cluttered the shelves of agencies and consultants' offices. Contestation from within local communities, such as the well-documented protests in Beel Dakatia, also contributed to international mobilisation against the plan by a range of groups (Adnan, 2000). A report in the UK weekly *New Scientist* by Pearce and Tickell (1993) explained that the very donors that had launched the FAP initiative four years earlier had finally lost confidence in the project. As Wood (1999) pointed out in a later overview, the FAP had been a contestation over water resources in which ordinary people had had very little voice in either problem diagnosis or the design of policy solutions. A key lesson was therefore that privileging the 'expert knowledge' of engineers, bureaucrats and development specialists was a poor substitute to an engagement with local communities, institutions and indigenous knowledge.

Policy history, lesson learning and development

Learning from the past is not a strong point of mainstream development agencies, which usually give more attention to the promised delivery of changes in the future than on the analysis of the history and fortunes of past development efforts, with the result that they live in a form of 'perpetual present' (Lewis, 2009). This is a condition in which there is an abundance of frequently changing jargon, constant excitement about a set of new approaches which promise better chances of success than those currently in place, and strong, and in many ways understandable, pressure to look to the future rather than dwelling on the past.

A key reason for this has been the infusion of ideologies of 'managerialism' into development (Roberts et al., 2005). Managerialism discourages engagement with the very ideas of past and present, through its focus on means-ends thinking, its reluctance to engage with questions of power, and its relentless emphasis on novelty and change. This has the effect of decontextualising development practice. For example, Cornwall and Brock (2005) show in their analysis of the ways in which development 'buzzwords' such as empowerment, participation and poverty reduction serve to maintain what they argue is a strongly 'imagined narrative' of development. It is one which relies on consensus rather than issues of politics and power, and on the coining of new terms that serve to separate the 'development present' from deeper historical references.

Planning tools such as 'logical frameworks' also form part of this process, alongside new types of 'progressive' language that mainly serve the purpose of indicating that development policy is 'moving forward'. For example, while the large numbers of people who live on Bangladesh's shifting silt islands (known as 'chars') have learned to cope with the frequent movements and migrations necessary to maintain a livelihood in what has long been an insecure and inhospitable environment, it is only during the last few years with the onset of climate change discourses that such people have come to be labelled 'climate change refugees' by donors and NGOs. There is a danger that this 'crisis discourse' of climate change is beginning to obscure other deep-rooted causes of insecurity, and the policy efforts to address these problems, such as the long-term problems of flooding in vulnerable areas due to poor water management policies, or the growth of salinity primarily caused by the expansion of commercial shrimp farming (c.f. Deb, 1998). Also as Hartmann (2010) points out, the term 'climate refugee' in fact replays an earlier policy idea from the 1990s about 'environmental refugees', which in turn recycled unhelpful colonial stereotypes of environmentally destructive peasants.

The FAP was part of an earlier chapter of policy history, and some people will argue that circumstances were very different from today's climate change and development agenda in Bangladesh. For example, there is now perhaps more participation of NGOs in planning discussions, and a far greater emphasis on community-based adaptation. The government is positioning itself in a more central position in relation to international donors in relation to climate change issues than it did in the years of the FAP, and is becoming more active in building a wider range of international linkages and relationships. Yet there are also continuities. A tendency towards generalised assumptions, technocratic solutions, and an essentialised 'crisis narrative' is strongly reminiscent of the FAP period. At the same time, critiques by local and international civil society actors of DFID/GoB climate change initiatives similarly pointed to top-down approaches, with an unbalanced emphasis on infrastructure development, all of which displayed striking parallels with earlier critiques of the FAP.[6]

By contrast, on a visit to Bangladesh in early 2010, I visited an area in Naogaon District where the NGO ActionAid has been undertaking community-level work with local partner organisations that seeks to build on local knowledge and histories in useful ways. The principle and practice of *gono gobeshona* (which means 'people's research' in Bengali) developed by ActionAid has encouraged and facilitated local community members to conduct their own enquiries into the processes of climate change, reflect on these and to take appropriate adaptive action (ActionAid, 2009). For example, a group of village women talked us through their reconstruction of the recent environmental trends in this drought-prone area, using picture maps and timelines that they had developed at community level, showing how drought is increasing and season lengths are changing. As a result, a range of local adaptation responses are being developed and implemented, including experimenting with new crop varieties such as wheat, new water-efficient cultivation methods, reduced-water latrines and adapted communally located tube-well pumps. At the same time, this approach seeks to raise awareness for embarking on local and international campaigning on mitigation as well as local level adaptation.

Author updates to the 2025 edition

Revisiting these issues in 2024, their relevance remains clear, and in at least two key respects, they have become even more urgent. The first theme that still resonates is the continuing presence of a set of crisis narratives around climate and migration. For example, one of the policy models that has emerged during the intervening years is that of 'managed retreat', seen as particularly relevant to densely populated areas of the Global South such as Bangladesh. This refers to the purposeful relocation of people, homes, businesses and infrastructure from locations judged to be hazardous to those judged to be safer.

A recent paper based on field research in Mongla, one of Bangladesh's key secondary cities, engaged with a new policy discourse around the idea of creating the 'migrant-friendly climate resilient cities' that is already beginning to reproduce some of the problems discussed in the earlier FAP case (Rahman et al., 2023). Informed by a Western-driven crisis narrative around climate migration, the managed retreat policies that are emerging similarly display a tendency to oversimplify complex realities and take on overly technical forms. The case of Mongla, where for example extensive port dredging efforts were found to have unforeseen detrimental effects on low income urban residents' access to clean well water, as a result of economic objectives overlooking social and community level livelihoods dimensions. There is a continuing risk that local decision-making, community participation and local organisation are overlooked in favour of top down infrastructure development. The authors argue that 'the design and implementation of equitable retreat policies will require a paradigm shift, away from cost–benefit and efficiency metrics toward ones better informed by values, ethics and social justice' (p.7).

The second continuing theme is the difficulty policy makers face in taking a long term view, and the concomitant tendency for opportunities to learn from history to be missed. The knowledge base around these issues has been significantly expanded by recent scholarship. Paprocki (2021) makes the case for seeing contemporary climate effects in the context of a long history of fragile livelihoods within Bangladesh's unstable yet dynamic ecological system. In order to understand the effects of climate change and the choices faced today, she argues, we must pay attention to the ways conditions have been shaped by 'historical power dynamics and inequalities that far predate what we today recognise as climate change' (p.6). Dewan (2023) shows how these 'climate reductive' narratives are deployed to favour technical, donor-driven interventions that imply that people are being forced to break with past behaviours, rather than building on and adjusting existing practices.

There is growing recognition of the importance of improving links between development policy decision makers and history, along with the need to explore in more depth the different kinds of reasons why this has often proved problematic – not only in relation to international environment and development policies, but also more widely. Approaching policy ethnographically can usefully draw our attention to important though less visible aspects of policy processes – such as the centrality of 'structural forgetting' within policy worlds, the prevalence of forms of policy amnesia, and the deliberate use of 'strategic ignorance' in justifying interventions (see for example McGoey, 2012; Epprecht, 1997).[7]

Conclusion

Dealing with the implications of climate change is likely to be crucial for securing a sustainable future for Bangladesh. The well-being of Bangladesh's people is likely to be better served by approaches that pay closer attention to recent development policy history. Of course learning lessons from history is not a straightforward matter, since such lessons can easily be manipulated by those with power. But as the historian Margaret Macmillan (2009: 169) argues: 'if the study of history does nothing more than teach us humility, scepticism, and awareness of ourselves, then it has done something useful' (p. 169).

It will perhaps be valuable to reflect further on three inter-linked issues. The first is the dangerous oversimplification implied by the 'crisis narratives' of climate change that are gaining ground in the media locally and internationally. The second is the need to better engage with the knowledge that has been built up over generations among the people who live within Bangladesh's rivers and deltas, and with the long-term policy experiences of those who have long worked alongside them. The third is to recognise, and begin to address, the tendency of development agencies to confine themselves to the realm of the 'perpetual present', in which development policy history and institutional memory is largely ignored in favour of present- or future-oriented discourse and action.

A little-documented but frequently overwhelming urge of policy (and of the development professionals that animate policy worlds) is to demonstrate action and forward movement, yet this urge contributes to potentially dangerous forms of what Lewis and Mosse (2006) term policy 'disjunctures'. These create discontinuities that unhelpfully break with the trajectories of longer-term development efforts and experience. This policy imperative tends to demand simple, rather than complex, stories in order to build momentum for action. Ideas which have not been systematically thought out, and that remain unsubjected to historical scrutiny, become attractive to policy actors – in this case donors, governments and NGOs – precisely because their simplicity carries an immediate power within the 'perpetual present' of a particular policy context. As Green (2008: 288) has argued, we will need a combination of 'public pressure and far-sighted leadership' if the capacities of governments are to be strengthened in ways that can equip the most vulnerable people with the means to cope with increasingly high levels of risk.

Notes

1 http://www.alertnet.org/thenews/newsdesk/DHA234479.htm (accessed 10 November 2008).

2 Although Sidr is believed to have been one of the severest hurricanes on record, due to improved warning and shelter facilities, the resulting loss of life (around 5,000–10,000 people) was a fraction of the 190,000 lives lost in 1991 to a similar event.

3 The last major activity had been the 1964 'Master Plan' undertaken during the period when Bangladesh was known as East Pakistan, after serious flooding occurred during 1954–56. The Plan was funded by USAID and World Bank (Adnan, 2000).

4 Such issues continue to cause controversy, as the IPCC found in 2009 when it was accused of reporting flawed predictions about the melting of Himalayan glaciers.

5 Boyce (1990) illustrated this point with the observation that unlike English, Bengali distinguishes between normal positive flooding which rejuvenates the land each year (*barsha*) and abnormal or harmful floods which cause distress (*bonna*).

6 See http://www.equitybd.org/feedback/feedback.htm#2.

7 The theme of policy amnesia and development is the subject of a forthcoming book by the author.

References

ActionAid (2009) 'Climate change adaptation in an uncertain environment: lessons from a targeted community based adaptation approach in Bangladesh', ActionAid, Dhaka.

Adnan, S. (1991) *Floods, People and the Environment: Institutional Aspects of Flood Protection Programmes in Bangladesh, 1990,* Research and Advisory Services, Dhaka.

Adnan, S. (2000) 'Explaining the Retreat from Flood Control in the Ganges-Brahmaputra-Meghna Delta of Bangladesh', unpublished paper, South Asian Studies Programme, National University of Singapore.

Boyce, J. (1990) 'Birth of a mega-project: political economy of flood control in Bangladesh', *Environmental Management* 14: 419–428.

Bradnock, R. and Saunders, P. (2002) 'Rising waters, sinking land? environmental change and development in Bangladesh', in R. Bradnock and G. Williams (eds.) *South Asia in a Globalizing World: A Reconstructed Regional Geography*, pp. 51–77, Pearson Education, Harlow.

Cornwall, A. and Brock, K. (2005) 'What do buzzwords do for development policy? A critical look at "participation", "empowerment" and "poverty reduction"'. *Third World Quarterly* 26: 1043–1060.

Custers, P. (1993) 'Bangladesh's Flood Action Plan: a critique', *Economic and Political Weekly* 28: 1501–1503.

Deb, A. (1998) 'Fake blue revolution: environmental and socio-economic impacts of shrimp culture in the coastal areas of Bangladesh', *Ocean and Coastal Management* 41: 63–88.

Dewan, C. (2023) 'Climate refugees or labour migrants? Climate reductive translations of women's migration from coastal Bangladesh'. *The Journal of Peasant Studies*, 1–22. https://doi.org/10. 1080/03066150.2023.2195555

Epprecht, M. (1997) 'Investing in amnesia, or fantasy and forgetfulness in the World Bank's approach to healthcare reform in sub-Saharan Africa', *The Journal of Developing Areas* 31(3): 337–356.

Green, D. (2008) *From Poverty to Power: How Active Citizens and Effective States Can Change the World*, Oxfam, Oxford.

Hartmann, B. (2010) 'Rethinking climate refugees and climate conflict: rhetoric, reality and the politics of policy discourse', *Journal of International Development* 22: 233–246.

Huq, S. and Ayers, J. (2008) 'Climate change impacts and responses in Bangladesh', European Parliament, DG Internal Policies, Policy Department Economy and Science, Brussels, [online] available from: http://www.europarl.europa.eu/activities/committees/studies/download.do?file=19195.

The Independent (1998) 'Dubious wave of flood relief to Bangladesh', 11 October.

Iqbal, I. (2007) 'The railways and the water regime of the Eastern Bengal Delta, c1845–1943', *Internationales Asienforum* 38: 329–352.

Lewis, D. (2009) 'International development and the "perpetual present": anthropological approaches to the rehistoricisation of policy', *European Journal of Development Research* 21: 32–46.

Lewis, D. and Mosse, D. (2006) 'Encountering order and disjuncture: contemporary anthropological perspectives on the organisation of development', *Oxford Development Studies* 34: 1–14.

Macmillan, M. (2009) *The Uses and Abuses of History*. Profile Books, London.

McGoey, L. (2012) 'The logic of strategic ignorance', *British Journal of Sociology* 63(3): 553–576.

Paprocki, K. (2021) *Threatening dystopias: The global politics of climate change adaptation in Bangladesh*. Ithaca, NY: Cornell University Press.

Pearce, F. and Tickell, O. (1993) 'West sinks Bangladesh flood plan', *New Scientist*, 21st August.

Rahman, M. Feisal, Lewis David, Kuhl Laura, Baldwin Andrew, Ruszczyk Hanna, Nadiruzzaman Md. and Mahid Yousuf (2023) 'Managed urban retreat: the trouble with crisis narratives', *Urban Geography* 45: 23–32. DOI: 10.1080/02723638.2023.2228094

Roberts, S., Jones, J. and Frohling, O. (2005) 'NGOs and the globalization of managerialism', *World Development* 33: 1845–1864.

Wood, G. (1994) *Whose Ideas, Whose Interests?* University Press Limited, Dhaka.

Wood, G. (1999) 'Contesting water in Bangladesh: knowledge, rights and governance', *Journal of International Development* 11: 731–754.

About the author

David Lewis is Professor of Social Policy and Development at the London School of Economics and Political Science. An anthropologist by training, he has worked on a range of theoretical and applied development issues in South Asia, including rural development, civil society and NGOs and the ethnography of policy. He is co-author with Katy Gardner of *Anthropology, Development and the Postmodern Challenge* (1996) and *Non-Governmental Organizations and Development* (2009, with Nazneen Kanji).

Chapter 14

Local perceptions and adaptation to climate change: A perspective from Western India

Dineshkumar Moghariya

People's perceptions of risk and their levels of concern can influence or constrain climate change policy. This study of risk perception in rural Saurastra and Kutch region of Western India reveals that rural people are able to detect the impact of climate change correctly; however, the extent to their knowledge and concern about climate change varies considerably, influenced not only by their local observations but also messages (sometimes misunderstood) from the mass media. Perceptions of risk range from moderate to high, but they are only moderately concerned regarding risks of climate change. Respondents in cyclone-prone areas express higher levels of perceived risk and slightly higher levels of concerns than their counterparts in drought-prone areas. Several people believed that technological innovations and the pursuit of non-farm income sources would protect them from adverse impacts of climate change. Overall, rural people use an integrated approach, incorporating both traditional and modern practices, for successful adaptation to climate change. There is a need for an inclusive approach to make people aware of causes, impacts and solutions to climate change.

Introduction

Despite scientific consensus, public acceptance of the existence of global warming is highly variable, influenced by controversies such as those over projections regarding the receding of Himalayan glaciers. Understanding climate change is especially a challenge in developing countries, where remoteness, limited communication infrastructure, illiteracy, and poverty hinder people's access to information. Yet, rural people in less developed societies are not disconnected from the wider world. Access to radio, TV and other mass media are reaching more people, but they are used more for entertainment rather than educational information. People perceive climate change within the local context, as filtered mainly by their local knowledge and socio-economic conditions. These perceptions are largely derived from their own observations and experience, as well as from knowledge accumulated locally through time. Nonetheless, outside sources of information are reaching further and more intensely into rural areas.

The value of local knowledge systems for development efforts has been recognized by many development practitioners and academics for decades, and its potential for climate change adaptation and mitigation is receiving attention (Salick and Anja, 2007). Rural people have developed and inherited complex traditional knowledge and practices over generations which help them to accommodate climatic variability (Altieri and Koohafkhan, 2008). The importance of local knowledge for adaptation to climate change is recognized in many international declarations, though it has yet to be mainstreamed into policy discussions concerning adaptation and mitigation (Srinivasan, 2004; Machi, 2008). Unfortunately, traditional knowledge and practices are still regarded by many people as primitive, inefficient and lacking in adaptation potential.

In this chapter I explore rural perceptions of climate change, identifying local knowledge and practices that facilitate adaptation. This is based on field research in the Saurastra and Kutch region of Gujarat state in Western India, as well as the findings of researchers from other parts of the world. In particular, I focus on rural people's knowledge, beliefs and perceptions of risk related to issues of climate change. Finally, I offer suggestions relating to the inclusion of local perspectives and knowledge in climate change policy.

Local risk perception and knowledge about climate change

Risk perception is the subjective evaluation of the probability of hazard occurring, including concern about its consequences (Sjoberg et al., 2004). Personal occurrence and other factors such as education and income, influence the way a person perceives risk (Garvin, 2001). Thus, risk perception is socially constructed; people do not rely only on assumed probability of occurrence of events alone, but situate risk within a complex mix of factors. To a large extent, the perception of risk is socially distributed, reflecting people's social milieu, including their personal experiences and culturally transmitted knowledge (including mass media), and their access to social networks and material resources. From both policy and scientific perspectives, it is important to know how people understand, detect, and perceive risks associated with climate change in order to better address mitigation or adaptation. This is particularly important for rural people, whose livelihoods depend on observing climate and weather patterns. Indeed they may be a good source of information for understanding climate change at the local level (Salick and Anja, 2007).

Human dimension of climate change

The Saurastra and Kutch region comprises eight districts of the Gujarat state along the coast of the Arabian Sea. For my doctoral research, I surveyed

410 participants from 16 villages across all eight districts regarding their perspectives about climate change. A multistage cluster sampling technique was used for village selection, and 10 per cent of the households from each village were selected randomly for the study.

From scientific perspectives, the distinction between weather and climate is a well understood concept. People in Saurastra and Kutch also have distinct words – *havaman* for weather and *abohava* for climate – for these concepts. However, *abohava* is not a part of regular discourse, which may hamper their spontaneous capacity to distinguish between these two concepts. In my study respondents often did not make the distinction, instead associated seasonal changes in weather parameters with longer-term climate change. The conflation of climate and weather does not apply to rural India alone, but was prevalent in studies carried out in developed societies such as the United States (Read et al., 1994). The apparent confusion of respondents concerning these two concepts does not mean that their understanding of long-term changes in climatic parameters is limited. All 410 respondents in my survey associated climate change with an increase in temperature, with some interviewees also mentioning long-term shifts in wind speed. More than 80 per cent of the respondents also identified a trend for rainfall to increase as local evidence of climate change. However, more than half of the 50 interviewees stated that rainfall has decreased, as did a smaller proportion of respondents in Porbandar and Jungadh districts. Some interviewees also cited changes in rainfall intensity and uncertainty of rain as indicators of local climate change. My interviews generally revealed a complex pattern regarding the local patterns of climatic fluctuation. People often stated that annual rainfall was higher 30 to 35 years ago, and then decreased for an extended period. It increased only in the past 10 to 12 years. In similar studies conducted in Egypt, Ghana, Kenya, South Africa, Nigeria and Senegal, people perceive temperature as increasing while rainfall was decreasing in their respective areas (Madison, 2007).

Rainfall data collected from two different online sources of Indian Meteorological Department (IMD) and Indiastate.com web pages revealed that rural people are correct in detecting recent changes in their local climate. Between 1997 and 2008 annual rainfall totals for the region have been on a general upward trend, suggesting that people's perceptions of increased rainfall match with the measured rainfall data. Analysis of the last 40 years (1969–2008) of regional climate data also shows an overall increase in seasonal rainfall totals, as well as a greater occurrence of heavy rainfall events that exceed 70 mm (Ray, 2009). A climate change scenario developed by Rupa Kumar et al. (2006) predicts both rising temperatures and more rainfall for North-western India, including my study area, in the 21st century. These scientific studies reinforce the fact that rural people observe and perceive changes in their local climate correctly. In another such study comparing climate data with farmers' responses, Madison (2007) found large numbers of farmers in Burkina Faso, Ghana and Zambia correctly stating that climate has become hotter and drier in their respective homelands. Even though the process of a long-term shift in the mean temperature and rainfall is slow and subtle, rural people can observe and identify such changes effectively.

Perceptions of causes and solutions

Most people surveyed considered deforestation as the main cause of climate change, followed by burning of fossil fuels. Interestingly, many people, irrespective of their belief about the main cause of climate change, see reforestation as the solution. A total of 45 per cent of the respondents believed that deforestation causes climate change, while 37 per cent cited burning fossil fuel as the main source. However, 53 per cent of respondents identified reforestation as the primary solution, compared to 21 per cent who mentioned burning less fossil fuel and 26 per cent who cited other measures to ameliorate climate change.

Scientific reports suggest that reducing carbon emissions from fossil fuel use is the primary step for halting climate change. In contrast, most people in the study area believe that reforestation offers the primary solution. To some extent they are right regarding their own circumstances, as their consumption of fossil fuel is very limited compared to people living in urban, industrialized societies. For these rural dwellers, reforestation does provide an important means for reversing the process of climate change. Nevertheless, forests are an important component of the global carbon cycle in terms of climate change mitigation. By absorbing carbon dioxide, forest ecosystems remove almost 30 per cent of all carbon dioxide emissions and are also a major contributor to the terrestrial carbon sink (Candell, 2008).

Gupta's study (1998: 264) of local agricultural knowledge in northern India concluded that it contained to some extent 'a mix of hybridity, mistranslations, and incommensurability,' reflecting an uneasy blending of ideas from a wide range of sources. This 'hybridity' is reflected in several interviews regarding climate change. For example, some respondents cited overpopulation as the main cause of climate change, while some others believe efficient use of energy to be a solution to climate change. In both cases they are right, as carbon emissions are connected to overall human consumption of resources and their use of energy. However, some respondents' explanation regarding contribution of overpopulation to climate change relied on a very different reasoning from scientists. Some respondents linked overpopulation with increased respiration emitting more heat into the environment. Similarly, several interviewees who cited efficient energy usage stated that light bulbs emit heat into the atmosphere, so having less lighting from a bulb means less heat. In identifying such beliefs, my purpose is not to belittle these rural people, or to demonstrate their ignorance. In fact, I am one of them, as I come from the study area. Rather, it is to show the pervasive influence of externally generated messages regarding climate change and the environment. Furthermore, rural Indians are not alone in apparent misperceptions of climate change phenomena, as demonstrated by Henry's (2000) study of American perceptions of this issue.

Many agricultural activities in these communities, including livestock-keeping, and the decomposing of farm waste, result in the emission of methane, one of the greenhouse gases responsible for climate change (Gibbs et al., 1989). Rural people, however, do not consider these activities as contributors to climate change. Instead, they generally assign causality for global warming to human actions such as cutting forests or industrial air pollution that appear to have a direct and visible impact on the environment. Methane emissions from rice fields or cattle dung are slow and invisible processes. That might be one of the reasons most people of rural Saurastra and Kutch do not consider agriculture as a contributing factor to climate change.

Overall, misconceptions regarding the causes of, and solutions to climate change suggest that even with the introduction of TV and radio in remote rural areas, people are still far from the reach of valid and reliable scientific information. The limited extent of formal schooling among many rural people in the region, means that they often lack the background information necessary to process fully scientific information on climate change, even if they receive it. Thus, as noted by Gupta (1998), such information may be 'mistranslated' or simply not comprehended due to cross-cultural differences in understanding. Once again, this phenomenon is not limited to the understanding of climate change, nor is it a unique feature of rural India, but occurs in all places as people seek to reconcile their local knowledge with external sources of information. My study shows that, in the short run, in these rural Indian communities, people correctly detect climate change but misunderstand some key aspects about it. The study also indicates that there is a need for increasing awareness about the role of burning fossil fuels in climate change.

Risk perception and concern

Perceiving risks from climate change is important for initiating action to reduce the process and mitigate its impacts. Study participants were asked to assess risks of climate change, exploring 15 issues about climate change, including whether agricultural productivity will decrease, or if new diseases will spread into the area in the next 25 years. I used the four-point Likert scale ranging from very unlikely (1) to very likely (4). Using this scale, district risk index scores were grouped in four subjective levels of perceived risk: less risk, moderate risk, high risk, and very high risk.

In general, rural people of Saurastra and Kutch perceive moderate to very high risk related to climate change. There is marked spatial difference in perceptions based on local climatic differences. Respondents in drought-prone Surendranagar and Kutch districts perceived less risk than people living in the cyclone-prone Junagadh and Porbandar districts.

The higher levels of perceived risk in cyclone-prone areas may be due to the catastrophic impacts of storms, including severe damage to property and loss of life. Drought impacts tend to be slower and less damaging to property. This pattern may be the reason for a lower level of perceived risk in drought areas. The high frequency of drought in these districts may mean that people are well adapted to such circumstances.

The study also probes people's level of concern regarding taking action for climate change risks. People may see high risk for example, but may not be concerned enough to start actions. Subjects were assessed for their levels of concern on the same four-point Likert scale ranging from not at all concerned (1) to very concerned (4). Respondents were generally less to moderately concerned about risk from climate change. Of those surveyed, 82 per cent of respondents reported that they are 'slightly' to 'somewhat' concerned. This means most people's level of concern is less than their degree of perceived risks from climate change. People perceive moderate to high risk, but they are concerned only moderately about it.

Why are people not strongly concerned? I asked many respondents for explanations. They generally do not think their livelihoods, including agriculture productivity, will suffer due to climate change, despite future increase in temperature, uncertain or heavy rainfall or possible spread of new plant diseases. Many respondents believe that innovations in agricultural science will address any unwarranted situations. Others assume that growth in off-farm sources of income will sustain their livelihood. This suggests that people underestimate the impact of climate change on non-agricultural sectors of the economy which may also prevent people from taking early adaptation action.

A difference existed in the level of concern between inhabitants of drought- and cyclone-prone areas, but it was not pronounced. Respondents in drought-prone areas were slightly less concerned than their counterparts in cyclone-prone districts. This low level of concern in drought-prone communities might be associated with recent trends. The study area has received generally good rainfall in the last decade perhaps making the villagers feel less worried about the possibility of future droughts (Weinstein, 1989). More than 50 per cent of the respondents believed that drought would not become more frequent or intense in next 25 years. Overall, people exhibited a moderate to high level of perceived risk from climate change, but only a moderate level of concern regarding it. They believe that agricultural innovation and non-farm income opportunities will protect them from climate change's adverse impacts.

Traditional knowledge and climate change adaptations

Local traditional knowledge for adaptation to climate change is also referred to as indigenous knowledge, farmers' knowledge, or rural people's knowledge (Srinivasan, 2004). It may be described as institutionalized local knowledge unique to a given culture or society, acquired through accumulation of experiences, informal experiments, and an intimate understanding of the natural systems stressed by climate change. This knowledge combines present-day observations with information passed on from one generation to the other by word of mouth (Osunade, 1994; Srinivasan, 2004).

The region is characterized by climatic variation, especially erratic rainfall, with recurring drought almost every four to five years. Although groundwater irrigation takes place in some areas, most of the agriculture is rain-fed due to lack of water supply and limited irrigation infrastructure. Regularly confronted by adverse climatic conditions, people in rural Gujarat have developed resilient farming systems that have the potential to accommodate new conditions brought on by climate change.

Most traditional farming practices are site-specific and represent farmers' experience in relation to local environment and to locally available resources. These traditional practices are primarily based on crop diversity, nutrient recycling, and water management, along with use of local plant varieties and locally suited soil and water conservation practices. This approach to farming averts or distributes risk, and it sustains crop yields under uncertain and adverse climatic conditions.

Crop diversity

Farmers of Saurastra and Kutch traditionally practise intercropping and mixed cropping as a safeguard against crop failure due to erratic and uncertain rainfall. Intercropping also allows farmers to use their land and available moisture optimally at different times. They combine cereals and leguminous crops depending on local soil conditions. It is very common in drought-prone Saurastra and Kutch to interplant cotton or cereals such as pearl millet with a leguminous crop, including green gram, black gram, or sesame. Intercropping of peanuts with pigeon pea also occurs on a large scale in this area. If one crop fails due to poor rainfall, the other may survive. For example, if rain terminates early, then cotton may fail, but sesame will still likely yield.

Use of local seed varieties is another mechanism to stabilize the production under extreme climate conditions. However, farmers nowadays often rely on hybrid crop varieties with a short life and less resistance to pest infestation. BT cotton, which is modified to contain a gene from the bacterium *Bacillus thuringiensis* as an insecticide, has been controversial yet widely adopted by farmers to sustain their yields. At the same time households commonly plant more than one cotton variety, usually three to four, to take advantage of different climatic conditions.

Changing planting dates according to rainfall and water availability is another important measure to cope with climatic variability. In Saurastra and Kutch, farmers cultivate cotton and groundnuts with the onset of monsoon, but if the rains are delayed, they switch to short duration and drought-tolerant crops such as sesame and castor. Sesame is also cultivated with the timely onset of the rains, but, when the rains are delayed, farmers prefer to cultivate its *purva* variety, which grows quickly and survives well with limited soil moisture. Some farmers, especially ones in drought-prone areas, who used to grow peanuts, are increasingly switching to sesame or cotton due to the increasing variability and uncertainty of rainfall. Peanut requires well-distributed rain for good crops, while sesame or cotton can withstand dry spells without much effect on its productivity. Farmers not only perceived rainfall as having increased in recent years, but also that rainfall uncertainty has increased.

Water management

In situ soil and moisture conservation through land levelling and farm bunds are common practices followed by farmers in the study region. These techniques increase water infiltration during rain and increase the moisture retention capacity of soil, thus increasing the ability of crops to withstand a prolonged dry spell. Using small water harvesting structures – century-old techniques to collect excess rain water for future irrigation or domestic use – is the most popular and commonly adopted strategy to cope with erratic rainfall. This practice is widely supported by government. People also drill bore wells or deepen existing wells for irrigation. Many farmers have adopted well recharge techniques, diverting runoff water in to the well though pipes and filters. They not only seek new sources of water for irrigation, but also change their irrigation methods depending upon the rainfall and water availability situation. Many farmers have started using drip or sprinkler irrigation to improve efficient water use. Others are alternating furrow irrigation, or making small basins for more efficient utilization of water.

Animal husbandry

Households engage in mixed farming, typically keeping cattle, goats or sheep for milking and bullocks for draught power. Cattle are fed with crop residues from pearl millet and sorghum, and they also graze on common land. Composted cattle dung is used as an organic fertilizer. Pastoralism is another traditional occupation of the area. In response to the area's dry climate, pastoralists migrate with their flocks and herds to grazing grounds in the middle or south Gujarat during summer. They might remain there the entire year during droughts. Others have reduced their herd size in response to the decreasing productivity and availability of pasture land.

Many pastoralists have diversified their occupation by taking up farming or employment in transport or mining sectors.

Socio-economic adaptations

The Aga Khan Rural Support Programme (India), a nationally recognized non-governmental organization working for enhancement of rural livelihoods, conducted participatory research in 2008 in Surendranagar district. People reported reducing their household expenses during drought, spending less on food, clothes and other requirements. They try to avoid attending social ceremonies such as weddings which require gifts or other obligations. Many survey respondents said that they have started decreasing social expenses for marriages, birth ceremonies, and funerals. Even during normal years they try to increase their savings base so that they can withstand shocks arising from drought, flood, or cyclones. Non-governmental organizations (NGOs) working in the area have initiated some community-based adaptations such as grain banks and micro-savings through self-help groups to reduce the impacts of present and future climatic extremes on local livelihoods.

Modern agriculture

Farmers in Saurastra and Kutch not only rely on traditional knowledge to cope with climatic variability, but have adopted a range of modern agricultural practices, which they utilize along with traditional ones. Most respondents are increasingly using chemical fertilizers and pesticides for protecting their crops. They plant BT hybrid cotton seeds and other short-duration varieties as a safeguard against rainfall uncertainty and pest infestation. Increased temperature is projected to increase the range and incidence of pest population, adding to local dependence on farm chemicals (IPCC, 2007). Many farmers adopt tractors, which they consider to be an important step in stabilizing their agriculture productivity. Tractors permit deep cultivation, allowing more water to be retained in the soil, helping crops withstand dry spells. Farmers are purchasing crop insurance for diversifying their risk of crop failures. Nevertheless, modern technologies require high investment, and many households cannot afford to adopt industrial farm inputs.

Both modern and traditional agriculture practices pose opportunities and risks. Use of modern practices such as genetically modified crop varieties, drip irrigation or fertilizers and pesticides are regularly portrayed as offering increased potential to withstand climate stress, more efficient use of water, and reduced damage in emergencies such as a sudden outbreak of pest or severe soil erosion due to flood. On the other hand, monocropping poses severe risk of crop failure under climatic extremes. Extensive use of fertilizers and pesticides not only increases cost, but also gives rise to other environmental problems such as water and air pollution. Pesticides kill both pests and their predators, and in the absence of natural predators, crops may be subject to increased pest infestation and reduced crop production. Externalities associated with modern farming, as well as its susceptibility to climatic extremes, suggest that it alone may not be fully capable of withstanding the impact of climate change (Saxena, 2009). Similarly, traditional practices are more resilient to climatic changes; however, their limited production potential, and susceptibility to sudden outbreak of diseases or pests necessitate integrated use of traditional and modern agricultural practices for successful adaptation to climate change.

Large uncertainties exist in climate change prediction in India. Climate predictions using the PRECIS model forecast a 20 per cent increase in rainfall and a 2°C rise in temperature for the west coast and the northeast of India (Kumar, 2006). Another regional climate model (HadRAM2/HadCM2) predicts no substantial change in India's monsoonal rainfall (Kumar, 2002). Looking at the projected variability of the monsoon, it is important to prepare for more severe droughts, floods and cyclones. Current adaptation measures might be useful, but they may be insufficient for meeting future challenges of climate change. When people were asked about future adaptation measures, they stressed increasing or strengthening present adaptations such as water harvesting, soil conservation, changes in cropping or irrigation methods. Many respondents suggested more focus on reducing social expenditures, increasing savings, buying crop insurance, expanding use of organic fertilizers, and greater reliance on non-farm employment; however, these practices are all currently at an early stage. Beyond addressing watershed and economic activities, more attention must be aimed at educating people and raising awareness about climate change. The capacity of local communities for adapting to climate change can also be improved by expanding their involvement in disaster preparedness planning. In addition, rural producers require improved weather forecasting specific to their spatial and temporal scales (Prabhakar and Shaw, 2008).

Conclusion

My research suggests that rural communities in Saurastra and Kutch are adapting to climate change by integrating their local knowledge and practices with modern technology. This process of mixing reflects the ongoing dynamism of so-called traditional knowledge systems, which have always been based on local experience and ideas obtained from external sources. Globalization is making external sources of information more available, sometimes supplanting traditional practices. But it also generates (agri) cultural hybridity at the local level. Both locally and externally generated systems of knowledge have their benefits as well as their limitations. The surveyed communities' successful use of local knowledge in coping with the region's climate variability suggests that policy makers and scientists need to give customary practices the respect and attention they deserve. Furthermore, a healthy relationship between local knowledge and scientific knowledge is desirable (Gyampoh et al., 2009). Many customary approaches that were considered primitive and useless are now seen as the appropriate solution for a specific locale (Nyong et al., 2007). Therefore inclusion of traditional knowledge in any response to climate change is important for preventing future catastrophes. At the same time, there needs to be an appreciation of the complex ways that farmers try to deal with their local climate.

Author updates to the 2025 edition

Research on climate change and livelihoods has grown since 2018 (Albugami et al., 2024). In the field site location of Western Indian, recent studies by climatologists and geographers show decreased rainfall, rising temperatures and a reduction of windspeed (Singh et al., 2024). Present over the last four decades, these trends are expected to continue and influence regional farming. In the original chapter, community members gave consistent and accurate accounts of climate change. However, their understanding of its causes and potential solutions varied. Since 2012, greater access to digital media in this region may have altered local knowledge of climate change. However, studies of Indigenous communities in other parts of the world have shown that workshops or other media have little effect on perceptions of climate change (Fernández-Llamazares et al., 2015).

Acknowledgement

This study was supported by generous fellowship and research grant from the Ford Foundation International Fellowship Program, New Delhi, India and partial research support from the Randolph G. Pack Environmental Institute at SUNY College of Environmental Science and Forestry, Syracuse, New York.

References

Albugami, H.F., Ali, K., Hossain, S., Zaffar, H., and Ahmad, N. (2024) 'Climate change and sustainable livelihood in south Asia: A bibliometric analysis'. *Environmental and Sustainability Indicators*, 24: 100524.

Altieri, M. and Koohafkhan, P. (2008) *Enduring farms: Climate change, small holders and traditional farming communities*, Environment and Development Series 6, Third World Network (TWN), Malaysia, [Online] http://www.agroeco.org/doc/Enduring%20farms.pdf [accessed 23 October 2011].

Candell, J. and Raupach, M. (2008) 'Managing forests for climate change mitigation', *Science* 320: 1456–57.

Fernández-Llamazares, A., Méndez-López, M.E., Díaz-Reviriego, I., McBride, M.F., Pyhälä, A., Rosell-Mele, A. and Reyes-García, V. (2015) 'Links between media communication and local perceptions of climate change in an indigenous society', *Climate Change*, 131(2): 307–320.

Garvin, T. (2001) 'Analytical paradigms: the epistemological distances between scientists, policy makers, and the public', *Risk Analysis* 21: 443–55.

Gibbs, M., Lewisa, L. and Hoffman, J. (1989) *Reducing methane emissions from livestock: opportunities and issues*, US Environmental Protection Agency, 400/1–89/002, Washington, DC.

Gupta, A. (1998) *Postcolonial Developments: Agriculture in the Making of Modern India*, Duke University Press, Durham, NC.

Gyampoh, B., Amisah, S., Idinoba, M., and Nkem, J. (2009) 'Using traditional knowledge to cope with climate change in rural Ghana', *Unasylva* 60: 70–4.

Henry, A. (2000) 'Public perceptions of global warming', *Human Ecology Review* 7: 25–30.

IPCC (Intergovernmental Panel on Climate Change) (2007) 'Summary for Policymakers', in M. Parry, O. Canziani, J. Palutikof, P. van der Linden and C. Hanson (eds), *Climate Change 2007: Impacts, Adaptation and Vulnerability. Contribution of Working Group II to the Fourth Assessment Report of the Intergovernmental Panel on Climate Change*, pp. 7–22, Cambridge University Press, Cambridge.

Kumar, R. (2002) 'Regional climate scenarios', *TERI Workshop on Climate Change, New Delhi, 5–6 Sept 2002*.

Kumar, R., Sahai, K., Krishna Kumar, A., Patwardhan, K., Mishra, S., Revadekar, P., Kamala, J., and Pant, G. (2006) 'High resolution climate change scenarios for India for the 21st century', *Current Science* 90: 334–45.

Macchi, M. (2008) *Indigenous and traditional peoples and climate change*, Issues paper, IUCN, [Online] https://portals.iucn.org/library/sites/library/files/documents/Rep-2008-011.pdf [accessed 14 April 2025].

Madison, D. (2007) *The perception of and adaptation to climate change in South Africa*, World Bank Research Group, Policy Working Paper 4308, Washington, DC.

Nyong, A., Adesina, F. and Elasha, B. (2007) 'The value of indigenous knowledge in climate change mitigation and adaptation strategies in the African Sahel', *Mitigation Adaptation Strategies and Global Change* 12: 787–97.

Osunade, M. (1994) 'Indigenous climate knowledge and agricultural practices in Southwestern Nigeria', *Malaysian Journal of Tropical Geography* 1: 21–8.

Prabhakar, S. and Shaw, R. (2008) 'Climate change adaptation implications for drought risk mitigation: a perspective for India', *Climatic Change* 88: 113–30.

Ray, K., Manorama, M. and Chincholikar, J. (2009) 'Climate variability over Gujarat, India', paper presented at the *ISPRS Workshop on Impact of Climate Change on Agriculture*, ISPRS archives XXXIII-8/W3, Ahmedabad, Gujarat, India.

Read, D., Bostrom, A., Morgan, M., Fischhoff, B. and Smuts, T. (1994) 'What do people know about global climate change? Survey studies of educated lay people', *Risk Analysis* 14: 971–82.

Salick, J., and Anja, B. (eds) (2007) *Indigenous People and Climate Change*, Tyndall Center for Climate Change Research, Oxford.

Saxena, N. (2009) 'Climate change and food security in India', in S. Narain, P. Ghosh, N. Saxena, J. Parikh and P. Soni (eds), *Climate Change*, pp. 37–45, United Nations Development Programme-India, New Delhi.

Singh, B.V.R., Agarwal, V., and Sanwal, V. (2024) 'Climatic shifts and vegetation response in Western India: a four-decade retrospective through GIS and multi-variable analysis', *Oxford Open Climate Change*, 4(1): 2–18.

Sjoberg, L., Moen, B. and Rundmo, T. (2004) 'Explaining risk perception – An evaluation of the psychometric paradigm in risk perception research', Rotunde No. 84, Norwegian University of Science and Technology, Trondheim.

Srinivasan, A. (2004) *Local knowledge for facilitating adaptation to climate change in Asia and the Pacific: Policy implications*; Institute for Global Environmental Strategy IGES-CP, Working Paper Series 2004–002, IGES, Kanagawa, Japan.

Weinstein, N. (1989) 'Optimistic biases about personal risks', *Science* 246: 1232–33.

About the author

Dineshkumar Moghariya is a postdoctoral fellow in the Department of Anthropology at the University of Manitoba. He holds a PhD from the Department of Environmental Science at the State University of New York College of Environmental Science and Forestry, Syracuse, New York.

Chapter 15

Ethno-ecology in the shadow of rain and the light of experience: Local perceptions of drought and climate change in east Sumba, Indonesia

Yancey Orr, Russell Schimmer and
Roland Geerken

Scholars are apt to consider pre-existing symbolic systems or the influx of external discourses in order to explain local knowledge of ecological relationships. This chapter proposes an alternative model that takes into account phenomenology to explain views of climate change among Sumbanese in eastern Indonesia. Phenomenological experiences such as shade, moisture, dew, heat, fire and sunlight, form the basis of their explanations for drought as well as a means to reorganize external information about global climate change. Their use of experience largely explains why the Sumbanese ecological model focuses largely on the role of vegetation in altering climate patterns and ignores industrial pollution and carbon emissions, both of which are commonly reported by the national media.

Introduction

People often depend upon their own experience to understand changes in their ecological context. Communities on the island of Sumba in eastern Indonesia interpret a perceived regional drought by using their experience of ecological interactions to formulate theories about climate change. Scholars are apt to consider pre-existing symbolic systems or the influx of exogenous discourses in order to explain local knowledge of ecological relationships. This chapter proposes an alternative model that takes into account phenomenology to explain Sumbanese ethno-ecology of climate change. Instead of explaining drought solely within their traditional religious beliefs or media reports of global warming, Sumbanese create an integrated ecological model for drought based on sensations of elements in the environment, or what is often termed phenomenological experience. We will define phenomenology as the experience of the world that is closely rooted in physical sensation and distinct from largely cognitive and symbolic cultural constructs. Phenomenological experiences such as shade, moisture, dew, heat, fire and sunlight, are the basis of east Sumbanese explanations for drought as well as a means to reorganize external information about global climate change. Their use of experience largely explains why the Sumbanese ecological model focuses solely on the role of vegetation in altering climate patterns and ignores industrial pollution and carbon emissions, both of which are commonly reported by the national media. The example of Sumba illustrates how local knowledge of ecological systems is, in many cases, not solely the result of cultural or exogenous discourses but instead is best described as an idiographic process of integration and analysis using multiple categories of knowledge such as sensation and discourse.

East Sumba

The island of Sumba is located in eastern Indonesia approximately 1,500 km south-east of the capital of Jakarta. Though it is nearly twice the size (11,153 square km) of the island of Bali, it has remained relatively isolated from Indonesian modernization. Modernization and integration into the Indonesian national economy have often been brought about by logging, industrial agriculture and mineral and oil extraction which have also collectively denuded forests and substantially impacted environments. On Sumba, the anthropogenic alteration of the environment, though present, has largely remained constant for generations and its environmental history is vague for local inhabitants as well as ecologists. This is not to imply that the environment of Sumba has not changed. Much of the sandalwood forests, which gave Sumba its colonial name, were felled before the 20th century but this remains unknown, or at the least, unmentioned by local communities. Thus, ecological isolation from development has left Sumba an appropriate place to examine local perceptions of climate change.

Differences in rainfall, subsistence strategies, language, culture and ancestry lead anthropologists and ecologists to divide Sumba into east and west cultural and ecological zones (Forth, 1981; Hoskins, 1996; Forshee, 2000). This chapter will focus on the district of east Sumba which is located in the rain-shadow of the western part of the island. In the largely tropical country of Indonesia, east Sumba has an atypically semi-arid climate (Monk et al., 1997; Fisher et al., 2006). This has resulted in two distinct features in east Sumba. Unlike much of the more humid regions of Indonesia, east Sumba has a low population density of 28/km^2 compared to the population density of 2,007/km^2 in Java. Subsistence activities in east Sumba are based upon smallholder livestock production of goats, cattle and pigs accompanied by gardens rather than intensive wet rice production common in western Indonesia (Onvlee, 1980; Kabupaten Sumba Timor, 2004). Though pastoral activities are a common adaptation to a semi-arid climate, the grasslands of east Sumba are not solely the result of low rainfall but rather managed by inhabitants through seasonal burning of brush to promote the growth of edible grasses for livestock (Fox, 1977; Dove, 1984). The experience of using fire to remove vegetation is significant to how communities in east Sumba conceptualize larger climatic variation regarding rainfall.

The closely related indigenous ethnic groups in east Sumba have blended in language and culture into what is now called the Kambera or east Sumbanese. The Leiden School of anthropology famously used east Sumbanese multifamily *uma* (households), monolithic tombs, symbolically organized villages, polygyny, and asymmetric marriage alliances to develop an early form of structuralism in the first half of the 20th century (van Wouden, 1968; Needham, 1987; Otterspeer, 1997). However, the great majority of east Sumbanese now live in dispersed homesteads, attend church in addition to performing indigenous rituals and practise monogamy which is no longer based on clan relationships. This generally describes the rural highland and lowland communities that were interviewed about climatic change. Their responses were compared to urban office workers, including agricultural professionals, in the district capital of Waingapu.

Perceived drought?

As we will examine more closely in this chapter, most east Sumbanese were adamant that there has been a decrease in rainfall over the last 5 to 15 years. Though how they link their experience of ecological interactions to larger processes is the subject of this chapter and not the accuracy of their assessments, we compared precipitation data for both east and west Sumba from two sources: rain stations and satellites. Rain station data provided by Global Precipitation Climatology Centre (GPCC) show that in the period from 1980 to 2007 Sumba received a mean rainfall of 1,435 mm and in the period 1998–2007 it received 1,473 mm.[1] NASA's satellite-based Tropical Rainfall Measuring Mission (TRMM) shows that this trend of increasing annual rainfall appears to have continued through 2009.[2] Using the GPCC dataset, we also examined longer trends in rainfall. During the 107-year period from 1901 to 2007, rainfall patterns were uniform with the only major spike in rainfall coming during the Second World War which may have caused measurement errors. Given the lack of evidence that Sumba has received less precipitation over the last 5, 15 or 100 years, this chapter will focus on how the east Sumbanese perceive drought. We argue that perceptions of drought are best explained as phenomenological observations and exposure to national media's coverage of global warming. Whatever the origin of east Sumbanese views on drought, they use the idioms of bodily experience and global warming to express them.

Method

During March 2010, individuals in the regency of east Sumba, Indonesia were interviewed about the local weather and its longer-term variation in the Indonesian national language of bahasa Indonesia. The interviews had three tiers designed to assess the subjects' 1) recognition of climatic characteristics and variation; 2) understanding of what caused such changes; and 3) means by which an individual came to hold those views. The informant's location, occupation and gender were also recorded. Only individuals who had lived or worked in Sumba for more than five years were used. In order to prevent leading questions, the interviews began as a conversation about the weather using the expression, '*matahari panas hari ini*' (the sun was hot this afternoon), which is a common invitation to talk about the weather regardless of the actual temperature. The informants were then engaged in a conversation about climate by asking if the weather was normal for this time of year and then in more general questions about whether it was atypical over a longer period of time. All informants, except one office worker in the city of Waingapu, said that the weather was drier than normal. The informants were then asked why they thought it was so dry or hot. If they did not mention global warming, they were asked at the end of the conversation if local weather was linked to other climate patterns at the provincial, national or global levels. After these conversations, individuals were informed that this was part of a research project and asked for permission to use their responses as part of this study. All informants consented.

Findings

We interviewed 35 participants; 24 from rural villages (14 lowland and 10 highland) in their local communities and 11 urban office or professional workers, including six agricultural professionals, in the city of Waingapu. The dispersion of these interviews covered an area of approximately 1,300 km^2. We interviewed an equivalent number of men and women in villages, though all agricultural professionals in Waingapu were men. We found no distinction between male and female responses. Although we inquired about both temperature and rainfall, respondents were less interested in discussing temperature than rainfall.

For this reason, we will focus on east Sumbanese perception of rainfall. All but one office worker said there had been less precipitation over the last 5 to 15 years. The singular explanation urban and rural east Sumbanese gave for what caused the decrease in precipitation was deforestation. When asked why it was becoming drier, 88 per cent of rural pastoral/horticulturalists thought it was a result of deforestation during the last 10 years in areas of Sumba, with only two answering that they did not know. Though rural villagers thought that deforestation was the origin of the perceived drought, where they placed the location of this critical deforestation differed. Of the 14 lowland villagers, 85 per cent said the deforestation took place in the highland regions of Sumba with the remaining two claiming they did not know why there was less rain. Of the 10 highland villagers, 90 per cent said that the critical deforestation is occurring in the adjacent district of west Sumba. When asked who was committing this deforestation, 75 per cent of villagers in the highlands and lowlands said it was the central government. Without prompting, 67 per cent mentioned *pemanasan global* (global warming) when talking about deforestation in the highlands or west Sumba, and all had heard of it.

Among urban residents in Waingapu, deforestation was also viewed as the cause of decreased rainfall. However, urban residents disagreed with one another regarding the location of deforestation. Urban residents who were not working in the agricultural industry did not specify where deforestation takes place. Conversely, urban residents of Waingapu working as government and private industry agricultural professionals said that deforestation in the distant and, at one time, heavily forested regions of Kalimantan and Sumatra caused the lack of rain. They also mentioned that Western corporations played the principal role in deforesting these areas. Urban residents and agricultural professionals mentioned global warming in their responses approximately 82 per cent of the time and all had heard of it from the news.

When asked how they knew that the loss of trees decreases rainfall, villagers used largely phenomenological experiences of heat, moisture, shade and vegetation to create an ethno-ecological response to this question. Eight stated that when one cuts down trees, the lack of shade makes the land hotter and thus less likely to rain. Ten answered that when one cuts down trees around the village, there is less moisture, fewer puddles and water overall. Two individuals talked about how fire, which is used to clear trees and other vegetation to encourage the growth of grass for cattle, heats up the environment and such heat keeps it from raining. One informant did not have an explanation why they thought deforestation reduced rainfall.[3] We emphasize the phenomenological basis of their ethno-ecology because their explanations revolve around the experience of sensations to link ecological cause and effect. Their use of the sensations of heat, moisture, fire and shade for evidence of the effect of vegetation on rainfall will be compared with other potential forms of evidence or justification that east Sumbanese do not employ.

Of the agricultural professionals, all six said local drought was the result of deforestation in other regions in Indonesia. Each explained that regional climatic patterns had been altered by changes in the hydrological cycle in large forests in Sumatra and Kalimantan. When asked how they knew this, they said that they had heard it from Indonesian news sources. Four also spoke about how it 'made sense' according to their knowledge of the hydrological cycle in which water is stored in vegetation and evaporates to cause rain. But none offered any explanation for how deforestation on one island would affect others 1,200 to 2,000 km apart.

When viewed at an aggregate level, these findings form the following basic ethno-ecological patterning regarding decreased rainfall:

- East Sumbanese view deforestation as a cause of their perceived decrease in rainfall.
- Distant deforestation affects local rainfall: lowland villagers attribute lack of rainfall to deforestation in the highlands; highland villagers attribute lack of rainfall to deforestation in west Sumba; and agricultural professional individuals, who work throughout the province, attribute lack of rainfall to deforestation in Sumatra and Kalimantan.
- A different type of agent causes deforestation: for villagers, it is the central government and, for both local businessmen and government employees, it is a foreign corporation.
- Most informants mentioned global warming in passing while focusing their responses on local and regional deforestation.

Analysis

The most obvious pattern we observed is that communities often place the responsibility for drought on distant areas and foreign entities. Because most communities extensively cut down trees and use fire to clear vegetation in the region (Dove, 1984; Fisher et al., 2006), this pattern could be expressed in the common Indonesian phrase *lempar batu, sembunyi tangan* (throw stone, hide hand) in which one's participation in a potentially condemnable activity is never admitted. If the analysis stops at this level in which east Sumbanese are only attempting to escape responsibility, consciously or not, fundamental insights into how they construct an ethno-ecology of climate variation would be ignored. The following section will address how phenomenological experiences of the environment are central to east Sumbanese's knowledge of ecology. Then, we will show how these experiences determine which parts of Indonesian media's climate change reporting are integrated into east Sumbanese ethno-ecological models. Finally, we will analyze how apparent similarities between east Sumbanese and the global climate change sciences, especially the importance they both place on deforestation, mask differences between the two.

Phenomenology in rural east Sumbanese ecology

Many people in east Sumba believe that a lack of trees results in a lack of rain. Whether true or not, this statement appears to be based on observed ecological relationships. However, the evidence and rationale for why this ecological relationship is true is established in phenomenological experience rather than experimental or empirical observation of solely vegetation and precipitation. Rural east Sumbanese do not simply make the statement that deforestation reduces rainfall and cite the interaction of these two variables. Nor do they reference a set of inherited cultural beliefs or the Indonesian news media's accounts of deforestation which we will discuss in a later section. Instead, they place their own experience as a physical body of how trees provide shade which is cool and this coolness is associated with wetness in the form of puddles, dew and moisture. For them, the antithesis to the sensations of a cool and wet environment is the experience of fire and sunlight. Fire, per se, provides heat and more importantly leaves the ground and people exposed to heat from sunlight. This is a hot and dry environment phenomenologically associated with a lack of trees. For rural east Sumbanese, their own bodies become the measuring instruments for understanding broader ecological relationships such as between trees and rainfall. This model is a different method of constructing an ecology than one based on a causal chain in which observably fewer trees result in observably less rain.

The absence of religious explanations also points to the importance of phenomenological experience in understanding the ecological interactions of drought. From early Dutch sources (see Onvlee, 1980) to ethnographies by contemporary anthropologists (Adams, 1970; Forth, 1981; Kuipers, 1990; Forshee, 2000), central to the *merapu* (spirit) religion is the role spirits play in protecting crops and livestock. According to this literature, nature was placed in a moral relationship to communities. Transgressions against spirits, such as incest or failure to conduct certain rituals, would cause drought, locusts and other events leading to crop failure and livestock death. Although people were not shy to talk about the traditional religion of *merapu*, during our interviews religious or moral explanations of decreased rainfall were never mentioned. In several interviews, we asked if a moral or religious transgression might result in a lack of rain. This question puzzled them. So we offered some examples: if someone failed to sacrifice the correct animal at a ceremony or a member of the community stole another's property, would this cause the *merapu* to withhold rain? In every instance, these suggestions were met with laugher and an exclamation that such a thing was absurd and amusing. Perhaps, the lack of religious explanation is the result of the growing presence of Christianity in the region. Though we cannot be certain, the fact that traditional *merapu* ceremonies and rites are practised openly suggests that this is not necessarily the sole cause of this change in view. Moreover, local experience strongly shapes what is assimilated from another cultural force in east Sumbanese communities – the Indonesian media.

Global context

These views of the relationship between forest and rain may appear to solely reflect Indonesian national media's reporting of deforestation and global warming. Though east Sumba is geographically isolated and comparatively poor by Indonesian standards, national media reach distant villages. Approximately one-third of rural homesteads have satellite dishes that pick up national programming and most villages have at least one dish and television that is communally used. All participants said that they watch the news for information about the environment. Since the 2007 United Nations Climate Change Conference in Bali and the 2009 World Oceans Conference in Sulawesi, Indonesian television comprehensively covers global warming. Moreover, deforestation receives even more coverage because it has a direct impact on economic and conservation efforts throughout Indonesia. This could lead one to believe that east Sumbanese are repeating the idioms of climate change from the national media to explain their local situation. Considering the discrepancy between the national media's coverage of climate change and the responses of our participants, it seems unlikely that east Sumbanese simply reiterate what they have heard and seen in the media.

Media likely shape how east Sumbanese understand ecological relationships, but are less likely to dictate how individuals understand their local ecology. Though not as central as deforestation to their reporting on climate change, the Indonesian media also attribute global warming to emissions generated by factories, gas engines and other industrial activities. However, these other sources of emissions are completely absent from east Sumbanese understanding of the perceived climate change. Sumba has a low population density, few automobiles and motorcycles and no factories, therefore descriptions of such factors altering the environment have little traction among east Sumbanese. Thus, deforestation is integrated with local experience while something too foreign, such as industrial pollution, is ignored. The lack of attention given to other forms of pollution could also be a result of not viewing their situation as related to global climate change. However, almost all mentioned *pemanasan global* (global warming) and all responded that they knew about it when asked. This suggests that they conceptualize perceived changes in their environment as part of global climate change – albeit with different causal components.

Deforestation is a critical element to both east Sumbanese and the scientific community's views on climate change. However, we observed critical distinctions in how the Sumbanese place deforestation in an ecological system. According to climatologists, the role of deforestation in climate change involves the destruction of carbon trapping plants and the release of stored carbon into the atmosphere (IPCC, 2007). The relationship between rainfall, temperature and forests in Sumba is of a different order: east Sumbanese do not attribute decreases in precipitation to deforestation because deforestation alters the composition of a global atmosphere through carbon emissions, but rather because it alters the rainfall patterns of a local ecology. This effect of trees on rainfall has been debated since the 19th century.[4] East Sumbanese describe their experience of moisture and heat and what may be called the hydrological cycle rather than climate change. For this reason, it is incorrect to take the view that east Sumbanese simply recapitulate similar scientific explanations on a local scale. This also suggests that they use their own experience of ecological interactions in preference to reiterating messages from the Indonesian media which place deforestation into a global carbon system. Thus, although exposed to a global explanation or model for climate change, east Sumbanese construct an ecological model based on their own sensations of the environment.

Conclusion

In this chapter, we demonstrate that east Sumbanese ethno-ecology of precipitation is a hybrid of their own phenomenological experiences and media reports on global warming. Though we found little evidence for long-term or recent changes in precipitation as stated by participants, the perceived lack of rain is constructed into a localized environmental shift that mirrors, to some degree, global climate change science. The importance placed on deforestation by east Sumbanese and climate change scientists overshadows considerable differences in how each views the effects of trees, forests and deforestation on ecosystems. The case of east Sumba demonstrates that, as scientific information explaining global climate change spreads over extensive geographic and cultural space, differing ethno-ecological knowledge systems result in a mosaic rather than uniform set of knowledge.

Author updates to the 2025 edition

In 2010, much of the research on climate change in Indonesia used *El Niño* oscillations as a proxy for the effects of climate change. The justification for such a method came from scholars' concerns that by the time that the effects of climate change were felt, it would be too late to act to reverse the chemical changes in the atmosphere that caused them. When writing the original article, we thought that within a decade, more empirical evidence would be available to show climate change outside of El Niño oscillations. Such data would make projecting climate change through proxies less necessary. This has not happened.

Studies of climate patterns in Sumba, Indonesia and the surrounding region of Nusa Tenggara Timur still rely on *El Niño* to describe the future of climate change (Yayasan Bambu Lingkungan Lestari, 2024). Over the last 15 years, these oscillations have been more intense than average, making understanding climate change in the region difficult. Current research still uses modelling about potential impacts of climate change (Sipayung et al., 2019) rather than evidence of climate change in Sumbanese rainfall patterns. The absence of studies within this region of Indonesia linking rainfall with climate change reflects the complexity of this climate interaction and the difficulty of conducting research in this area. Although considerable attention has been brought to climate change within Indonesia, this has had little effect on greenhouse gas production. While the United States and Europe have reduced greenhouse gas emissions, since the first publication of this volume Indonesia has seen a per-capita CO^2 emission increase of approximately 50 per cent.

Notes

[1] ftp://ftp-anon.dwd.de/pub/data/gpcc/PDF/GPCC_intro_products_2008. pdf (last accessed June 24, 2010).

[2] http://trmm.gsfc.nasa.gov/3b43.html; http://trmm.gsfc.nasa.gov/ overview_dir/background.html (last accessed June 24, 2010).

[3] The association of cool weather and rain may also come from the experience of the rainy season which is generally cooler in east Sumba as well as the pre-existing dyadic relationship between cool-wet and hot-dry common in the Austronesian world (Forth, 1981) or both.

[4] For a summary of such studies, see *Forest Hydrology* (Chang, 2006), chapter 8.

References

Adams, M. (1970) 'Myths and self-image among the Kapunduk people of Sumba', *Indonesia* 10: 81–106.

Chang, M. (2006) *Forest Hydrology*, Taylor & Francis Group, Boca Raton.

Dove, M. (1984) 'Man, land and game in Sumbawa: some observations on agrarian ecology and development policy in Eastern Indonesia', *Singapore Journal of Tropical Geography* 5: 112–24.

Fisher, R., Bobanuba, W., Rawambaku, A., Hill, G. and Russell-Smith, J. (2006) 'Remote sensing of fire regimes in semi-arid Nusa Tenggara Timur, eastern Indonesia: current patterns, future prospects', International *Journal of Wildland Fire* 15: 307–17.

Forshee, J. (2000) *Between the Folds: Stories of Cloth, Lives, and Travels from Sumba*, University of Hawaii Press, Honolulu.

Forth, G. (1981) *Rindi: an Ethnographic Study of a Traditional Domain in Eastern Sumba*. Martinus Nijhoff, The Hague.

Fox, J. (1977) *The Harvest of the Palm; Ecological Change in Eastern Indonesia*. Harvard University Press, Cambridge.

Hoskins, J. (1996) 'The heritage of head hunting: History, ideology, and violence on Sumba, 1890–1990', in J. Hoskins (ed.), *Headhunting and the Social Imagination of Southeast Asia*, pp. 216–48, Stanford University Press, Stanford.

Intergovernmental Panel on Climate Change (IPCC) (2007) 'Summary for policymakers'. In: S. Solomon, D. Qin, M. Manning, Z. Chen, M. Marquis, K.B. Averyt, M. Tignor and H.L. Miller (eds), *Climate Change 2007: The Physical Science Basis. Contribution of Working Group I to the Fourth Assessment Report of the Intergovernmental Panel on Climate Change*, Cambridge University Press, Cambridge, and New York.

Kabupaten Sumba Timor, Badan PS (2004) *Sumba Timur in Figures 2003*, Percetakan Usaha Mulia, Waikabubak, Sumba.

Kuipers, J. (1990) *Power and Performance*, University of Pennsylvania Press, Philadelphia.

Monk, K. and De Fretes, Y. (1997) *The Ecology of Nusa Tenggara and Maluku*, Periplus Press, Hong Kong.

Needham, R. (1987) *Mamboru: History and Structure in a Domain of Northwestern Sumba*, Clarendon Press, Oxford.

Onvlee, L. (1980) 'The significance of livestock in Sumba', in J. Fox (ed.), *The Flow of Life: Essays on Eastern Indonesia*, pp. 195–207, Harvard University Press, Cambridge, MA.

Otterspeer, W. (1997) *Leiden Oriental Connections, 1850–1940*, Brill Academic Publishers, Brill.

Sipayung, Sinta Berliana, Indah Susanti, Edy Maryadi, Amalia Nurlatifh, Bamban Siswanto, Muhammad Nafayest, Fanny Aditya Putri, Eddy Hermawan (2019) 'Analysis of Drought Potential in Sumba Island until 2040 Caused by Climate Change'. *Journal of Physics: Conference Series* 1373: 012004.

Wouden van, F.A.E (1968) *Types of Social Structure in Eastern Indonesia*. (trans. Rodney Needham). Koninklijk Instituut voor Taal-, Landen Volkenkunde Translation Series, vol. 11. Martinus Nijhoff, The Hague.

Yayasan Bambu Lingkungan Lestari (2024) 'El Niño in East Nusa Tenggara 2023: A Climate Challenge Requiring Action' [blog], 7 March 2024. https://www.bambuvillage.org/blog/2024/03/07/el-nino-in-east-nusa-tenggara-2023-a-climate-challenge-requiring-action/

About the authors

Yancey Orr is an anthropologist and associate professor of environmental science at Smith College. His research investigates how individuals develop knowledge and perceptions of their physical environment. He has conducted research in Southeast Asia, Australia and the United States.

Russell Schimmer is the head of SIAS Global, a remote sensing and consulting company. His primary research is in resource extraction, land use and climate change in Indonesia, the Southwestern United States and on the Horn of Africa.

Dr Roland Geerken is a geologist and remote sensing scientist. His expertise is in multitemporal land cover and vegetation coverage analysis and climate modeling. Dr Geerken has worked extensively in North Africa, and Central and West Asia with organizations such as the Deutsche Gesellschaft für Technische Zusammenarbeit (GTZ). He is currently Director of Geomatics for SIAS Global.

Chapter 16

Local knowledge and technology innovation in a changing world: Traditional fishing communities in Tam Giang Cau Hai lagoon, Vietnam

Thanh Vo and Jack Manno

Vietnam is among the most vulnerable countries to climate change, with forecasted shifts in the spatial and temporal pattern of rainfall, increasing frequency of extreme weather events, and rising sea levels. This chapter presents a case study of fishing/aquaculture communities in Tam Giang Cau Hai lagoon, the largest coastal lagoon in Southeast Asia. The people of this region are attempting to adapt to climate change in the context of sweeping political, social and market changes. Adaptation occurs through innovation that draws upon local knowledge of weather patterns, sea currents, and fish behaviour, as well as upon social norms and values that guide local resource management. Not waiting for national policy on climate adaptation, local people have adapted to multiple contextual changes through innovative structures known as net enclosed ponds (NEPs) that combine prawn aquaculture with traditional fish corrals. However, their success, popularity and density have brought additional problems to the lagoon, further challenging local social and ecosystem resilience.

Introduction

Approximately 100,000 people, one-third of the population of Vietnam's Thua Thien Hue province, live near, around and in floating communities on the surface of Tam Giang Cau Hai lagoon. At 80 kilometres in length, it is the largest coastal lagoon in Southeast Asia. For centuries, thousands of families have depended on its aquatic resources, particularly fish and prawns. This chapter describes a complex, nested social-ecological system being severely challenged by shifting currents and intensifying storms, globalizing markets and enclosing commons, political socialism and market capitalism, sustaining traditions and creative innovations. In this chapter we focus on how individuals and communities have drawn on their traditional and local knowledge to adapt their livelihood and resource management practices in response to climate change, coinciding with dramatic shifts in Vietnamese social/economic policies and the globalization of fish and prawn markets. The changes in climate, policies, and economy that we describe are all driven by forces operating at system levels beyond the influence of local actors. Yet these forces have dramatic effects on their lives and livelihood opportunities to which they must react creatively or suffer the consequences.

In this case study we confirm the findings of other researchers; that communities retain a cultural resilience enabled by long, intense and shared observations of ecological information. In combination with local norms and values, this information has guided an understanding of proper behaviour regarding use and management of the commons. It also indicates that the capacity to continue to innovate and organize effectively to sustain livelihoods from Tam Giang Cau Hai lagoon in the face of climate change is not unlimited. Social change, like ecological and climate change, has a way of accumulating and reaching thresholds where new system dynamics suddenly predominate. This chapter documents a case where such change is occurring. Finally, it suggests how and why traditional ecological knowledge and social norms remain essential elements for communities as they respond to the risks and opportunities of climate change in the context of simultaneous political, social and economic change.

Vietnam is considered to be among the countries most vulnerable to climate change. Climate forecasts predict shifts in the spatial and temporal pattern of rainfall, increasing frequency of extreme weather events and rising seas (Imamura and Dang, 1997; Cruz et al., 2007; Dasgupta et al., 2007; DOST, 2004). The study area experiences hot summers and rainy winters, with a large range of seasonal variability and several tropical depressions, including some of hurricane strength. From August to December, the region receives an average of four to six storms with heavy rain that create the potential for severe flooding (DOST, 2004).

Beginning in the mid-1980s, the Government of Vietnam encouraged commercial based decision-making and discipline as it integrated its resource economy, including agriculture and fisheries, with global markets. The industrial-scale aquaculture model these global markets preferred, and which the government introduced, encouraged, promoted and focused on one single species, black tiger shrimp, with strict quality standards and high-volume production. This model required significant up-front cash investments from households. In addition, black tiger shrimp aquaculture also consumes large quantities of energy and chemical inputs which require large and constant capital investments. As we will see, as the environmental, economic and health consequences of this production shift became increasingly apparent to local producers, individual and community innovators drew upon their local knowledge and traditional fishing methods to design and engineer an alternative aquaculture model. This innovation, locally named *ao vay* or net enclosed pond (NEP), helped local producers steer a middle path that supported livelihoods through expanded market access, increased use of a broader range of native lagoon species and grounded this practice in traditional knowledge of lagoon ecology and society.

While the NEP model of mixed aquaculture and wild capture demonstrates how traditional environmental knowledge and social institutions can help produce innovative solutions in changing environments, this chapter suggests that climate change may increasingly stress the resilience of natural resource-dependent communities already reeling from political and economic change. We believe that sustainable livelihood strategies will require many creative new ways to integrate and synthesize traditional environmental knowledge and scientific knowledge.

Local knowledge of weather and climate variability and change

Fisherfolk and aquaculturalists use daily observations of weather, in combination with expectations based on past experiences of local climate patterns in specific months and seasons, to guide their livelihood activities on the lagoon and elsewhere. Knowledge of local climate constitutes a foundation for understanding the local lagoon ecological system and the interactions between elements of this system. Vo's (2009) field research over several years demonstrated that local fisherfolk and aquaculturalists know their local weather in great detail. They read the water's colour, salinity, surface motion, deep currents and many other signs in which they find meaning. Each cue is understood in relation to other signals and in the context of expectations drawn from past experiences. In other words, they read the ecological system in the context of their knowledge of climate.

Even though fisherfolk and aquaculturalists rarely use the Vietnamese term for 'climate', fisherfolk interpret lagoon resources and make decisions based on a seasonal reference point, framed by their observation and memory of local weather patterns. They assess potential opportunities and hazards, choosing appropriate fishing sites and gear. Aquaculturalists decide how to operate their NEP production, feeding their stock based on experience and expected weather patterns. They also receive daily weather forecasts from national and provincial television stations, though mainly as warnings for severe weather events such as tropical depressions, hurricanes, storms and floods. Daily weather forecasts from meteorological sources generally do not provide information at the scale useful to local fisherfolk and aquaculturalists in daily livelihood decision-making. Local weather on the coast is highly variable day and night, and local fisherfolk must make predictions about their micro-climates on the scale of hours, even minutes.

Local fisherfolk have experienced changes in weather patterns, including more frequent and severe storms and floods, and longer and more intense heatwaves over the two decades prior to Vo's research. They described the historic storm of 1985 and the flood of 1999 that wreaked havoc, causing massive loss of life and property. Community residents report that life on the lagoon has grown more perilous and that this has altered safety practices, arrangements for mutual support, lending and borrowing norms, design and use of fishing gear, general fishing strategies and rules and, most significantly, settlement patterns. The 1985 storm occurred early in the storm season and left many homeless. Local government responded to the crisis by resettling the most severely affected communities away from the water. Those who still lived in traditional floating villages of small houseboats on the surface of the lagoon were moved ashore. Shoreline villages that had been destroyed or badly damaged were moved to higher ground. This marked one of the most significant changes in the centuries-long history of these fishing communities (Imamura and Dang, 1997). The floodwaters of 1999 reached historic heights and remained above flood levels longer than any in recorded or remembered history. The flood destroyed numerous communities throughout six provinces in the Central region of Vietnam (DOST, 2004). Waves breached the sand barrier on the eastern shore of the lagoon, exposing it to the Pacific Ocean, altering its salinity and circulation characteristics and creating an entirely new estuary.

In 2005, the region experienced an extreme high flood season with five consecutive floods within two months. The 2006 season featured consecutive floods, none of which reached the levels of 1999 or 2005. However, cumulatively, they grounded fishing and aquaculture for extended periods and wiped out most of the NEPs after the third or fourth consecutive flood of the season. Several NEP aquaculturalists reported that extreme heat and longer drought periods had also become more frequent and damaging. Most NEP aquaculturalists interviewed by Vo agreed that heatwaves were reducing their harvest by stunting fish and shrimp growth.

Fish corrals, traditional adaptation to local climate

Local fisherfolk have developed and used many types of gear and fishing strategies such as bottom nets, jump nets, lift nets and fish corrals which are highly adapted to the local weather–water system. In this chapter we focus on fish corrals, one strategy for large-scale fishing in the lagoon, from which has evolved a new technology, the net enclosed pond (NEP) system. This is an example of creative livelihood adaptation to the systemic effects of the political, economic and climate stresses faced by the people of the lagoon.

A fish corral is a large, complex, arrow-shaped structure that can enclose from 1 to 10 hectares of otherwise open fishing ground. People build these structures using thousands of bamboo poles in patterns designed to drive desired fish species into species-specific enclosures. To design and build a large fish corral one must adapt its structure to the micro-conditions of a particular location in the lagoon to take full advantage of river and ocean currents that will carry fish into your corral. At the same time, the design must minimize pressure on the structure itself, particularly through the five months of turbulence in rainy and stormy seasons. Fisherfolk must have extensive knowledge of bottom morphology and water currents in the complex channels that regularly change by tide, season and salinity. Success also depends on detailed knowledge of species-specific fish behaviour, life cycles, and reproductive strategies. They utilize this knowledge which is embedded in the fisherfolk's frame of reference of climate-water cyclic systems within daily, monthly and seasonal timeframes.

In addition to climate-sensitive physical constraints, Vo found that a set of informal but widely understood social rules require fisherfolk to communicate with each other as they design and build their corrals. These rules constrain the placement and size of corrals, and their location relative to the direction of the tide and the distance between corrals. These coordinated fishing practices help avoid and resolve lagoon conflicts by defining shared access to common resources within the corrals and in the lagoon. Fisherfolk report that for centuries these rules have been respected by fishing communities because they work. The rules derive from the proven efficiencies of the corral designs in relation to shared understanding of the physical features of the lagoon and the social organization of the Vietnamese *van* or traditional fishing institution. Within the local community, these rules have been accepted and followed as part of the social interactions of daily life. Furthermore, these rules help to develop and maintain relatively cohesive and resilient fishing communities to cope with their harsh natural environment, particularly during the flood and storm seasons. Changing climate and social conditions in the lagoon stress these institutions, requiring innovations in fishing practice to best exploit the new opportunities brought by changing markets and ecosystems.

The evolution from *tro no* (fish corral) to *ao vay* (net enclosed pond)

In the late 1980s, the Vietnamese government began a transition from a centralized, planned economic model to a market-based economy to facilitate integration into international markets. Government policies provided incentives, including preferential financing, extension services and new land use arrangements for small agricultural businesses, to encourage farmers to adopt intensive aquaculture (EJF, 2003). In addition, land reforms granted long-term land use rights to individual farmers, creating functional property rights that could be inherited, transferred or used as collateral.

By the late 1990s, these policies led to rapid expansion of intensive industrial aquaculture focused on exporting large volumes of a single commercial species – black tiger shrimp. It required large amounts of chemicals to manipulate water quality, antibiotics, and a waste management infrastructure that demanded greatly expanded commercial energy use and high input costs, as well as much higher waste outputs than traditional local production and harvesting techniques. After a few years of initial success, failures increased due to a combination of increased energy costs, waste management and health maintenance problems, poor fingerling quality, unstable international shrimp markets, and an immature Vietnamese link to global markets. According to Vo's field research, as of 2008, most farmers in the region who had participated in intensive aquaculture had fallen into a classic debt trap.

After cautiously observing the initial success of early adopters and some failures of intensive tiger shrimp cultivation and marketing, several local fisherfolk had, by 1992, rejected the government- and investor-preferred methods of building earthen ponds around the edges of the lagoon. Instead, they began to experiment with enclosing their existing fish corrals with netting, transforming them into net enclosed ponds in the shallow lagoon. In the process, they developed a mixed system of aquaculture they believed to be better suited to the lagoon and their existing practices. Unlike the earthen ponds, the NEPs did not create artificial energy- and labour-intensive habitats, they merely enclosed existing natural habitat that varied little from a traditional fish corral.

From mobile fisherfolk, they purchased fry and fingerlings and released them into their net enclosed ponds to grow, thereby creating a market for catch that had previously been released. They experimented with several high-value native and culturally familiar species, such as groupers, snappers, rabbit fish and mullet. In this mix, they included black tiger shrimps and other species valued by distant consumers. Thus the NEP households earned income both from the fish that entered their corrals on their own and grew naturally inside their 'ponds' and from the fish and prawns that they bought, released and stocked in their ponds. For feed, NEP fisherfolk used food sources such as sea grass and algae that grew naturally in the 'ponds,' and then supplemented it with algae collected from other locations in the lagoon. By using this model, these fisherfolk cum aquaculturalists were better able to maintain natural processes in the lagoon, while improving the economic situation for their families, a potential model of sustainable fish production.

After 1992 the first NEP families were beginning to succeed economically. By enclosing their corrals, they created new property with clear boundaries, enclosing what was formerly a commons and creating property rights for themselves and their families that they now wanted recognized and formalized by the government. Many others joined them. The lagoon fishery that had been a relatively well-regulated commons before the economic and climatic changes, now experienced a resource boom with little in the way of formal lagoon resource management. In the rush to invest in the NEPs and gain property and use rights for their households, fisherfolk transformed the open lagoon fishing grounds in the shallow areas into a dense aquaculture zone. The number of NEPs exploded from the first 24 households in Tan Duong Village to thousands, without adequate control over new entries or coordination between existing fisherfolk.

As families invested their time, attention and resources, they became increasingly dependent on the NEPs. NEP expansion was approaching the physical limits of the lagoon. Scarcity of shallow bottom space and continued demand for NEP sites led to rising prices and increased pressure on families to sustain and protect their NEPs. Options for collective action to address the rapid increase in pond enclosures and overexploitation of the lagoon were now constrained. NEPs had rapidly become the livelihood practice of most fishing families and represented a significant investment of money, time, creativity and social capital. Almost all of a fishing household's spending, investment, savings, labour, and even education were now dependent on their net enclosed ponds. Predictably, fisherfolk began to notice reduced capture of free fish moving into their corrals and poor growth in their 'ponds', increased pollution, animal disease, loss of critical sea grass and dramatic decreases in open lagoon area.

The thousands of net layers erected in the lagoon slowed, and in places, blocked the free movement and exchange of water between rivers and ocean, the movement of fingerlings and mature fish from ocean to lagoon, and led to significant changes of sediment and benthic vegetation in the lagoon. In addition, large quantities of highly concentrated, unprocessed wastewater from hundreds of intensive aquaculture ponds on adjacent banks in agricultural villages have been added into the now stagnant lagoon.

The challenge became how to establish new rules to manage the impacts of the NEP-dominated system. Could a new and effective management regime be built on the remnants of the traditional *van*? The government, having undermined the traditional *van* fishing system, failed to create an effective fishery management regime. Local NEP 'owners' seemed collectively unable to establish and enforce rules to deal with lagoon use rights that might balance the new private ownership in the NEP system with the commons management that had long functioned in the lagoon. Although many of the fisherfolk interviewed had thought about potential solutions to the increasing water stagnation, all involved reducing the extent of NEP coverage and re-establishing circulation. Social and economic tension arising from the fear of losing the right to their 'ponds' kept fisherfolk from initiating discussion about these solutions and participating in efforts to reopen lagoon areas.

In addition, local government tried to respond by forcing families to reopen natural space in the lagoon. Their attempts were resisted, causing conflict between local government and fishing families, and among families. These conflicts hindered fisherfolk attempts to hold discussions about a potential solution. As a result, there was no improvement in the lagoon environment and the quality of the fishery. Meanwhile the pressure on the lagoon was exacerbated by climate change.

Environmental change and vulnerability

Days of extreme heat in recent summers have apparently become more frequent, intensifying the environmental impacts associated with aquaculture. An increased number of storm events leads to increased run-off. The combination of adding nutrients from agricultural and aquacultural run-off stimulates algal production. While the NEPs expanded, the intensive upland aquaculture ponds have continued in some areas, releasing their wastes, mostly untreated, into the lagoon, including chemical residues and disease organisms. Temperature extremes, variable precipitation and high winds have also stressed the cultured fish and shrimp, causing farmers to increase the additives they use. In addition, the thousands of net layers in the region also contribute significantly to the pollution of the lagoon by slowing circulation and recharge. Extreme heatwaves and large temperature swings are identified by NEP owners as one of the most important causes of lost production and therefore lost summer income since the turn of the 21st century.

As the NEP is a fixed structure throughout the year, it is strongly affected by natural hazards such as storms, floods, hurricanes and combinations of these. While fisherfolk continue to learn and improve their techniques for strengthening NEP structures, the increasing frequency and severity of these natural hazards in recent decades has kept ahead of their innovations. The damage to NEP systems from these extreme events has been increasingly severe.

Vo's research showed how weather stress affects the decisions fisherfolk, buyers and lenders make. Fisherfolk learn to adapt. They adjust their seasonal calendar of production and maintenance to reduce losses and increase their chances of success. Recently, NEP fisherfolk have been adjusting the timing of their harvest to avoid more losses due to the anticipated large storms. Before the flood season in late July (lunar calendar), NEP families concentrate on repairing and strengthening their NEPs against floods and storms. They hope to hold on to some of the younger, smaller fish trapped in the NEPs to harvest later for badly needed winter income. They harvest and sell all the larger shrimp, fish and crabs before the storms that might destroy their NEPs.

Weather also appears to have become a factor in lending and borrowing decisions. The fisherfolk of Tam Giang Cau Hai lagoon depend on local lenders for cash for ongoing household expenses and production. These relationships were traditionally based primarily on trust built over years and backed by one's position in the community. Natural disasters had been an 'acceptable risk factor' in informal money lending. If fisherfolk lost their gear or their NEP was severely damaged due to floods or storms, they could borrow additional money to rebuild or buy new gear without collateral. However, Vo's research suggests that increasingly unpredictable and severe weather is eroding the trust and confidence on which these informal institutions are based.

Planning changes and collective community action

In 2006 and 2007 researchers from Hue University initiated an effort to support local fisherfolk/aquaculturalists in solving the growing problems of stagnant water and its impact on the open water fishery and NEP productivity (Vo, 2009). They facilitated a dialogue between local government and fisherfolk with the intention of developing a plan to increase water and resource exchanges between the ocean tides and the lagoon, while ensuring for households the continued 'rights of use' of NEPs. In fact, these scientists had played two major roles, as knowledge brokers and mediators in these highly contentious relationships. As knowledge brokers, these scientists integrated the knowledge of local people with the resource management knowledge of government in discussing the ecological processes needed for potential solutions. As conflict mediators, they facilitated discussions that respected both parties and led to a compromise that addressed the concerns and interests of both local fisherfolk and the local authority.

After about a year, some fisherfolk, working with Hue University scientists, proposed a plan to redesign their NEPs, to better align them with natural water currents in the lagoon. The scientists estimated that doing so would help restore approximately 20 per cent of the lagoon to open area. Drawing again on their intimate knowledge of water circulation and fish movement, the fisherfolk helped determine where water channels needed to be re-opened in order to return estuarine flow to the shallow areas of the lagoon. The fisherfolk believe that the resulting increase in water and resource exchanges will ease the cumulative impact of pollution during the hot summer and reduce the impact of floods and storms during the winter. It bears noting that in this process of change, the fisherfolk negotiated among themselves, drawing on their shared understanding of the lagoon system, common values, interests and goals. Each family then adjusted the NEP themselves without any apparent conflict, and without enforcement by local authorities. The university group recorded the agreements both in writing and as digital maps which could be used to inform local authorities about the changes.

Based on their local knowledge of the ocean, river and lagoons, the fisherfolk adjusted their NEP using two major principles. First, they narrowed their NEP to provide greater open space to the community while reshaping their NEP in a way so that fisherfolk could still use their fish corrals and natural capture practices. Second, all the newly returned open space had to connect together in the correct direction and size in accordance with water flows and currents. These direction, size and connectivity requirements allowed more natural exchange of water from the ocean, river and the lagoon, preventing stagnation of the lagoon water during the dry summer time. During this process of reestablishing open space among the NEPs, the fisherfolk took into account currents and flows during both dry and rainy seasons. They also used their knowledge of local coupled climate-hydrological systems, making it possible to protect their property, net enclosures, and harvests. The agreement also reduced the potential damage from high flood currents and opened access for rescue transportation in case of floods.

This effort hopefully will return about 20 per cent of open space to the lagoon from NEPs at critical water pathways which will resolve the detrimental stagnant water in the area and help increase water and resource exchanges. Fisherfolk believe that the opening of these waterways will ease the cumulative impact of pollution during the hot summer time, and reduce the impact of floods and storms during the winter.

Discussion

In this chapter we have described an example of how the fishing communities of Tam Giang Cau Hai lagoon depend on their detailed knowledge of climate, weather and ecosystems in making livelihood decisions. While still depending on traditional environmental knowledge, local fisherfolk have welcomed, evaluated and sometimes adopted or adapted new technologies or methods to increase their productivity or to reduce the personal and economic risks to their livelihood. We presented two examples in which fisherfolk have responded to change: first, the development of NEPs as a locally appropriate system to meet external market demand; and, second, by responding to the accumulated detrimental environmental consequences of the success of NEPs. In each example, solutions were based on traditional ecological knowledge held in individual and institutional practice and memory. People who depend on the aquatic resources of Tam Giang Cau Hai lagoon know how to read its surface, depths, temperature, and air and water currents. They use this information to make decisions that greatly affect their lives. Weather and climate are critical elements of local people's knowledge of, and concerns for, the lagoon. This local knowledge is used in the design of fishing gear, techniques and strategies and in the response by local financial institutions to the needs of fisherfolk.

Climate is one of many factors local people consider when making decisions, but it is central to the context in which all the other drivers assert their influence. The innovation and use of aquaculture technology in traditional fishing communities in Tam Giang Cau Hai are much more complicated than simply adapting to, and coping with, climate change. Technical innovation is part of complex household livelihood strategies drawing on their assets, skills and knowledge of the lagoon ecosystem and resources. This process has also been mediated and influenced by an array of changing institutions responding to political, social, economic and environmental dynamics. While the sources of this change lie beyond the control of local fisherfolk, they react as best they can, using their creativity and the knowledge accumulated through millennia of human interaction with Tam Giang Cau Hai lagoon.

Conclusion

Although climate change is global, adaptation will always be local, place-based, and involve complicated decision-making. Governments should recognize the diversity of ecological systems and therefore support ecosystem-based adaptation of local communities, especially as these ecosystems are stressed and reconstituted in unfamiliar and perhaps unforeseeable ways. Perhaps ironically, as local ecological knowledge becomes less reliable for predicting change, the source of that knowledge, ongoing experimentation and observation by people with long-term intimate experience with local ecosystems, may become an ever more important source of innovation as governments and communities attempt to adapt and hopefully thrive.

Updates to the 2025 edition

Yancey Orr

Recent studies of climate change in Vietnamese fishing villages show vulnerability to increased water temperature, storms and runoff (Thi Ngoc et al., 2022). According to this research, the state has not demonstrated the ability to respond to these impacts on communities. Given the state's absence, local communities are adapting using different strategies. Estuary fishers are increasingly turning to diversifying their labour activities to include paid labor while larger fishing industries are more likely to embrace technological solutions involving capital investment (Lam Pham and Saizen, 2023). Fisheries are both sources of protein for the poor and export industries. Historical studies of fishing in Vietnam suggest that as communities that produce such domestic protein sources are put under stress, the welfare of consumers in the region will reduce ((Ha Nguyen, 2022).

References

Cruz, R.V., Harasawa, H., Lal, M., Wu, S., Anokhin, Y., Punsalmaa, B., Honda, Y., Jafari, M., Li, C., and Huu Ninh, N. (2007) 'Asia. Climate change 2007: Impacts, adaptation and vulnerability', in M. Parry, O. Canziani, J. Palutikof, P. van der Linden and C. Hanson (eds), *Climate Change 2007: Impacts, Adaptation and Vulnerability. Contribution of Working Group II to the Fourth Assessment Report of the Intergovernmental Panel on Climate Change*, pp. 469–506, Cambridge University Press, Cambridge.

Dasgupta, S., Laplante, B., Meisner, C., Wheeler, D., and Yan J. (2007) *The Impact of Sea Level Rise on Developing Countries; A Comparative Analysis*. World Bank Policy Research Working Paper 4136, Washington: Development Research Group, World Bank.

DOST (Department of Science and Technology) (2004) *Characteristics of Climate and Hydrology of Thua Thien Hue Province*, Thuan Hoa Publisher, Hue.

EJF (Environmental Justice Foundation) (2003) *Risky Business: Vietnam Shrimp Impact and Improvement.* Environmental Justice Foundation, London.

Ha Nguyen, T.V. (2022) 'Welfare impact of climate change on capture fisheries in Vietnam', *PLoS One* 17(4): e0264997.

Imamura, F. and Dang, T. (1997) 'Flood and typhoon disasters in Vietnam in the half century since 1950', *Natural Hazards* 15: 71–87.

Lam Pham, T., and Saizen, I. (2023) 'Coastal fishers' livelihood adaptations to extreme weather events: an analysis of household strategies in Quang Ngai Province, Vietnam', *Humanities and Social Sciences Communications*, 10: 759.

Thi Ngoc, N., Xuan Binh, N., and Thi Thu Ha, N. (2022) 'Impacts of Climate Change on Fishing Villages in the North Vietnam', *Environment and Urbanization ASIA*, 13(1): 179–189.

Vo, T. (2009) *Living with Change: Local Knowledge, Institutions, Livelihoods and Coastal Resources in Tam Giang Cau Hai Lagoon System under Context of Institutional and Global Climate Change,* unpublished PhD dissertation, State University of New York, College of Environmental Science and Forestry, Syracuse.

About the authors

Thanh Vo is a Senior Environmental Scientist with IM Systems Group, Inc., focusing on institutional development for climate adaptation and sustainability and programme evaluation related to ocean and climate policies.

Jack P. Manno is Associate Professor of Environmental Studies at SUNY College of Environmental Science and Forestry. His research focuses on incorporating ecological and indigenous perspectives into policy and governance and understanding patterns that drive overconsumption.

Chapter 17

Conclusion: Some reflections on indigenous knowledge and climate change

*Dan Taylor, A. Peter Castro,
and David W. Brokensha*

The case studies in this volume have examined communities under threat
from climate change, including exploring the nature of their vulnerabilities,
their capacities for response, and the kinds of actions they have taken. While
the individual chapters have highlighted specific settings and issues, it is
important to bear in mind similarities among the cases. These communities
are often socially and politically marginalized, including in environmental
planning processes. A great risk in climate change adaptation and mitigation
efforts is that policymakers, planners, and technical experts will ignore
or disregard local priorities and capacities. Past experience and present
circumstances demonstrate that outsiders often all too easily assume that
communities and their members lack agency. In contrast, the case studies
presented here have shown that communities not only possess considerable
capacity for action, but are already engaged in a wide range of efforts to deal
with the challenges of climate change. These actions include adjustments
to livelihood strategies and techniques, economic diversification, and social
mobilization to ensure a stronger voice in policy processes. Overall, poor
and marginalized communities possess insights and technologies that can,
and must, form part of global solutions.

One of the fundamental capacities possessed by communities is their
detailed and dynamic environmental knowledge, which has served as the
basis for livelihoods and other cultural practices. In concluding, we wish
to reflect on the nature of indigenous knowledge, including debates about
its nature and continued relevance. The tendency to treat indigenous
knowledge as traditional and therefore as primitive and unchanging
suggests a continuity with the past that is not reflected in reality. On the
contrary, indigenous knowledge is constantly changing as new knowledge
is appropriated into the repertoire of practices, skills and ideas of farmers,
pastoralists and fisherfolk whose learning derives from their own and their
community's experience, as well as from external sources. Hence knowledge

is always situated, invariably contested and arguably provisional (see Long and Long, 1992; Scoones and Thompson, 1994; Cruikshank, 2005) as contexts change, new meanings are ascribed, additional information is acquired and practices evolve.

There is a debate in academic circles as to what constitutes indigenous (or local) knowledge, its links to place, its gendered nature, and whether in a globalized world all knowledge is 'hybrid' knowledge (Hannerz, 1987; Dove, 2006). Similarly, the notion that knowledge may either be indigenous or scientific creates a false dichotomization that, in assuming discrete categories of knowledge, pits the one against the other. This type of representation does not serve either. Neither can indigenous knowledge be broken down into its component parts for its commoditization, for in divorcing knowledge from its source in the social relations of its production we lose the context in which it is produced, and thus its 'social life' (Appadurai, 1989).

These points are important for they allude to the purpose of this volume, highlighted in the contributions to this book: the value and importance of indigenous knowledge in addressing the current crisis of climate change. It should be clear that the contributors wish neither to cling to a romanticized view of a primordial past nor to dismiss critiques that argue that the problem is too all encompassing to rely on indigenous knowledge alone. Based on their own research in various parts of the globe, they also all acknowledge one imperative: the inclusion of marginalized people in the discourse and action around the many problems facing humankind including climate change adaptation and mitigation. Some of these solutions rely more on past practices than others; some are decidedly technologically 'modern'. For example Burnham (Chapter 2), has shown that interventions adopting global positioning systems (GPS) technology to delineate forest boundaries incorporate new technologies for mapping forests and forest cover and contribute to changing local understandings.

The problems associated with climate change are immense and therefore it is understandable that solutions may be articulated on a national or global scale, but this is exactly the problem: it overlooks or ignores local people and their indigenous knowledge. Lewis (Chapter 13) calls for an historical analysis of preceding interventions which evaluates past development actions to inform new strategies that do not override community perceptions and aspirations – the disjuncture between past and present impacts negatively on the poor or those who can least afford failed interventions. Similarly Taylor (Chapter 5) demonstrates that the maintenance of agricultural biodiversity (and with it cultural diversity) is both socially and culturally important, and offers resilience in the face of climatic uncertainties. But he too warns against a dominant discourse – or meta-narrative – which, in prioritizing climate change, ignores local priorities. These are the seemingly less important constraints, when viewed nationally or globally, which impinge on the lives of the poor.

Vo and Manno (Chapter 16) show how fisherfolk adapt to changing opportunities and circumstances through a process of innovation and improvisation in which new ways of catching and maintaining fish stocks are introduced, but they also go on to the dangers of fishing beyond ecological limits. The need for good and appropriate policy is evident in this chapter as is the need for timely and appropriate external expertise. This is an important point because this case study – in accordance with the views of the many contributors to this volume – shows that local communities have an impressive stock of indigenous knowledge which should provide a foundation for any intervention – but it also acknowledges additional needs which cannot be met from local sources and resources.

The call for inclusion of communities and/or indigenous peoples into deliberations about climate change is emphasized in our introductory chapter in which we reinforce their right to inclusion and not just the efficacy of their involvement in instrumental terms. Nonetheless, many studies of international development interventions do show that where there has been effective participation by 'beneficiaries' there is a greater chance of success (for example Brokensha et al., 1980; Kottak, 1991; Msukwa and Taylor, 2011). For effective involvement to take place, issues of both power and capacity need to be addressed with respect to communities and their members; otherwise, such supposedly 'participatory' endeavours may prove not only disappointing, but even potentially destructive for their intended 'beneficiaries' (Cooke and Kothari, 2001).

There is no doubt that communities are aware of the changing weather patterns, in terms of temperature, total rainfall and its distribution, as Wellard and her co-authors have shown (Chapter 4). However, perceptions and records often diverge, because communities use a different register to interpret these changes with resulting incommensurability. We should be aware though, that communities' awareness of climate change may only become an issue once the interventions of external agencies define the phenomenon for them. Hence, climate change could justifiably be regarded as one of the many problems faced by poor people, albeit a very important one. And there is the further danger that technological responses to climate change – the dominant paradigm – will overlook the social, political and economic changes that are necessary to safeguard our 'common future'. The technical and technological determinism inherent in current mitigation and adaptation strategies overlooks the structural inequalities that have caused the problem in the first place. The negation, in policy terms and practical actions, of the food, fuel and financial crises – along with current climate change – takes the form of a relentless pursuit of economic growth and poses a grave threat to long-term sustainable development.

In drawing our conclusions, we do not wish to understate the tremendous challenges that face humankind in mitigating and/or adapting to climate change; neither do we need to restate the compelling scientific evidence for human-induced global warming. But we do want to challenge the exclusion of poor communities across the globe in planning our collective future and the global discourse of climate change that is disassociated from their voices. The call for an alternative to the 'business as usual' approach (see IAASTD, 2008) resonates with an alternative vision espoused in the voices of many marginalized peoples whose current struggles are captured in the chapters of this book.

The intention of this book is not to map out the course of action that needs to be taken to address the challenges of climate change but rather to highlight the continued marginalization of the global poor whose collective contribution to the problem is relatively insignificant, yet whose contribution to the solution is essential. As population pressure puts increasing pressure on our global resources; as information and communication technologies shorten and shrink time and distance; and as the aspirations of poor people grow as they bear witness to the discrepancies between rich and poor, there is a dire need for change. Climate change is part of a greater challenge without which there can be no resolution: the struggle for social justice in an unfair world.

Author updates to the 2025 edition

The ability to examine the same locations and issues more than a dozen years apart allows this volume to explore social and environmental change. Original contributors, emerging scholars, and the editor updated these case studies with how the local community had altered their relationship to the environment, how academic fields have developed and the history of national and international climate change policy. Such updates provide a glimpse into the diversity of the processes that govern human and environmental interactions as well as the ways in which it is understood by researchers. Yet, there is an implicit and sometimes explicit sentiment that although there has been so much change over the last 12 years, many believe that it has not made much of a difference in the causes of climate change or its potential impact on vulnerable communities. The emotional tone of the scholarship ranges between resignation and pessimism. Yet, it is difficult to imagine addressing climate change without going through such scholarship and the feelings that it can evoke.

The revised volume's theme is change.

References

Appadurai, A. (1989) *The Social Life of Things: Commodities in Cultural Perspective*, Cambridge University Press, Cambridge.

Brokensha, D., Warren, D. and Werner, O. (eds) (1980) *Indigenous Knowledge Systems and Development*, University Press of America, Lanham.

Cooke, B. and Kothari, U. (eds) (2001) *Participation: The New Tyranny?* Zed, London.

Cruikshank, J. (2005) *Do Glaciers Listen? Local Knowledge, Colonial Encounters, and Social Imagination*, University of British Columbia Press, Vancouver.

Dove, M. (2006) 'Indigenous people and environmental politics', *Annual Review of Anthropology* 35: 191–208.

Hannerz, U. (1987) 'The World in Creolisation', *Africa* 57: 546–59.

International Assessment of Agricultural Knowledge, Science and Technology for Development (IAASTD) (2008) 'Agriculture at a Crossroads', Island Press, Washington DC [Online] Available from: http://www.agassessment.org/reports/IAASTD/EN/Agriculture%20at%20a%20Crossroads_Global%20Report%20%28English%29.pdf [accessed 9 June 2010].

Kottak, C. (1991) 'When people don't come first: Some sociological lessons from completed projects', in M. Cernea (ed.), *Putting People First: Sociological Variables in Rural Development*, pp. 431–64, Oxford University Press for the World Bank, New York.

Long, N. and Long, A. (eds) (1992) *Battlefields of Knowledge: The Interlocking of Theory and Practice in Social Research and Development*, Routledge, London.

Msukwa, C. and Taylor, D. (2011) 'Why can't development be managed more like a funeral? Challenging participatory practices', *Development and Change* 21: 55–67.

Scoones, I. and Thompson, J. (eds) (1994) *Beyond Farmer First: Rural People's Knowledge, Agricultural Research and Extension Practice*, Intermediate Technology Publications, London.

Resources for Communities on the Frontlines of Climate Change

Compiled by Wendy B. Miles

This curated list of freely available online resources is designed to support local and Indigenous communities in their climate resilience goals, offering access to both introductory and advanced climate science. Since the first edition of this book, the availability and quality of public climate data and planning tools have advanced significantly. Communities around the world can now access regionally downscaled climate projections, interactive risk assessment tools, and step-by-step guides to develop adaptation strategies tailored to their local context. Climate resilience planning is no longer the sole domain of technical experts; it is increasingly grounded in community leadership and place-based knowledge. The tools shared here are credible and practical—intended to support, not replace, the leadership of communities charting their own climate resilience paths.

Indigenous-Led and Community-Centered Platforms

Indigenous Climate Hub (indigenousclimatehub.ca): An Indigenous-led online platform developed by and for Indigenous Peoples. Focused on Canada, it hosts climate resiliency resources, funding information, and stories from an Indigenous perspective. The Indigenous Climate Hub is designed to support Indigenous communities in monitoring environmental changes and planning adaptation on their lands and waters.

Local Communities and Indigenous Peoples Platform (lcipp. unfccc.int): An official United Nations Climate Change web portal that facilitates the exchange of adaptation experiences, best practices, and tools to build local climate resilience. The global platform advocates for increased representation of Indigenous and local communities in national and international climate policies and actions.

Practical Action (practicalaction.org): Practical Action is a global development organization that advances its mission by collaborating with communities to develop locally appropriate climate resilience solutions. They publish multilingual content, including technical guides addressing climate resilience in the domains of water, agriculture, energy, and disaster risk reduction on the Practical Answers platform (practicalaction.org/learning/practical-answers).

They also create school resources and toolkits specifically designed to help marginalized groups adapt more effectively to environmental and market-driven changes, so as to build community resilience (practicalaction.org/learning).

Global Knowledge Platforms & Learning Hubs

CARE Climate Justice Center (careclimatechange.org): The CARE Climate Justice Center hosts a wide range of free, online, self-paced multilingual courses through the Climate & Resilience Academy (careclimatechange.org/academy). Trainings and associated resources address topics that include locally led adaptation planning, monitoring and evaluation for adaptation, youth leadership in adaptation, climate and disaster risk finance and insurance, climate and gender justice, building climate-smart organizations, and the Green Climate Fund. The site also includes a multilingual toolkit for youth on adaptation leadership (careclimatechange.org/toolkit-for-youth-on-adaptation-leadership-website), and the widely used *Climate Vulnerability and Capacity Analysis Handbook* (careclimatechange.org/cvca).

Climate Adaptation Knowledge Exchange (CAKE) (cakex.org): CAKE is a collaborative knowledge-sharing platform that offers an extensive digital library of climate adaptation case studies, guides, tools, and training materials for practitioners working at the frontlines of climate change. Users can create profiles, contribute new resources, and exchange job and funding opportunities through the platform's community section. Founded by the U.S.-based nonprofit EcoAdapt in 2010, CAKE's primary audience includes professionals from across the United States and Tribal/First Nations, though its global reach has grown in recent years. EcoAdapt also convenes the National Adaptation Forum (nationaladaptationforum.org), the leading climate adaptation conference in the United States.

Climate Change Knowledge Portal (climateknowledgeportal.worldbank.org): Designed to support development planning, this portal hosted by the World Bank provides public access to climate projections, historical climate data, and socio-economic indicators for most countries. While it does not generate original climate science, it compiles data from authoritative sources, including the IPCC, and shares this information in user-friendly formats.

Climate & Development Knowledge Network (CDKN) (cdkn.org): An international initiative focused on mobilizing knowledge, resources, and leadership for climate-resilient development in the Global South. Established in 2010, CDKN works with public, private, and non-governmental sectors to promote locally led climate-resilient action. Their multilingual resource library shares geographically diverse stories and publications at the nexus of climate and development.

Global Hub on Locally Led Adaptation (llahub.gca.org): An information hub hosted by the Global Center on Adaptation, an international organization supported by the Government of the Netherlands, development banks, private donors, and philanthropic organizations. The website provides curated technical reports and white papers on locally led adaptation, stories of community resilience efforts, and guides relevant to community-based climate planning. *(See also: GCA entry under the United Nations and International Climate Institutions section.)*

International Institute for Environment and Development (IIED) (iied.org): A collection of research reports, policy briefs, and toolkits on community-based adaptation and climate justice. These resources are curated by the IIED, a 50-year-old nonprofit organization that was an early and influential advocate for sustainable development. IIED works primarily in the Global South and hosts the Community-Based Adaptation Conference every year. The IIED also hosts the NAP Global Network (napglobalnetwork. org), an independent international initiative that supports developing countries in advancing their National Adaptation Plans.

weADAPT (weadapt.org): One of the longest-running online platforms for climate adaptation knowledge exchange, weADAPT shares high-quality climate change information. The platform is designed to support adaptation learning and collaboration among practitioners, researchers, and decision-makers, and encourages users to share lessons learned in local adaptation initiatives.

Regional Portals and Climate Hubs

Africa Adaptation Initiative (AAI) (africaadaptationinitiative.org): AAI is a continent-wide, African-led initiative that aims to strengthen collaboration on climate adaptation across the continent. Areas of focus include fostering high-level dialogues, enhancing climate information services, implementing on-the-ground climate adaptation, and increasing access to adaptation finance. Other sources of online climate adaptation resources for the African continent include ICLEI Africa (africa.iclei.org), Africa Adaptation Acceleration Program (gca.org/programs/aaap), and WWF Africa Adaptation Hub (africa.panda.org/our_work/programs_and_initiatives/africa_adaptation_hub).

Climate Action Latin America and Caribbean (Climate Action LAC) (accionclimatica-alc.org): Funded by the United Nations Environment Program (UNEP), Climate Action LAC is a multilingual online platform focused on providing climate change information, case studies, and strategic guidance tailored to Latin America and the Caribbean. Areas of focus include climate adaptation in urban communities, as well as mitigation, transparency, and sustainable development.

ICLEI - Local Governments for Sustainability (iclei.org): The International Council for Local Environmental Initiatives (ICLEI) Local Governments for Sustainability works with local and regional governments to advance sustainable development and climate adaptation through peer-to-peer learning, tools, and trainings. It hosts online resources like the Resilient Cities Action Package (ReCAP), Urban Resilience Learning Hub, and Climate Risk and Vulnerability Assessment (CRVA) Framework to provide guidance on community-led adaptation and climate risk assessments, with a focus on urban areas. ICLEI has country offices in Africa (africa.iclei.org), East Asia (eastasia.iclei.org), Europe (iclei-europe.org), Mexico, Central America and the Caribbean (iclei.org.mx), North America (icleicanada.org), Oceania (icleioceania.org), South America (americadosul.iclei.org), South Asia (southasia.iclei.org), and Southeast Asia (icleiseas.org).

Pacific Climate Change Centre (PCCC) (sprep.org/pacific-climate-change-centre): The new PCCC serves as the regional hub for climate change information, research, and innovation in the Pacific Islands. The Centre aims to enhance the flow of practical information on climate change mitigation and adaptation between policymakers, researchers, practitioners, and the public, thereby strengthening the resilience of Pacific Island communities. The PCCC hosts the Pacific Climate Change Portal (pacificclimatechange.net), which provides resources and decision-support tools tailored to the resilience needs of the Pacific Islands, and emphasizes solutions that are driven by Pacific Island communities. It also facilitates networking in the region and includes a roster of regional climate experts and information on upcoming trainings and events. *(See also: Pacific Climate Change Portal entry under the Climate Science, Data, and Projections section.)*

U.S. Climate Resilience Toolkit (toolkit.climate.gov): A U.S.-focused toolkit that hosts frameworks and tools that are globally applicable. Useful for communities seeking examples of structured climate adaptation planning processes, the site offers step-by-step guidance on identifying climate hazards, assessing vulnerability and risk, exploring solutions, prioritizing and planning, and taking action and tracking progress. The website features community case studies, sector-specific guides, trainings, and interactive tools for data visualization and mapping.

Climate and Social Justice Networks

Climate Action Network (CAN) (climatenetwork.org): Founded in 1989, CAN is a global network of civil society organizations working to address the climate crisis while promoting social justice. Their offerings include publications, webinars, and a civil society newsletter as well as organized campaigns and events to raise awareness. There are national and regional CAN networks – accessible through the CAN website – with resources and activities tailored to place-specific priorities.

Rights and Resources Initiative (RRI) (rightsandresources.org): RRI is a global coalition focused on securing legal recognition of community natural resource rights for Indigenous Peoples, Afro-descendant Peoples, local communities, and women within these communities. Recognizing that local land rights are critical for climate resilience, the RRI coalition works to secure community tenure rights and support communities in managing their lands sustainably. Their website hosts a wide range of relevant resources, including the LandWise Law Library (resourceequity.org/#elementor-tab-title-2101) and RRI Tenure Tool (rightsandresources.org/rri-tenure-tool).

United Nations and International Climate Institutions

United Nations (UN) (un.org/en/climatechange): The United Nations has served as a global convener and support system for the international response to climate change. Key UN mechanisms designed to mitigate the impacts of and prepare for climate change include:

- **UN Framework Convention on Climate Change (UNFCCC)** (unfccc.int): A global treaty that establishes international climate goals, hosts negotiations, and coordinates international adaptation and mitigation mechanisms like **REDD+** (Reducing Emissions from Deforestation and Forest Degradation) (redd.unfccc.int) and **National Adaptation Plans** (NAPs) (unfccc.int/national-adaptation-plans).

- **Intergovernmental Panel on Climate Change (IPCC)** (ipcc.ch): The world's most robust and agreed upon climate change assessment reports, used as the scientific foundation for global climate policies and actions. The IPCC also publishes summary reports for policymakers and fact sheets for regional and sector-specific action.

- **UN Development Program (UNDP)** (adaptation-undp.org): UNDP is tasked with supporting low- and middle-income countries in designing and implementing their National Adaptation Plans and meeting their nationally determined contributions under the UNFCCC. The UNDP's thematic areas of focus on climate change include food security resilience, climate change and health, climate information and early warning systems, ecosystem-based adaptation, climate-resilient livelihoods, climate-resilient infrastructure, and adaptation planning and policy.

- **UN Environment Programme (UNEP)** (unep.org): The UNEP promotes ecosystem-based climate adaptation and hosts the Global Adaptation Network (GAN) (unep.org/gan), a knowledge-sharing platform for climate adaptation.

- **International Union for the Conservation of Nature (IUCN)** (iucn.org): The IUCN has expertise in the role of Nature-based Solutions (NbS) and Ecosystem-based Adaptation (EbA) in addressing climate change. In addition to resources on both NbS and EbA, the IUCN has co-developed tools, resources, and frameworks at the nexus of community resilience, biodiversity conservation, and climate change, which can be explored on their resources page (iucn.org/resources).

- **Green Climate Fund (GCF)** (greenclimate.fund): The largest climate fund in the world, GCF finances climate mitigation and adaptation efforts in developing countries.

- **Global Center on Adaptation (GCA)** (gca.org): While not a UN agency, the GCA is a close partner to UN institutions and national governments, co-leading initiatives such as the Africa Adaptation Acceleration Program (gca.org/programs/aaap), Youth Adaptation Forums, and Global Hub on Locally Led Adaptation (llahub.gca.org).

Climate Analytics (climateanalytics.org): Climate Analytics is an international climate science and policy institute that works to advance the Paris Agreement goal of limiting global warming to 1.5°C. Climate Analytics hosts open-access resources and tools designed to help local-to-national governments understand regional climate risks and visualize future climate scenarios. Their tools include the Climate Action Tracker (climateactiontracker.org), 1.5°C National Pathway Explorer (1p5ndc-pathways.climateanalytics.org), Climate Risk Dashboard (climate-risk-dashboard.iiasa.ac.at), and Global Mitigation Potential Atlas (mitigationatlas.org).

Community Monitoring and Participatory Mapping Platforms

RAISG (Amazon Network of Georeferenced Socio-Environmental Information) (raisg.org): Established in 2007, RAISG is a consortium of civil society organizations from Amazonian countries dedicated to the region's socio-environmental sustainability. The RAISG website serves as a platform for sharing socio-environmental GIS data, and hosts a range of geospatial information, analyses, maps, and tools for communities, researchers, and policymakers in the Amazon.

Local Environmental Observer (LEO) Network (leonetwork.org): The LEO Network is a global platform that enables people to share observations of unusual environmental events in the communities where they live. The network was established in 2012 by the Alaska Native Tribal Health Consortium. Today, its interactive map documents observations of extreme weather, environmental hazards, and changes in wildlife behavior from around the world.

Climate Crowd - World Wildlife Fund (WWF) (wwfclimatecrowd. org): As one of the world's largest environmental conservation organizations, WWF is focused on nature-based and conservation-integrated climate adaptation. WWF's Climate Crowd (wwfclimatecrowd.org) is an online platform for gathering observations of environmental change, including climate change.

Global Atlas of Environmental Justice (EJAtlas) (ejatlas.org): Developed and managed by volunteers, students, and researchers, the EJAtlas is an interactive map of environmental justice (and climate justice) struggles globally.

Community Climate Finance

USAID Climate Ready-PIDP Small Grants Guide (eastwestcenter. org/publications/small-grants-guide): This guide was written for local governments, civil society organizations, and community groups in Pacific Islands, but its approach is not region-specific. The freely accessible book is designed to help communities access funding to support their climate resilience goals. It provides step-by-step guidance on identifying suitable funding opportunities, crafting compelling proposals, and effectively managing grants. While designed for first-time grant writers, this guide also offers skills and a clear process relevant for larger funding proposals.

Climate Science, Data, and Projections

Global

Intergovernmental Panel on Climate Change (IPCC) (ipcc.ch): The IPCC provides the world's most authoritative climate science reports. Their "Assessment Reports" are published every 5–7 years. The accompanying "Summary for Policymakers" reports summarize the lengthy climate assessment reports in language that is more accessible. The IPCC's interactive atlas and regional fact sheets provide clear summaries of climate projections by region. The IPCC's Special Report on *Global Warming of 1.5°C* (ipcc. ch/sr15) shows how even half a degree of additional warming (2°C versus 1.5°C) would dramatically increase risks of extreme heat, sea level rise, and ecosystem loss. *AR6 Synthesis Report: Climate Change 2023* brings together the latest scientific consensus from the entire Sixth Assessment Cycle of the IPCC to provide a comprehensive summary of the causes, impacts, and solutions to climate change (ipcc.ch/report/sixth-assessment-report-cycle). The *Climate Change 2022: Impacts, Adaptation and Vulnerability* report provides region-specific chapters for Africa, Asia, Europe, North America, Central and South America, Australasia, Polar Regions, and Small Islands (ipcc.ch/report/ sixth-assessment-report-working-group-ii).

Copernicus Climate Data Store (C3S) (cds.climate.copernicus.eu): C3S provides comprehensive climate data and tools with global coverage. The Climate Data Store (CDS) hosts open-access climate data, climate analysis tools, and the ability to create custom climate maps. The Copernicus Interactive Climate Atlas enables users to visualize and analyze climate variables across time and in different geographic regions.

North America

NOAA Sea Level Rise Viewer (coast.noaa.gov/slr): A user-friendly tool that enables the public to create tailored maps of local coastal flooding under different downscaled climate projections.

The Climate Explorer (crt-climate-explorer.nemac.org): An interactive, web-based tool designed to assist communities in the U.S. – including U.S. Territories – in understanding and planning for climate change impacts at the local scale. The Climate Explorer provides localized climate information in accessible formats that can be incorporated into community climate adaptation plans.

ClimateData.ca (climatedata.ca): An online portal that enables Canadians to access, visualize, and analyze climate data. Using ClimateData.ca, local communities can create custom graphs and high-resolution projections to inform their adaptation decision-making.

National Climate Assessment (NCA) (nca2023.globalchange.gov): The U.S. National Climate Assessment reports provide regional climate projections and summaries of climate adaptation needs nationally and regionally.

Latin America & Caribbean

Caribbean Community Climate Change Centre (CCCCC) (caribbeanclimate.org): The CCCCC (also known as the "5Cs") serves as a hub for coordinating the region's response to climate change. Established in 2002, they have maintained a repository of regional climate data to support adaptation decision-making. Their interactive tools include the CCORAL (Caribbean Climate Online Risk and Adaptation Tool), CLIE'nT (Caribbean Climate Information Education and Tools), CREWS (Coral Reef Early Warning System), and Clearinghouse Search Tool (see: caribbeanclimate.org/tools).

Observatorio Andino (observatorioandino.com): Observatorio Andino is a collaborative network that provides environmental monitoring and forecasting for Andean countries to improve climate risk and vulnerability assessments and support climate adaptation decision-making.

Centro de Previsão do Tempo e Estudos Climáticos (CPTEC) (cptec. inpe.br): CPTEC delivers climate and weather forecasts to Latin American countries. Part of the National Institute for Space Research in Brazil, it provides valuable climate data and analyses to improve knowledge of climate variability and climatic changes in the region.

Africa

Climate Information Platform (CIP) (cip.csag.uct.ac.za): Developed by the University of Cape Town, the CIP hosts climate data and information for Africa and Asia. The CIP platform includes raw databases, interactive maps and graphs, and guidance on how to use these resources to inform climate-resilient planning.

IGAD Climate Prediction and Applications Centre (ICPAC) (icpac. net): The Intergovernmental Authority on Development (IGAD)'s ICPAC is an accredited Regional Climate Center of the World Meteorological Organization. ICPAC serves East Africa by providing climate services and knowledge to support community resilience. ICPAC provides both seasonal forecasting and real-time monitoring of climate indicators and their impacts.

Europe

Climate-ADAPT European Climate Data Explorer (climate-adapt. eea.europa.eu): Part of the European Union's Climate-ADAPT platform, this interactive dashboard can be used to explore climate impact indicators across sectors and regions in Europe. It draws on data from the Copernicus Climate Change Service and supports climate risk assessment and adaptation planning.

UKCP18 (UK Climate Projections) (metoffice.gov.uk): The Met Office hosts the most up-to-date climate data and information for the United Kingdom, which can be accessed through their interactive portal.

Asia & Southeast Asia

Asia-Pacific Climate Change Adaptation Information Platform (AP-PLAT) (ap-plat.nies.go.jp): AP-PLAT provides access to climate science data and interactive climate adaptation planning tools for the region. For example, AP-PLAT's ClimoCast is a climate projection tool with downloadable data for the Asia Pacific, and their Climate Impact Viewer tool helps visualize the impacts of climate change on different sectors in the region.

Singapore V3 Study (mss-int.sg/v3-climate-projections): The Centre for Climate Research Singapore (CCRS) released Singapore's Third National Climate Change Study (V3) in 2024. The report and interactive website utilize downscaled global models from the IPCC's most recent report (AR6) to provide state-of-the-art, high-resolution climate projections for Singapore and Southeast Asia.

Oceania

Australia CSIRO (Commonwealth Scientific and Industrial Research Organization) (csiro.au/en/research/environmental-impacts/climate-change?start=0&count=12): The Australian Government's national science agency CSIRO provides climate data, downscaled projections, and interactive planning tools in support of climate adaptation in Australia. Their work extends beyond Australia, with contributions to climate knowledge in the broader Oceania region.

New Zealand Ministry for the Environment (environment.govt.nz): Aotearoa's National Adaptation Plan and high-resolution downscaled climate projections can both be accessed on the Ministry for the Environment's website.

Pacific-Australia Climate Change Science and Adaptation Planning Program (PACCSAP) (bom.gov.au/climate/pacific): PACCSAP supports the development of climate information resources and scientific tools, such as the Pacific Climate Futures web tool (pacificclimatefutures.net). Climate data for the Pacific Islands can also be accessed through the Pacific Climate Change Data Portal, hosted by the Australian Bureau of Meteorology (bom.gov.au/climate/pccsp). The portal supports improved access to downscaled projections in the region.

Pacific Islands Regional Climate Assessment (PIRCA): National and jurisdictional climate assessments for Palau, the Marshall Islands, the Federated States of Micronesia, Guam, American Samoa, and the Northern Mariana Islands are available at eastwestcenter.org.

Pacific Climate Change Portal (PCCP) (pacificclimatechange.net): A climate information hub for Pacific Island nations, this portal is hosted by the Secretariat of the Pacific Regional Environment Programme's Pacific Climate Change Centre. The PCCP's extensive library includes regional climate reports and country profiles for Pacific Island climate planning. *(See also: Pacific Climate Change Centre entry under the Regional Climate Hubs section.)*

About the author

Wendy B. Miles is an independent Hawai'i-based consultant specializing in community-led climate resilience, policy evaluation, and science-based decision support for governments and frontline communities. She has led adaptation initiatives across Hawai'i and the U.S.-Affiliated Pacific Islands, advancing national climate assessments, Indigenous-led resilience planning, and cross-sector conservation partnerships. Dr. Miles holds degrees from the University of Oxford and the University of Hawaiʻi, and is a former Fulbright Fellow.

Index

Action Aid 201
adaptation 5, 20, 59, 107
adaptive capacity 86–88, 90
Aga Khan Rural Support Program 170
agriculture
    cultural significance 150
    employment in 102
    industrial 222
    intensification 44, 53, 176
    irrigation-based 165
    Mayan 177
    modern 215
    and rainfall variability 176
    traditional practices 215
agro-ecology 39, 41, 76
Alaska 165
all terrain vehicles, see ATVs
'Amazon Chernobyl' 11
American Indians 163–71
    effect of climate change 164–65
    effect of historical exploitation 10, 164, 169–70
    legal position 164, 166–69
    poverty 170
    renewable energy 10, 166–67
    vulnerability 166
Amhara 40, 43, 45
Amharic language 38
Anaya Hernández A. 145, 176, 182, 190–92
Andes 9, 115, 117, 149–56
animal husbandry 40, 120, 214
aquaculture, intensive 234, 237 190, 191 238–39
archaeological research 11, 175–76 142, 145 178, 181

Badjwe people 21
Baker River 118
Banda, Dr Hastings 75
Bangladesh 195–99, 201, 203
Bangladesh Flood Action Plan, see FAP
Barbour, M. 103
BASIS project 40, 43, 47

beekeeping 91
biodiversity 18–20, 76, 88, 91, 121
bio-fuels 166
birds, migration of 110
Bond, I., Grieg-Gran, M., Wertz-Kanounnikoff, S., Hazlewood, P., Wunder, S. and Angelsen, A. 25
Boyce, J. 204
Brown, L. and Wolf, E. 45

Calakmul 140, 142, 145, 146, 147
Cameroon 17, 19–23, 25, 30
    community forestry 7, 21, 23
    forestry law (1994) 19–21
    REDD 16–17, 20–3
Campeche 175–78, 180–82, 189
    maize 180–81
    Mayan canal systems 177–78, 189
    population density 179
Canada 136, 139–40, 144
Canada geese 136
canal system, Mayan 11, 141–2, 145–8 177–78, 181–82, 188
caribou 140
CARPE (Central African Regional Program for the Environment) 22
cash crops 57, 104, 106, 175
Castro, A. P. 101, 111
Cauich 175–76, 182
CBNRM (community-based natural resource management) 91
Central African Regional Program for the Environment, see CARPE
Centre for Research on the Epidemiology of Disasters see CRED
CEPA (Centre for Environment Policy and Advocacy) 61
Chevron Corporation 11
China 77
Chocolate Glacier 123
Christianity 38, 227
'climate change refugees' 197, 201
'climate equity' 5
'climate justice' 5
colonialism 73, 170

Colorado 165–66
commoditization 8, 78
community-based natural resource management, see CBNRM
Community Forestry Development Unit 21
compensation 22–23
Concrete 118–19, 122–23
conflict 9, 99–100, 104, 107
Congo Basin 17
consultation, local, lack of 20, 200
contamination, water 178
Cook-Lynn, Elizabeth 169
Coordinating Unit for Rehabilitation of the Environment see CURE
Cordillera Blanca 115, 117, 119, 124
Cornwall, A. and Brock, K. 200
'cosmovision' 10, 149–50, 152–53, 155
Cotacachi 149–50
cotton 143, 147, 169, 170, 171
CRED (Centre for Research on the Epidemiology of Disasters) 44
Cree people (Eeyouch)
    coastal hunting and climate change 140
    and indigenous knowledge 137
    population 131
    traditional skills 132
    travel and climate change 111-12, 113
crops
    combining 76
    diseases 46
    diversity 213
    experimental 120
    GM 72
    hybrid 76, 213
    and rainfall variability 7, 63–64
cultural change 156
cultural reinforcement 139
Cuomo, C., Eisner, W. and Hinkel, W. and Hinkel, K. 93
CURE (Coordinating Unit for Rehabilitation of the Environment) 61
cyclones 212

Daltabuit , M., Ríos, A. and Pérez, F. 190–1
Darfur 99–103, 105–8, 111
    conflict 9, 102, 106
    infrastructure 84
    onion and potato cultivation 106, 108
    population increase 100
    rainfall 100
    response to climate change 104–6
    role of climate change in conflict 107
    water supply 102
'de-agrarianism' 8, 78
debt 238
decentralisation 23
deforestation
    East Sumba 222
    and farming 79
    Himalayan 198
    and industrialization 2
    Malawi 56, 65
    media coverage 228
    Mexico 180
    phenomenology 226–27
    and public perception 211, 224–25
    and religious belief 154
Degradation Programme see REDD
Democratic Republic of Congo 18, 20, 22, 25
Department for International Development see DFID
Derg 37, 42–43
desertification 9, 99, 105, 107
Dessie 38, 42
Devereux, S. and Sharp, K. 41
de Wachter, P. 20
DFID (Department for International Development) 196
Dhaka 198, 200
diet, changes in 151
disease, and European contact 140
displacement, internal 9, 89, 100, 102 107,188
diversification 76, 93
Dja 21
donor aid 198–99
drought
    Bangladesh 201
    Ethiopia 2, 37, 42–45
    India 12, 208, 212, 215
    Indonesia 12, 221, 223–27, 236
    Malawi 53–54, 56, 60, 62–64
    Mayan 177, 188
    Mexico 176

Mozambique 89–90
Somalia 4
Southern Africa 73, 76, 78, 80
Sudan 101, 105, 107–8
Dryden, John 166

Eastmain 138
East Sumba 221–29
    geography 222
    perceptions re climate change 12,
    224–26
    rainfall 223–24
'Ecological Indian' 166
ecosystems, changes to 19, 135
ecotourism 90–91
Ecuador 10, 149–50, 152
Edzná 176, 178, 181–82
Eeyouch see Cree people
Ekoko, F. 19
energy, renewable 163–71
    funding 167–68
    and indigenous knowledge 164
    and need for capital 167
ENSO (El Niño Southern Oscillation)
    72
environmental impact studies 168
EPRDF (Ethiopian Peoples
    Revolutionary Democratic Front)
    34, 35 42–43
erosion, coastal 165
Ershad, General H. M. 156, 157
Ethiopia 37–45, 47, 49
    coalition 42
    drought 2, 37–38, 43–44
    education 40
    employment 40
    famine 42–45
    farming practices 39, 44
    food aid 43
    geography 39
    government policies 7
    income 40
    land scarcity 40
    plough-based agriculture 7
    population 38
    poverty 38, 40
    public services 44
    religion 38
    rural income 39
    vulnerability of rural
    communities 41–44
    war with Eritrea 43
Ethiopian Peoples Revolutionary
    Democratic Front see EPRDF

evangelicalism 152
extension services 9, 57, 75, 99, 107

'fair trade' production 179
famine 2, 4, 7, 37, 41–44
FAP (Bangladesh Flood Action Plan)
    11, 153, 154, 156–8
Faust, B. 176
Faust, B. and Bilsborrow, R. 179
FEICOM (Fonds d'Intervention et
    d'Equipement Communal) 23
fertilizer 53, 75, 215
fishing 233–42
    breeding 165
    corrals 233, 236–39, 241
    and decrease in water 89
    and extreme weather 197
    Quebec 133
    traditional practices 237
        see also aquaculture
Flavier, J. M. et al. 164
flooding
    Bangladesh 195–96, 198–99
    India 192, 193 241
    Malawi 54–56, 61–62
    Mexico 176, 181, 188
    Mozambique 88–90
    Southern Africa 76
    United States 123, 165, 169
    Vietnam 234–37
Fonds d'Intervention et
    d'Equipement Communal see
    FEICOM
food insecurity, chronic 37, 54, 105
foraging 88
forestry 19, 21, 23, 25, 30
    community 7, 21, 23
    and indigenous knowledge 17
    local effects 19
    management 18
    national plan 20
    subarctic 133
    sustainability
Forest Stewardship Council 25
fossil fuels 2, 12, 104, 210–11
Fukayama, Francis 169
fur communities 9, 82, 99, 101–2,
    104–8
fur trade 131

G-7 summit (1989) 198
Gabon 22
Gates, M. 180
gender differences 7, 40–41, 57

genetically modified (GM) crops 72
169, 171 213, 215
Geovannini Acuña, H. 176, 181, 185
glacial retreat 115–26
  Andean 152
  effects of 9
  evidence for 116–17
  meltwater 120, 122, 124
  published accounts 121
  rainfall 124
Glacier (town) 119, 122
Global Humanitarian Forum (2009)
82
GM crops, see genetically modified
  crops
GoB (Government of Bangladesh),
154, 155
GPS (global positioning system), 112
Green, D. 204
Green Belt Initiative (Malawi) 60
green house gas emissions 77
ground water irrigation 213
Gujarat 208, 213
Gupta, Akhil 11, 210–11

Haile Selassie 38, 41–42
hakura land tenure 102, 106, 108
Hari, Johann 197
Hartmann, B. 201
harvest, extension of 76
health 93, 105
HELVETAS 91
Henry, A. 211
herding 100, 104
Hue University 241
hunter gatherers 20
hunting 132, 137, 139
hybrid crops 75, 213
hydroelectric development 133
HYVs (high yielding varieties) 73

IAASTD (International Assessment
  on Agricultural Knowledge,
  Science and Technology for
  Agricultural Development) 76
ice, decrease of and travel 111–13
IK (indigenous knowledge)
  and adaptation 53–54, 59–62,
  64–66, 245
  and adaptive capacity 86, 88,
  92–93
  American Indians 163
  Bangladesh 195–96
  and community capacity 90–92

cosmovision 155–56
  definition 164, 213
  ecological disruption to 165
  importance of 19, 200
  India 213
  Indonesia 222
  local 25
  loss of 9, 124–26, 137
  Mayan civilization 177–78
  and place names 121
  and relationship with land 125
  and response to climate change
  119, 121–24
  and scientific knowledge 115, 241
  undermined 90
  as under used 87
  Vietnam 234
income generation 77, 88, 103
India 207–11, 215–16
  agriculture 11
  MDGs 77
  modern agriculture 216
  rainfall 209
  views re climate change 208–9,
  211
Indian Promotion and Parity Act
  (2010) 168
indigenous knowledge, see IK
Indonesia 11, 221–23, 225–26,
  228–29
industrialized nations
  as cause of climate change 225–26
  effects of climate change 115
  inertia 3
  response 196
infant mortality 54
information 12, 112, 163, 167 93;
  see also media
infrastructure 42, 48, 88, 93, 105–6,
  109, 133, 143, 199, 202
insects 46, 107
intercropping 213
International Union for
  Conservation of Nature, see IUCN
International Union of Soil Scientists
  188
Inuit people 137
IPCC (Inter-Governmental Panel on
  Climate Change) 2, 196
irrigation
  adaptation and mitigation 107
  Africa 3
  change of method 214
  Green Belt Initiative (Malawi) 60

and intensification of agriculture
44, 53
South Asia 3
subsurface 182
wadis
Islam 102
Italy 118, 127–28
IUCN (International Union for
Conservation of Nature) 91

James Bay 131, 133–34
Jebel Marra Rural Development
Project 9, 99, 102–3, 107
Joiris, D. 21
justice, social 4–5

Kambera 223
Karsenty, A., Lescuyer, G., Ezzine
de Blas, L., Sembres, T., and
Vermeulen, C. 22
Kasungu 65
Kichwa community 10, 126, 149–51,
155
Kombolcha 38, 42, 50
Kutch 12, 207–9, 211, 213, 215–16
land
degradation 45
levelling 214
ownership 150
redistribution 43
reforms 237
resources 107
scarcity 43
tenure 118
titling 44
language 126
Lebon, J. and Robertson, V. 103
Leiden School of anthropology 223
Lewis, D. and Mosse, D. 203
Lewis, J. 7, 25
liberalization, economic 38, 237
logging 18, 22, 25, 133, 222
LULUCF (land use, land use change,
and forestry) 5

Macmillan, Margaret 203
Madison, D. 209
Mahalanobis, Professor Prasanta C.
157
maize
Campeche 179–81
dependency upon 8, 71–75, 77–80
gender differences 73
hybrid 73, 179

importance of 150, 179–80
increased growth of 63
production predictions 89
resilience 73
yield 73
malaria 89
Malawi 53–57, 59–61, 63, 66
climate variability 55–58
community response to climate
change 61–62
cropping system 63–64
crop predictions 57
donor aid 78
government response to climate
change 59–60
maize 8
NGO response to climate change
61
population increase 54
poverty 54
projections 57
rainfall 54
smallholders 7
tree planting 65–66
managerialism 200
Manitounuk Sound 135
Maputaland Centre of Endemism 88
Maputo 88, 90
Marcara 120
marginalization 5, 12, 47, 79, 171
197, 200 248
Marxism 37, 42
Matheny, R., Gurr, D., Forsyth, W.,
and Hauck, F. 182
Mathewson, K. 189
Matutúine 8, 85, 88–91
Maya people 175–76, 178
Mbendjele people 25
McCann, J. 39
MDG (Millenium Development
Goals) 77
MDTF (Multi-Donor Trust Fund), 155
media 207–8
data 209, 227–28
indigenous knowledge 213,
215–16
and risk perception 208, 211–12
Meles Zenawi 42
Mesfin Wolde Mariam 43
mestizos 188
Mexico 175, 177–81, 191
archaeological excavations 11,
175–76
farming 180–81

Revolution 182
Michaelowa, A. and Michaelowa, K. 62
migration, labour 40, 77, 90
migratory patterns, changes in 113–14, 131 139–40, 165
Millenium Development Goals, see MDG
millet 71, 74, 103
mining 133, 166
mitigation strategies, definition 59
mixed cropping 213
mobility, seasonal 20–21
'modernization,' agricultural 152
monocropping 74, 215
Mozambique 85, 87–93, 96
  and adaptive capacity 86–90
  Civil War 88, 90
  community capacity 90–92
  conservation policies 90
  decentralization 92
  living conditions 88
  rainfall predictions 88
  temperature predicted increase 88
Mt Baker 122–23
Mt. Baker-Snoqualmie National Forest 118
Multi-Donor Trust Fund, see MDTF
Mzimba 63

NAPA (National Adaptation Programmes of Action) (Malawi) 43, 48, 76 55, 60, 92
National Environmental Action Plan (Malawi) 59
National Forestry Action Plan for Cameroon 19
nationalization, land 34
Native Communities and Climate Change 143, 163, 165, 168, 172–73
National Renewable Energy Laboratory 166
National Research Council 72, 74
Navajo Tribe 168
Ndong, Ondo 23
NEP (net enclosed ponds) 186–7, 189–93
Nepal 198
New, M., et al. 55
New Scientist 158
NGOs (non-governmental organizations)
    consultation with 201

ecotourism 90–91
  as source of information 91
India 170, 171 215
Malawi 61, 78
Nooksack River 96
North American Free Trade Agreement 175, 179
North Americans, indigenous, see American Indians
North Bengal floods (1922) 157
North Cascades
  climate 117
  glacial retreat 122–25
  local view re climate change 126

Obama, President Barack 167
ODA (Overseas Development Aid) 76
oil 222
onion cultivation 9, 99–10
  geography of area 101–3, 105
  irrigation 103
  response to climate change
Ontaneda, G. 152
Operational Directive on Indigenous Peoples (World Bank 1991) 19
oral history 119
'organic' production 179
Oromiya 39–40, 43
Osbahr, H., Dorward, P., Stern, R., and Cooper, S. 57
Overseas Development Aid, see ODA
Oyono, P., Cerutti, P. and Morrison, K. 23

participation 4, 8–9, 19, 92, 188
pastoralism 104, 214
patrimonialism 75
payment for ecological services, see PES
peanuts 214
Pearce, F. and Tickell, O. 200
People Mattered (Schumacher) 3
  smallholders 53–54, 56–65, 67
  geography of area 54
  perceptions 55–58
  responses 59–60, 62–65, 67
'permaculture' 178
permafrost, melting of 135
'permanent forest estate' 20
Peru 129, 158–60
PES (payment for ecological services) 23
pesticides 215
pests, crop 151

phenomenology 221, 226
Pich 176, 181
planting dates, changing 214
pollution 12, 211, 216, 222, 239
polycropping 178
polycultures 76
polynyas 138
population, decrease 198
population movement, enforced 34
potato cultivation 9, 99–100, 103–4,
    108
    irrigation 103
    and Jebel Rural Development
    Project 106
Prasad, Raekha 197
Pre-Columbian system 188
PRSP (Poverty Reduction Strategy
    Paper) 196
PTCs (Production Tax Credits) 168

Quebec 132–33, 135, 137, 139, 144
    environmental change 10, 133,
    135–36
    landscapes 135
    wildlife 132

Radwanski, S. and Wickens, G. 103
Rahman, Dr Atiq 197
rainfall variability 45, 177, 180–81,
    213, 215, 234
recreation 122–23
REDD (United Nations Reducing
    Emissions from Deforestation and
    Forest Degradation Programme)
        Cameroon 17–22, 24–25, 28
        effectiveness 7
        and equity 22, 24
        policies 18–19
        scale 24–25
regulation, federal 118, 123
religion 227
REM (Reserva Especial de Maputo)
    88
reservations, American Indian
    10,129, 130, 132, 133, 134, 136
    163–64, 166–68, 170
resources, local 5, 12, 19–20, 89, 102,
    108
Revkin, Andrew 3
Rhoades, Robert E. 207
Rio Declaration 24
Rio Grande Pueblos 165
risk perception 207–9, 211–13, 215
Ronga people 85, 88, 91

root crop agriculture 21

Sahel 100
salinity 74, 197
Samuelson, R. 74
Sandovai, J. M. 180
Santa Valley 117
satellite phone systems 139
Satti, Y. H. 101
Sauk River 123
Saurastra 12, 207–9, 211, 213,
    215–16
Schumacher, E. F. 3
sea ice travel 137, 139
sea levels 2, 9, 11, 115, 187, 196–97
seasons, unpredictability of 98
seeds
    local 213
    saving of 151
sesame 214
Seventh Day Adventist church 119
shadoof 85, 86
Shahabuddin, Justice 199
shaman (yachak) 155
Shaw, J. 180
Shewa 43
Siemens, A. and Puleston, D. 175
Siete Imperios 117, 119, 124–26
Simlemba 62
Sioux people 170
Skagit River 118, 123
snowcaps, melting of 165
snowmobiles 137, 139
soil
    erosion 78, 198
    fertility 63, 66, 78, 107
    types 107, 188
Somalia 4
sorghum 71, 74–75, 103
South Africa 8, 77–78, 89–90
Southern Maya Lowlands 175
Southern Ute Tribe 166
South Tirol 115, 117–18, 121–22,
    124,
    125–26
soya 63
stewardship 163–64, 166
Stimulus Package 167
Stockholm Environment Institute
    49, 50 61–62
storage, crops 100, 105, 109
subsidies 10, 54, 75
subsistence farming 95, 107, 176
Sudan 99–100, 103–4, 106–8, 111

geography 103–4
onion and potato production 9, 107–8
responses to climate change 104–6
sugarcane cultivation 64
Sulden glacier 121
support, technical 87
Surendranagar 215
Swaziland 89
swidden 88, 175, 178–80

Tadross, M., Jack, C. and Hewitson, B 56
Tam Giang Cau Hai Lagoon 233–42
adaptation 236–39
local knowledge 235–36
vulnerability 240
Tangail 200
taxation, redistribution of 20, 21
temperature increase
Africa 55–56, 105–6
Bangladesh 196
India 216
Mexico 187
Quebec 132, 134
United States 165
TFAP (Tropical Forestry Action Plan) 17
TFCA (Transfrontier Conservation Area) 89
timber production 19
tobacco cultivation 57, 64
tourism 118–19, 122–24, 180
tractor cultivation 179–80, 185
Transfrontier Conservation Area, see TFCA
travel and climate change, 131 137, 139
tree planting 65–66
tribal codes, model 169
Tribal Nations Conference 2009 167
TRMM (Tropical Rainfall Measuring Mission) 223
Tropical Forestry Action Plan, see TFAP

UNDP (United Nations Development Programme) 3
UNFCC (United Nations Framework Convention on Climate Change) 48, 154 60
United Kingdom 196, 259

United Nations Climate Change Conference (2007) 181
United Nations Climate Change Conference (2010) 58
United Nations Development Programme see UNDP
United Nations Environmental Programme 106
United Nations Framework Convention on Climate Change, see UNFCC
United Nations Reducing Emissions from Deforestation and Forest Degradation Programme, see REDD
United States, 144, 166 119, 210
University of Colorado 165
urban culture, as attractive 74
urban population, food provision 89
USAID (United States Agency for International Development) 198

vegetable cultivation 73, 100, 188
Vertisols 185
Vietnam 233–37, 239, 241
climatic forecasts 234
fisheries 236–37, 239
indigenous knowledge 235–36
violence 3, 9, 107
Vo, T. 235–37, 240
volcanoes 153
vulnerability 4, 7, 38, 164

Waswanipi people 135
water
contamination 89
distribution 155
infrastructure 124
levels 151
management 214
pumping, cost of 181
redistribution of 120
supply 177
water-borne diseases 89
waterfowl 136, 139–40
waterlogging 74
weather forecasts 66, 123, 235, 259
wells 64, 103–4, 107, 214
wildlife migration 135, 139–40
Wilk, R. 190
wind energy 166
Winterbottom, R. 19
Wollo 37–45

Wood, G. 200
World Bank 19, 23, 57, 196, 198
World Development Report, World
    Bank (1992) 19
World Oceans Conference (2009)
    228

Yucatan 177, 179, 181, 187

Zakieldeen, S. 105
Zalingei 99–105, 107–9, 111
    agriculture 103, 106
    onion and potato cultivation 108
    rainfall 102, 107
Zapatista 179
Zimbabwe 8, 75

www.ingramcontent.com/pod-product-compliance
Lightning Source LLC
Chambersburg PA
CBHW051256020426
42333CB00026B/3232